P9-CLO-421

# SAN FRANCISCO

| | |
|---|---|
| Orientation | 4 |
| Civic Center/Hayes Valley | 16 |
| South of Market (SOMA) | 26 |
| Union Square | 38 |
| Financial District | 58 |
| Chinatown | 70 |
| Nob Hill/Russian Hill | 78 |
| Fisherman's Wharf/Telegraph Hill/North Beach | 88 |
| Upper Fillmore/Pacific Heights/Marina | 108 |
| The Haight/Japantown | 126 |
| The Mission/Potrero Hill/Bernal Heights | 136 |
| Noe Valley/Castro/Upper Market | 144 |
| Sunset/Twin Peaks | 154 |
| Golden Gate Park | 160 |
| The Richmond/The Presidio | 168 |
| Gay San Francisco | 180 |
| Architecture Tours | 194 |
| Day Trips | 197 |
| History | 208 |
| Index | 210 |

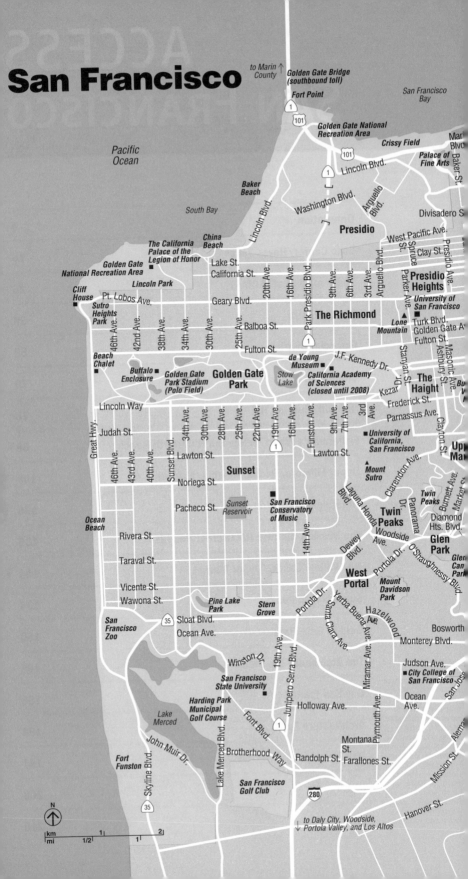

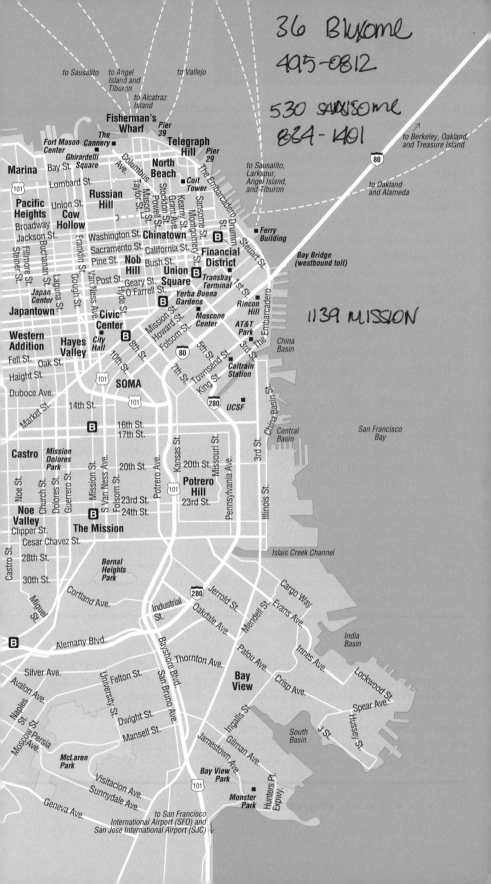

The City by the Bay's stature as one of the US's most attractive, welcoming destinations is well deserved. Honeymooners continue to be lured by San Francisco's romantic charm, seasoned travelers like the civilized pace and dramatic views, families appreciate the many attractions for children, gays and lesbians flock to this tolerant town for its vibrant subculture, and executives *love* to have their conventions here year after year.

San Francisco covers a 47-square-mile peninsula, with the **Pacific Ocean** to the west, the **Golden Gate Strait** to the north, and the **San Francisco Bay**, a large estuary, stretching north to east. Its 791,684 inhabitants make it the second-largest city in the nine-county **Bay Area,** a region that continues to thrive. Many new civic projects and improvements by internationally acclaimed architects are under way.

Originally inhabited by the Ohlone Indians and reputedly visited by British admiral Sir Francis Drake in 1579, the region saw five flags fly—representing England, Spain, Mexico, the Republic of California, and the United States—from 1579 through 1850. Ever since gold was discovered at Sutter's Mill in 1848, San Francisco has drawn adventurers and gold-seekers. It became known as a place to get rich quick—and a place to spend it all, as miners and other high rollers flooded to the saloons and dance halls of the Barbary Coast. When the city was largely demolished by the 1906 earthquake and fire, attention was again riveted on the city. But San Francisco was quickly rebuilt, sowing the seeds of the indomitable image that persists today.

Since then, San Francisco has cultivated its freewheeling reputation and made news on different fronts, from the kitchens of famous restaurants to the violent scenes of labor unrest on the docks and the 1978 assassinations of Mayor George Moscone and Harvey Milk, a gay member of the Board of Supervisors. The city has been in the forefront of social movements from the arrival of the flower children and the "summer of love" in 1967 to gay couples exchanging wedding vows at City Hall. San Francisco ranks in the front lines of culture, with a world-class opera house, symphony, and ballet company, as well as the country's best Asian, European, and modern art museums. New Yorkers love San Francisco, and they frequently compare it to the Big Apple. Europeans feel comfortable because, in many respects, it is the most European of American cities. Hispanics gravitate to the Spanish-speaking Mission District, and Asians also feel at home, since the city has one of the largest Chinese populations in the country, a substantial Japanese community, and increasing numbers of Vietnamese, Cambodian, Laotian, and Filipino immigrants. These ethnic neighborhoods keep San Francisco fresh and vibrant.

Locals have been accused of being smug about their city, and the charge is probably valid. San Franciscans know and love the Bay Area, and enjoy sharing its attractions. By boat, kayak, hiking trail, or bike path, it's easy to take advantage of the city's parks and scenic waterways. And, as the visitor quickly discovers, the famed city by the bay shares its many pleasures with visitors. Check www.sfvisitor.org for travelers' discounts. For information on transportation, call 510/817.1717 (no area code required if calling in the Bay Area), or look online at www.511.org.

---

**Area code 415 unless otherwise noted.**

# How to Read This Guide

ACCESS SAN FRANCISCO° is arranged by neighborhood so you can see at a glance where you are and what is around you. The numbers next to the entries in the following chapters correspond to the numbers on the maps. The type is color-coded according to the kind of place described:

Restaurants/Clubs: Red

Hotels: Purple | Shops: Orange

Outdoors/Parks: Green | Sights/Culture: Blue

& Wheelchair accessible

## WHEELCHAIR ACCESSIBILITY

An establishment (except a restaurant) is considered wheelchair accessible when a person in a wheelchair can easily enter a building (i.e., no steps, a ramp, a wide-enough door) without assistance. Restaurants are deemed wheelchair accessible *only* if the above applies, *and* if the rest rooms are on the same floor as the dining area and their entrances and stalls are wide enough to accommodate a wheelchair.

## RATING THE RESTAURANTS AND HOTELS

The restaurant ratings take into account the quality, service, atmosphere, and uniqueness of the restaurant. An expensive restaurant doesn't necessarily ensure an enjoyable evening; a small, relatively unknown spot could have good food, professional service, and a lovely atmosphere. Therefore, on a purely subjective basis, stars are used to judge the overall dining value (see the star ratings at right). Keep in mind that chefs and owners often change, which sometimes drastically affects the quality of a restaurant. The ratings in this guidebook are based on information available at press time.

The price ratings, as characterized at right, apply to restaurants and hotels. These figures describe general price-range relationships among other restaurants and hotels in the area. The restaurant price ratings are based on the average cost of a dinner entrée for one person, excluding tax and tip.

Hotel price ratings reflect the base price of a standard room for two people for one night during the peak season. Expect a 40 percent discount in hotel rates in January and February. Hotel rates fluctuate based on occupancy. A $65 room will fetch $145 when a big convention is in town and hotels are fully booked. Most hotels post the best available rates on their web sites.

## RESTAURANTS

| | |
|---|---|
| ★ | Good |
| ★★ | Very Good |
| ★★★ | Excellent |
| ★★★★ | An Extraordinary Experience |
| $ | The Price Is Right (less than $10) |
| $$ | Reasonable ($10-$18) |
| $$$ | Expensive ($18-$28) |
| $$$$ | Big Bucks ($28 and up) |

## HOTELS

| | |
|---|---|
| $ | The Price Is Right ($100-$150) |
| $$ | Reasonable ($150-$200) |
| $$$ | Expensive ($200-$250) |
| $$$$ | Big Bucks ($250 and up) |

## MAP KEY

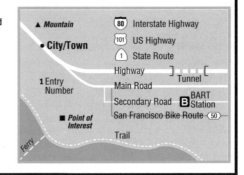

---

# Getting to San Francisco
# Transportation
# Airports

## San Francisco International Airport (SFO)

Fourteen miles south of San Francisco on the peninsula is **SFO,** the seventh busiest airport in the country. This important Asian transportation hub provides weekly flights year-round to Taipei, Hong Kong, and Seoul. And larger gates accommodate the new wide-bodied aircraft. Most overseas flights, as well as many domestic flights, arrive and depart from **SFO.** All domestic flights depart from terminals 1 and 3, while terminal 2 is closed for renovation. Ticket counters and gates are located on the upper level and baggage claim on the lower level. On view in 20 galleries are rotating exhibits of folk art, crafts, and historic artifacts. Overseas flights

depart from the **International Terminal,** the signature winglike building, from boarding areas G and A. Two upscale food courts feature outposts of the Bay Area's top eateries such as Ebisu (Japanese), Emporio Rulli (Italian), and Andale (Mexican). Note the terminal's cherrywood paneling and stop by the Louis A. Turpen Aviation Museum, housed in a replica of the 1937 airport terminal. There is Wi-Fi throughout the terminals. **AirTrain,** a hydroelectric-powered people mover, and the **BART** trains are in Concourse H. The AirTrain stations are located at all terminals, terminal parking garages, the Rental Car Center, and SFO's BART station and operates 24 hours a day. Travel time on BART from SFO to downtown is 30 minutes.

## AIRPORT SERVICES

Airport information and paging ..............650/821.8211

Airport Police ........................................650/821.7111

Lost and Found ....................................650/821.7014
Parking................................................650/821.7900

## AIRLINES

Air Canada ...................................................Terminal 1
888/247.2262 ...............................www.aircanada.ca

Air China .........................................................International
800/986.1985 ...............................www.airchina.com.

Air France............................................................International
800/237.2747..........................www.airfrance.com/us

Air New Zealand ..............................................International
800/262.1234 .......................www.airnewzealand.com

AirTran Airways .............................................Terminal 1
800/247.8726 ...................................www.airtran.com

Alaska Airlines (Domestic & Canada Flights) ..Terminal 1
800/426.0333 ...............................www.alaskaair.com

Alaska Airlines (Mexico Flights)...................International
800/426.0333 ...............................www.alaskaair.com

America West Airlines ..................................Terminal 1
800/235.9292 ....................www.usairways.com/awa

American Airlines...........................................Terminal 3
800/433.7300 .........................................www.aa.com

ANA (All Nippon Airways) ..........................International
800/235.9262 .........................www.fantaskyweb.com

Asiana ..............................................................International
800/227.4262 ...................................us.flyasiana.com

British Airways ...............................................International
800/247.9297 .......................www.british-airways.com

Cathay Pacific Airways ...............................International
800/233.2742 ..........................www.cathaypacific.com

China Airlines.................................................International
800/227.5118.........................www.china-airlines.com

Continental Airlines .....................................Terminal 1
800/525.0280 ...........................www.continental.com

Delta Airlines.................................................Terminal 1
800/221.1212 ......................................www.delta.com

EVA Airways ...................................................International
800/695.1188 ....................................www.evaair.com

Frontier Airlines ............................................Terminal 1
800/432.1359 ......................www.frontierairlines.com

Hawaiian Airlines...........................................Terminal 1
800/367.5320 ............................www.hawaiianair.com

Horizon Air......................................................Terminal 1
800/547.9308 ...............www.horizonair.alaskaair.com

Japan Airlines.................................................International
800/525.3663.................................www.japanair.com

KLM Airlines ...................................................International
800/447.4747 .........................................www.klm.com

Korean Air ......................................................International
800/438.5000...............................www.koreanair.com

LACSA ..............................................................International
800/225.2272...........................................www.taca.com

Lufthansa .........................................................International
800/645.3880 ...............................www.lufthansa.com

Mesa Airlines..................................................Terminal 1
800/637.2247 ................................www.mesa-air.com

Mexicana ........................................................International
800/531.7921...............................www.mexicana.com

Midwest Airlines ..............................................Terminal 1
800/452.2022 .....................www.midwestairlines.com

Northwest (Domestic) ...................................Terminal 1
800/225.2525 .........................................www.nwa.com

Northwest (International) ............................International
800/225.2525 .........................................www.nwa.com

Philippine Airlines............................................International
800/435.9725 ...................www.philippineairlines.com

Qantas ..............................................................International
800/227.4500 ....................................www.qantas.com

Singapore Airlines .........................................International
800/742.3333................................www.singaporeair.com

Spirit .................................................................International
800/772.7177 ...................................www.spiritair.com

Sun Country Airlines ....................................Terminal 1
866/FLY-N-SUN (866/359.6786)...www.suncountry.com

TACA ................................................................International
800/535.8780..........................................www.taca.com

Ted (Domestic) ...............................................Terminal 3
800/225.5833 ....................................www.flyted.com

Ted (International) ..........................................International
800/225.5833 ....................................www.flyted.com

United Airlines (Domestic) ...........................Terminal 3
800/241.6522 .....................................www.united.com

United Airlines (International) ....................International
800/241.6522 .....................................www.united.com

United Express.................................................Terminal 3
800/241.6522 .....................................www.united.com

US Airways ......................................................Terminal 1
800/428.4322 ...............................www.usairways.com

Virgin Atlantic...................................................International
800/862.8621..........................www.virgin-atlantic.com

## Getting to and from San Francisco International Airport (SFO)

### BY BART, BUS, SHUTTLE

An extension to **Bay Area Rapid Transit (BART)** connects San Francisco International Airport to the city as well as to destinations in the East Bay and the Peninsula. You can board BART at the **International Terminal** and arrive downtown in 30 minutes. For more information visit www.bart.gov or call 650/992.2278. **SamTrans** provides bus service to San Francisco's Transbay Terminal at **First** and **Mission Streets** 24 hours every day with limited service between 1AM and 5AM. SamTrans bus stops are located on the Arrivals level of terminal 3, and International. SamTrans buses 292, 397, and the KX also serve the airport. For information, call 650/508.6200 or 800/660.4287 elsewhere in California. Door-to-door shuttle service is generally reasonably priced and is available on a walk-up basis on the Departures/Ticketing level from the roadway center island at all terminals. Contact the shuttle company for service after 11PM. Shuttle operators include:

Airport Express .............................................775.5121

American Airporter Shuttle.........................202.0733 or
800/282.7758

Bay Shuttle ......................564.3400 or 877/467.1800

Bayporter Express ...........................................467.1800

Lorrie's Airport Shuttle....................................334.9000

M&M Luxury Shuttle ......................................552.3200

For information, call 495.8404. Also www.transitinfo.org.

## BY CAR

The most direct way to get from the airport into San Francisco is by **Highway 101.** Depending on traffic and weather conditions a typical ride into town will take 30 to 45 minutes; it takes longer during rush hour.

## RENTAL CARS

Most national and local car-rental agencies are located at and around **SFO,** and most major hotels have car-rental counters. Options run the gamut—everything from your basic Ford to a Rolls-Royce, Ferrari, or a classic two-seater T-Bird. Weekly (a minimum of five days) or three-day weekend rates are usually the best deals, but you should always shop around. Contact the following major companies for their current rates:

Dollar..........................650/244.4131, 800/800.4000

Hertz ..........................650/624.6600, 800/654.3131

National ................................................650/616.3000

Thrifty..........................650/259.1313, 800/847.4389

**AirTrain** (blue line) services SFO's **Rental Car Center,** the pick-up and drop-off place for all rental car companies.

## BY LIMOUSINE

A luxurious transportation alternative, limousine or town car service between **SFO** and downtown San Francisco can cost approximately $55 to $70 (not including tax and tip), depending on the size of the car. Contact one of the following companies for further information:

Airport Commuter............... 759.5463, 888/876.1777
www.airportcommuter.com

Associated Limousines Inc. ..703.9200, 888/544.5466
www.sflimo.com

Bauer's Limousine ................................. 800/LIMO.OUT
www.bauerslimousine.com

Elite Limousine............866/964.7433, 650/777.0977
www.elitelimousineinc.com

## BY TAXI

Taxis are available on the lower level of the airport to downtown San Francisco. Taxis to downtown cost approximately $37. For getting to the airport call **Luxor Cab Co.** (282.4141), **Yellow Cab** (626.2345), **National Cab Co.** (643.4874), or **Big Dog City** (city-wide dispatch; 920.0700).

## Oakland International Airport (OAK)

Located five miles south of downtown Oakland on **Highway 880,** this airport is smaller than **SFO,** making it

less confusing to navigate. The airport just completed a $350 million project to improve runways. The airport's two terminals are linked by an indoor corridor. Wi-Fi access has been installed throughout the terminals. A convenient shuttle service is also available between both terminals.

## AIRPORT SERVICES

Airport Information .................................510/563.3300

Airport Police .........................................510/563.2900

Customs...................................................510/563.3300

Ground Transportation
and Parking Availability ...........................888/IFLYOAK

Lost and Found.......................................510/563.3982

Parking....................................................510/663.2571

Web Site ...............................www.oaklandairport.com

## AIRLINES

Alaska Airlines (Horizon Air) .................800/426.0333

Aloha Airlines .........................................800/367.5250

America West (US Airways)....................800/235.9292

American Airlines ...................................800/433.7300

ATA ....................................................... 800/435.9282

Azores Express .......................................800/762.9995

Continental..............................................800/525-0280

Delta Air Lines .......................................800.221.1212

Harmony..................................................866/868.6789

Jet Blue...................................................800/538.2583

Mexicana ................................................800/531.7921

Southwest Airlines..................................800/435.9792

United Airlines .......................................800/241.6522

US Airways .............................................800/428.4322

## Getting to and from Oakland International Airport (OAK)

## BY BART, BUS, SHUTTLE

**AirBART** (510/465.BART) runs approximately every 20 minutes to the **Coliseum/Oakland BART** station. The bus picks up passengers at **Terminals 1** and **2** and at **Airport Drive** and **Neil Armstrong Way.** The fare is $2. **AC Transit** (510/817.1717, www.actransit.org) operates in the East Bay. **American Airporter Shuttle** (202.0733) serves Oakland Airport.

## BY CAR

The easiest way to reach downtown San Francisco from the Oakland airport is to take **I-880** at the airport to **I-80** west across the **San Francisco–Oakland Bay Bridge** into San Francisco.

## RENTAL CARS

Most national car-rental agencies are located at and around **Oakland International Airport.** Weekly (a minimum of five days) or three-day weekend rates are usually the best deals, but you should always shop around. Contact the following major companies for their current rates:

Avis ........................................................800/331.1212
Budget ...................................................800/527.0700
Dollar .....................................................800/800.4000
Hertz.......................................................800/654.3131
National ..................................................800/227.7368

## BY LIMOUSINE

Limousine services are also available; the cost ranges from $50 to $90 depending on the size and type of car.

ABC Chauffeured Limousine & Sedan ....888/401.6200
Avalon Transportation 650/579.2677, 800/445.0444
Carey Limousine San Francisco..............800/872.3090
Grand Limousine ........650/588.8333, 888/754.1700

## San Jose International Airport (SJC)

This airport is located about 2 miles from downtown San Jose and approximately 50 miles south of San Francisco via Highway 101. Although farther from the city than either **SFO** or **OAK**, it often offers less expensive flights to some destinations.

## AIRPORT SERVICES

Airport Administration ............................408/277.5366
Airport Information ................................408/277.4759
Currency Exchange ......408/287.0748, 408/287.3748
Customs .................................................408/291.7388
Lost and Found and Paging....................408/277.5419
Parking ..................................................408/277.3145

## AIRLINES

Alaska/Horizon Airlines...........................800/547.9308
American.....................408/291.3808, 800/433.7300
American Trans Air ................................800/435.9282
America West (US Airways)....................408/295.4171, 800/235.9292
Continental ............................................800/525.0280
Delta ...........................408/286.6981, 800/221.1212
Frontier Airlines .....................................800/432.1359
Hawaiian Airlines ...................................800/367.5320
JetBlue ..................................................800/538.2583
Mexicana.....................408/293.8474, 800/531.7921
Northwest/KLM ............408/282.1903, 800/225.2525
Southwest ....................408/283.5910, 800/435.9792
United, United Express...........................800/241.6522

## Getting to and from San Jose International Airport (SJC)

### BY BUS, SHUTTLE

Several companies provide direct transportation to downtown San Francisco. **South and East Bay Shuttle** (800/548.4664) and **M&M** (552.3200, 800/286.0303) can be found opposite **Terminal C.** Fares run $69 to $79 per person. **San Jose Express Shuttle** (800/773.0039) also travels to San Francisco.

### BY CAR

The easiest way to reach downtown San Francisco from San Jose is to exit the airport on **Airport Boulevard** going northeast to Highway 101, which leads directly into San Francisco.

### RENTAL CARS

Most national car-rental agencies at **San Jose International Airport** are in **Terminal C.** Weekly (a minimum of five days) or three-day weekend rates are usually the best deals, but you should always shop around. Contact the following major companies for their current rates:

Alamo ....................................................800/327.9633
Avis ........................................................800/831.2847
Budget ...................................................800/527.0700
Dollar .....................................................800/800.4000
Hertz ......................................................800/654.3131

### BY LIMOUSINE

A luxurious transportation alternative, limousine service between San Jose and San Francisco can cost anywhere from $70 to $95.

AA Executive Transportation ....................408/979.1269
First Choice Limousine ............................888/795.5466

## Getting Around San Francisco

### BAY AREA RAPID TRANSIT (BART)

A clean, reliable, easy-to-use underground transportation system. BART has 43 stations throughout the Bay Area. All stations have facilities for people with disabilities. Trains serve parts of San Francisco, **Daly City, San Francisco International Airport,** and the **East Bay.** The system operates Monday through Friday from 4AM to 1:30AM, Saturday from 6AM to 1:30AM, and Sunday from 8AM to 1:30AM.

On weekdays, trains run on all six routes approximately every 15 minutes, and extra service is offered during rush hours. After 7PM and on Sunday, you may have to transfer to another train to get to your final destination. Brochures about using the system and train schedules are available at all BART stations. You can also download BART schedules to your Apple iPod and web-enabled mobile devices such as a phone, PDA, or BlackBerry.

To buy a ticket, check the prominently displayed information chart to determine your destination and the ticket value required for a one-way trip. Ticket machines sell tickets for any amount between $1.40 and $40. *Save the ticket to exit the station.*

Discount tickets are available for senior citizens (age 65 and older), people with disabilities, and children ages 5 to 12. You can also buy discounted high-value tickets. All discounted tickets are sold *only* at participating institutions (for information call 989.2278), and *not* at BART stations. An excursion-ride ticket allows you to tour the entire system, visiting any of the 34 stations for up to 3 hours as long as you enter and exit at the same station. If you get out en route, the fare gate will compute the normal fare (obviously, this is a good deal for hard-core train buffs only). For information about BART and connecting bus service, call 415/989.2278; www.bart.gov.

## BICYCLES

Bicycles in San Francisco, with its infamous steep streets, may seem overly ambitious for all but the most physically fit, but if you plan your route to avoid the hills, a bicycle can be one of the best ways to see the city. San Francisco's Department of Parking and Traffic has a bicycle program that sets out these routes. Even-numbered routes travel east/west and odd-numbered routes north/south. (See "Plum Paths for Pedal Pushers in the City by the Bay" on page 146 and the individual chapter maps for the designated routes.) **The Embarcadero** and the **Golden Gate Promenade** both provide breathtaking views of the bay. **The Presidio** and **Golden Gate Park** are also bicycle-friendly. Bicycles can be rented from **Adventure Bicycle Company** (734 Lombard at Columbus Ave, 771.8735) and **Blazing Saddles** (1095 Columbus, at Francisco St, Pier 39½ and Pier 41, 202.8888). Cyclists are allowed to take their bikes on most trains except those highlighted on the BART schedule and crowded cars.

## BY ELECTRIC CAR AND SCOOTER

You won't go more than 25 to 30 mph, but two- and four-seater electric cars are a fun way to scoot out to **Crissy Field,** the **Golden Gate Bridge,** up to **Coit Tower,** and out to **Golden Gate Park.** Along with your rental you get a map of the most popular routes. Some cars offer computer-guided, "talking" guidance. The cars easily climb the toughest hills. Operators usually charge $40 an hour and then $20 for each additional hour. The companies include **Electric Time Car Rentals** (2800 Leavenworth St between Beach and Jefferson Sts, 674.8800, www.etcars.com), **GoCar Rentals** (2715 Hyde St at Bay St, 800/91-GoCar, www.gocarsf.com), and **Scootcar Rentals** (431 Beach St at Taylor St, 567.7994, www.scootcar.net).

## DRIVING

Driving in San Francisco's **Downtown** and **Financial Districts** is suitable for extremely patient people who can handle slow-moving traffic. **North Beach, Chinatown,** and **Telegraph Hill** are also congested, and parking is difficult. Many parking meters provide only a half hour of parking, and traffic cops patrol frequently. Unless otherwise posted, meters operate Monday through Saturday, usually from 7AM to 6PM (check to be sure).

Some curbs are painted colors that have specific meanings, and violators incur costly fines. A **white curb** indicates a drop-off zone for passengers. This code is in effect only when the facility it fronts (a restaurant, theater, or office building) is in operation. If closed, it's okay to park. A **green curb** signifies parking for 10 minutes only. **Yellow curbs** are for loading and unloading commercial vehicles, and **blue curbs** are reserved for drivers or passengers with disabilities who have an official placard prominently displayed in their car window. Unless information is otherwise posted, it's usually legal to park in green or yellow zones after 6PM.

When parking on San Francisco's hilly terrain, always turn the tires toward the street when facing uphill, and toward the curb when facing downhill.

## FERRIES

Ferries still are popular means of transportation to and from the city for commuters from the East Bay and **Marin.** And though they do not have recorded commentary describing the sights, ferries are a less expensive alternative to sight-seeing cruises. The landmark **Ferry Building** on The Embarcadero (at Market Street) is one terminus for the **Golden Gate Ferries** (925.5575, www.goldengate.org), while the **Blue & Gold Fleet** (773.1188) and **Red & White Fleet** (447.0591, 877/855.5506) dock at **Fisherman's Wharf/Pier 39.** The **Ferry Building Line** operates sight-seeing cruises from Gate E.

## MUNI PUBLIC TRANSPORTATION SYSTEM

**Muni** operates a variety of transit vehicles: cable cars, buses (diesel and electric), streetcars, and Metro light-rail vehicles. No other city in the world can match San Francisco in offering such extensive transit with two types of vintage vehicles: cable cars and electric streetcars. The **F-line,** which opened in 1995, runs vintage streetcars from around the world from Jones and Beach Streets in Fisherman's Wharf, through the Financial District to Upper Market Street, to the renowned gay and lesbian Castro district. For recorded information, call the **Muni Hotline** at 554.6999; for a live operator, call 673.6864. Visit Muni online at www.sfmuni.com. Click on Routes & Schedules, then Trip Planner, for assistance with mapping out the best route to points of interest. Refer to the partial Muni map on the inside back cover of this book.

## CABLE CARS:

Muni operates two lines: the **Powell-Hyde** cable car and the **California Street** cable car. The one-way fare is $3 for adults, $1 for seniors before 7AM and after 9PM, and free for children under 5. No transfers are issued or accepted on cable cars.

## BUSES, ELECTRIC TROLLEY BUSES, STREETCARS, AND METRO LIGHT-RAIL VEHICLES:

Diesel buses cover the majority of the bus lines operating within city limits. Trolley buses are powered by overhead electric wires.

Historic streetcars (F-Market) run along Market Street and the Embarcadero to Fisherman's Wharf. Light-rail vehicles and modern Breda streetcars (J-Church, K-Ingleside, L-Taraval, M-Ocean View, N-Judah) run under Market Street in the Metro stations located a level above BART and on the surface throughout various neighborhoods. A new line now runs along Third Street.

Purchase tickets at the fare windows at the Muni Metro subway stations and at vending machines at all high-level surface platforms. You can use your ticket to board through any door of the streetcar or pay your fare by boarding through the front door of the first car and depositing cash in the cash box. Exact change is required. Bus, streetcar, and Muni metro fare is $1.50 for adults; 50 cents for seniors, the disabled, and youth aged 5 to 17; and free for children 4 and under. Ask for a transfer at the time you pay your fare. Transfers are valid for 90 minutes for two boardings in any direction.

## OPTIONS FOR UNLIMITED ACCESS:

If you plan to use public transportation extensively, for convenience and unlimited access purchase a Muni pass, Passport, CityPass, or a token 10-pack.

For unlimited rides on buses only, purchase a Muni pass, which is available as a 1-day, 3-day, weekly, or monthly "Fast Pass." Discounted Muni passes for children, seniors, and people with disabilities are also available.

For unlimited rides on buses *and* cable cars, purchase a "Passport," which is sold as 1-day, 3-day and 1-week passes.

Tokens can be used any time, don't expire, and cost $1.50 apiece; they can be purchased in 10-packs. Coupon booklets with 10 coupons per booklet have expiration dates.

## WHERE TO BUY:

Muni passes, Passports, and tokens are available at the City Hall Information Booth (401 Van Ness Ave at McAllister St), Cable Car Ticket Booth (Market St at Powell St), San Francisco News and Gifts (350 California St at Sansome St), and Snacks on First (455 Market St, Suite 110, at First St). Check online at www.sfmuni.com for other locations around the city.

The San Francisco CityPass includes a 7-day Muni passport for hop-on, hop-off privileges on cable cars, streetcars, and light-rail trains and is valid 9 days from first use. The booklet has discount admission to five attractions and you can visit the de Young and Legion of Honor on a single ticket if you go on the same day. The cost is $59 for adults, $39 for children 5 to 17, and free for children under 5. Purchase at the San Francisco Convention & Visitors Bureau at 900 Market St (Hallidie Plaza, at Powell and Market Sts) or by calling 707/256.0490; they can also be purchased online at www.citypass.com or call 888/330.5008.

## TAXIS

In San Francisco taxis are expensive and sometimes impossible to hail. In general it's best to call and make arrangements for a pickup. It's relatively easy to get a cab at any of the major hotels; however, plan on waiting a long time for one during the rush hours and when the weather is foul. Taxi companies include **Yellow Cab**

(626.2345), **Luxor** (282.1224), and **Veteran's Cab** (552.1300).

## WALKING

Exploring the city on foot reveals the rich detail that makes San Francisco memorable. The main tourist areas are within a half-hour walk of each other, making walking practical. The steep streets of **Telegraph Hill, Russian Hill,** and **Nob Hill** leave many pedestrians gasping for breath, but the views are worth the climb. (See tours on page 14.)

# FYI

## ACCOMMODATIONS

San Francisco offers a wide variety of places to stay, from inexpensive motels to charming bed-and-breakfast inns to world-class luxury hotels. Rooms should be reserved at least two months in advance from July through October. Be aware that hotels charge up to $48 a day for parking. For budget lodging, try the motel strip along Lombard Street. In the Marina, renovated motels are a great bargain and provide the rare offer of complimentary parking. Many hotels are 100% non-smoking, and they have free wireless Internet access in lobbies and guest rooms. To make hotel reservations, call 888/782.9673; 800/637.5196.

## CLIMATE

San Francisco's mild marine climate boasts temperatures that seldom rise above 70 degrees or fall below 40 degrees. Morning and evening fog are common from June through August, and rain is not unusual from November through March.

| MONTHS | AVERAGE TEMPERATURE (°F) |
|---|---|
| January-March | 59-48 |
| April-June | 62-50 |
| July-September | 65-54 |
| October-December | 62-51 |

## DRINKING

The legal drinking age is 21. Bars stay open until 2AM. Wine and liquor can be purchased in most grocery stores and supermarkets.

## HOURS

Most shops in San Francisco are open from 10AM to 6PM Monday through Saturday. The large department stores, as well as some shops, are open on Sunday.

## MONEY

**Deak International, Foreign Exchange, Associated Foreign Exchange,** and many major banks handle currency exchanges. Traveler's checks are available at banks and at **American Express** and **Thomas Cook Travel** offices. Banks are open Monday through Friday, generally until 4PM, and often on Saturday morning (usually until 1PM).

## PARKING

There are some relatively inexpensive city-owned parking garages, particularly for short-term parking, but parking in congested areas tends to be costly. Here are some low-cost 24-hour parking facilities:

**Ellis-O'Farrell Garage** 123 O'Farrell St (between Powell and Stockton Sts), 986.4800

**Fifth & Mission Garage** 833 Mission St (between Fourth and Fifth Sts), 982.8522

**North Beach Garage** 735 Vallejo St (between Stockton and Powell Sts), 397.5102

**Portsmouth Square Garage** 733 Kearny St (between Clay and Washington Sts), 982.6353

**Sutter-Stockton Garage** 444 Stockton St (between Sutter and Bush Sts), 982.8370

**Union Square Garage** 333 Post St (enter on Post St or Geary St between Stockton and Powell Sts), 397.0631

## PERSONAL SAFETY

Drugs and crime are unfortunate components of urban living, and San Francisco is no exception. In general, neighborhoods that could be troublesome look it (of course, there are exceptions). In **Golden Gate Park,** stay on well-populated paths and avoid walking there after dark. Surrounding the downtown side of the **Civic Center** is a high-crime neighborhood called the **Tenderloin** that's often a way station for undesirable types. Toward the west side, the neighborhood is improving, but caution is still advised. Once you're past the busy downtown area (from about **Fifth Street** and going west to **Gough Street**), **Market Street,** San Francisco's main thoroughfare, is distressingly seedy. At night there's a virtual parade of vagrants. And the **Haight-Ashbury** neighborhood, still filled with its share of panhandlers and lost youth, can be somewhat intimidating.

## PUBLICATIONS

The city's morning newspapers are the *San Francisco Chronicle* and the *San Francisco Examiner. San Francisco Magazine,* a monthly lifestyle magazine, covers politics and personalities, fashion and food. *7×7 Magazine* covers the fashion and social scene. *S.F. Weekly* and the *Bay Guardian* are both liberal, free, alternative newspapers that provide good listings of entertainment events. The *San Francisco Arts Monthly* lists hundreds of arts events and exhibits at downtown hotels, available at the Visitor Information Center on the lower level of Hallidie Plaza and at the TIX Bay Area booth in Union Square. It's also available online: www.sfarts.org. The *Nob Hill Gazette* is a monthly that covers the society scene. The weekly *Sun Reporter* serves the black community, *Hokubei Mainichi* is a daily Japanese-English publication, and the daily *Chinese Times* is the largest of several Chinese newspapers. The *Jewish Bulletin* is published every Friday. Gay and lesbian newspapers include the weekly *Bay Area Reporter,* the *San Francisco Sentinel,* and *Bay Times.* The weekly *San Francisco Business Times* is the business-oriented publication. All are available on newsstands.

## RESTAURANTS

There are over 4,375 restaurants and drinking establishments in San Francisco offering a variety of cuisine at a wide range of prices. Fresh local produce, especially seafood, has contributed to the city's well-deserved reputation as a culinary capital whose multiethnic citizens bring an international flavor to the dining scene. You can reserve a table at many top restaurants at www.opentable.com, an online reservation service, after you set up an account and create a user-ID.

## SHOPPING

Cutting-edge fashions can be found at boutiques along **Maiden Lane, Powell, Post,** and **Stockton Streets.** This area, known as **Union Square,** caters to every taste and budget and is home to **Macy's, Saks Fifth Avenue,** and **Neiman Marcus.** Across Market Street are **Bloomingdale's** and **Nordstrom** in Westfield San Francisco Centre. **The Embarcadero Center, Pier 39,** and **Ghirardelli Square** showcase everything from museum-quality artifacts to the latest designer wear. Other shopping areas include **Japan Center,** noted for art galleries and bookstores.

## SMOKING

San Francisco has stiff antismoking regulations. Minors cannot buy cigarettes. It's illegal to light up in offices, public buildings, banks, lobbies, stores, sports arenas, stadiums, theaters, restaurants, and on public transportation. The smoking ban extends to bars, cocktail lounges, and nightclubs.

## STREET PLAN

With the exception of certain residential neighborhoods, most of San Francisco is laid out on a grid plan, with **Market Street** dividing the north and south segments of the city. Each block increases its numbering by 100, so buildings on the first block of a street might start with number 1, the second block with 100, and the third with 200. Newcomers may be confused by the numerical streets and avenues, which are in two different neighborhoods. When San Franciscans speak of "the avenues," they are referring to the numerically named avenues—**Second Avenue, Third Avenue,** etc.—that extend through the **Richmond** and **Sunset** districts. But other numerical streets, **First Street** to **30th Street,** span the **South of Market** area.

## TAXES

An 8.5 percent sales tax is added to purchases in San Francisco. If your purchases are shipped to a destination outside of California, you will be exempt from the sales tax. Foreign visitors may have to pay duty in their home country. An 8.5 percent tax is added to restaurant bills, and hotels tack a 14 percent room tax to the bill.

## TICKETS

The main source for tickets to concerts, theater, and sports events is **City Box Office** (392.4400; www.city boxoffice.com). Tickets can also be charged by phone (there is a charge for each ticket) or purchased at the theater box offices.

# MAIN EVENTS

San Francisco, always abuzz with activity, hosts a wide variety of special events and festivals throughout the year. The following is a sampler of the many treats available in and around the city. The dates for some events vary from year to year; for up-to-the-minute information call the **San Francisco Convention and Visitors Bureau** (391.2001).

### January

**San Francisco Sports and Boat Show** presents large floating toys for affluent adults during two weekends in mid-January at the **Cow Palace.**

**Ballet season** begins at the **War Memorial Opera House.**

During the three-week **dine-about-town** event, the city's top restaurants offer deeply discounted prix-fixe menus at lunch and dinner. You can choose from among more than 150 restaurants. For more information, visit www.sfdineabouttown.com.

### February

The **Chinese New Year** takes place sometime between late January and late February.

The **Golden Gate Kennel Club Dog Show,** considered the largest dog show west of the Mississippi, is held the first weekend in February at the **Cow Palace.**

The **San Francisco Crab Celebration** features a marketplace festival with food and wine tastings, cooking demonstrations, and competitions, all in honor of Dungeness crab season. For more information, call 391.2000 or visit www.sfvisitor.org.

### March

**St. Patrick's Day Parade** marches down **Market Street,** where the bars are filled with merrymakers.

The **San Francisco Flower and Garden Show** transforms the Cow Palace into a 5-acre gallery of 23 astonishing gardens, complete with waterfalls, metal sculpture mermaids, and a miniature Tuscan village. Tickets to the preview party, 750.5441. Tickets to the garden show, 771.6909.

The last week of the month heralds the **Cherry Blossom Festival,** which is observed in the **Japanese Tea Garden** at **Golden Gate Park.**

### April

Sunrise services are held at dawn on **Easter Sunday** on **Mount Davidson,** the highest hill in the city.

The **San Francisco International Film Festival** (931.FILM) presents cinema at various venues around the city through mid-May.

### May

**Cinco de Mayo Parade and Celebration,** commemorating Mexico's defeat of French troops in 1862, takes place throughout the **Mission District** during the first week of the month.

Latin American and Caribbean cultures blend in the Mission District for the very festive **Carnavale** on the last weekend of the month.

### June

Take the kids to the **Pier 39 Street Performers Festival.** Comedians, jugglers, and unicyclists gather the first weekend in June at Pier 39 to do their zany acts (705.5500).

The annual **Father's Day Kite Festival** enjoys a perfect (and windy) setting at **Marina Green,** at the edge of San Francisco Bay (956.3181).

Summer concerts at **Stern Grove** (www.sterngrove.org) bring San Franciscans with picnic baskets for free performances of opera, ballet, and music from classical to jazz, bluegrass, and African beat (252.6252).

At the **Juneteenth Festival,** the African-American community celebrates the 1865 announcement of emancipation outdoors with entertainment, food, and booths (931.2729; www.sfjuneteenth.org).

With more than 300,000 participants, the **Lesbian/Gay Freedom Day** parade and celebration is the biggest show in San Francisco and the largest of its kind in the US. Annual events are held at the **Civic Center** and on the Market Street parade route in late June (864.3733).

### July

Fireworks explode during the **July 4th** celebration along the waterfront from the **Ferry Building** to **Fisherman's Wharf.**

**San Francisco Symphony Pops** concerts are summer events at the **Civic Auditorium** (974.4060).

A **Summer in the City** popular music series is held at **Davies Hall** three weeks in July (864.6000). Concerts feature artists such as Bobby McFerrin, Johnny Mathis, Audra McDonald, and Little Richard.

The last Sunday in July is the **San Francisco Marathon.** Over 6,000 athletes race from the **Golden Gate Bridge** to **Golden Gate Park.**

### August

Early August is the popular **Nihonmachi Street Fair** at **Japantown,** where Japanese-style fun and games are the order of the day.

The **Ringling Brothers and Barnum & Bailey Circus** is presented at the **Cow Palace** for five days in late August, ending on Labor Day.

## September

**Piers 30** and **32** come alive with the **San Francisco Fair** during Labor Day weekend.

**Shakespeare in the Park** (Saturday and Sunday from Labor Day weekend through the last Sunday in September) is performed at the temporary outdoor theater in the **Liberty Meadow** of **Golden Gate Park.**

**Opera Season** begins with a gala formal ball on opening night at the **War Memorial Opera House.**

**Symphony Season** begins in **Davies Hall** and runs until June (864.6000; www.sfsymphony.org).

The **San Francisco Performances** presents 200 events from September to May. The web site lists chamber music, vocal and instrumental recitals, jazz, and contemporary dance (392.2545; www.performances.org).

**San Francisco's Blues Festival** attracts some of the world's best blues stars to the **Great Meadow** at **Fort Mason** for two days the last weekend of September (979.5588; www.sfblues.com).

At the **Autumn Moon Festival,** during the Chinese "Thanksgiving" (the last weekend of September), Grant Avenue in **Chinatown** is thronged with booths and stages where you can see Chinese opera, martial artists, magicians, and an hourly lion dance.

## October

**Litquake,** the city's most audacious and irreverent celebration of the written and spoken word, takes place over nine days of readings, storytelling, and literary happenings and concludes with the Lit Crawl, a three-hour literary pub crawl through 30 venues on Valencia Street in the Mission District on the final night (www.litquake.org).

**Castro Street Fair,** one of the city's largest and longest-running street celebrations, is held the first week of the month.

**Fleet Week** floats into the city with its parade of ships under the **Golden Gate Bridge.**

Head to **North Beach** and **Fisherman's Wharf** for the annual **Columbus Day** celebrations and parade.

**Halloween Night** is among the city's more colorful celebrations, with thousands of costumed revelers converging on Market and the **Civic Center.**

The last week of October and the first week of November, the **San Francisco Jazz Festival** takes place in venues throughout San Francisco and Oakland. Free noon concerts of world-class jazz take place at Justin Herman Plaza, at the Embarcadero Center, during the festival (788.7353, 800/850.7353, www.sfjazz.org).

On every weekend throughout the month, visual artists open their workplaces to the public. Sponsored by **ArtSpan's Open Studios,** the event attracts 800 artists who are on hand to discuss and sell their work (705.0686, www.sfopenstudios.com).

## November

**Día de los Muertos** (Day of the Dead) is held in the Mission District at the beginning of November. It commences with the celebration-of-life procession leading to ornately decorated altars (826.8009).

At **HolidayFest,** enjoy a big-city holiday with 100 holiday events (800/637.5196; www.onlyinsanfrancisco.com).

The annual **Holiday Lights Celebration** at **The Embarcadero** includes the illumination of the waterfront with more than 17,000 lights.

**Kristi Yamaguchi Embarcadero Center Holiday Ice Rink** opens at Justin Herman Plaza, offering skating sessions, classes, and birthday parties (956.2688).

## December

**Huntington Park Tree Lighting Ceremony** takes place the first week in December atop Nob Hill. Festivities begin at Grace Cathedral at California and Taylor Streets at 5:30PM, then move to the park, where over 10,000 twinkling lights adorn the park's trees. Christmas carols are sung by the San Francisco Girls Chorus, and there's complimentary hot chocolate (474.5400).

**Christmas at Sea** is held the second weekend at Hyde Street Pier, with caroling, storytelling, hot cider, kids' crafts, and a visit from Saint Nick aboard a historic ship (561.6662).

**Sing-It-Yourself Messiah** is held in early December at **Davies Symphony Hall** with the audience performing under the direction of various conductors (864.6000).

The **Dickens Christmas Fair** depicts a Victorian holiday with entertainment, food, and drink. It runs through the last weekend of December (800/510.1558; www.dickensfair.com).

**The San Francisco Bowl** matches teams from two of the country's strongest college football conferences: the Big East and Mountain West. They play on New Year's Eve at AT&T Park. For more information, call 947-BOWL (www.sfbowl.com).

## Phone Book

## EMERGENCIES

Ambulance/Fire/Police ..........................................911

AAA (road service) ................................800/222.4357

Highway Patrol ...............................................557.1094

Auto Theft.............................................707/551.4100

Children's Emergency Services ......................558.2650

Handicapped Crisis Line ........800/426.4263 (CA only)

Hospitals

California Pacific Medical Center,
Pacific Heights ..........................................923.3333

San Francisco General Hospital, Potrero ....206.8000

UCSF Medical Center, Parnassus ..............476.1037

Pharmacy (open 9-6) ................................392.4137

Poison Control Center
(Northwest CA only) ..........................800/523.2222

Police (Nonemergency)..................................553.0123

Towed vehicles ...........................................553.1235

## VISITORS' INFORMATION

Adult Immunization Clinic & Travel
Clinic .............................................................554.2625

AC Transit Bus Lines (Alameda-Contra
Costa) .....................510/891.4777; www.actransit.org

Amtrak .....................800/872.7245, www.amtrak.com

Bay Area Rapid Transit (BART) ...........415/989.2278;
650/992.2278; www.bart.gov

Better Business Bureau ...............................243.9999

Caltrain Peninsula Commuter Rail Service
(Bay Area) ..............800/660.4287; www.caltrain.com

Golden Gate Transit (Marin and Sonoma
Counties)...................415/923.2000; 415/921.5858

MUNI Bus Lines (San Francisco) ..................673.6864

Road Conditions ..................................800/427.7623

San Mateo County Transit
(SamTrans) ..........800/660.4287; www.samtrans.com

Toll-free numbers ..............800, 877, and 888 prefixes

US Customs ....................782.9210; www.customs.gov

US Passport .................................................538.2700

Visitors' Information Center ..........................391.2001

Chaperon Multilingual Guide (www.chaperon.com), a guide to walks, excursions, nightlife, and restaurants in five editions: German, Japanese, French, Italian, and Spanish

24-hour foreign-language hotlines:

French ......................................................391.2003

German ....................................................391.2004

Japanese ..................................................391.2101

Spanish ....................................................391.2122

Weather .......................................................364.7974

Youth Hostels.............................788.5604, 771.7277

---

The **TIX** booth at Union Square sells half-price tickets to theater, dance, and music performances on the same day of the performance only (cash only), or full-price in advance to select shows. TIX is also a Ticketmaster outlet. You can also purchase half-price tickets in advance at www.TheatreBayArea.org. For more information call 433.1235.

### TIME ZONE

San Francisco is in the Pacific time zone, three hours earlier than New York City.

### TIPPING

A 15 percent tip is standard for taxi fares and restaurants. Hotel porters and station porters expect $1 per bag. Concierges expect tips based on the quality of their service and the generosity of the guest. If you've used the concierge's advice a lot and he or she has recommended places that made your stay more pleasurable, tip at least $5.

### TOURS

There's something here for everyone. Here's a sampling of what's offered:

One of the largest operators of tours, **Gray Line** (reservations 888/428.6937; www.grayline.com) offers city tours and multilingual tours.

**All About Chinatown** (982.8839) offers daily two-hour visits to the city within a city. Discover an herbal pharmacy, a fortune cookie factory, and the **Stockton Street** food markets, and enjoy a dim sum lunch. Also in Chinatown, cooking instructor and food writer Shirley Fong-Torres conducts cooking classes and leads the **Wok Wiz Chinatown Tours** (650/355.9657, www.wokwiz.com). Highlights include area history, plus visits to an herbal emporium, dim sum lunch, produce markets, and food stores.

**Cruisin' the Castro** (255.1821, www.cruisinthecastro.com) features insights into gay contributions to the city. kathy Amendola leads four-hour visits to the Harvey Milk camera shop, Castro Theatre, and Victorian homes.

**Victorian Home Walk** (252.9485, www.victorianwalk.com) is a 2.5-hour tour by Muni and on foot where you learn to distinguish Queen Anne, Italianate, and Stick-style Victorians. You'll see more than 200 Victorians.

For a unique look at San Francisco's nightlife, join **3 Babes and a Bus** (800/414.0158, www.threeBabes.com) on

Saturday. Partygoers can dance the night away at four hot clubs and then be whisked back to their hotel.

Explore San Francisco on foot for free with the **City Guides** (557.4266, www.sfcityguides.org). **Barbary Coast Trail** (454.2355), and **Dashiell Hammett Tour** (510/287.9540, www.donherron.com) are other walking tours you'll enjoy.

The **Urban Safari** (866/697.2327; www.TheUrbanSafari.com) offers city tours off the beaten track to famous home sites, distinctive Victorians, murals, architecture, and forays into San Francisco's celebrated past. Choose from dozens of pre-planned routes.

For a novel experience, cross the Golden Gate Bridge on a beautifully restored open-air 1955 Mack fire truck whose owners, Robert and Marilyn Katzman, live in a 107-year-old Victorian firehouse. The 75 minute-tour departs from Beach Street in front of the Cannery (333.7077; www.fireenginetours.com).

**Extranomical Adventures** provides affordable one-day tours for those who want to explore outside the city. Tours include Muir Woods, the Wine Country, Yosemite (from $75), and historic Sonoma. The company will pick you up at your hotel either in San Francisco or Oakland. For more information, call 866/231.3752 or visit www.extranomical.com.

The gray whale migration can be witnessed June through November off the Pacific coastline; **Oceanic Society Expeditions** (474.3385) conducts trips to the Farallones from Fort Mason pier October through April.

Kayak from Pier 38 with **City Kayak** (357.1010; www.citykayak.com) on an adventurous crossing to Alcatraz Island or paddle along the downtown waterfront.

Explore the bay with **Hornblower Cruises** (Pier 33, The Embarcadero near Bay St, 788.8866, www.hornblower.com) and **Hawaiian Chieftain** (3020 Bridgeway, Sausalito, 331.3214, www.hawaiianchieftain.com).

## VISITORS' INFORMATION CENTER

The Visitors' Information Center is open Monday through Friday from 9AM to 5PM and Saturday and Sunday from 9AM to 3PM; closed Sunday in winter. The staff provides maps, information on lodging, and various discounts including the **CityPass,** which contains discounted admission tickets to six museums and a seven-day Muni Passport valid on all Muni vehicles and cable cars. The **Go San Francisco Card** (800/887.9103, www.goSanFranciscoCard.com) includes admission to 45 museums, tours, and historic sites plus discounts on shopping, dining, and tours. It comes with a guidebook with full details. The center is located at Hallidie Plaza, lower level, at Powell and Market Sts (391.2000, 974.6900). The mailing address is PO Box 429097, San Francisco, CA 94142-9097.

Visitor information on the web:

www.onlyinsanfrancisco.com ........................................
.................San Francisco Convention & Visitors Bureau

www.flysfo.com ..........San Francisco International Airport

www.thinker.org ........M.H. de Young Museum in Golden Gate Park, and California Palace of the Legion of Honor in Lincoln Park at 34th Ave and Clement St

www.fishermanswharf.org....................Fisherman's Wharf

www.sfmuseum.org ..............San Francisco City Museum

# CIVIC CENTER/ HAYES VALLEY

San Francisco's **Civic Center** complex is acclaimed by critics as America's finest collection of Beaux Arts buildings. **Daniel Burnham,** the architect commissioned to design the city's master plan, combined a highly developed aesthetic sense with the know-how of a skilled politician. He was invited to the city for consultation by millionaire and former mayor James Phelan, who, along with other prominent citizens, had become concerned about the ugliness of the building construction that was blighting the city. Burnham came with his young assistant, **Willis Polk** (himself a Westerner), and was immensely impressed with the potential of the natural setting. In 1904 he set up a cottage

office on Twin Peaks so he could look down on the terrain as he worked out his vision of the city's future. He was generations ahead of his time in suggesting such ideas as one-way streets, downtown subways, and residential areas where backyards would be merged into a common park. Polk wished to preserve the crest of the hills with access roads that curved to follow the contours of the land rather than conventional gridiron patterns. He designed a huge park for Twin Peaks with landscaped slopes and a special watercourse that would carry the city's water supply from reservoirs. But before any real action could be taken, much of San Francisco, including the old City Hall, collapsed in the 1906 earthquake and fire, literally burying Burnham's plans. However, with his enthusiastic supporters (John McLaren, first superintendent of **Golden Gate Park;** Phelan; sugar czar Claus Spreckels; and others), Burnham set a campaign in motion to rebuild the city. Political scandal delayed their plans, but he finally salvaged part of his project and convinced the supervisors to finance the monumental **Civic Center.** Alas, it was not until after his death that his recommendations were acted upon.

The man largely responsible for actually getting **City Hall** built was "Sunny" Jim Rolph. He was the mayor for two decades, and he considered the hall his proudest achievement. (Other projects launched by Rolph were the first San Francisco Public Library, **Civic Auditorium, Hetch Hetchy Aqueduct,** the yacht harbor, and the campaign to build the **Bay Bridge.**) City Hall's architect was **Arthur Brown Jr.,** a designer who had what colleague **Bernard Maybeck** admiringly called "perfect taste." Brown attended the Ecole des Beaux Arts in Paris along with his fraternity brother **John Bakewell Jr.,** and garnered more prizes than had ever been received by an American. Upon their return, the two young men set up the architectural firm of **Bakewell and Brown.** They soon won a contest for designing the City Hall in Berkeley, and though they felt they had no chance of winning, they competed for the greater prize: the key building in San Francisco's Civic Center master plan, City Hall. Ignoring sensible restrictions, they produced a plan for a spectacular structure that even by today's standards was exorbitant in design and expense. The new team won out over established stars in the field, and their victory catapulted Brown to the front ranks of American architects. By 1936, when the **War Memorial Opera House** and **Veteran's Building** were in place, a unified square of stately and ornate Beaux Arts architecture had been built. And it was in this opera house that the charter creating the United Nations was signed nine years later.

The **San Francisco Public Library** took up residence in 1996 in its contemporary new headquarters, designed by **James Ingo Freed** of **Pei Cobb Freed and Partners.**

The building, with its gray granite façade, is a modern interpretation of the classic Beaux Arts style. Two blocks away in the performing arts district, the 1981 **Louise M. Davies Symphony Hall** breaks completely with this design tradition. In the plaza across from the gilded-dome City Hall, protestors gather for demonstrations and festival-goers attend outdoor events. West of the Civic Center, Hayes Valley bustles with many fine restaurants, galleries, and antiques shops. East and north of the Civic Center is a portion of the **Tenderloin,** where Asian immigrants, many from Vietnam and Cambodia, have settled, opened restaurants, and brought a new respectability to the neighborhood.

## 1 St. Mary's Cathedral

Built in 1971 by **Pietro Belluschi, Pier Luigi Nervi,** and **McSweeney, Ryan and Lee,** this modern cathedral consists of four hyperbolic paraboloids creating a 190-foot roof over a square plan on a podium. It seats 2,500 people around a central altar and is similar to other contemporary cathedrals in Liverpool and Brasília. ♦ Geary St (at Gough St). 567.2020 ♿

## 2 The Opal San Francisco

$$ An early 1900s ambience pervades this 164-room hotel, where children under 18 stay free when sharing a room with a parent. The coffee bar serves continental breakfast and is open daily. ♦ 1050 Van Ness Ave (at Geary St). 673.4711, 888/673.4711. www.theopalsf.com ♿

## 3 Monarch Hotel

$$ Modern conveniences are combined with 1920s charm in this attractive hotel, which is close to the Civic Center and other activities. The 101 rooms have the feel of a European hostelry—there are canopied beds, shuttered windows, and an open courtyard. The lower lobby has facilities for meetings. The hotel's restaurant serves a hearty breakfast. ♦ 1015 Geary St (between Polk St and Van Ness Ave). 673.5232, 800/777.3210. www.themonarchhotel.com ♿

## 4 Mitchell Brothers O'Farrell Theatre

This infamous sex palace was rendered even more infamous by the slaying of one Mitchell brother by the other. As the sign warns, "Admission is limited to adults who will not be offended should they observe any type of sexual activity." The innocent mural outside belies the steamy action within. ♦ Cover. Daily. 895 O'Farrell St (at Polk St). 441.1930 ♿

## 5 Great American Music Hall

Top talent appears at this premier music club, which showcases rock, pop, jazz, and comedy. Robin Williams, Leon Russell, Buddy Rich, and Count Basie have all performed here. It's a large place with a balcony, but the sights and sounds are excellent from almost any table. A dinner menu offering "hip bar food" such as french fries, California-style quesadillas, spareribs, pizza, and salads is available. There is a full bar. ♦ Cover. Box office: M-Sa (Su if there is a show). 859 O'Farrell St (between Larkin and Polk Sts). 885.0750. www.musichallsf.com

## 6 Vietnam II

★★$ Of all the restaurants cooking up *pho* and other Vietnamese dishes along the stretch of Larkin Street dubbed Little Saigon, Vietnam II's menu shines with all-star dishes. Come here for giant bowls of star anise–scented broth with noodles, rare beef, brisket, or other seasonal meat and seafood. Other offerings are the deep-fried boneless duck, and abalone and crab, live from the tanks. ♦ Vietnamese ♦ Daily, breakfast, lunch, and dinner. 701 Larkin St (at Ellis St). 885.1274 ♿

## 7 Bodega Bistro

★★$ Jimmy Kwok, the Hanoi-born chef/owner, makes creations from Vietnamese food staples. Try the noodle soup with chicken, beef, or seafood. He makes a paste of crab and shrimp that melts into the crab soup, then tosses in fresh herbs and finishes with Vietnamese garnishes. The dishes on the Hanoi Street Cuisine menu, such as the stuffed pancakes, show the culinary creativity of this Asian culture. ♦ Vietnamese ♦ Daily, lunch and dinner. 607 Larkin St (at Eddy St). 921.1218 ♿

## 8 The Phoenix Hotel

$$ The 44-room urban inn in "Tendernob" borders the disparate neighborhoods of Nob Hill and the Tenderloin. The presence of the Phoenix and its popular **Bambuddha Lounge** started the new urban identity. The hotel has a resortlike feel, with a pool, outdoor café, garden, and massage and other bodywork services on-site. Popular with the artistic and celebrity sets, it often hosts rock stars. The bedrooms and grounds feature original art from Bay Area artists, and the hotel has its own video channel featuring movies made in San Francisco. On-site parking and continental breakfast are included. The hip, trendy Bambuddha Lounge, a retro-LA poolside lounge with ebony benches and tables, serves Southeast Asian cuisine and party cocktails (885.5088). ♦ 601 Eddy St (at Larkin St). 776.1380, 800/CITY.INN ♿

## 9 California Culinary Academy

★$$ The students at San Francisco's best-known cooking school may change, but standards remain uncompromisingly

Dense afternoon and evening fogs are common in San Francisco during the summer months, sometimes causing the temperature to drop by as much as 30 degrees in a matter of hours.

Poet Maya Angelou was San Francisco's first black female street-car conductor.

high. You have a choice of two restaurants: The **Academy Grill** offers a lunch menu of sandwiches, salads, and other straightforward fare, as well as a buffet dinner; the more formal **Careme Room,** surrounded by a glass-enclosed kitchen, serves a prix-fixe three-course lunch and dinner on most weekdays and a classic European buffet dinner on Friday (the menu reflects what students are learning to make that week). Be forewarned: Prices are not as low as many diners think they ought to be for student labor. ◆ Continental ◆ M-F, lunch and dinner. Reservations recommended for the Academy Grill, required for the Careme Room. 625 Polk St (at Turk St). 771.3500 ᙠ Weekend Gourmet at the Academy holds one-day cooking classes every Saturday. 354.9198

## 10 BOOKS INC.

This shop is popular with bibliophiles looking for the latest good read. Signings and readings by authors are often held. ◆ Daily. Opera Plaza, 601 Van Ness Ave (at Golden Gate Ave). 441.6670 ᙠ

## 10 MAX'S OPERA CAFÉ

★$$ Jeans and evening gowns mix in this upscale New York–style deli and bar, a popular pre- and post-performance haunt for those attending events at the nearby **Performing Arts Center.** Specials include ample portions of barbecued brisket of beef—enough for two. Calorie counters can choose from such low-fat—but equally large—selections as salads with an oil-free mustard dressing, broiled chicken breast with tomato vinaigrette, and a turkey Salisbury steak. The waitstaff also provides entertainment, breaking into song throughout the evening. Takeout is available. ◆ American/Deli ◆ Daily, lunch and dinner. Opera Plaza, 601 Van Ness Ave (at Golden Gate Ave). 771.7301 ᙠ

## 11 FEDERAL OFFICE BUILDING

This building was constructed in 1959 by **Albert F. Roller, Stone/Marraccini/Patters,** and **John Carl Warnecke.** The bland face of the federal government building—a Miesian slab block set back from the street—offers a somber contrast to the ornate designs of the Civic Center. A new 18-story federal building just opened at 1000 Mission Street. ◆ 450 Golden Gate Ave (between Larkin and Polk Sts)

## 12 EDMUND G. BROWN STATE OFFICE BUILDING

**Skidmore, Owings & Merrill** were the architects for this complex, which was built in

1986. Their design complements the **Louise M. Davies Symphony Hall** down the street by facing diagonally toward **City Hall** and completing the Beaux Arts composition of civic buildings along this stretch of Van Ness Avenue. Clad in white precast concrete, it has a large seal of the State of California above the entry to the courtyard, which is disappointingly institutional in scale. ◆ Van Ness Ave (at McAllister St) ᙠ

## 13 ABIGAIL HOTEL

$$ Built in 1926 to house members of visiting theater groups, this Howard Johnson hotel was remodeled in an arty European style. Gone are the smiling moose head and family of stuffed elk; now there's a cozy, British feeling, complete with antiques, down comforters, and turn-of-the-century English art. While still not exactly luxurious, the 60-room hotel is a good value and conveniently located. ◆ 246 McAllister St (between Hyde and Larkin Sts). 626.6500

## 14 HIBERNIA BANK

At the time of its construction in 1892, **Willis Polk** described **Albert Pissis**'s design as "the most beautiful building in the city." Notice how it turns the corner of Jones and McAllister Streets at Market Street with a domed vestibule. ◆ Jones St (at McAllister St)

## 15 WAR MEMORIAL VETERANS BUILDING

Built in 1932 to honor World War I soldiers, this Beaux Arts–style edifice has a near identical twin in the **War Memorial Opera House.** In addition to housing the **Herbst Theater** (see below), the building is home to the offices of veterans' groups. ◆ 401 Van Ness Ave (at McAllister St). 621.6600. City Hall: 554.4000 ᙠ

Within the Veterans Building:

## HERBST THEATER

Built in 1932, this minor component of the **Performing Arts Center** was refurbished in 1978. But the orchestra seats are raked, and the balconies sit too far back in this 916-seat theater. It's best for small theatrical performances, dance groups, lectures, and recitals. The hall is adorned with murals depicting Earth, Water, Air, and Fire, the four elements of the ancient world. They were executed by British painter Frank Brangwyn for the Panama-Pacific Exposition of 1915. ◆ First floor. 392.4400 ᙠ

## 16 ASIAN ART MUSEUM

The museum reopened in its new home after a $160.5 million transformation of the 1917 Beaux Arts building, the former main library. Architect **Gae Aulenti,** who converted a Paris train station into the celebrated Musée d'Orsay, reprised that accomplishment in San Francisco. The museum's core collection of 13,000 objects spans 6,000 years and a hundred countries and cultures. The second- and third-floor galleries house 2,500 works from the museum collection. In the Japanese galleries, during the monthly tea ceremony, visitors learn about the Japanese ritual and drink sweet bowls of whisked green tea. The ground floor has a museum store and a café with an outdoor dining terrace overlooking the Fulton Street mall. ◆ Tu-Su, 10AM-5PM; Th until 9PM. Admission includes a complimentary audio tour of the galleries. Free first Tuesday of the month. 200 Larkin St (at McAllister St). 581.3500. www.asianart.org

## 17 INN AT THE OPERA

$$$ This 47-room hotel was built in 1927 to house visiting opera stars. Elegantly restored, its luxuries include queen-size beds, large bathrooms, wet bars, small refrigerators, microwaves, 24-hour room service, concierge services, and parking. Rates include a continental breakfast buffet. Just a few steps away are the **Opera House** and **Davies Symphony Hall.** ◆ 333 Fulton St (between Franklin and Gough Sts). 863.8400, 800/325.2708. www.innattheopera.com ও

Within the Inn at the Opera:

## OVATION AT THE OPERA

★★$$$$ Filled with wonderful oil paintings and flower arrangements, an ornate bar, dark wood appointments, an oversize fireplace, and deep, plush banquettes, it's appealing at any time, and the perfect spot for a nightcap and a light bite after a concert or evening on the town. The seasonal menu might include roasted free-range chicken breast with chicken and pistachio sausage, butter-whipped yams, and caramelized apples; or seared Maine scallops with blood orange glaze and braised greens. Free valet parking. ◆ Californian/American Grill ◆ Daily, dinner. Reservations recommended. 863.8400 ও

## 18 JARDINIÈRE

★★★$$$ Traci Des Jardins's restaurant does more than just fill the need for dinner before a performance or after an afternoon on trendy Hayes Street. Warm, weathered brick helps create a backdrop for a classy celebration at this two-story restaurant. Backlit champagne buckets were built into a ribbonlike railing on the mezzanine level, and the dome over the oval bar is fitted with fiber optics, tiny champagne-bubble lights. Chef Des Jardins, who was "born into a family that took pride in eating well," changes the menu daily. Starters can include lobster-leek-chanterelle strudel, and entrées range from pan-roasted squab with baby turnips and tatsoi to lamb loin with squash blossoms, cranberry beans, and tomato confit. An inventive cheese course features more than 50 choices that are kept in a temperature-controlled "cave." For dessert try the bittersweet Scharffen Berger chocolate torte, or brown butter walnut cake with crème fraiche and caramel ice cream, or sip a glass of Vin de Glacière. ◆ French-Californian. ◆ Daily, dinner. Late-night menu until midnight. Reservations recommended. 300 Grove St (at Franklin St). 861.5555. www.jardiniere.com ও

## 18 SAN FRANCISCO BALLET ASSOCIATION BUILDING

Architect **Beverly Willis** designed this modest addition to the **Civic Center** composition in 1984. It contains administrative offices, a ballet school, and state-of-the-art rehearsal studios. The facilities are not open to the public. ◆ 455 Franklin St (at Grove St). 861.5600

## 19 WAR MEMORIAL OPERA HOUSE

This splendid and ornate house is the crown jewel of San Francisco's **Performing Arts Center.** With seating for 3,176, it opened on 15 October 1932, and like the **Veterans Building** it is dedicated to the memory of World War I soldiers and is now home to the city's renowned opera and ballet companies. The opera season opens in September with a gala—replete with splendidly gowned and bejeweled patrons—and runs through December. The ballet season immediately follows. For tours during opera season, call 552.8338. ◆ 301 Van Ness Ave (at Grove St). 861.4008 ও

## 20 CITY HALL

The focal point of the **Civic Center** complex was designed in 1915 by **Bakewell and Brown.** This magnificent symbol of government has a huge dome (modeled after

St. Peter's in Rome), Baroque stairs, and echoing marble-clad corridors. The building underwent a $175 million seismic renovation. Visit the City Hall Store in the lobby. History was made at City Hall in 2004 when smiling single-sex couples posed for the camera on their wedding day. The plaza in front of the building has gardens and playgrounds, and is often used for fairs and festivals. ◆ Van Ness Ave (at McAllister St). 554.4000

## 21 SAN FRANCISCO PUBLIC LIBRARY

Opened in April 1996, San Francisco's library, designed by **Pei Cobb Freed and Partners** with **Simon Martin-Vegue Winkelstein Morris Associated Architects,** has double the capacity of the former library across the street, housing more than two million books and audiovisual materials. Note that the gray granite façades on Larkin and Fulton Streets blend with the Beaux Arts style of the **Civic Center,** while the stark geometric formation along Grove and Hyde Streets complements the modern commercial buildings on nearby Market Street. The library's interior is organized around two major spaces: a great open staircase and a five-story skylit open space that connects the library's various divisions. The library is divided into several centers, including **Art and Music, Business and Technology,** the **Environmental Center,** the **Government Information Center,** and **Humanities and General Collections.**

There are also centers for the blind and visually impaired, and for the deaf and hearing impaired; a **Chinese Center;** an **African-American Center;** a **Gay and Lesbian Center;** and the **Children's Center,** which features a storytelling room and the **Children's Creative Center** with live performances and crafts programs. The **Exhibit Gallery** showcases rare artwork and artifacts from the library's own collection, as well as those on loan from other institutions such as the Smithsonian and the Library of Congress. A café offers beverages and light snacks. ◆ 100 Larkin St (at Fulton St). 557.4400 ⑤

Within the San Francisco Public Library:

## SAN FRANCISCO HISTORY ROOM AND SPECIAL COLLECTIONS DEPARTMENT

In this combination document-and-photograph museum and research library you'll find glass cases filled with memorabilia, including photos of some of the city's classic buildings that no longer exist and of historic events such as the opening of the Golden Gate Bridge. ◆ Free. Tu-W, F, afternoon; Th, Sa, morning and afternoon. 557.4567 ⑤

## 22 ORPHEUM THEATER

**B. Marcus Priteca** designed this 2,503-seat theater in 1926. In bygone days, it was an important part of the vaudeville scene. Today, the huge space is used for large-scale theatrical productions. ◆ 1192 Market St (at Hyde and Eighth Sts). Call 551.2000 for current and upcoming plays. 512.7770. www.bestofbroadway.com

## 23 UNITED NATIONS PLAZA

This plaza memorializes the fact that the UN Charter was written and signed in this city in 1945. The plaza has become a hangout for panhandlers. ◆ Market St (at Fulton St) ⑤

In United Nations Plaza:

## HEART OF THE CITY FARMERS' MARKET

Fresh fruits and vegetables, direct from the growers, are sold at low prices. ◆ W, Su. Market St (between Grove and Fulton Sts). 558.9455 ⑤

## 24 SAN FRANCISCO PERFORMING ARTS LIBRARY AND MUSEUM

Exhibitions related to the performing arts of the Bay Area are featured here. ◆ Free. Tu-Sa. 399 Grove St (at Gough St). 255.4800 ⑤

## 25 CITIZEN CAKE

★★★$$ Elizabeth Falkner presides over the city's favorite patisserie, restaurant, and bar. She dares you to walk past her tortes and mile-high layer cakes oozing with butter cream and mousse without ordering a slice. The San Francisco institution devoted to fabulous desserts has also become a good place for cocktails, wine, and dinner. The dinner menu features seasonal Californian cuisine and may include rib-eye steak with potatoes and leeks or a classic duck breast with cippolini and turnips. ◆ Desserts/American ◆ Tu-Su, breakfast and lunch; Tu-Sa, dinner. 399 Grove St (at Gough St). 861.2228. www.citizencake.com ⑤

## 26 LOUISE M. DAVIES SYMPHONY HALL

Designed by **Skidmore, Owings & Merrill,** this hall, which is named after arts patron Louise M. Davies, who contributed $5 million toward its construction, opened in 1980 after more than a decade of squabbling. It cost $33 million to build (all but $5 million of it was raised privately), and in 1992 the hall underwent a $10 million acoustical and architectural face-lift. The renovations included a new sound and video system as well as a computer-assisted resculpturing of the walls to improve acoustics. The hall is the official home of the **San Francisco Symphony,** whose season runs from September through May. Besides the symphony, the 2,743-seat Davies regularly books other musical and touring groups. ♦ Admission charge for tours. Tours of the Performing Arts Center (Louise M. Davies Symphony Hall, War Memorial Opera House, and Herbst Theater) meet at the Grove Street entrance M on the hour, 10AM to 2PM. Van Ness Ave (at Grove St). Tours 552.8338, box office 431.5400 &

# 27 BILL GRAHAM CIVIC AUDITORIUM

Designed by architect **John Galen Howard,** the auditorium was completed in 1915 during the architectural renaissance that followed the destruction of the 1906 earthquake and fire. In 1993 the **Civic Auditorium**'s name was changed to honor Bill Graham, the local rock music impresario who promoted such legends as the Grateful Dead, Miles Davis, and Jimi Hendrix. The auditorium serves as the city's main conference center and has seating for 7,000 people. ♦ 99 Grove St (between Larkin and Polk Sts). 974.4000 &

# 28 PLACE PIGALLE

★$ This artsy café has a back room dedicated to monthly art exhibits, poetry readings, and live entertainment on the weekends. The copper-topped bar and sofas arranged in conversational groupings add warmth, as do the wines, beers, and coffee drinks. The small menu includes smoked salmon, quiche, and cheese plates. ♦ Café ♦ Daily, lunch and dinner. No credit cards accepted. 520 Hayes St (between Octavia and Laguna Sts). 552.2671 &

# 29 OCTAVIA BOULEVARD

Ⓟ When Hayes Valley residents voted to demolish the quake-damaged Central Freeway, Octavia Boulevard was offered as an alternative, and construction began on the four-lane roadway. The central median dividing the roadways is a green oasis of poplars, elms, flowering plants, park benches, and cobblestone-like paving. A one-acre neighborhood park, Patricia's Green at Hayes Valley, now blooms at the junction of Octavia and Hayes Streets. Patricia Walkup was a neighborhood activist who was a central figure in the demolition of the Central Freeway and the building of the boulevard.

# 30 OCTAVIA'S HAZE GALLERY

Enter this light-filled gallery that displays vessels in a thousand colors and you'll have a hard time departing without a purchase. The fine art of handblown glass is alive in the Bay Area. Starbursts of color bring the bowls, vases, and platters to life. The gallery features the work of San Franciscan glass artists. Even the glass earrings and handblown pendants dazzle. Director Kelly Yount holds exhibitions for internationally acclaimed glass masters, such as Tsuchida Yashuhiko and Orlando Zennaro. ♦ 498 Hayes St at Octavia St. 255.6818. www.octaviashaze.com

# 31 ABSINTHE BRASSERIE AND BAR

★★$$ Popular with a diverse clientele, this attractive restaurant has an interesting menu that changes daily. Showstoppers include grilled chicken stuffed with herbs in a champagne sauce. Excellent oyster bar. ♦ French/Mediterranean ♦ Tu-F, lunch and dinner; Sa, dinner; Su, brunch and dinner. Reservations recommended. 398 Hayes St (at Gough St). 551.1590. www.absinthe.com &

# 32 F. DORIAN, INC.

Unique ethnic folk art and jewelry from around the world are sold here. ♦ Daily. 370 Hayes St (between Franklin and Gough Sts). 861.3191. www.fdorian.com &

# 33 AMPHORA WINE MERCHANT

Neil Mechanic charms patrons with his encyclopedic knowledge of wine. Tell him your host is serving spring rolls and roast crab and he'll pull five bottles off the shelf ranging in price from $15 to $75 and expound the merits of each. He holds weekly wine-tasting seminars and offers a daily wine flight. Check out his table of $15-or-less wines. ♦ Daily. 384-A Hayes St (between Franklin and Gough Sts). 863.1104. www.arlequinwine.com

# 34 HAYES STREET GRILL

★★$$$ One of the city's most renowned seafood houses, it has built a reputation for serving the freshest fish with a choice of a half dozen sauces.  Salads all have unusual twists, such as grilled calamari with fennel, red onion, and arugula, or shrimp with grapefruit and lime. The 1930s-style light fixtures, bentwood chairs, white walls, and white tablecloths give the place a comfortable look. The service is erratic—anywhere from grill-room surly (heaven help you if you want to send anything

# The Best

**Dianne Feinstein**
United States Senator

I'm a native San Franciscan and terribly in love with my city. Selecting a favorite place is consequently very difficult, since there are simply miles and miles of pleasures and delights packed into our 47-square-mile area.

However, caveats aside, I always recommend that visitors stroll through **Golden Gate Park,** with its more than 1,000 acres of magnificent trees, plants, and greenswards. The park also houses our renowned **Japanese Tea Garden,** a special park within a park whose ambience is unmistakably Eastern—a wonderful place to reflect and relax.

San Francisco's finest museum is also located within Golden Gate Park—the **de Young Museum.**

I also highly recommend visiting San Francisco's **Chinatown**—one of the largest outside of Asia—where you can eat exquisitely for very low prices and shop for virtually anything.

And don't forget to ride one of San Francisco's cable cars. The city, with tremendous support from the private sector, has rehabilitated this century-old

transportation system—America's only national monument—and it remains a g to see San Francisco's incredibly hilly str spectacular views.

Visit **Fisherman's Wharf** too and sample our incomparable Dungeness crab, sourdough bread, and succulent seafood. Be sure to take a boat ride on **San Francisco Bay,** one of the world's most beautiful deep-water bodies. You can sail right under the **Golden Gate Bridge**—as well as the equally impressive **Bay Bridge.** Views of San Francisco from the bay are breathtaking.

As for restaurants, we have more per capita than any city in America and they range fully across the world's most exciting cuisines. We have food for literally every palate!

Shopping is also excellent, particularly in **Union Square,** one of the nation's leading retail centers, located in the heart of downtown San Francisco.

My final recommendation is probably the most important one: Be sure to meet our citizens. San Francisco is a cultural cornucopia of the world's people, most of whom are friendly, helpful, and eager to share their insights about life in San Francisco.

back!) to diner-friendly. ♦ Seafood ♦ M-F, lunch and dinner; Sa, Su, dinner. 320 Hayes St (at Franklin St). 863.5545. www.hayesstreetgrill.com &

## 35 Suppenküche

★★$$ This German restaurant is popular for its venison with red cabbage and cranberry sauce, chicken stew, and pork schnitzel with spaetzle. ♦ German ♦ Daily, dinner; Sa, Su, brunch. 525 Laguna St (at Hayes St). 252.9289. www.suppenkuche.com &

## 36 Fritz Fries and DJ Art Teahouse

★★$ Share a large cone of thick Belgian fries and platter of dipping sauces like strawberry mustard, pesto mayonnaise, curry ketchup, and Kalamáta olive ketchup. Also popular are the sweet and savory Belgian crepes. This hip café names its fare after famous artists—try the Basquiat sandwich or the Duchamp crepes. Wash it down with a pitcher of Belgian beer. In sunny weather, head for the mosaic-lined courtyard. ♦ Belgian ♦ Daily, lunch and dinner. 579 Hayes St (between

Octavia and Laguna Sts). 864.7654. www.FritzFries.com & Also at Ghirardelli Sq, 900 Northpoint (at Larkin St). 928.3886

## 37 Alabaster

Furnishings and antiques fill this amazing store. The street-front room displays vintage fragrance bottles, alabaster lamps, and French comic books. A back door leads through a courtyard to the shop's remaining rooms, crowded with owner Nelson Bloncourt's collections. Handle the Venetian treasures, ornate mirrors, Art Deco housewares, and teapots with care. ♦ Tu-Su. 597 Hayes St (at Laguna St). 558.0482. www.alabastersf.com &

## 38 Flight 001

This 747-shaped shop houses a great selection of wheel-aboard luggage, such as Hideo Wakamatuse trolleys in blossom patterns. Browse the shelves for aero therapy and other provisions for en-route comfort that you didn't think you needed but can't live without. ♦ Daily. 525 Hayes St (between Octavia and Laguna Sts). 487.1001. www.flight001.com &

**Restaurants/Clubs: Red | Hotels: Purple | Shops: Orange | Outdoors/Parks: Green | Sights/Culture: Blue**

# TROLLEYS TO YESTERYEAR

Matt Morrow/NORTH MARKET STREET GRAPHICS '98

The cheerful clang of historic trolleys once again sounds on Market Street, thanks to the donations of vintage cars from various US cities and other countries. Originally introduced in 1935 at a time when a fleet of 1,000 electric cars plied Market Street, a hundred streetcars were brought back into operation in 1995 to launch MUNI's new F-line service. These Presidential Conference Cars (PCCs), affectionately called "green torpedoes," run from Castro Street, past the Civic Center area, through the Financial District to the Ferry Building, then rumble north along The Embarcadero to Pier 39, with its terminus at Fisherman's Wharf.

Some examples of trolleys from other places include Car 351 from Johnstown, Pennsylvania; the popular "boat" car of the English seaside resort of Blackpool; two 1927 trams from Japan; and a 1928 tram all the way from Australia. As a result, no city comes close to matching San Francisco's collection of Art Deco–era streetcars. So hop aboard one for a riotous ride through the scenic heart of the city.

## 39 EVELYN'S ANTIQUE CHINESE FURNITURE

For a good selection of Chinese pieces, this is the place. ♦ M-Sa. 381 Hayes St (at Gough St). 255.1815 ♿

## 40 BLUE BOTTLE COFFEE CO.

This tiny sidewalk kiosk serves the most sought-after coffee in the city. Blue Bottle evokes obsessive loyalty from its patrons not only for its quality but the baristas' froth art. They use organic milk and sell cookies and biscotti for dipping. Linden is between Hayes and Fell Sts. ♦ Coffeehouse ♦ Daily. 315 Linden St (at Gough St). 252.7532. www.bluebottlecoffee.net ♿

## 41 SAN FRANCISCO CONSERVATORY OF MUSIC

This prestigious school joins the symphony, ballet, and opera in the city's burgeoning Performing Arts district. Each year SFCM serves 1,300 students through its collegiate division and summer programs. Public performances take place in the Osher salon, the Recital Hall, and the large Concert Hall. The performance schedule is available online, or call 503.6277 for recorded information. You can purchase tickets an hour before performances at the SFCM box office. ◆ 50 Oak St (between Van Ness Ave and Franklin St). 503.6275. www.sfcm.edu &

## 42 ARTS COMMISSION GALLERY

Indoor and outdoor exhibitions of work by both emerging and established Bay Area artists are presented here. ◆ Tu-Sa. 25 Van Ness Ave (between Oak and Hickory Sts). 252.2590 &

## 43 BISTRO CLOVIS

★★$ The setting is pure Parisian wine bar, where classic country flavors come alive in the onion soup gratinée, sweetbread and scampi casserole, and duck filet with green peppercorn sauce. Be sure to do some wine sampling too: Three two-ounce tastes of different wines are available at a modest fee. ◆ French ◆ Tu-F, lunch; Tu-Su, dinner. 1596 Market St (at Franklin St). 864.0231 &

## 44 ZUNI RESTAURANT & BAR

★★★$$$ Since opening Zuni's in 1979 with a menu of Southwestern fare (hence the name), Judy Rodgers has developed a Mediterranean style of cooking that includes a grand selection of oysters, roast chicken cooked in a wood-burning oven with bread salad (bread and greens in a champagne vinaigrette), juicy ground-to-order hamburgers on house-baked focaccia, and frosty espresso granita (coffee-flavored shaved ice). ◆ Californian/Mediterranean ◆ Tu-Su, lunch and dinner. Reservations recommended. 1658 Market St (at Rose St, between Franklin and Gough Sts). 552.2522 &

## 45 CAV WINE BAR & KITCHEN

★$$ Chef Christine Mullen's seasonal menu traverses the Mediterranean. She makes everything in-house from pickles and mustards to pasta. Charcuterie items include chicken liver mousse, rabbit rillettes, and boar pâté. The true aficionado will go for the salami platter. Other popular dishes are cheese-filled mission figs, fondue for two, and pork belly with shiitake mushrooms. Pamela Busch masterminded the wine list, picking 300 wines from locales around the globe. ◆ Mediterranean ◆ M-Sa, dinner. 1666 Market St (near Gough St) 437.1770. www.cavwinebar.com &

## 46 EDWARDIAN SAN FRANCISCO HOTEL

$ This pleasant European-style hotel has 36 small, cheerful rooms with shared bathrooms (there are 9 rooms and 4 bathrooms on each floor). ◆ 1668 Market St (between Franklin and Gough Sts). 864.1271; 888/864.8070. www.edwardiansfhotel.com

---

Restaurants/Clubs: Red  |  Hotels: Purple  |  Shops: Orange  |  Outdoors/Parks: Green  |  Sights/Culture: Blue

# SOUTH OF MARKET (SOMA)

**P**opularly known as SOMA, but familiar to earlier generations as "South of the Slot," the South of Market area has evolved into one of San Francisco's most eclectic new neighborhoods. It incorporates a new shopping center, high-rise hotels, trendy restaurants, a wholesale flower market, a train terminal, a baseball park, a convention center, warehouses, and rock, comedy, and jazz clubs, as well as ultramodern condominium towers.

Close to **The Embarcadero** and the bay, SOMA has always been home to industry. Several foundries were located here in the 1850s, along with row after row of tiny houses, many prefabricated in the East, which the city's first industrial population occupied. Author Jack London, born on **Third Street** in 1876, reflected his rough-and-ready neighborhood in his work. But when it became apparent that the climate was warmest on this side of town, **Rincon Hill** became a prestigious address. Small, elegant shops filled **Second Street**. Adjacent **South Park** was a pioneer real-estate development promoted by George Gordan, an Englishman who modeled residences for 64 families on the plan of terraces in London. Stately Georgian houses rose around an enclosed park to which only the residents had a gate key. Here lived cattle king Henry Miller, Senator William McKendree Gwin, and Hall McAllister, until he lost his mansion in a poker game.

But before the park was half built, the decline of Rincon Hill set in because of the persistent industrialization of the neighborhood. Its residents fled to Nob Hill, abandoning their homes to Japanese immigrants. Rooming houses and machine shops took over, although remnants of grandeur can still be seen here and there, especially on Third Street between **Bryant** and **Brannan** Streets.

Creative professionals have bought and gentrified their South Park homes. Several residential projects have opened, bringing in hundreds of new residents. Infinity, a 35-story tower at Folsom and Main Streets, offers urban living for $560,000 for a studio condo. At One Rincon at First and Harrison Streets, one-bedroom condos go for $800,000.

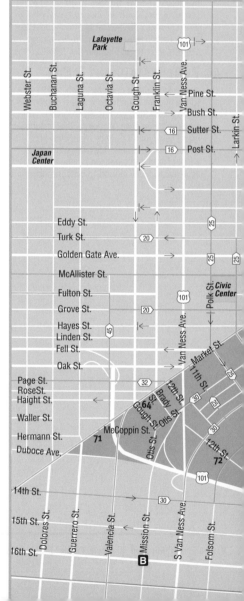

The **Yerba Buena** neighborhood surrounds **Yerba Buena Gardens,** the arts and cultural center, which opened its doors in October 1993 and is now the most concentrated arts district outside New York City. The center's striking visual-arts building was designed by renowned Japanese architect **Fumihiko Maki,** and a theater by highly acclaimed New York architect **James Stewart Polshek,** while across Third Street, Swiss architect **Mario Botta** designed the massive brick **Museum of Modern Art.**

Also fueling SOMA's emerging prestige is **AT&T Park** baseball stadium, luxury residential towers along King Street and on Rincon Hill, and the **University of California San Francisco (UCSF)** campus in Mission Bay. Muni has opened the new Third Street line and plans are underway to build a new cruise ship terminal at Pier 30/32.

## 1 ONE MARKET RESTAURANT

★★★$$$ Celebrity chef Bradley Ogden created a hit restaurant that, despite its grand size, gets so packed you often have to make reservations weeks in advance. The view and the sounds set the mood: The airy dining room lined with huge windows overlooks the side of **Justin Herman Plaza** and the end of bustling Market Street, and jazz piano music dominates the attractive bar in the evenings. Mark Dommen is making his menu more casual, with such dishes as meat loaf, pork chops, roasted vegetables, and grilled beef tenderloin. This venture is every bit as successful as Ogden's others, but the food quality is more variable—sometimes marvelous, sometimes just okay. ♦ Californian ♦ M-F, lunch and dinner; Sa, dinner; Su, jazz brunch and dinner. Reservations recommended. 1 Market St (at Steuart St). 777.5577. www.onemarket.com &

## 2 SAN FRANCISCO RAILWAY MUSEUM

Rarely seen photographs from the Municipal Railway archives cover the walls and give visitors a glimpse of pre-1906 San Francisco. Exhibits include fare boxes, the Wiley birdcage traffic signal, and vintage travel posters. Railway memorabilia is for sale in the gift shop. At the Steuart St F-line stop south of the Ferry Building. ♦ W-Su, 10AM-6PM. 77 Steuart St (at Mission St). 974.1948. www.streetcar.org &

## 3 HOTEL VITALE

$$$ Three reasons to book a room at the city's newest full-service luxury hotel: breathtaking views of San Francisco Bay, a rooftop garden with a day spa, **Spa Vitale** (278.3788; www.spavitale.com), and circular suites with 270-degree water-and-light views. Designers chose a soothing décor of blue-gray and pale-green tones in the Vitale's 199 spacious guest rooms and suites. All the home-away-from-home necessities, such as Wi-Fi in all the rooms, spa-style bathrooms with soaking tubs, natural fabrics on bed linens and pillows, are here. A fitness center, yoga studio, business center, outdoor living-room café, restaurant (**Americano**), and bar are conveniently located in-house. The relaxing indoor lounge is a good place for afternoon tea. ♦ 10 Mission St (at The Embarcadero). 278.3700; 800/738.7477. www.hotelvitale.com &

## 4 AUDIFFRED BUILDING

Built in 1889 by Hippolyte d'Audiffred, this brick building was the only one south of Market to survive the fire after the 1906 earthquake. Ironically, it burned down in 1981, but has since been restored. ♦ Mission St (at Steuart St)

## 5 RINCON CENTER

The old **Rincon Annex Post Office Building,** built here in 1940 by **Gilbert Stanley Underwood,** is one of the city's masterpieces, and was incorporated into a massive complex of offices, shops, restaurants, and apartment towers in 1989 by **Johnson, Fain, and Pereira Associates.** The historic murals that were in the annex lobby are the centerpiece of the 85-foot-high skylighted atrium from which falls a magnificent cascade of water. The post office has moved to 2 Rincon Center. ♦ Spear St (at Mission St) &

## 5 COSMOPOLITAN CAFE

★$$ This café, tucked between office towers, is a favorite of the Financial District lunch crowd, who love the sophisticated menu and surroundings of deep taupe walls covered with oversized artwork of lovers embracing. Chef Steven Levine creates a fine dining experience and satisfying menu from local ingredients. Try the cornmeal-crusted rainbow trout, lamb loin with grilled artichokes, or seared ahi with jasmine rice. There are great appetizers to nibble on in the piano lounge, like the Dungeness crab enchiladas and the grilled flatbread with chanterelles and crescenza cheese. ♦ American ♦ M-F, lunch; M-Sa, dinner. 121 Spear St (between Howard and Mission Sts). 543.4001. www.thecosmopolitancafe.com &

## 6 HOTEL GRIFFON

$$$ Originally built in 1907, making it the oldest hotel on the waterfront, this 62-room place is part of the expanding Financial District, which has moved south of Market Street. It is a block from the **Ferry Terminal** and a scant two blocks from the **California Street Cable-Car Line.** The **E-Line** passes right in front. The rooms have minibars, and complimentary services include morning coffee and daily newspaper delivery. ♦ Reservations only. 155 Steuart St (between Howard and Mission Sts). 495.2100; 800/321.2201 &

Within the Hotel Griffon:

## FAZ RESTAURANT

★★$$ Everything prepared on the fireplace grill at this cozy eatery is wonderful. Food is plentiful and tastes home-cooked. Try the roasted artichokes or the roasted salmon salad tossed with spinach, mango, onion, cucumber, hard-boiled eggs, dried cranberries, and toasted pine nuts, or the saffron cheese croquettes, the grilled prawns, or the smoked Petaluma duck with pomegranate sauce. The most popular dishes are the filet mignon with portobello mushrooms and the lightly smoked rack of lamb. ♦ Mediterranean

♦ 155 Steuart St (between Howard and Mission Sts). 495.6500. www.fazrestaurants.com &

## 6 THE CONTEMPORARY JEWISH MUSEUM

SOMA arts institutions will welcome a new member when architect **Daniel Libeskind** completes the transformation of the 1907 brick Power Substation into a state-of-the-art museum. Libeskind is the architect responsible for creating the master plan for the reconstruction of the World Trade Center in New York. The Jewish Museum will include space for changing exhibitions, a media project, art workshops, lectures, films, and performances. ♦ 121 Steuart St (at Mission St). & (Note: This is a temporary location through 2009.)

## 7 HARBOR COURT HOTEL

$$ When the despised Embarcadero Freeway was torn down due to damage caused by the 1989 quake, this hotel gained some great bay views. Housed in a 1907 building, it has 131 small guest rooms (30 have the views) and a magnificent lobby with a stone fireplace. Patrons have gym privileges at the adjacent **YMCA,** complimentary wine every evening from 5 to 7PM, and daily limousine service to the Financial District. ♦ 165 Steuart St (between Howard and Mission Sts). 882.1300, 800/346.0555. www.harborcourthotel.com &

## 8 YANK SING

★★★$$ One of the best dim-sum houses in San Francisco, this place just happens to be south of Market Street. All the dishes arrive on carts, and virtually everything is delicious. Don't miss the Peking duck, steamed pork buns, chicken wrapped in foil, and the custard tarts for dessert. At the end of the meal, your server tallies up the plates and totals the bill. ♦ Chinese ♦ Daily, lunch. 49 Stevenson Pl (between Mission and Market Sts; between First and Second Sts). 541.4949. www.yanksing.com. Also at 101 Spear St at Mission St in Rincon Center. 957.9300

## 9 TRANSBAY TERMINAL

When the Bay Bridge was opened, this austere, functional 1939 building by Timothy Pflueger (with consulting architects Arthur Brown Jr. and John L. Donovan) replaced the Ferry Terminal as the gateway to the city. The city wants to replace the structure on this site and add a tunnel for CalTrain, and has

plans for a high-speed rail from Los Angeles. ♦ Mission St (at First St) &

## 10 GORDON BIERSCH

★★$$ This branch of the popular Palo Alto–based brewery-restaurant was a word-of-mouth success even before it opened. Beer, brick, and business suits dominate the ground floor, while diners herd upstairs to sample the sparse but tempting menu. Visually stimulating but acoustically devastating, this place—located in the old Hills Brothers coffee factory—seems to reach rock-concert decibel levels even at lunch. ♦ Californian ♦ Daily, lunch and dinner. Reservations recommended. 2 Harrison St (at Steuart St and The Embarcadero). 243.8246 &

## 11 BAY BRIDGE

Charles H. Purcell was chief engineer for this bridge, which eliminated the isolation between the cities of San Francisco and Oakland. The longest steel high-level bridge in the world, and one of the most costly structures ever built, it took three years to construct. The 8-mile span from approach to approach is, in fact, two bridges separated by a tunnel through Yerba Buena Island. The foundations of one of the piers extend 242 feet below water, deeper than those of any other bridge ever built. The pier is bigger than the largest of the world's pyramids and required more concrete than the Empire State Building in New York City. The San Francisco side consists of a double-suspension bridge; the Oakland side is a cantilever bridge. The bridge has two levels, with five lanes in each direction. Originally, electric trains and trucks ran on the lower deck and cars on the upper deck, but the tracks were removed in the late 1950s when the trains were replaced by buses. During the October 1989 quake, an upper section of the bridge collapsed onto the lower one, sending motorists fleeing from their cars and killing one person; the damage was repaired in just one month. Today it's the busiest thoroughfare in the area. Tolls have raised enough revenue to pay for other means of public transportation, including the **BART** tube, the **San Mateo/Hayward Bridge,** and most of the **Dumbarton Bridge.** The best views of the bridge are from Yerba Buena Island and from below on **The Embarcadero** in San Francisco. ♦ Toll westbound

## 12 FOUR SEASONS HOTEL SAN FRANCISCO

$$$$ Housed in a new 40-story mixed-use complex, the hotel occupies 10 floors while residents occupy the other floors. The

sprawling Sports Club/LA, to which hotel guests have free use, takes over the lower floors. The rooms are elegant and comfortable, with down comforters, terry robes, and Bulgari toiletries. The spacious bathrooms have a deep soaking tub, and a vanity of Italian marble. The **Seasons Restaurant** serves three meals a day, serving products from Bay Area farms, ranches, and dairies. This is a favorite lunch stop for downtown shoppers. ♦ 757 Market St (between Third and Fourth Sts). 633.3000; www.fourseasons.com

## 13 WESTIN SAN FRANCISCO MARKET STREET

$$$$ Formerly the Argent Hotel, this sleek hotel was built in 1983 by Air France and features 667 rooms and suites, many with sweeping city views. Within walking distance of Union Square, the Financial District, and the **Moscone Convention Center,** it offers guests valet parking, a health club, room service, and a business center. The hotel caters to allergy sufferers and the environmentally conscious by offering "green suites": Special air- and water-filtration systems are featured in 19 rooms along with toiletries that have not been tested on animals. The elegant **Jester's** restaurant is off the lobby. ♦ 50 Third St (between Mission and Market Sts). 974.6400, 877/222.6699; fax 543.8268; www.starwoodhotels.com/westin &

## 14 CALIFORNIA HISTORICAL SOCIETY

Exhibits feature memorabilia, art, and artifacts culled from 300 years of California history. The photography collection comprises more than 500,000 images, including works by Eadweard Muybridge and Ansel Adams. The fine arts collection depicts the state's history from pre–Gold Rush days to the early 20th century. After visiting the galleries, stop by the well-stocked store. ♦ Free. Library, W-F; galleries and store, W-Sa. 678 Mission St (between New Montgomery and Third Sts). 357.1848. www.californiahistoricalsociety.org &

## 15 MUSEUM OF THE AFRICAN DIASPORA

The museum occupies three floors of the Saint Regis museum tower. The three-story glass atrium features compelling photography. The museum showcases African experiences in media-based photographic, and art exhibits that honor the African Diaspora and document the scattering of Africans from their ancestral homelands. Exhibits include Ethiopian paintings, West African and southern US textiles, and Afro-Latino films. Painter Grafton Tyler Brown (1841-1918)

migrated west during the Gold Rush. His 1886 painting of Cliff House beach is among the works on display. The museum store has books about photography, food, adornment, and celebration, as well as handcrafted items that help revive nearly forgotten craft techniques and traditions. ♦ W-M. 685 Mission St (at Third St). 358.7200. www.moadsf.org &

## 15 ST. REGIS HOTEL SAN FRANCISCO

$$$$ Guest rooms are housed in the lower 20 floors of this 40-story building. While residents command views from the top 20 floors, the lower floors lack views and feel cramped. The corner rooms are larger, and have floor-to-ceiling windows and plasma TVs, but the furnishings and gray color palette are more suited to a boardroom than a bedroom. However, everyone warms up to **Ame,** an excellent restaurant off the lobby. There's also a swimming pool, a café, and two lounges. Patrons of the stark white **Remède Spa** (284.4060; www.remede.com) are presented upon check-in with champagne, truffles, and cashmere throws. The signature Remède facial includes a warm foot wrap, foot and scalp massages, and eye and lip treatments. The automatic gratuity of 20 percent detracts from the welcome. ♦ 125 Third St (at Mission St). 284.4000; 877/STREGIS. www.stregis.com &

## 16 THE CARTOON ART MUSEUM

This second-floor exhibition space is devoted to art that tickles the funny bone. There is a children's gallery where budding artists can get hands-on experience using markers and crayons. Classes and tours are available. The first Tuesday of every month is pay-what-you-wish day. ♦ Admission; reduced for children 5 and under. Tu-Su. 655 Mission St (between Third and New Montgomery Sts). 227.8666. www.cartoonart.org &

## 17 PACIFIC TELEPHONE BUILDING

One of the most beautiful skyscrapers in San Francisco, this 1925 building, by **Miller & Pflueger** and **A.A. Cantin Architects,** owes much to **Eliel Saarinen**'s celebrated design proposed for the Chicago Tribune Tower, particularly in the building's profile, detailing, and vertical emphasis. Notice the modern entrance lobby with its Chinese decorated ceilings. ♦ 130-140 New Montgomery St (between Howard and Mission Sts)

## 18 TEMPLE

Set in the former DV8 space, this is *the* address for global electronic music. The club's Martin Audio Sound System is the best one available, and no expense was spared on the décor. The DJ booth on the main dance floor is housed in a 16th-century Indian temple façade. One lounge has white leather banquettes, while the below-ground-level catacombs have stone walls and wood floors. The VIP mezzanine has museum-quality antiques. Temple offers designer drinks such as shakti sparkler with orange-infused vodka, lavender essence, and vanilla bean. Also on offer are organic teas and non-alcoholic wine and beer. Owner Paul Hemming also runs Zen City Records. ♦ W-Sa, 9PM-2AM. 540 Howard St (between First and Second Sts). 978.9953. www.templesf.com &

## 19 HOTEL PALOMAR

$$$$ This sleek Kimpton boutique hotel brings a welcome urbanity to the bustling Yerba Buena neighborhood. Secluded five floors above Market Street in a refurbished 1907 landmark building is a 198-room hotel. You'll find a clean, artful design that includes walnut parquet floors, hand-tufted wool carpets, and headboards with green velvet panels. ♦ 12 Fourth St (at Market St). 348.1111, 877/294.9711. www.hotelpalomar-SF.com

## 20 OLD NAVY

This four-story flagship store has a fun, energetic atmosphere throughout. The ground floor contains the menswear line and the Old Navy General Store. ♦ 801 Market St (at Fourth St). 344.0375

## 21 THE JEWISH MUSEUM OF SAN FRANCISCO

Another of **Willis Polk's** masterpieces, this 1907 building was originally the Pacific Gas and Electric Substation. It is being restored as part of the Yerba Buena Redevelopment Project and will open as the Contemporary Jewish Museum in 2010. ♦ 222 Jessie St (bounded by Third and Fourth Sts, and Mission and Market Sts). www.jmsf.org

## 21 MUSEUM OF CRAFT AND FOLK ART

This unique museum provides museum-goers with craft and folk art from a variety of ethnically diverse communities. Kate Eilertsen oversees a rich offering of focused and unique exhibitions of traditional and contemporary folk art and crafts. The museum's gift shop supports folk artists from around the world. ♦ Tu-Su. 51 Yerba Buena Lane (at Mission St between Third and Fourth Sts). 227.4888. www.mocfa.org &

## 22 SAN FRANCISCO MARRIOTT HOTEL

$$$$ This controversial hotel went up in 1989 amid considerable architectural acrimony. Critics lambasted **Anthony J. Lumsden's** design, comparing its 40 stories to a jukebox. The hotel opened ahead of schedule after the October 1989 earthquake, when it sprang into use as an emergency shelter, thereby muting some critical voices. The imposing structure has 1,500 rooms and suites, an indoor swimming pool, a spa and health club, a 40,000-square-foot ballroom, and more than 85,000 square feet of meeting and exhibition space. Food and beverage facilities on premises include the **Garden Terrace, Fourth Street Bar and Deli,** the **Atrium Lobby Lounge,** and the **View Lounge** (on the 40th floor). ♦ 55 Fourth St (at Mission St). 896.1600, 800/228.9290. www.marriott.com &

## 23 THE MOSSER VICTORIAN HOTEL OF ARTS AND MUSIC

$$ This landmark hotel's small rooms are more than made up for by its prices (which border on the philanthropic) and its superb location near the **Westfield San Francisco Centre** and **Yerba Buena Gardens.** The 165 rooms are decorated with rattan furniture and floral fabrics, and the restaurant features a cabaret show in the evenings (hence the hotel's rather misleading name). Hotel guests receive a complimentary continental breakfast. Beware—some floors have shared baths. Ask about reduced weekly rates. ♦ 54 Fourth St (between Mission and Market Sts). 986.4400; 800/227.3804 &

## 24 SAN FRANCISCO MUSEUM OF MODERN ART (SFMoMA)

In January 1995, in celebration of its 60th year, the museum relocated to the **Yerba Buena neighborhood.** Its handsome brick box home was designed by internationally acclaimed Swiss architect **Mario Botta** and features a 125-foot cylindrical skylight that channels light down to the first-floor atrium court. More than 17,000 works of art are housed on the museum's four floors of gallery space. The permanent collection contains works by Pablo Picasso, Henri Matisse, Wassily Kandinsky, the Abstract Expressionists (including large holdings of Clyfford Still), Josef Albers, Isamu Noguchi, Alexander Calder, and distinguished California artists. The museum functions as a cultural center for contemporary art, films, and live music. The active photography department presents frequent exhibitions from its extensive permanent collection and temporary shows of 20th-century photography. **MuseumStore,** on the main floor, is open daily and has the city's best selection of modern-art books and catalogs, gifts, and jewelry. A pleasant, inexpensive café is located on the fourth floor (open during museum hours). The **San Francisco Museum of Modern Art Gallery** (see page 111) is located at Fort Mason, Building A. ♦ Admission; free first Tuesday of the month. M, Tu; F-Su; Th until 9PM. Tours daily. 151 Third St (between Howard and Mission Sts). 357.4000

Within the San Francisco Museum of Modern Art:

## CAFFÈ MUSEO

★$ The eye-catching décor consists of wooden pegboards, a slatted ceiling, a striped granite floor, and leather directors' chairs. Sandwiches, including an excellent grilled vegetable version, are made with focaccia, and the salad choices range from barley with mushrooms and artichokes to saffron rice studded with bits of zucchini and whole rock shrimp. ♦ Mediterranean ♦ M, Tu, F-Su, breakfast, lunch, tea, and dinner until 6PM; Th until 9PM. 357.4500 ♿

## 25 W HOTEL SAN FRANCISCO

$$$$ Uniquely designed, this ultradeluxe 423-room hotel is convenient to Moscone Center for high-end conventions. Hotel guests experience unparalleled service, a 24-hour fitness center, **Bliss Spa,** beautifully furnished rooms that include Internet access, and goose-down comforters. **XYZ** restaurant serves breakfast, lunch, and dinner with a Mediterranean-influenced menu. W is part of Starwood Hotels and Resorts, as are most of the hotels in SOMA. ♦ 181 Third St (at Howard St). 777.5300, 888.625.5144. www.whotels.com

## 26 HAWTHORNE LANE

★★★$$$ A hot place for daring California cuisine since it opened in 1995, this establishment has a menu that features boldly flavored American fare with a few Asian accents mixed in. Try grilled tenderloin of beef with spicy greens in fresh spring rolls; seared Maine scallops with mâche, Cabernet sauce, and horseradish crème fraiche; or slices of Sonoma lamb with artichoke risotto and tomato tarragon sauce. Desserts also have an artistic bent: A light cheesecake, topped with a rich lemon curd, is accompanied by swirls of blueberry sauce and berries. ♦ Californian ♦ M-F, lunch and dinner; Sa, Su, dinner. Reservations recommended. 22 Hawthorne La (at Howard St). 777.9779 ♿

## 27 SPA BAR

One of the best hair salons and luxury day and night spas in the area. Treat yourself to a 15-minute session at their oxygen bar, which generates 97% pure oxygen for an all-natural boost. Swedish massage runs $90 for an hour. ♦ Daily, 10AM-10PM. 246 Second St (at Folsom St). 975.0888. www.spa-bar.com ♿

## 28 THE FLY TRAP

★★★$$ Named after a long-closed but once popular Financial District restaurant, this is one of the area's more upscale spots, with a mirrored, casually elegant interior and a menu that borrows some culinary inspiration from its namesake. Main courses include sautéed sweetbreads with mushrooms, calves' livers with bacon and onions, and chicken Jerusalem (with artichoke hearts). ♦ Californian/Italian ♦ M-F, lunch and dinner; Sa, Su, dinner. Reservations recommended. 606 Folsom St (at Second St). 243.0580 ♿

## 29 SAILORS' UNION OF THE PACIFIC BUILDING

**William S. Merchant's** 1950 building symbolizes the power that unions gained after the bitter struggles and strikes of 1934. It is reminiscent of European Constructivist buildings of the 1930s. ♦ 450 Harrison St (at First St)

## 30 76 TOWER UNION OIL COMPANY BUILDING

A landmark on top of Rincon Hill, the triangular tower designed in 1941 by **Lewis P. Hobart** is directed toward the approach ramp to the Bay Bridge. It is clad in white porcelain enamel—a material that architects have rediscovered. ♦ 425 First St (at Harrison St)

## 31 WESTFIELD SAN FRANCISCO CENTRE

The seven-story Emporium opened in 1896; a grander version opened in 1908 after the earthquake and remained opened until 1996. When the Westfield San Francisco Centre opened in 2006, the ornate 1908 Market

Street façade, grand rotunda, and 102-foot-wide glass-and-steel dome were once again unveiled. Westfield's $420 million shopping hub gathers retail, restaurants, and entertainment under one roof. It has the largest Bloomingdale's outside New York, the second-largest Nordstrom, a Burke Williams day spa, and a nine-screen Century Theatre and CinéArts. A unique curved escalator carries shoppers to 170 specialty stores and a gourmet marketplace. Entrances on Market and Mission Sts. ♦ Daily, 845 Market St (between Fourth and Fifth Sts). 512.6776. www.westfield.com/sfc &

Within Westfield San Francisco Centre:

## STRAITS RESTAURANT

★★$$ On the fourth floor you enter an Asian oasis through a hand-carved door. The teak chandeliers, dark wood, and rich silk are a sensual contrast to the mall outside. Chef Chris Yeo serves the Singapore dishes of his youth. Order the origami sea bass baked in parchment, the edible fruit of a southeast Asian evergreen tree. Also delicious is the chicken with lemongrass chili, tamarind beef, whole lobster, and shrimp *pad thai*. The bar lounge has comfortable low sofas and Thai silk pillows inviting you to kick off your shoes and stay awhile. The libations, such as lemongrass mojitos or lychee martinis, are as exotic as the food. ♦ Singaporean ♦ Daily, lunch and dinner 11AM-2AM. 845 Market St. 597.668.1783. www.straitsrestaurants.com &

## 32 HOTEL MILANO

$$$ Originally constructed as a hotel in 1920, this building's latest incarnation was conceived to play host to movie production companies filming on location in San Francisco. It contains a private screening room and other facilities for film crews. Most business travelers who come here enjoy the convenience of walking to the nearby **Moscone Convention Center.** The 108 spacious, airy rooms have picture windows, fax and computer connections, and a two-line speakerphone with voice mail. Other amenities include a two-story fitness center. ♦ 55 Fifth St (between Mission and Market Sts). 543.8555, 800/398.7555 &

## 33 THE PICKWICK HOTEL

$$ This 192-room hotel is well located—mere footsteps from Market Street shopping, and just a block away from the **Moscone Convention Center** and the **Yerba Buena Gardens**—and has been renovated. It's a terrific value, which many European visitors have discovered. The hotel restaurant serves breakfast and a light lunch. ♦ 85 Fifth St (at Mission St). 421.7500, 800/227.3282 &

## 34 METREON

This entertainment complex has 12 movie screens, an IMAX, and various attractions, including The Way Things Work—in Mammoth 3D, the Sony store, and an upscale food court. At press time, Westfield, the new owner, plans to introduce new attractions. ♦ 101 Fourth St (between Minna and Mission Sts). &

## 35 YERBA BUENA GARDENS

This $87 million arts and cultural center is the result of 30 years of public planning and debate and is intended to feature the work and talents of San Francisco's diverse ethnic and artistic communities. Many of the major structures were designed by internationally acclaimed architects, including the 55,000-square-foot **Center for the Arts Galleries and Forum** by Japanese architect **Fumihiko Maki; James Stewart Polshek and Partners'** 755-seat **Center for the Arts Theater;** and the home of the **San Francisco Museum of Modern Art,** designed by Swiss architect **Mario Botta,** which opened in January 1995 to commemorate the museum's 60th anniversary. The five-and-a-half-acre Esplanade, bordered by Howard and Mission Streets, and Third and Fourth Streets, features a memorial to Martin Luther King Jr., a 20-foot-high, 50-foot-wide waterfall made of Sierra granite; the **Sister City Garden,** which is planted with flowers and plants from San Francisco's 13 sister cities from around the world; and a number of public artworks. On the Esplanade, the Yerba Buena Gardens Festival gives free youth concerts, world music, theater, and spoken-word performances. At the **Yerba Buena Center for the Arts,** arts organizations both traditional and "on the fringe" have a welcome home. Dance companies that perform here include Smuin Ballets/SF, Margaret Jenkins Dance Company, ODC/SF, and Alonzo King's Contemporary Ballet. Tickets 978-ARTS. Samovar Tea Lounge, on the upper terrace, is open daily (227.9400. www.samovartea.com) ♦ Bounded by Folsom and Mission Sts, and Third and Fourth Sts. Program information 978.ARTS

## 36 CHEVYS

★★$$ This popular restaurant has found a formula for success and repeated it many

times throughout the Bay Area. Tortillas are made on the premises, along with terrific fajitas and other Mexican fare. They're offered in substantial portions in a deliberately funky setting, where beer cases serve as room dividers. It's a casual dining experience that's especially enjoyable when everything is washed down with a pitcher of the slushy (although not too potent) margaritas. ◆ Mexican/Take-out ◆ Daily, lunch and dinner. Reservations required for eight or more. 201 Third St (at Howard St). 543.8060. Also at Two Embarcadero Center, Promenade level (between Clay and Sacramento Sts). 391.2323; Stonestown Galleria (at 19th Ave and Winston Dr). 665.8705 ♿

## 37 MOSCONE CONVENTION CENTER

This 1.2-million-square-foot facility anchors the vast **Yerba Buena Gardens** complex. Named after assassinated mayor George Moscone, it was designed by **Hellmuth, Obata & Kassabaum.** The city's premier meeting and exhibition facility was expanded in 1992 by **Gensler & Associates** and **DMJM** to the tune of $200 million. Although it is largely underground, the center's imaginative use of skylights and other light-maximizing features keeps conventioneers from feeling like troglodytes. Alas, it was too small. Moscone West; on the northwest corner of Fourth and Howard Streets; adds 300,000 square feet, creating a total of over 900,000 square feet of convention space. ◆ 747 Howard St (between Third and Fourth Sts). 974.4000 ♿

## 38 INTERCONTINENTAL HOTEL

$$$ This new hotel (opening early 2008) next to Moscone Center West has a street-level restaurant with a bar wrapping around the corner of Fifth and Howard. Convention-goers will have all the comforts of a brand-name hotel with a spa and sixth floor swimming pool. ◆ 888 Howard St (at Fifth St). 800/972.3124. www.intercontinental.com ♿

## 39 YERBA BUENA SQUARE

With lots of discount and outlet shopping for men, women, and children under one roof, this is a bargain hunter's heaven. The largest store in the complex is the **Burlington Coat Factory Warehouse** (495.7234), which carries a huge supply of coats and just about everything else. ◆ Daily. 899 Howard St (at Fifth St). 543.1275

## 40 LULU

★★★$$ One of the best meals in San Francisco can be had at this recently expanded spot. Formerly three separate eateries, they are now connected throughout and serve the same menu. Fish and tender cuts of meat come slow-cooked from a rotisserie or a wood-burning oven. The food, presented on Italian pottery platters, is served family style. For entrées, consider the roast chicken or the grilled rib eye for two, served over a bed of thinly sliced potatoes and artichokes. Don't miss the fire-roasted chestnuts with white truffle honey. Warm chocolate cake, with a gush of molten chocolate in the center, is the most popular dessert. The dramatic Main Room has a soaring ceiling with a skylight, seating on two levels, and an open kitchen. ◆ French/Italian ◆ Daily, lunch and dinner. Reservations recommended. 816 Folsom St (at Fourth St). 495.5775. www.restaurantlulu.com ♿

## 41 BONG SU RESTAURANT AND LOUNGE

★★$$ This long, narrow space with a wall of windows overlooking Third Street is sleek and modern. Vietnamese art adorns the walls, and bronze, orange, and champagne-colored sheers separate the seating areas and enclose a spacious booth. Two communal tables are reserved for walk-ins. At Bong Su's, where chef Tammy Huynh's dishes edge toward couture cuisine, a gong sounds when the kitchen door opens. Each intensely flavored dish stimulates the senses. Good choices on a first visit are roasted quail, duck salad rolls, and shaking beef—cubed filet mignon with garlic and onions. The wine list features boutique wineries from Croatia and Hungary. ◆ Vietnamese ◆ M-F, lunch; daily, dinner. 311 Third St (at Folsom St). 536.5800. www.bongsu.com ♿

## 42 PAZZIA

★★$$ This Tuscan-inspired trattoria makes fantastic thin-crust pizza and is a favorite spot of pizza lovers. Other specialties to emerge from the wood-burning oven include chicken with mushrooms, calamari, salmon, and filet mignon. ◆ Italian ◆ M-Sa, dinner. Reservations recommended. 337 Third St (between Harrison and Folsom Sts). 512.1693 ♿

## 43 SUPPERCLUB SAN FRANCISCO

★$$ The first American debut of this Dutch-born sexed-up concept combines visual entertainment with fine dining. In a stark white dining room, the wait staff entertains guests as they await courses from a five-course set menu. On occasion, chef Jon Stevens brings out his aphrodisiac-inspired menu. After dinner, the staff replaces tables with oversized plush beds and out come the aerialists, dancers, and drag queens. Reservations required. ◆ Supper club ◆ 657 Harrison St (between Second and Third Sts). 348.0900. www.supperclub.com ♿

## 44 SOUTH PARK CAFÉ

★★$$ Here's a little bit of Paris overlooking the urban oasis of **South Park.** With the long, narrow room painted in ochre, the cozy bar, and the brief menu, the atmosphere is French café all the way. There's blood sausage, steamed mussels, roast pork tenderloin with potato purée, and duck breast with honey, ginger, and cinnamon. Desserts include a classic crème brûlée, profiteroles, and a bittersweet chocolate cake. ♦ French ♦ M-Sa, dinner. 108 South Park Ave (between Second and Third Sts). 495.7275

## 45 JEREMYS

Jeremy Kidson started selling samples purchased from local clothing companies in 1987. Her expanded location in a warehouse with hardwood floors, exposed brick, and wooden tresses became a hit through word-of-mouth. Women's and men's clothing, couture gowns, and designer shoes are all sold as is; some are damaged and some are customer returns. Lucky you if you wander into Jeremys on a 30-percent discount day. Join the mailing list if you want advance notice. ♦ Daily. 2 South Park (at Second St). 882.4929. www.jeremys.com &

## 46 21ST AMENDMENT BREWERY

★$ Two blocks north of AT&T Park, this brewery has beer and much more. In summer they serve strawberry lemonade and ice-cream-sundae martinis. Good post-game fare includes New York steak, ahi tuna, roasted jerk chicken, fish and chips, and clams steamed in ale. ♦ American ♦ Daily, lunch and dinner. 563 Second St (between Bryant and Brannan Sts). 369.0900. &

## 47 DELANCEY STREET RESTAURANT

★★$$ This self-described "ethnic American bistro" makes a social statement as well as a culinary one. It's run by residents of the Delancey Street Project, a residential community and training program for former down-and-outers. The handsome copper bar, handcrafted by the residents, and the wood and brass appointments create a modern bistro look. The outdoor patio provides a lovely view of the Bay Bridge and the water-front area. On any given day, the menu might include matzo-ball soup, Szechuan noodles with peanut sauce, Moroccan vegetable stew, or salmon mousse in phyllo. The American fare includes such staples as meat loaf, pot roast, barbecued baby back ribs, and chicken. ♦ American ♦ Tu-F, lunch

and dinner; Sa, Su, brunch and dinner. Reservations recommended. 600 Embarcadero (at Brannan St). 512.5179 &

## 48 US COURT OF APPEALS BUILDING

This neoclassical federal building boasts a stone-clad façade and a fine marble-faced postal lobby. The structure, by **James Knox Taylor,** sustained serious damage in the 1989 earthquake and underwent extensive renovations by the architectural firm **Skidmore, Owings & Merrill.** It reopened in 1998. ♦ Seventh St (at Mission St)

## 49 CLUB 1015

This is the place to go on weekend nights if you're young and hip and love to dance. The three dance floors each have their own theme (1970s disco, modern, jazz). Underclad, libidinal dancers hover in wrought-iron cages above the dance floors. It is straight on Friday, gay on Saturday. ♦ Cover. F, Sa, 10PM to 7AM. 1015 Folsom St (at Sixth St). 431.1200

## 50 FRINGALE RESTAURANT

★★$$$ Loosely translated, *fringale* means "I'm starving" in French. Well, anyone who's feeling a mite peckish is in for a treat at this intimate, soothing restaurant. The Basque owners describe their food as "Gallic exotic," and although it's far removed from nouvelle cuisine, the kitchen has an equally light hand with sauces, turning out intriguing dishes such as sautéed sweetbreads and split Basque sausages. ♦ French ♦ Tu-Sa, lunch; M-Sa, dinner. Reservations recommended. 570 Fourth St (between Brannan and Bryant Sts). 543.0573

## 51 Coco500

★★★$$ In a modern bistro with chocolate tones, rich teak finishes, art-glass light fixtures, and Italian glass tile, Loretta Keller prepares crowd-pleasing favorites. Try the squash-blossom flatbread Catalan shrimp and the fresh guacamole tacos. The slow-simmered and gently baked dishes are just the thing on a foggy day. Keller is a whiz with vegetables, and devotes a section of the menu (California Dirt) for farm-fresh kale, green beans, zucchini and German butterball potatoes. Desserts are memorable, especially the chocolate pudding cake and crème brûlée. ♦ Californian ♦ M-F, lunch and dinner; Sa, dinner. Reservations recommended. 500 Brannan St (at Fourth St). 543.2222. www.coco500.com &

## 52 Bacar

★★★$$$ Bacar is one of the most high-profile restaurants to open in San Francisco in the past couple of years. The expansive multilevel restaurant features an open kitchen, and a dramatic wine wall and wine salon that looks like a living room. The American menu by chef-owner Arnold Wong offers an interesting mix of French and Italian flavors, with a touch of Asia thrown in. Specialties include duck and foie gras sausage, wok-seared mussels, pan-roasted monkfish with braised endive, and whole roasted lobster. ♦ American ♦ M-F, lunch; daily, dinner. 448 Brannan St (between Third and Fourth Sts). 904.4100

## 53 Jack London's Birthplace

A plaque on the Wells Fargo Bank marks the birthplace of this legendary writer. ♦ Brannan St (at Third St)

## 54 San Francisco Fire Department Pumping Station

This stripped-down classical building houses pumps for the city's elaborate water system designed after the 1906 earthquake and fire. It was built in 1920 by **Frederick Meyer** to ensure that the city would never again be left without adequate means of fighting a massive fire, even if the water mains from outside were ruptured. ♦ 698 Second St (at Townsend St)

## 55 Sea Change

This welded steel sculpture by international artist Mark di Suvero is the entrance to **South Beach Yacht Harbor** and marks the southern end of The Embarcadero. The 70-foot-tall bright red object, standing on four legs that converge at the top, contains a kinetic piece that moves with the wind. Columnist Herb Caen has likened the sculpture to chopsticks impaling a giant dim sum. ♦ King St (between The Embarcadero and Second St)

## 56 Rolo

Definitely not for the introverted, this shop offers fashions for men who like to push the outer limits of style. ♦ Daily. 1235 Howard St (between Eighth and Ninth Sts). 335.1122

## 57 Brain Wash

★$ This combination launderette and café makes great sense for busy singles who want to accomplish something while they socialize. The 49-seat café, separated from the washers and dryers, offers simple foods such as sandwiches, pasta, and chili. The last call for dryers is 9:30PM, but the merriment continues for another hour and a half in the café. ♦ Californian ♦ Daily. 1122 Folsom St (at Seventh St). Café 861.3663. Launderette 431.WASH

## 58 Julie's Supper Club

★$$ The deliberately funky retro décor, heavy on 1950s icons that might have come from a pine-paneled rec room of that era, attracts an upwardly mobile crowd of singles to this noisy restaurant and bar with a courtyard. The food aims to be interesting: Try fried wontons, fried calamari, and chicken brochettes. For the main event, the grilled New York steak, leg of lamb, or pork chops will provide the fuel for partying the night away. ♦ American ♦ M-Sa, dinner. Reservations recommended. 1123 Folsom St (at Seventh St). 861.0707. www.juliessupperclub.com

## 59 Rainbow Grocery and General Store

Collectively owned and operated, these two-stores-in-one reflect strong environmental positions and countercultural tastes. The grocery stocks a sizable assortment of organic produce and health foods, while the general store carries a staggering variety of items, from housewares, toiletries, and natural-fiber clothing to toys and gemstones. Vitamins and cast-iron ware are offered at particularly attractive prices. ♦ Daily. 1145 Folsom St (between Seventh and Eighth Sts). 863.9200 ♿

## 60 Antonio's Antiques

Very fine 17th- to 19th-century French, English, and continental antiques, including furnishings and accessories, fill three floors here. ♦ M-Sa. 701 Bryant St (at Fifth St). 781.1737

## 61 O'Neill's Irish Pub

★★$$ After a day at AT&T Park, linger over a pint or try some of O'Neill's nachos or a New York steak sandwich. Free Wi-Fi. ♦ American ♦ Daily, 10AM-2AM. 747 Third St (at King St). 777.1177

## 62 AT&T Park

Known as "the Miracle on Third Street," AT&T Park combines the feel of an old-fashioned ballpark with splendid bay views. Its doors opened 11 April 2000, when the San Francisco Giants played their season opener against the Los Angeles Dodgers. It is located beside the bay at China Basin. One-hour tours take place daily. 10AM-2PM. $10 per person. Buy your tickets online. April to October. ♦ King and Third Sts. 972.2000, 800/734.4268. www.sfgiants.com ♿

## 63 Acme Chophouse

★★★$$$ Award-winning chef Traci Des Jardins opened a traditional chophouse grill outside the gates of PacBell Park to accommodate a range of appetites and budgets. The spacious dining room overlooking Willie Mays Plaza is furnished simply with banquettes and wooden tabletops for a casual ambience.

Locals come here for wood-grilled steaks, chops, whole fish, braised meats, and rotisserie meats. An impressive wine list complements the menu and includes Bordeaux blends, Rhône varietals, Super Tuscans, and Cabernet. You can order grilled sandwiches, fish and chips, and burgers from the bar menu. ◆ American ◆ Daily, dinner. 24 Willie Mays Plaza (corner of King and Third Sts). 644.0240

### 64 BELL'OCCHIO

All kinds of things you never knew you needed but suddenly can't live without, such as imported ribbons, silk roses, unusual toiletries, and curious trinkets—mostly European—are here to tempt you. ◆ Tu-Sa. 8 Brady St and 10 Brady St (off Market St, between 12th and Gough Sts). 864.4048

### 65 NEW LANGTON ARTS

This nonprofit gallery specializes in experimental (and sometimes controversial) works by American and international artists. The theater presents performance art, literary readings, and jazz in the evenings. ◆ Daily. 1246 Folsom St (between Eighth and Ninth Sts). 626.5416. www.newlangtonarts.org Ꮬ

### 66 GRAND CENTRAL STATION ANTIQUES

Two floors are filled with French, English, and Belgian furniture and collectibles from the 18th to 20th centuries. ◆ Tu-Su. 333 Ninth St (between Ringold Alley and Folsom St). 252.8155

### 67 THE STUD

Rock, funk, oldies, New Wave, and world-beat music draw a crowd your mother might not approve of. There are some women, but the clientele is mostly male, mostly gay. Drag shows at midnight. ◆ Cover on some nights. M-Sa until 2AM. 399 Ninth St (at Harrison St). 252.7883. www.studsf.com

### 68 THE SAN FRANCISCO FLOWER MART

This area is fragrant with blossoms and abloom with activity when most of the city sleeps. It's the wholesale center for the floral trade, but some shops also sell retail at attractive prices. ◆ M-Sa, mornings. Sixth St (at Brannan St). 392.7944. www.sfflmart.com Ꮬ

### 69 TRAIN DEPOT

The terminal for the former **Southern Pacific Railroad** line now houses the commuter trains to San Jose. Originally this was the starting point for the famous Coast Starlight and Daylight Express trains to Los Angeles. The old Mission-style station was demolished in 1979 to make way for the current utilitarian structure. ◆ At Fourth and Townsend Sts

### 70 CHINA BASIN BUILDING

If this 1922 warehouse/office building by **Bliss & Faville** were put on end, it would be 850 feet high and one of the city's tallest structures. In 1988, it was repainted in blue with white stripes to resemble an ocean liner. ◆ 185 Berry St (between Third and Fourth Sts)

### 71 LIMELIGHT

This bookstore specializes in film and theater books. ◆ M-Su. 1803 Market St (between McCoppin and Guerrero Sts). 864.2265. www.limelightbooks.com Ꮬ

### 72 MANORA'S THAI CUISINE

★★★$$ Many cognoscenti think this is one of the best Thai restaurants in the city. Try the Pooket Skewer—vegetables, scallops, prawns, calamari, mussels, and other seafood served with spicy lemon-garlic and sweet chili sauces; the pork infused with garlic and pepper; or the minced fish steamed in banana leaves. ◆ Thai ◆ M-F, lunch and dinner; Sa, Su, dinner. 1600 Folsom St (at 12th St). 861.6224. Also at 3226 Mission St (at Valencia St). 550.0856 Ꮬ

### 73 SLIM'S

Rocker Boz Scaggs is a part owner of this live music-and-dance club, which bills itself as the "home of roots music." Country, jazz, and blues musicians, some well-known, some up-and-coming hopefuls, have played here, as has Scaggs himself. ◆ Cover. Daily, to 2AM. 333 11th St (between Harrison and Folsom Sts). 522.0333. www.slims-sf.com

### 74 DNA LOUNGE

Clubgoers are flocking to the new DNA Lounge, which was remodeled into a multimedia playground, outfitted with a potent sound system, video screens, and Internet kiosks. Balconies ring the spacious dance floor, and there's also a candlelit lounge in the back. ◆ Nightclub. 375 11th St (at Harrison St). 626.1409. www.dnalounge.com

### 75 GIFT CENTER

Formerly a warehouse, this 1917 **Maurice Couchot** building was renovated in 1984 by **Kaplan/McLaughlin/Diaz** with the construction of a large atrium in place of the original light well. Designed in Art Deco style, its shops are open to wholesalers only (although the restaurants are open to the public); the center is often used for large parties. ◆ 888 Brannan St (at Eighth St). 861.7733

Restaurants/Clubs: Red | Hotels: Purple | Shops: Orange | Outdoors/Parks: Green | Sights/Culture: Blue

# UNION SQUARE

San Francisco's famous shopping district is the nearest thing to a crossroads you'll find in the city. The bronze statue *Victory* presides over Union Square, where sunshine beams on pavilions, garden terraces—and flocks of visitors. Radiating from the square are streets lined with flagship stores, hotels, restaurants, and theaters, along which flow uninterrupted streams of shoppers. Some of the world's most prestigious names in retailing command Post, Stockton, and Market Streets. International fashion houses line Maiden Lane and fill three floors of Crocker Galleria (Post Street). On the Galleria's third floor, steps lead up to a Parisienne rooftop garden (page 48). West of the square, the theater district bustles with year-round performances at Curran Theater, American Conservatory Theater, Geary Theater, Post Street Theatre, Marine's Memorial Theatre, EXIT Theatreplex, and SF Playhouse.

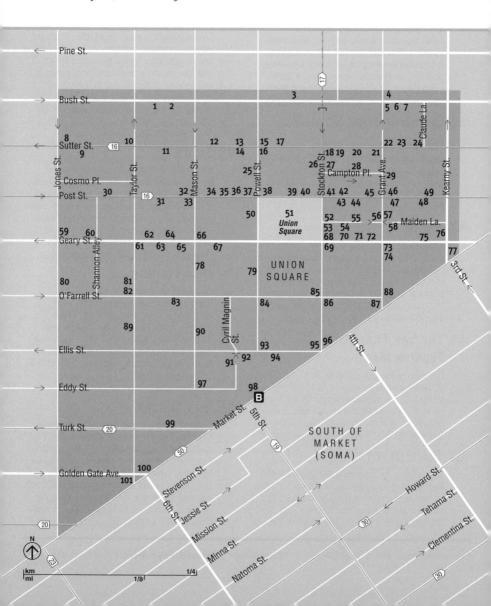

Musicians, some of outstanding caliber, enliven the area. Many, in fact, work professionally in the evening and use their street time for practice and pocket money. Adding to the local color, both literally and figuratively, are the curbside flower stands selling tulips, gardenias, and springtime calla lilies. The flower stands owe their beginning to civic leader and publisher Michael de Young, who in the late 1800s allowed the vendors—usually youngsters of Italian, Belgian, Irish, or Armenian descent—to sell their flowers in front of the de Young building and protected them from the police. They were licensed in 1904, and, as with the cable cars, any attempt to suppress the stands has been halted by a sympathetic public.

**Maiden Lane** is an elegant, tree-lined alley that extends two blocks east of Union Square from **Stockton** to **Kearny Streets.** City dwellers scorned the area in the 19th century, when it was called Morton Street, but now French couture and modern art adorn the windows of former bordellos.

## 1 PETITE AUBERGE

$$ Just a few doors up Bush Street from the **White Swan Inn** is another Joie de Vivre property, with a French country theme. You'll find the same kind of warmth and elegant hospitality that characterize its neighbor. A full breakfast is served, but there is no restaurant. In the evening, wine and hors d'oeuvres are served in a cozy parlor with a welcoming fireplace. ◆ 863 Bush St (between Mason and Taylor Sts). 928.6000, 800/365.3004. www.petiteaubergesf.com

## 2 WHITE SWAN INN

$$$ In this era of bustling hotels, this is an exciting and romantic find. This 1900 hotel on downtown Bush Street is an English garden retreat oozing charm and quiet good taste. There are 26 rooms, each with a bath, a fireplace, and a refrigerator, all furnished in handsome antiques and lovely fabrics. There's a stunning common room adjacent to a tiny garden, where a bountiful breakfast and tea, including home-baked breads and pastries, are served (there is no restaurant). You may also have sherry and wine by the fireplace and browse through the latest periodicals. The feeling of a family welcome surrounds every service. ◆ 845 Bush St (between Mason and Taylor Sts). 775.1755. 866/276.3887, 800/999.9570. www.jdvhospitality.com

## 3 MASA'S

★★★★$$$$ Chef Gregory Short turns out dazzling multi-course menus of three, six, or nine courses. Start the evening with a tasting of foie gras, or an heirloom tomato feast with several presentations. Two examples of the chef's mastery with flavor, texture, and color are the seared scallops with melted leeks, Granny Smith apples, and lemon vinaigrette. Or try the arctic char (a white fish from Iceland) served with lentils, fennel, and sunchokes in a red wine essence. Alan Murray has a sixth sense about choosing the perfect wine from Masa's legendary wine cellar to pair with the various dishes. A bronze sculpture by Albert Buibara is the centerpiece of the small dining salon, furnished with red silk lanterns, toile fabric chairs, and mohair banquettes. Jackets recommended. Reservations recommended. ◆ French ◆ Tu-Sa, dinner. 648 Bush St (between Stockton and Powell Sts). 989.7154. www.masasrestaurant.com &

## 4 ORCHARD GARDEN HOTEL

$$ California's first hotel built "green" from the ground up is just one block from Union Square. The 10-story building adheres to standards set by the US Green Building Council, including the use of chemical-free cleaning products. The "all green" building has 86 guest rooms and 4 suites, plus a fitness center, rooftop garden, and restaurant. Complimentary amenities include European-style breakfast buffet, morning paper, town-car service to the Financial District, Wi-Fi Internet access, and a complimentary DVD library. ◆ 466 Bush St (at Grant Ave). www.theorchardgardenhotel.com &

## 5 HOTEL TRITON

$$$ The 140 smallish rooms at this Kimpton property are stocked with playful and sophisticated modern furniture decorated in a blue-and-gold color scheme. The hotel works hard to ingratiate itself with the fashion and entertainment industry, so expect to rub shoulders with some glitzy folk. Better yet, stay in a celebrity-designed suite. The collection includes The Wyland Suite by ocean artist Wyland, the J. Garcia Suite, and the Black Magic Bedroom by

---

Restaurants/Clubs: Red  |  Hotels: Purple  |  Shops: Orange  |  Outdoors/Parks: Green  |  Sights/Culture: Blue

Carlos Santana. The Triton has adopted eco-friendly practices in all its rooms. Café de la Presse serves breakfast, lunch, and dinner. ♦ 342 Grant Ave (at Bush St). 394.0500, 800/433.6611. www.hoteltriton.com &

## 6 HOTEL DES ARTS

$ To make up for tiny rooms with no views, the owners commissioned artists to paint bedroom walls in whatever motif struck their imagination. Artistic expression surrounds hotel guests. One room has become a canvas for a Japanese pleasure garden with cherry blossoms and geisha girls. Hallways serve as rotating galleries for up-and-coming artists. The art community anticipates the monthly receptions in the tiny hotel lobby. The five-story hotel has 51 rooms, most with private baths, queen-size beds, TVs, phones, and Wi-Fi access. Continental breakfast is served in the small lobby and **Le Central,** a French brasserie, is next door. Ask for a painted room upon booking. ♦ 447 Bush St (between Kearny St and Grant Ave). 956.3232; 800/956.4322. www.sfhoteldesarts.com &

## 7 LE CENTRAL

★★$$$ Regularly patronized by former San Francisco mayor Willie Brown and the late Herb Caen, this place turns out hearty, tasty fare. The grilled steak topped with Roquefort sauce is great, though the Provençal cassoulet (a crock of white beans with sausage and duck confit) is even better. ♦ French ♦ M-Sa, lunch and dinner. Reservations recommended. 453 Bush St (between Claude La and Grant Ave). 391.2233 &

## 7 THE IRISH BANK BAR & RESTAURANT

★★$$ San Francisco's most authentic Irish bar serves Irish and Californian cuisine outdoors in warm weather, when the alley fills with tables and canvas umbrellas, becoming a great spot for Saturday and Sunday brunch. ♦ Irish ♦ Daily, lunch and dinner. 10 Mark La (off Bush St, between Claude La and Grant Ave). 788.7152. www.theirishbank.com &

## 8 OBIKO

One-of-a-kind high fashion clothing inspired by Japanese art, some of it created by Bay Area designers, is offered at this cutting-edge shop. ♦ M-Sa. 794 Sutter St (between Taylor and Jones Sts). 775.2882 &

## 9 FLEUR DE LYS

★★★★$$$$ An impressive arrangement of fresh flowers at the center of the dining area makes a perfect setting for the stunning French/Californian menu. In addition to the impressive à la carte selections, there are three-, four-, and five- course tasting menus, including a five-course vegetarian feast. The tasting menu begins with a spectacular "Symphony of Fleur de Lys Appetizers" (which may include the cucumber-and-tomato gazpacho with melon pearls and Sonoma foie gras prepared in a terrine, with a pistachio crust and with smoked duck), followed by an entrée such as venison tournedos on braised endive, herb-crusted rack of lamb, or sautéed veal medallion. The setting is beautiful and the wine list is the best in the city. ♦ French/ Californian ♦ M-Sa, dinner. Reservations and jacket required. 777 Sutter St (between Taylor and Jones Sts). 673.7779. www.fleurdelyssf.com &

## 10 AUSTRALIA FAIR

Shop here for RM Williams dress boots and Blundstone boots. Andy Murray, who manages this outpost of the Queensland, Australia–based company, also stocks Drizabone oilskin coats. But the one item he has a hard time keeping in stock is Tim Tams, the favorite tea-time Australian biscuit. ♦ Daily. 700 Sutter St (at Taylor St). 441.5319. www.australiafairinc.net &

## 11 HOTEL BERESFORD

$ This modest, European-style hotel is located downtown near the theater district. The 114 rooms are small but pristine and comfortable. It's a good value, and family rates are available. ♦ 635 Sutter St (between Mason and Taylor Sts). 673.9900, 800/533.6533. www.beresford.com &

Within the Hotel Beresford:

## THE WHITE HORSE TAVERN AND RESTAURANT

★★$$ This place replicates an Edinburgh pub, and as might be expected, the cooks do a splendid job with grilled meats. Portions are large. Try the grilled brochette of prawns with a spicy mango sauce or the filet mignon with Cabernet sauce. ♦ American ♦ Daily, dinner. Reservations recommended. 673.9900 &

## 11 ACADEMY OF ART UNIVERSITY GALLERIES

Find excellent deals on oil paintings, sculpture, and photography at the three galleries run by this nonprofit institution. Many of the Academy's students, alumni, and faculty sell their work at all three locations. Artist receptions are held the first Thursday of the month from 5:30PM to 7:30PM. ♦ M-Sa, 8:30AM-5:30PM. 625 Sutter St. 618.6305. www.academyart.edu. & Also at 688 Sutter (at Taylor St); 79 New Montgomery (at Mission St)

## 12 THE REX

**$$** This full-service hotel resurrects the name and times of San Francisco's beat poet Kenneth Rexroth. The 1907 building has 94 elegant rooms decorated with mauve and red-wine hues, custom wall coverings, and hand-painted lampshades. The lobby is reminiscent of art and literary salons of the 1920s and 1930s, with bookcases for the hotel's antiquarian book collection. Amenities include a daily wine hour and continental breakfast. ♦ 562 Sutter St (between Powell and Mason Sts). 433.4434, 800/433.4434. www.thehotelrex.com &

Within The Rex:

### CAFÉ ANDRÉE

★★$$ Named for Rexroth's wife, Andrée Dutcher, the intimate jewel-box dining room is perfect for romantic trysts. Rexroth claimed at first meeting that she would be his wife. Inspired by Franco-Latino cuisine, chef Jim Jardine pairs ingredients from both traditions in intriguing dishes. Try the Argentine chimichurra or the grilled rib-eye steak with fire-roasted corn on the cob, and for dessert the banana and walnut empanadas with rum sauce. ♦ Latin Fusion ♦ M-F, breakfast and lunch daily, dinner; weekend brunch. 433.4434. &

## 13 CARTWRIGHT HOTEL

**$$** This is yet another downtown hotel that has been redone and prides itself on personal touches. The lobby incorporates large arched windows, giant plants, Oriental rugs, and comfortable seating and reading areas. The 114 rooms are homey, each decorated with antiques and vases of fresh flowers. A continental breakfast is available for a modest price. Complimentary afternoon tea and cakes are served, and there is a wine hour daily. ♦ 524 Sutter St (between Powell and Mason Sts). 421.2865, 800/919.9779; www.cartwrighthotel.com &

## 14 PASQUALE IANNETTI GALLERY

An extensive collection of prints by old masters up through the 20th century, including Goya, Daumier, Picasso, Miró, and Klee, is housed in this gallery. It also presents changing exhibitions of graphic art. ♦ M-Sa. 531 Sutter St (between Powell and Mason Sts). 433.2771. www.pascualeart.com &

## 15 CROWNE PLAZA HOTEL

**$$$** One block from the square, this 400-room hotel offers an ideal location as well as fabulous views of the city. Business travelers love this hotel for its 24-hour business center, fitness club, swimming pool, and convenient dining. ♦ 480 Sutter St (at Powell St). 398.8900, 800/972.3124; www.crowneplaza.com

## 16 SIR FRANCIS DRAKE HOTEL

**$$$** To preserve some of the flair of its namesake, this Kimpton hotel keeps a doorman in full yeoman-of-the-guard attire. The lobby, with murals, crystal chandeliers, mirrors, sweeping marble staircase with bronze balustrade, and vaulted gold-leaf ceiling, reflects the splendor and romance of the 1930s. Because it is small by the standard of many of its neighbors (435 rooms and suites), it is able to integrate the luxurious advantages of a larger hotel with a more personal approach to hospitality. For the business traveler, there are special rooms available with a desk and seating area for interviews or briefings. **Scala's Bistro** (www.scalasbistro.com) offers northern Italian and southern French dishes, and **Harry Denton's Skylight Lounge** offers martinis at sunset and dancing to live music (www.harrydenton.com). ♦ 450 Powell St (at Sutter St). 392.7755, 800/227.5480; www.sirfrancisdrake.com &

## 17 450 SUTTER STREET OFFICE BUILDING

This medical/dental office building clad in undulating terra-cotta was designed by **Timothy Pflueger** and built in 1930. It is a good example of Art Deco architecture. Notice the elaborately designed entrance lobby with its Pre-Columbian styling. ♦ Between Stockton and Powell Sts

## 18 RICHART

Chocolate lovers become weak in the knees on entering this store, so redolent is the scent of chocolate and so glamorous the gallery-like displays. Spiced ginger, ylang-ylang, basil, and vanilla are some of the taste sensations the French aesthetic has applied to chocolate. Introduce yourself to the Richart world of art chocolate with a reasonably priced *petit Richart* sample box. ♦ Daily. 393 Sutter St (near Stockton St). 291.9600. www.richartchocolates.com &

## 19 WILKES BASHFORD

Six levels of beautiful and expensive designer clothes for men and women are sold in lush surroundings complete with music and wine. Wilkes Home, on the second level, sells antiques and gifts. Even if your budget can't take the strain of shopping here, stop by to

---

Restaurants/Clubs: Red | Hotels: Purple | Shops: Orange | Outdoors/Parks: Green | Sights/Culture: Blue

see the witty and surreal window displays. ♦ M-Sa. 375 Sutter St (between Grant Ave and Stockton St). 986.4380 &

## 20 METIER

This elegant boutique sells women's clothing by European and American designers such as Italian designer Anna Molinari. The jewelry cases display unique works of artists Cathy Waterman and Annette Ferdinandsen. ♦ M-Sa. 355 Sutter St (between Grant Ave and Stockton St). 989.5395. www.metiersf.com

## 21 TEUSCHER CHOCOLATES OF SWITZERLAND

Expensive and delectable Swiss chocolates, such as champagne truffles and wine truffles, tempt the most discriminating sweet tooth. ♦ Daily. 307 Sutter St (at Grant Ave). 834.0850. www.teuschersf.com &

## 22 BANANA REPUBLIC

This specialty chain of shops got its start selling safari-style clothing in an atmosphere that's a lot more comfortable than any jungle. Now much of the Indiana Jones–style gear has been replaced by well-crafted, reasonably priced contemporary fashions. ♦ Daily. 256 Grant Ave (at Sutter St). 788.3087. www.bananarepublic.com &

## 23 HACKETT FREEDMAN GALLERY

This fourth-floor gallery displays modern American paintings and sculpture. ♦ Tu-Sa. 250 Sutter St (between Kearny St and Grant Ave). 362.7152 &

## 24 CAFÉ CLAUDE

★★$ SF's authentic Parisian bistro has specials chalked on a blackboard. Grazers will love the charcuterie platter, which includes pâté. If cassoulet is on the menu, don't pass it up, and wash it down with a Côtes du Rhône. And for dessert, what else but choco-late mousse, *bien sûr!* ♦ French ♦ M-Sa, lunch and dinner. 7 Claude La (between Sutter and Bush Sts). 392.3505. www.cafeclaude.com

## 24 MARGARET O'LEARY

The Irish farm-girl-turned-designer who says, "A good sweater is like an old friend," shows her stunning collection of soft, elegant chenille sweaters and knitwear. ♦ Tu-Sa. 1 Claude La (between Sutter and Bush Sts). 391.1010. www.margaretoleary.com

## 25 CHANCELLOR HOTEL

$$$ A fixture on Union Square since 1914, this hotel has an intact Edwardian exterior, which is both solid and soundproofed. Its 137 rooms are fresh and contemporary. The Art

Deco **Clipper Ship** room—once a popular meeting place for World War II servicemen—has been restored to serve as a party and meeting room. It still contains an 85-foot aerial-photo mural of San Francisco from 1935. Rates, always a bargain for those in the know, have not changed much and are definitely moderate for this prime location. **Luques** serves breakfast and lunch. ♦ 433 Powell St (between Post and Sutter Sts). 362.2004, 800/428.4748. www.chancellorhotel.com &

## 25 SEARS FINE FOOD

★★$$ Silver-dollar-size pancakes with maple syrup and whipped butter is a San Francisco treat. In 1938, Ben Sears retired from the circus and his wife Hilbur whipped up airy, dollar-size cakes, which became a much-heralded 18 Swedish pancakes. The black-and-white tiled floors, the red swivel stools, and the old-fashioned milk-shake mixers help retain the 1930s diner theme. ♦ American ♦ Daily, breakfast, lunch, and dinner. 439 Powell St (between Post and Sutter Sts). 986.0700. www.searsfinefood.com &

## 26 GRAND HYATT HOTEL

$$$$ Rising 36 stories above Union Square, this 693-room hotel is in the heart of the city and offers extensive services for business travelers, including language translation, business-equipment rental, and shipping and mailing, plus all the latest news on business and investor services. Within the hotel is the elegant **Grandview Restaurant and Lounge,** with a breathtaking view. The **Regency Club** comprises floors set aside for guests who pay a surcharge. These smartly decorated rooms include honor bars, concierge services, and complimentary breakfasts. There are also six penthouse suites serviced by trained butlers. ♦ 345 Stockton St (between Post and Sutter Sts). 398.1234, 800/233.1234. www.grandsanfrancisco.hyatt.com &

Within the Grand Hyatt Hotel:

## GRANDVIEW

★★★$$$ This 36th-floor restaurant offers incredible views of Golden Gate Bridge, Alcatraz, Coit Tower, Nob Hill, and to the west dramatic sunsets. Chef Richard Slusarz's cuisine is as visually arresting. Some of his more innovative creations include heirloom tomato seviche, salmon confit, truffle fettuc-cine, and rack of lamb. Try the sorbet tasting for dessert. ♦ California/French ♦ Daily, breakfast, lunch, and dinner. 398.1234

In the Grand Hyatt Hotel plaza:

## RUTH ASAWA FOUNTAIN

Created by and named for the noted San Francisco artist, a bronze-relief frieze made

# STREETCARS OF DESIRE

San Francisco's beloved cable-car system made its maiden voyage on 1 August 1873. With its Scottish inventor, Andrew Hallidie, at the grip, the car successfully tackled five hilly blocks along **Clay Street** to **Portsmouth Square** in **Chinatown.**

Hallidie, a mine-cable designer during the Gold Rush days, decided to invent the system after witnessing an unfortunate accident on a steep hill: A horse-drawn wagon had rolled backward, dragging the helpless horses behind. Hallidie's system was safer, and it opened up areas in the city previously thought unsuitable for building homes.

Just before the 1906 earthquake, cable cars had reached their peak, with 600 cars traveling a 110-mile route. But the system sustained heavy damage during the quake and fire, and many lines were not rebuilt. Electric trolleys took over some of the lines, and the number of cable cars dwindled over the next 50 years. But in 1955 the city voted to preserve the famed hill-climbers, and in 1964 they became the first moving National Historic Landmark in the United States.

Starting in 1984, at a cost of more than $60 million, the system underwent two years of head-to-toe renovations. Old track and cable vaults were pulled up and replaced. For extra strength, deeper-grooved rails and more flexible curves were installed. The track was also realigned or moved to avoid interfering with traffic, and the pulleys and depression beams that guide each cable were replaced. The historic Washington-Mason car barn was completely renovated and its traditional appearance preserved. The cars themselves were given a shiny coat of maroon, blue, and gold paint, as well as new brakes, seats, and wheels.

Today you can choose from three lines: the **Powell-Mason Line;** the **Powell-Hyde Line,** which is said to offer the best views and the most thrilling curves; and the **California Line.** There are 44 cable cars in all, with 27 used at peak times. An average of 13 million passengers travel on the 17 miles of track in a year—about 35,616 people a day.

Each six-ton car attaches itself to a cable beneath the street, moving along at a steady 9.5 miles per hour by the turning of 14-foot wheels located in barns. A cable-car operator starts and stops the car by mechanically gripping the cable to make the car go forward and by releasing it to stop the car. Tension can be adjusted if necessary to keep the cable from slipping.

### Cable Car Climbs Hyde Street

up of 41 plaques covers the circular wall of the fountain bowl. Thousands of sculptured figures on the plaques charmingly depict different aspects of the city, from the swaying palms of Mission Dolores to Victorian houses with gingerbread trim. The plaques were modeled from bread dough before being cast in metal, expressing the artist's philosophy that art and everyday life are interrelated.

## 27 CAMPTON PLACE

$$$$ This small and luxurious hotel a half block from **Union Square** used to be the **Old Drake Wilshire.** Although the ambience and décor are stunning, it is the service and extra touches usually found only in Europe's top hotels that the staff likes to emphasize. Professional valets pack and unpack for you, a French laundry and dry-cleaning service is available in-house, secretarial assistance is immediate, shoes are shined every night, and each of the 136 rooms contains a desk and fresh flowers. Corner suites are cozy. Tea is served daily from 2:30PM to 4:30PM in the bar. ♦ 340 Stockton St (at Campton Pl). 781.5555, 866/332.1670. www.camptonplace.com &

Within Campton Place:

### CAMPTON PLACE RESTAURANT

★★★$$$$ The hotel's dining room is the epitome of conservative elegance: quiet, understated, and comfortable, a perfect venue for gourmet Californian cuisine. Recommended are the duck breast with baby turnips, kumquats, and Kaffir lime leaves or pork chops with cardamom, cabbage, apples, bacon, and chestnuts. Stop by the bar bistro. The wine list is extensive and is considered one of the best in town. ♦ Californian ♦ Daily, breakfast, lunch, and dinner. Reservations recommended. 955.5555 &

## 28 ANJOU

★★$$$ Enjoy a charming French ambience in this two-level dining room. The menu created by chef-owner Pierre Morin strikes a balance between tradition and innovation: There's tender duck confit on Portobello mushrooms and herb polenta; asparagus with puff pastry in a morel-studded cream sauce; and a casserole of prawns and artichokes. On the classic side, consider the thin-cut New York steak with extra-crisp fries or the calves' brains sautéed with sage, with the *tarte tatin* (upside-down apple tart) for dessert. ♦ French ♦ Tu-Sa, lunch and dinner. 44 Campton Pl (off Stockton St, between Post and Sutter Sts). 392.5373. www.anjou-sf.com

## 29 JOHN BERGGRUEN GALLERY

This prestigious gallery occupies the second, third, and fourth floors and handles some of the most celebrated names in American art. ♦

M-Sa. 228 Grant Ave (between Post and Sutter Sts). 781.4629 &

## 30 THE ANDREWS HOTEL

$$ In a city rife with the posh and chic, the principal charm of this 48-room Joie de Vivre hotel lies in its atmosphere of civilized informality. For example, the complimentary breakfast can be carried back to bed on trays from hallway buffets. The cozy rooms are decorated in floral chintz, and each one has a desk, upholstered armchair, wireless Internet access, and satellite TV. The staff is knowledgeable about the city and happy to recommend many favorite places known only to locals. ♦ 624 Post St (between Taylor and Jones Sts). 563.6877, 800/9.ANDREWS. www.andrewshotel.com

Within The Andrews Hotel:

### FINO BAR AND RISTORANTE

★★$$ The arched windows and blazing fireplace make this a romantic place to dine, although the Italian fare is only so-so. Each dish is a variation on a theme: *Piccata* (lemon-caper) sauce is served on veal, chicken, scallops, salmon, and even beef. Many of the pastas have three too many ingredients; the simpler ones are by far the most successful. One reliable menu choice is the *contadini* (seafood, chicken, or both, served with sausage, prawns, whole garlic cloves, mushrooms, peppers, and other vegetables). ♦ Italian ♦ Daily, dinner. 928.2080 &

## 31 THE PRESCOTT HOTEL

$$$ This 164-room hotel is close to Union Square. The Edwardian-era décor features deep jewel tones; amenities include minibars, dryers, and terry-cloth robes. Complimentary evening wine, coffee, and tea are served. Executive-club level includes a private lounge, concierge, continental breakfast, and full-bar manager's reception. The hottest attraction, however, is that guests have an easier time than ordinary mortals getting a table at **Postrio,** the exciting hotel dining room. There is also room service (provided by the restaurant), and limousine transportation to the Financial District can be arranged. ♦ 545 Post St (between Mason and Taylor Sts). 563.0303, 866/271.3632. www.prescotthotel.com &

Within The Prescott Hotel:

### POSTRIO

★★★★$$$ Wolfgang Puck's northern California outpost looks like a slice of LA.

However, although the ambience is influenced by Hollywood, the inventive food is rooted in San Francisco's strong Italian and Asian heritage. Chef Mitchell Rosenthal has put his own spin on Puck's signature cuisine with such creations as garlic lamb stir-fried with mint and fresh chilies, smoked salmon served on giant blini, and grilled quail accompanied by a soft egg ravioli (pierce the pasta, and the yolk of a quail egg oozes forth). While everyone seems to come here for lunch or dinner, most people don't realize it's also a great downtown breakfast spot. ♦ Californian ♦ M-F, breakfast, lunch, and dinner; Sa, Su, brunch and dinner. Reservations recommended. 776.7825 &

## 32 JW MARRIOTT HOTEL SAN FRANCISCO

$$$ Formerly the **Pan Pacific,** this 338-room hotel was designed and built in 1987 by well-known architect **John C. Portman Jr.** The bathrooms are marble with large dressing areas, built-in cabinetry, and telephones. One personal valet is provided for every seven rooms, and room service is available 24 hours a day. Exemplary personal service, such as having a private car waiting at the airport to drive you into town, is stressed here, but the hotel staff doesn't always live up to this reputation. Business facilities include four conference suites and a boardroom with a private dining facility that provides continuous buffet service for all meetings. Secretarial, translation, and audiovisual services are offered, and computers are available. In addition, there is a solarium, a ballroom, and a rooftop club with breathtaking views for breakfast, tea, or cocktails. ♦ 500 Post St (at Mason St). 771.8600, 800/228.9290. www.marriott.com &

## 33 DONATELLO HOTEL

$$$ This is indeed a polished jewel. Throughout the hotel there is a tasteful blend of Italian marble, Murano glass, European antiques, and contemporary art. The 95 rooms and 9 suites are larger here than in any other hotel in the city, although some of them could do with new furnishings. Especially appealing are the fifth-floor rooms, which open onto a private terrace. The hotel is the creation of A. Cal Rossi Jr., the hotelier who masterminded the **Stanford Court Hotel,** but here, in the absence of a Nob Hill view, the staff compensates with extraordinary service. ♦ 501 Post St (at Mason St). 441.7100, 800/792.9837 in CA, 800/227.3184 &

Within the Donatello Hotel:

# ZiNGARi
### r i s t o r a n t e

## ZINGARI RISTORANTE

★★$$$ Owner/chef Giovanni Scorzo of this place, named after the Italian word for "gypsy," has chosen to feature dishes from all over Italy, presented in an elegant, refined style with such menu offerings as broiled calamari topped with fresh tomatoes and basil, grilled and smoked mozzarella cheese served with Portobello mushrooms and radicchio (which the menu calls "wild chicory"), and veal loin stuffed with truffles and fontina cheese, as well as risottos, pasta dishes, and salads. The intimate dining room boasts Venetian marble accents. ♦ Italian ♦ Daily, breakfast, lunch, and dinner. Reservations recommended. 885.8850. www.zingari.com &

## 34 POST STREET THEATER

Just a half block from Union Square, this 800-seat house has enlivened San Francisco theater by bringing in quality off-Broadway shows. ♦ 450 Post St (between Powell and Mason Sts). 771.6900 &

## 34 KENSINGTON PARK HOTEL

$$ This former Elks Lodge has 92 spacious rooms and one elegant suite with a queen canopy bed, a beautiful formal dining room, a large living room with a pull-out sofa, a whirlpool bath, two fireplaces, and expansive views overlooking San Francisco's Union Square. The views of the city and bay are especially good from the upper corner rooms. Amenities include tea and sherry served among the palms every afternoon in the beautifully restored lobby with its hand-painted Gothic ceiling. Guests also enjoy the 24-hour business center, complimentary use of the Hotel Diva fitness center, valet parking, laundry/dry-cleaning services, twice-daily maid service, irons, newspapers, and preferred seating at **Farallon** next door. ♦ 450 Post St (between Powell and Mason Sts). 788.6400, 800/553.1900. www.kensingtonparkhotel.com &

## 34 FARALLON

★★★★$$$$ From Bristol Bay salmon to Willapa Bay oysters, diners indulge in some of the world's finest piscean pleasures. You will find fish imported from as far away as New

---

Zealand. Since the cuisines of the Americas, Europe, and Asia have influenced seafood cookery, the menu extends to all parts of the globe. Try the Spanish mackerel tartare as an appetizer and continue with pan-seared Alaskan sea scallops. Desserts, particularly the passionfruit cake, are first-rate. In keeping with this high-styled coastal cuisine, the restaurant's illuminated pillars simulate sea kelp and the handblown lighting, jellyfish. ◆ Seafood ◆ M-Sa, lunch; daily, dinner. Reservations required. 450 Post St (between Powell and Mason Sts). 956.6969. www.farallonrestaurant.com &

## 35 THE INN AT UNION SQUARE

$$$ This Georgian-style hotel with excellent personal service offers complimentary continental breakfast, as well as wine and hors d'oeuvres (but no restaurant). There are 30 rooms and suites, all individually decorated with an emphasis on a cozy English-country look, and all equipped with minibars. The concierges have a good inside track on the city. ◆ 440 Post St (between Powell and Mason Sts). 397.3510, 800/288.4346. www.unionsquare.com &

## 36 MORTON'S

★★★$$$ Historic photos, hardwood paneling, and deep leather banquettes give this subterranean restaurant the feel of a 1940s men's club. The San Francisco branch of the famous Chicago steakhouse chain is popular with conventioneers. During a table-side cart presentation, diners select the size and cut of beef, which ranges from a 24-ounce porterhouse to a 14-ounce double-cut filet. Seafood portions are large, especially the whole baked Maine lobster and swordfish steak with Béarnaise sauce. Vegetables are fresh and lightly steamed. The desserts harken back to the '40s with hot upside-down apple pie, chocolate velvet cake, New York cheesecake, and Key lime pie. ◆ American ◆ Daily, dinner. Reservations recommended. 400 Post St (at Powell St). 986.5830 &

## 37 BORDERS BOOKS AND MUSIC

If you can't find it here, it probably isn't in print: This mammoth store carries over 160,000 book titles and an extensive music and video selection. There's also an espresso bar. ◆ Daily. 400 Post St (at Powell St). 399.1633. Also at Stonestown Galleria, 19th Ave (at Winston St). 731.0665; www.borders.com &

## 38 SAKS FIFTH AVENUE

**Hellmuth, Obata & Kassabaum** designed this building in 1981. The upscale store has escalators that can drive shoppers to distraction, forcing them to walk halfway around the store on each floor to ascend or descend; take the elevator if you're in a hurry. On the fifth floor is a pleasant, sunny restaurant with sometimes good, sometimes so-so food, popular with ladies-who-lunch. ◆ Daily. 384 Post St (at Union Sq). 986.4300 &

## 39 TIFFANY & CO.

Blue bloods come here for their blue-ribbon baubles. ◆ M-Sa. 350 Post St (at Union Sq). 781.7000 &

## 40 WILLIAMS-SONOMA

In this four-story atrium, cook's tools, linen, barware, books, and gourmet food are displayed on three open galleries. The top floor has fresh and frozen food, so head upstairs if you are looking for truffle cake or seasonal offerings from the farmers' market. Cooking classes, held Tuesday and Thursday from 6PM to 8PM, show you how to prepare, for example, autumn soups or great-tasting last-minute meals. ◆ 340 Post St (between Stockton and Powell Sts). 362.9450. www.williamssonoma.com

## 41 NIKETOWN

Opened in 1997, this athletic-ware shop offers Nike shoes and apparel on three shopping levels. ◆ M-Sa, 10AM-8PM; Su, 11AM-7PM. 278 Post St (at Stockton St). 392.6453 &

## 42 ZARA

Clothing from this Spanish retailer is displayed like art in this spacious gallery. Designer knockoffs and chic basics are sorted by color: black, gray, plum, brown, and off-white. ◆ Daily. 250 Post St (between Grant Ave and Stockton St). 399.6930. www.zara.com &

## 43 ERIKA MEYEROVICH GALLERY

Works by the biggest names in the art world—including Pablo Picasso, Henri Matisse, Marc Chagall, David Hockney, Frank Stella, and Andy Warhol—are shown by this sleek gallery owned by Russian émigrés. ◆ M-Sa. 251 Post St (between Grant Ave and Stockton St). 421.7171 &

## 44 CARTIER

The jewelry, watches, and other trinkets from this renowned French firm are for those who don't have to look at price tags. ◆ M-Sa. 231 Post St (between Grant Ave and Stockton St). 397.3180 &

## 45 SHREVE & CO.

Established in 1862, this retailer showcases fine jewelry, crystal, and silver in a setting suffused with grand architectural touches from a bygone era. ◆ Daily. 200 Post St (at Grant Ave). 421.2600 &

## 46 COACH LEATHER

This chain store offers a wide variety of sturdy leather bags, including ergonomic shoulder bags, and small leather goods. ♦ Daily. 190 Post St (at Grant Ave). 392.1772 &

## 47 MAXMARA

Prices are steep here at the first US retail store opened by this Italian manufacturer of high-quality women's clothing. But fashionables swear the values are terrific when compared with other big names in the garment business. ♦ M-Sa. 177 Post St (between Kearny St and Grant Ave). 981.0900 &

## 48 GUMP'S

S.G. Gump & Company was founded in 1865 by German immigrants and former linen merchants, and is now world-famous for jade and pearls, Asian treasures, and the largest collection in the country of fine china and crystal, including such prestigious names as Baccarat, Steuben, and Lalique. There is a bridal registry. ♦ M-Sa. 135 Post St (between Kearny St and Grant Ave). 982.1616 &

## 49 BROOKS BROTHERS

Classic clothes for men and women are the stock in trade at this refined haberdashery. ♦ Daily. 150 Post St (between Kearny St and Grant Ave). 397.4500. www.brooksbrothers.com &

## 50 WESTIN ST. FRANCIS HOTEL

$$$$ The second-oldest hotel in the city, this has been a focal point for the social events in San Francisco's history for many years. Royalty, political leaders, literati, and theatrical stars have all made it their headquarters. The hotel was built in 1904 by Charles T. Crocker and his friends to cope with what they felt were inadequate accommodations for the new class of bonanza kings and their entourages. Much effort was made to initiate new ideas for better service: electric grills that cooked a steak in 5 minutes, perambulators that brought food to the tables, a pneumatic tube that sent service orders to the dining room instantly, and pipes that dumped ocean water into the Turkish baths. After severe earthquake damage in 1906, the reconstructed hotel was so successful that an addition brought the room total to 750, making it the largest hotel on the Pacific Coast. Now the hotel has 1,192 rooms, 83 suites, and **Alexandra's,** the ultimate party room. The St. Francis Health Club (774.0357) offers La Stone therapy at this new full-service spa. The

fitness center is stocked with Cybex machines and training equipment. Outdoor glass elevators offer a stunning view of the city at a spritely 1,000 feet per minute. ♦ 335 Powell St (at Union Sq). 397.7000, 800/228.3000. www.westinstfrancis.com &

Within the Westin St. Francis Hotel:

## MICHAEL MINA

★★★$$$$ Glamour is the word for the evening, from the dining-room hues of shimmering grays to the beautiful place settings that change with every course. They offer a three-course prix-fixe menu and two tasting menus. The seasonal eight-course tasting menu gives you two variations of each main ingredient, with palate refreshers. The chef achieves perfection with osetra caviar parfait (paired with Veuve Clicquot rosé), ahi tuna tartare, black mussel soufflé, Maine lobster pot pie, miso-glazed sea bass in consommé with Muscat, pan-fried poussin, truffle macaroni and cheese, and Burgundy steak. Sommelier Rajat Parr's suggestions enhance the dining experience. ♦ American ♦ Daily, dinner. 397.9222. www.michaelmina.net &

## 51 UNION SQUARE

Since 1850, this plaza has been the heart of downtown San Francisco. The 2.6-acre park, filled with grassy terraces, a bandshell, café cart, and grand staircases, is in the midst of the city's most bustling shopping area. Its name commemorates a Civil War rally during which demonstrators pledged their loyalty to the Union. A granite shaft celebrating the victory of Admiral Dewey's fleet at Manila Bay during the Spanish-American War marks the center of the square. The face of the bronze statue of *Victory* (pictured on page 50) atop the monument was modeled after a well-known San Francisco benefactor, Mrs. Adolph de Bretteville Spreckels. ♦ Bounded by Stockton and Powell Sts, and Geary and Post Sts. www.unionsquaresf.net

On Union Square:

## SAN FRANCISCO TICKET BOX OFFICE SERVICE

The TIX booth at Union Square near Powell Street sells half-price tickets to theater, dance, and music performances on the day of the performance, or full price in advance to select shows. For more information call 433.7828. www.tixbayarea.com

## HARRY AND DAVID

Store shelves laden with gourmet food and organic produce are a refreshing sight on

---

**Restaurants/Clubs: Red | Hotels: Purple | Shops: Orange | Outdoors/Parks: Green | Sights/Culture: Blue**

# ROOFTOP PLEASURES

Views and abundant greenery beckon visitors to nine rooftop gardens.

There's something about the wind-in-your-hair freedom of a rooftop. Eileen Kaufman, wife of Beat poet Paul Kaufman, recalls the '50s and '60s in San Francisco as a time "of dancing, singing, poetry, parties, people, painting, music, sunshine, moonlight, and rooftops." My memories of working downtown include a rooftop garden where I shared dim sum with my beau at the time, under the bougainvillea.

Downtown, you are bound to be within a few blocks of one of the nine rooftop gardens described here. Ride the elevator to these small aeries where you can enjoy a box lunch amid fountains, romantic greenery, and beautiful views. You'll be eye to eye with some of the city's most interesting landmarks.

**San Francisco Art Institute**    An art lover's rooftop in Russian Hill.

Italian cypress, lavender, and rosemary line the façade of the San Francisco Art Institute. This **Julia Morgan** building has an inner courtyard that opens to a Moroccan-tiled fountain and artwork along a colonnade. The first gallery on the left holds Diego Rivera's 1931 fresco *The Making of a Fresco*. Beyond the gallery is the rooftop quadrangle with a café and a stadium-style sun terrace. At the top of the steps the views are of Alcatraz, Angel Island, Treasure Island, Coit Tower, Telegraph Hill, and the twin spires of Saints Peter and Paul Church. Such a wide vista opens the imagination, which has perhaps sparked the creative talent everywhere you look. Exhibits and receptions take place every Tuesday during the school year from 5PM to 7PM. Not only the view and the art but the burgers at **Pete's Café** make up for the lack of greenery atop this roof. ♦ 800 Chestnut St (between Jones and Leavenworth Sts). 749.4563. A short walk from Fisherman's Wharf or from North Beach, where you can walk up Chestnut St from Columbus Ave.

**Crocker Galleria Roof Terrace**    A lunchtime sanctuary.

Circular planters filled with flax, pyracantha, and perennials keep this urban sanctuary colorful year-round. A gravel trail forms the perimeter, which hotel guests occasionally use for jogging. More often office and retail workers are having lunch on the wooden-slat park benches. The roof terrace is one flight up from San Francisco's finest food court. Take-out lunch spots line **Crocker Galleria**. With a box lunch of cashew chicken or homemade tortilla soup, repair to a park bench beneath

the jasmine-covered arbor. In this sheltering spot, you are only vaguely aware of the concrete jungle, so well do the New Zealand Christmas trees camouflage the hotel wall and the escallonias hedge the street. ♦ 50 Post St. Enter from Post or Sutter Sts. Also accessible to hotel guests of the Galleria Park Hotel at 191 Sutter St

**Wells Fargo Roof Garden**    A classic pleasure garden.

Birdsong wins out over car horns and streetcars in this elegant enclave. You can sit on long, circular benches by the medieval astrolabe under the canopy of a myoporum tree or amid the periwinkle. Coral bougainvillea covers the arched trellis at the parapet, and cherry trees flank the central walkway. Adding a merry sound is the water gushing from a lion's mouth into a basin. An astonishing collection of 20th-century office architecture rises beyond the greenery. The Romanesque/French-château office building with the tiled mansard roof is the 1926 **Hunter-Dulin Building.** Across Market Street, **Willis Polk and Company** designed the 1914 **Hobart Building.** ♦ One Montgomery (at Market and Post Sts). Go through the Wells Fargo doors to the elevators and push *R*. M-F. Closes at 6PM

**One Market Plaza Steuart Tower**    Lawns and patio garden above the waterfront.

In the lobby, a giant white aluminum pavilion rises 11 stories under a glass rotunda. Walk under it to Steuart Tower, pick up a visitor pass, then take the elevator to the seventh-floor rooftop garden, where you can view the top of the aluminum sculpture. This large open space alternates between open paved plazas, intimate seating areas, and lush circular lawns. At the railing, take a moment to admire the sweeping grandeur of the Oakland Bay Bridge. Dylan Thomas said, "You wouldn't think that such a place as San Francisco could exist— the wonderful sunlight here, the hills, the great bridges." At this rooftop garden, you enjoy a prized view of the water and share the poet's enthusiasm for the architectural wonder spanning the bay. ♦ One Market St (at Steuart St), Steuart Tower, seventh floor. A photo ID is required to obtain a visitor pass at the security desk. Enter on Market St between Spear and Steuart Sts

**First and Mission Streets**    A pocket-size sun terrace.

Follow the laughter and sunshine to this open terrace, well appreciated by workers and students around Mission Street. Enter from Mission Street (up the steps) or from First Street up the lobby escalator and down a small art gallery hallway onto a garden terrace. The absence of a view is of little concern because this cozy rooftop terrace remains flooded with sunlight well into the afternoon. The ocean-wave fountain is a highlight, as well as grass-filled terraces and comfortable patio tables and chairs. ◆ 100 First St (at Mission St). 243.8803

**343 Sansome Street**  Upscale rooftop patio.

Clear marine air and sparkling views combine to create no finer venue for outdoor dining in sunny weather. Look for Treasure Island between the Maritime Plaza Building and Embarcadero Two. In the central plaza, an obelisk—a mosaic of bright blue, yellow, and red tiles by Joan Brown—represents the four seasons. You'll find more intimate seating on the plantation-white benches that encircle giant planters holding full-grown olive trees. Patio tables and chairs line the guardrail so you can view the skyline at your leisure. By 4PM in summer, this pleasant scene can quickly be replaced by howling wind and fog. Before leaving the building, stop in the museum lobby to view sarsaparilla bottles, clay pipes, and other artifacts unearthed during construction. ◆ 343 Sansome St (between California and Sacramento Sts), 15th floor. M-F, 7AM to 5:30PM

**Embarcadero Center and Maritime Plaza**  Outdoor sculpture garden.

Approach from Sansome Street, between Sacramento and Clay Streets. Cross Sansome Street and ascend a regal stone staircase with Roman columns, an arched pergola, and a stair-step fountain cascading with water. On your right is the Old Federal Building and on your left the Park Hyatt Hotel. The staircase deposits you on Embarcadero Center's promenade level. Ahead is the cinema and beyond that the black metal grid of the Maritime Plaza Building. Follow the walkway left through the Embarcadero Center Building 2 (2EC). The rooftop garden sits atop the garage at the end of the footbridge, taking you from gray to green. The path winds through a grove of poplars and another footbridge crosses Davis Street. Walkways are lined with rhododendron and flower beds planted with foxglove and begonia. One of the pieces of modern sculpture was a friendship gift from the South Korean government. The path ends at street level at Clay and Drumm Streets, where you can continue exploring Embarcadero Center.

**Fairmont Hotel**  A Nob Hill retreat.

The Fairmont's contribution to the greening of San Francisco is a turn-of-the-century oasis with the style of a private estate. Royal palms spread enormous canopies. The wind-tossed fountain spray and the distant view of the bay add to the grand air, as do the olive trees, the birds-of-paradise, and the manicured lawn. Notice the granite façade of the Fairmont Hotel. On the top floor you can see the terrace belonging to the penthouse suite, rumored to be San Francisco's most expensive set of rooms. Inside the hotel, wander the corridors on the lobby level, where historic photos are exhibited. ◆ 950 Mason St (at California St). At the entrance on California St, take the elevator to the lobby level and follow the corridor on your right to the rooftop garden

**Yerba Buena Gardens**  A rooftop meadow at street level.

Coming from the concrete corridors onto this lush oval meadow, you stumble into a magical place. Pines, fruit trees, and berry shrubs dot the meadow, and sweet-scented grasses and lilies, carnations, roses, mint, peonies, tulips, violets, and butterfly-attracting plants line the walkways. You can hop across stepping-stones behind a waterfall. The fountain is a 50-foot-tall memorial to Martin Luther King Jr., whose words are inscribed into the granite wall. Above, a reflecting pool forms the edge of the raised terrace and overlooks the meadow. Cross the footbridge to Howard Street and you can hop on a 1903 carousel with exquisitely carved giraffes, camels, horses, and rams. This bounty of pleasures rests atop **Moscone Convention Center**. A special blend of compost, mulch, and spongelike ingredients—which weighs less than regular topsoil and retains more water—separates the gardens from throngs of conventioneers below. From the garden terrace you can peer below through the glass pyramids into the exhibition halls. ◆ Mission St (between Third and Fourth Sts)

Victory

Union Square. Harry and David fruit baskets have been a common sight in homes all over the US since this Oregonian mail-order company began shipping its scrumptious fruit. ♦ Daily. 355 Powell St (between Geary and Post Sts). 296.9233

## 52 YVES SAINT LAURENT

Maiden Lane meets Rue Saint-Honoré as Yves Saint Laurent joins French designers and boutiques with outposts here. You can see the sexy ultra-hip clothing a few weeks after the collection made news on Paris runways. ♦ Tu-Sa. 166 Maiden La (near Stockton St). 837.1211. www.ysl.com

## 53 DIPTYQUE

This tiny emporium resembles the shops you may encounter while strolling Paris's narrow streets. The gold lettering on the door and polished wood shelves within, all with fine artfully displayed wares, are a strong temptation. Christiane Gautorte sells the soaps, scented candles, and essential oils in the currently trendy fragrances of the French capital. ♦ Tu-Sa. 171 Maiden La (near Stockton St). 402.0600. www.diptyqueusa.com

## 53 ARTHUR BEREN

This upscale manufacturer sells footwear, leather goods, and clothing for men and women. ♦ Daily. 222 Stockton St (across from Union Sq). 397.8900. www.berenshoes.com ♿

## 54 MAIDEN LANE

When this exclusive lane was known as Morton Street, it enjoyed a less-than-chic reputation. Up until 1906, when a fire gutted the area, prostitutes sat at open windows and solicited passersby, and there was an average of two murders a week. Gradually, shops took the place of bordellos, and as entrepreneurs struggled to change their street's image, Morton was changed to Maiden in the hopes of sparking a new era—and it has. Except for the occasional delivery truck, today it is a pedestrian-only way lined with fashionable boutiques. On nice days, tables are set out in front of **Mocca** and other luncheonettes for alfresco dining. ♦ Between Kearny and Stockton Sts

## 54 CHANEL

One of Maiden Lane's most elegant and exquisite boutiques has three floors of women's clothing and cosmetics by the famous French design house. Some men's accessories are sold here as well. ♦ Daily. 155 Maiden La (between Grant Ave and Stockton St). 981.1550 ♿

## 55 FRANK LLOYD WRIGHT BUILDING

This exquisite building designed by **Frank Lloyd Wright** in 1948 has a spiral ramp leading to the upper floor; it was one of the prototypes for the architect's Guggenheim Museum in New York City. The brick exterior has a superbly detailed arched entrance. ♦ Daily. 140 Maiden La (between Grant Ave and Stockton St). 392.9999 ♿

Within the Wright Building:

### FOLK ART INTERNATIONAL, XANADU GALLERY AND BORETTI AMBER & DESIGN

These galleries offer a collection of ethnographic and tribal art from around the world. Ceramics, textiles, furniture, and jewelry are the draws here. ♦ M-Sa; Su, noon-6PM in summer. ♿

## 56 DAVID STEPHEN

This menswear shop caters to an exclusive clientele who need infallible advice on selecting perfectly tailored suits and dress shirts. If you like an old-fashioned shave, they have all the accoutrements plus shaving cream with lemon essential oil. ♦ Tu-Sa. 50 Maiden La (near Grant Ave). 982.1611 www.davidstephen.com ♿

## 56 HERMÈS OF PARIS

The prices are heart-stopping at this internationally based boutique, where finesse and quality reign supreme in leather goods, scarves, gloves, ties, and clothing for men and women.

It is also one of the few places in town where equestrians can purchase a saddle. ♦ M-Sa. 125 Grant Ave (at Maiden La). 391.7200 &

## 57 CHRISTOFLE

Merchandise from the Paris-based silversmiths (purveyors to the courts of Louis Philippe and Napoléon III) is offered for those with a taste for fine things. ♦ M-Sa. 140 Grant Ave (at Maiden La). 399.1931. www.christofle.com &

## 58 BISTRO 69

★$$ Oversize sandwiches, salads, and espresso draw regulars to this pricey but unpretentious cafeteria with alfresco dining. ♦ American ♦ M-Sa, breakfast and lunch. 69 Maiden La (near Grant Ave). 398.3557 &

## 59 SAVOY HOTEL

$$ This elegant 92-room hotel in a 1915 building now has the feel of a country inn in Provence, with down comforters, old-fashioned etchings, and other homey touches. A continental breakfast is served every morning, and the hotel prides itself on excellent service. ♦ 580 Geary St (at Jones St). 441.2700, 800/227.4223. www.thesavoyhotel.com &

Within the Savoy Hotel:

### MILLENNIUM

★★★$$ Chef Eric Tucker's seasonal menu is his paean to vegetarian world cuisine. Whether you choose a dish from Tokyo or Tuscany, every dish is a multi-layered sensation. The samosa is made with seitan "sausage," roasted eggplant, zucchini, brown basmati pilaf, cardamom-scented tomato coulis and coconut mint raita. The flageolet gratin is garlic-chive polenta topped with marinated tempeh, herb-roasted tomato and sweet corn, and sherried cashew cream. Another plus is the Old World elegance of the Savoy's wood-paneled dining room. ♦ Vegetarian ♦ Daily, dinner. 345.3900. www.millenniumrestaurant.com. Reservations online at www.opentable.com

## 60 HOTEL ADAGIO

$$ Joie de Vivre took the **El Cortez Hotel** under its wing, and keeping the 1929 Spanish colonial revival façade, thoroughly modernized the interior. The lobby, overlooking Geary Street, provides modern sofas under colossal white shades. Two penthouse suites and 171 guest rooms are decorated in a minimalist modern fashion in taupe and brown with vibrant Thai silk pillows. End tables, chairs, and bathroom commodes are in dark-stained Indonesian hardwood. Modern needs are well provided for with high-speed Internet access, CD players, Egyptian cotton linens, and Aveda bath amenities. Executive-level guest rooms have the best views, as well as complimentary continental breakfast and Frette bathrobes. You can't bed down better at a better address in the heart of the theater district. ♦ 550 Geary St (between Taylor and Jones Sts). 775.5000, 800/228.8830. www.thehoteladagio.com &

Within Hotel Adagio:

### CORTEZ RESTAURANT AND BAR

★★★$$ Downtown habitués flock to this favorite haunt for a tantalizing selection of small plates. The flavors are unabashedly Mediterranean, and prices encourage you to order several dishes. Start with the herbed baby green salad with roasted pistachios, oven-dried strawberries, and feta, and then move on to the rack of lamb in a date-and-mint crust with garlic chive purée. Chef Pascal Rigo also pulls out all the stops on seafood, such as the poached yellowtail served with shallots in thyme foam. Desserts transcend the ordinary, especially the pear and hazelnut brown butter cake with chestnut ice cream. ♦ Mediterranean ♦ Daily, breakfast and dinner. Reservations recommended. 292.6360. www.cortezrestaurant.com &

## 61 THE CLIFT HOTEL

$$$$ It's been a San Francisco landmark for almost 80 years. As always, its high standards and individualized attention bring its loyal following back time and time again. Guests call their own shots here. If celebrities wish to come and go so no one knows they are in town, the hotel protects them. If they want a press conference, the hotel can arrange that too. Ian Schrader renovated the hotel, which has an LA look. **Asia de Cuba** serves Latin-Asian fusion cuisine and is open for breakfast, lunch, and dinner. Another plus is the location—two blocks from Union Square and the theater district. ♦ 495 Geary St (at Taylor St). 775.4700, 800/332.3442. www.clifthotel.com &

Within the Clift Hotel:

### REDWOOD ROOM

★$$ Soaring 22-foot fluted columns and an elegant 75-foot bar decorated with fine Italian marble highlights and Klimt reproductions complete the magnificent Art Deco look. The "bistro" menu from Asia de Cuba next door lists a nice selection of snacks and light lunch choices. 775.4700 &

## 62 THE WARWICK REGIS HOTEL

$$$ This hotel offers 80 rooms and suites in the heart of the theater district, and within

strolling distance of Union Square. The décor is a mix of French and English antiques, including canopied beds and armoires. Some suites offer fireplaces. There are facilities for business travelers, 24-hour room service, and a concierge. ♦ 490 Geary St (between Mason and Taylor Sts). 928.7900, 800/203.3232. www.warwicksf.com

Within The Warwick Regis Hotel:

## LA SCENE CAFÉ AND BAR

★★$$$ A pleasant spot before or after the theater, this richly appointed room is graced with sketches of performers who have appeared at the **Curran Theatre.** The ever-changing à la carte menu features such dishes as apple and fennel salad with Gorgonzola and walnuts dressed with a pear vinaigrette; spicy calamari dipped in lemon-caper aioli; polenta napoleon with goat cheese, pesto, and mushroom ragout; and grilled salmon in butternut squash sauce with roasted Peruvian potatoes. The pre-theater three-course fixed-price menu is a great deal. ♦ Mediterranean ♦ Tu-Sa, dinner. 292.6430 &

## 63 CURRAN THEATRE

Coproducers Carole Shorenstein Hayes and James M. Nederlander advertise this 1,678-seat theater as the chief pit stop for their *Best of Broadway* series. The live and sometimes lively productions can be worth the hefty ticket price. Avoid the rear balconies unless you're a lip reader—the acoustics are impossible. ♦ 445 Geary St (between Mason and Taylor Sts). Call 551.2000 for current and upcoming plays. 512.7770. www.bestofbroadway-sf.com &

## 64 HOTEL DIVA

$$ This hotel's leather, marble, glass, and chrome Euro-tech look often lures the style-conscious business traveler, but there are also classic creature comforts like down comforters and VCRs in all of the 110 rooms and suites, including the Little Divas suite for kids. Valet parking is available. The choice location, opposite the **Curran** and **Geary Theaters** and two blocks from Union Square, and the accommodating staff make for a most rewarding stay. The hotel's restaurant, **Colibri** provides the room service. ♦ 440 Geary St (between Mason and Taylor Sts). 885.0200, 800/553.1900; fax 885.3268 &

## 65 GEARY THEATER

Home to the renowned **American Conservatory Theater (ACT),** this Edwardian-style

> "One day if I do go to heaven . . . I'll look around and say, 'It ain't bad, but it ain't San Francisco.'"
>
> —Herb Caen

theater opened in 1910 during the city's renaissance after the devastating earthquake and fire of 1906. The theater regained its lost glamour after a $27.5 million restoration and seismic upgrade. ♦ 415 Geary St (at Mason St). ACT box office 749.2228. www.act-sfbay.org &

## 66 RUBY SKYE

Built in the 1890s, the club features Art Nouveau architecture and plush modern furnishings, and is one of the most elaborate clubs in the Union Square area. Dance on the main floor or socialize in the Jungle Room. ♦ Nightclub ♦ 420 Mason St (at Geary St). 693.0777. www.rubyskye.com

## 66 THE MAXWELL

$$ America's jazz age was the inspiration for this newly restored hotel with midnight colors, plush bedding, and hand-painted lamp shades in 153 rooms. **Max's on the Square,** the hotel's American restaurant, serves breakfast, lunch, and dinner in a 1940s interior. Try the lemon meringue pie. ♦ 386 Geary St (at Mason St). 986.2000, 888/SF-4-MAXX. www.maxwellhotel.com

## 67 HANDLERY UNION SQUARE

$$$ Some poetic license has gone into the naming of this 375-room hotel, which, strictly speaking, is near but not on Union Square. There is a heated outdoor pool and a multi-lingual staff. Californian food, as interpreted in San Francisco, is served in **The Daily Grill.** There is also a cocktail lounge. ♦ 351 Geary St (between Powell and Mason Sts). 781.7800, 800/843.4343. www.handlery.com/sf &

## 68 GUCCI

The expanse of brass, marble, and fine woodwork at this world-renowned retailer creates a luxurious environment for those with lots of money to spend on clothes, leather goods, and accessories. ♦ Daily. 200 Stockton St (across from Union Sq). 392.2808 &

## 69 NEIMAN MARCUS

**Philip Johnson** and **John Burgee**'s architecturally underwhelming design—both inside and out—has provoked heated debate among San Franciscans since it was built in 1982. Many opposed the destruction of the **City of Paris,** a popular store occupying the site since 1896. A compromise stipulated that the building should incorporate the enormous glass dome that surmounted the old store. At Yuletide, the store erects the most dramatic Christmas tree in the city. ♦ Daily. 150 Stockton St (at Geary St). 362.3900 &

Within Neiman Marcus:

## THE ROTUNDA

★$$ The centerpiece of this elegant restaurant on the fourth floor is the impressive stained-glass dome from the **City of Paris** department store, the site's former occupant. The dome lends a warm, romantic glow to the tiered dining room that wraps around the atrium. Popular dishes include the lobster club sandwich, the oven-roasted chicken with mustard sauce, and the smoked-salmon salad. This is one of the most elegant places for afternoon tea. They serve popovers warm from the oven with strawberry butter. ♦ Californian ♦ Daily, lunch. Reservations recommended. 362.4777. www.rotundarestaurant.com &

## 70 LACOSTE BOUTIQUE

While the popularity of most clothing logos has ceased, the green alligator has gained cachet with the younger generation. This store carries a full range of colors and styles in Lacoste polo shirts, dress shirts, blouses, and dresses for grandparents as well as grandchildren. ♦ Daily. 172 Geary St (near Stockton St). 677.9004. www.lacoste-usa.com &

## 71 BETSEY JOHNSON

Special-occasion party dresses and flirtatious blouses and skirts come in a seductive range of colors and fabrics. Check out the rack of silk-ruffle blouses and bustiers. ♦ Daily. 160 Geary St (between Grant Ave and Stockton St). 398.2516. www.betseyjohnson.com &

## 71 PRADA

This minimalist-designed store with a marble staircase is a stunning showcase for the boots, bags, and wearable-art clothing of this Milan fashion house. ♦ Daily. 140 Geary St (between Grant Ave and Stockton St). 391.8844. www.pradaUSA.com &

## 71 BRITEX FABRICS

Everything to tempt the well-heeled seamstress and tailor is lavishly displayed on floor-to-ceiling bolts at Britex's headquarters. Lose yourself in the sight and feel of exquisite imported and designer fabrics. Let the profes-

sional sales team help you decide. If the prices leave you breathless, check out the remnant department. The notions counters carry one-of-a-kind buttons and decorative accessories. ♦ M-Sa. 146 Geary St (between Grant Ave and Stockton St). 392.2910 &

## 72 BOTTEGA VENETA

Handmade and pricey leather bags and shoes, scarves, ties, and luggage are available from this famed Italian manufacturer. ♦ M-Sa. 108 Geary St (between Grant Ave and Stockton St). 981.1700 &

## 73 871 FINE ARTS GALLERY AND BOOKSTORE

Contemporary and modern artists are represented here. The gallery was originally at 871 Folsom Street until earthquake damage in 1989 forced a move but not a change of name. ♦ Tu-Sa. 49 Geary St, Suite 513 (between Kearny St and Grant Ave). 543.5155

## 73 FRAENKEL GALLERY

This gallery exhibits 19th- and 20th-century fine photography exclusively, including the work of Diane Arbus, Garry Winogrand, Carleton E. Watkins, and Edward Weston. ♦ Tu-Sa. 49 Geary St (between Kearny St and Grant Ave), fourth floor. 981.2661

## 74 TED BAKER

If you want to see what young urban professionals are wearing across the Atlantic, visit Ted Baker's shop. This London clothier makes his American debut with unique designs. The youthful sales staff will help you put together an outfit for the right look. ♦ Daily. 80 Grant Ave (between Market and Geary Sts). 391.1256. www.tedbaker.co.uk &

## 75 GALLERY PAULE ANGLIM

Celebrated contemporary American artists as well as emerging artists are showcased. ♦ Tu-Sa. 14 Geary St (between Kearny St and Grant Ave). 433.2710 &

## 76 DISCOUNT CAMERAS

In business for more than 40 years, this firm deals in new and used cameras and does video transfers and camera repairs. ♦ M-Sa. 33 Kearny St (between Geary St and Maiden La). 362.4708 &

## 77 RITZ-CARLTON RESIDENCES AND CLUB

In 1890 the 16-story **Chronicle Building** was the first skyscraper in the West. Willis Polk restored the Romanesque building after the 1906 earthquake. The historic façade of brick and stone was recently restored as part of a $90 million project. Ritz-Carlton added 8 new stories, creating 49 club residences and 52 privately owned one- to three-bedroom condos. Fractional ownerships (1/12) sold for $200,000 to $300,000, and the condos for $1.1 million to $5 million. ♦ 690 Market St (at Kearny St). www.ritzcarltonrealestate.com &

## 78 KING GEORGE HOTEL

$$$ This quaint hotel lives up to its billing as a unique antique in the center of the city. Its location is superb—in the theater district and within walking distance of the many restaurants and shops on Union Square. The hotel, built in 1914 for the Panama-Pacific Exposition, is tall and narrow, much like an Amsterdam canal house. Its nine floors house 143 rooms, all with private baths and in-room safes. Continental breakfast is available daily, and English high tea is served Wednesday through Sunday, complete with scones, crumpets, and finger sandwiches (but there's no restaurant). ♦ 334 Mason St (between O'Farrell and Geary Sts). 781.5050, 800/288.6005 &

## 79 VILLA FLORENCE

$$ Part of the Kimpton boutique hotel collection, this is a princess of a hotel only a few yards from Union Square. The lobby is pretty, with wood-burning fireplaces, a wine bar, murals of Florentine scenes, and fresh flowers abloom everywhere. The 183 bedrooms are gracious, with high ceilings and country-house chintz. Amenities include complimentary morning limousine service to the Financial District and coffeemakers and refrigerators in every room. ♦ 225 Powell St (between O'Farrell and Geary Sts). 397.7700, 800/553.4411. www.villaflorence.com

Within the Villa Florence:

### KULETO'S ITALIAN RESTAURANT

★★$$ Crowds and a large open kitchen makes this trattoria boisterous, yet a seat at the counter can be fun: watch the always-harried chefs pull wonderful pizzas from the oven and exceptional roasted meats from the rotisserie. Pastas are good too—especially the penne with lamb sausage and red chard in a marinara sauce—though on particularly busy nights the food can be lackluster. The adjoining **Caffè Kuleto** serves espresso drinks, focaccia, panini, and gelato at outdoor tables during the day. ♦ Italian ♦ Daily, breakfast, lunch, and dinner. Reservations recommended. 397.7720 &

## 80 PACIFIC BAY INN

$ Simple, unpretentious, and very inexpensive, this family-owned, European-style inn with 84 rooms is located a few blocks from Union Square. Amenities include 24-hour desk and concierge service, and free in-room videos. For the price, location, and quality, this is one of the best deals in the city. ♦ 520 Jones St (at O'Farrell St). 673.0234, 800/343.0880 in CA, 800/445.2531 &

Adjoining the Pacific Bay Inn:

### DOTTIE'S TRUE BLUE CAFÉ

★★★$ Pancakes and house-baked breads are the lure of this breakfast and lunch spot. A recent change in ownership has brought an increase in vegetarian offerings, especially at lunch, like the roasted eggplant sandwich with goat cheese and tomatoes, black bean chili, and vegetable-filled tarts. ♦ American ♦ W-M, breakfast and lunch. 522 Jones St (at O'Farrell St). 885.2767 &

## 81 NAPA VALLEY WINERY EXCHANGE

This retail wine boutique features hard-to-find wines, mostly from (surprise!) the Napa Valley. It will ship them too. ♦ Daily. 415 Taylor St (between O'Farrell and Geary Sts). 771.2887 &

## 82 PONZU

★★★$$ From Bangkok to Beijing, diners can snack their way around the Pacific Rim on the chef's selection of small plates. These may include Saigon shrimp with green papaya and chili-mint sauce; rice-paper crab and green mango spring rolls with tamarind dip; and red curry clay pot with Kaffir lime and green sauce. The restaurant's velvet drapes and table lighting are dramatic and as seductive as the menu. ♦ Californian/Asian ♦ Daily, dinner. Reservations recommended. 401 Taylor St (at O'Farrell St). 775.7979. www.ponzurestaurant.com &

## 83 SAN FRANCISCO HILTON AND TOWERS

$$$$ Popular with conventioneers, this block-square hotel is the largest on the West Coast (2,000 rooms total, of which 156 are suites). Forty-four guest rooms are equipped for guests with disabilities, and 110 nonsmoking rooms are available. Some rooms are located poolside. The **Towers** form a hotel within a hotel, with seven floors of exclusive services, including a private lounge with complimentary continental breakfast and a cocktail hour. A health club, four ballrooms, and several restaurants are among the facilities. Don't miss the **Cityscape** restaurant and bar, which offers a stunning 360-degree view of the city. ♦ 333 O'Farrell St (between Mason and Taylor Sts). 771.1400, 800/HILTONS &

## 84 H&M

This Swedish fashion giant offers inexpensive yet fashionable clothing. An abbreviation for Hennes & Mauritz, H&M has clothing for women and men. Noted designers like Karl Lagerfeld and Dutch designers Viktor & Rolf create clothing lines exclusive to H&M. ♦ Daily. 150 Powell St (at O'Farrell St). 986.4215. www.hm.com/us &

## 85 MACY'S

A wide variety of merchandise, mostly in the middle-to-high price range, can be found in two buildings across the street from each other. The store that extends to Union Square includes mini-boutiques of designer fashions for women, cosmetics, and home furnishings. The food court in the basement has outlets for **Boudin's Bakery and Café, Ben and Jerry's Ice Cream, Jamba Juice,** and **Wolfgang Puck.** The other structure focuses on menswear, children's clothing, and electronics. ♦ Daily. 170 O'Farrell St (at Stockton St). 397.3333 &

Within Macy's:

### CHEESECAKE FACTORY

★★$$ A huge hit with locals and visitors, the restaurant has a terrace overlooking Union Square for outdoor dining. The menu features over 200 items (salads, pizza, chicken) and 40 varieties of cheesecake. ♦ American ♦ 391.4444 &

## 86 BARNEY'S NEW YORK

After two years of construction, the Manhattan clothier opened in the long-vacant F.A.O. Schwarz building, bringing top designers to Union Square. ♦ Stockton St (at O'Farrell St). www.barneys.com &

## 87 EMPORIO ARMANI BOUTIQUE

This opulent mini-emporium is the product of a multimillion-dollar renovation of the former **Security Pacific Bank,** built in 1911 and designed by **Bliss & Faville.** The result is breathtaking—racks of beautiful clothes surrounding a beautiful café staffed by an army of beautiful people. If you're hungry (and if you have any money left), take a seat at the counter and share a platter of *antipasti misti* (assorted appetizers) with a glass of Merlot. ♦ Shop: daily. Café: daily, lunch. 1 Grant Ave (between Market and O'Farrell Sts). 677.9400 &

## 87 PHELAN BUILDING

One of San Francisco's best flatiron buildings, designed by **William Curlett** and built in 1908, this cream-colored, terra-cotta-clad building may have been the inspiration for more recent flatirons, such as the one at 388 Market Street. ♦ 760 Market St (at Grant Ave)

## 88 WELLS FARGO BANK BUILDING

**Clinton Day's** Beaux Arts design presents a gently curved façade on Market Street. The building complements its classical neighbor, the former **Security Pacific Bank** across the street (now the **Emporio Armani Boutique**). ♦ 744 Market St (at Grant Ave)

## 89 EXECUTIVE HOTEL MARK TWAIN

$$$ Formerly the **Hotel Mark Twain,** this hotel has a pleasant lobby and 119 comfortable rooms, all appointed with refrigerators and coffeemakers. Its historical distinction is that it was where the late jazz singer Billie Holiday was arrested for drug possession in 1949. A suite has been named in her honor. The restaurant serves breakfast, lunch, and dinner. ♦ 345 Taylor St (between Ellis and O'Farrell Sts). 673.2332, 800/2RAMADA &

## 90 HOTEL NIKKO SAN FRANCISCO

$$$$ The luxurious expanse of white marble in the vast two-story lobby, punctuated by the lulling sound of water falling from a fountain, may remind some visitors of a mausoleum, but the management believes it calls forth a sense of serenity. Accommodations include 522 guest rooms, including 22 suites, and two authentic Japanese tatami suites. A fitness center, which the public may patronize, has the city's only glass-enclosed indoor pool. Other amenities are Japanese soaking tubs, the **Fountain Lobby Lounge,** and the **Nikko Lounge,** which is reserved for guests on floors 23 to 25. The restaurant, **Anzu,** serves Californian and Japanese cuisine. ♦ 222 Mason St (near Ellis St). 394.1111, 800/NIKKOUS. www.hotelnikkosf.com

## 91 RENAISSANCE PARC FIFTY FIVE

$$$$ Part of Marriott, this imposing 1,005-room hotel is the third-largest in town, and is mere footsteps from the **San Francisco Shopping Centre** and the **Powell Street cable-car** turntable. Facilities include a fitness center, two lounges, a business communications center, a **Concierge Club** level, and two restaurants. The intimate **Piazza Lounge** offers grand piano music and cocktail service. The hotel boasts a million-dollar art collection,

---

Restaurants/Clubs: Red | Hotels: Purple | Shops: Orange | Outdoors/Parks: Green | Sights/Culture: Blue

## THE BEST

### Robert and Marilyn Katzman

Tour Operators, San Francisco Fire Engine Tours & Adventures

At any moment, San Francisco's dramatic views and unique weather can infuse familiar sights with eye-catching splendor. A stiff sea breeze brings the ideal conditions to the waterfront. If you enjoy an invigorating walk, as we do, the bay is the place to go.

From the end of the *F-Line* streetcar at Beach and Jones, every direction promises a wonderful walk. If you're up for a challenge, walk up the **Filbert Steps** from Sansome Street off The Embarcadero. At the top, tour **Coit Tower,** a gift to the city from Lillie Hitchcock Coit. Lillie was an avid fire buff and bequeathed money to beautify the city.

If you're looking for a nice stroll without hills, head west beyond Aquatic Park to Fort Mason, then follow the Marina Green promenade to **Fort Point.** Watch the container ships cruise under the Golden Gate Bridge and the pelicans skimming the water.

If you head east, walk through **Fisherman's Wharf** and continue along The Embarcadero. On Tuesday and Saturday, when farmers' stalls line The Embarcadero and **Ferry Building** arcades, treat yourself to organic produce, artisan cheese, and brick-oven-baked bread. As you continue toward **SBC Park,** say hello to the firefighters at the fireboat under the Oakland Bay Bridge at the foot of Harrison Street.

When we aren't on our vintage fire engine, you'll find us walking the streets of San Francisco.

---

including vases, custom-made mirrors, sculpture, weavings, and paintings that recall an elegant Italian Renaissance theme. A handsome pair of Italianate lions stand guard in the travertine-marble lobby. At the carriage entrance is a seven-panel bas-relief sculpture by San Francisco artist Ruth Asawa, chronicling San Francisco's past, present, and future. ◆ 55 Cyril Magnin St (between Eddy and Ellis Sts). 392.8000, 800/650.7272. www.marriott.com &

Within the Parc Fifty Five:

### THE VERANDA BISTRO

★$$ The inspired garden setting, with its lovely pastel hues, thriving plants, urns, and fountain, delights the eye and makes this an exceptionally pleasant place to have lunch. Order the cioppino (this tomato-and-white-wine-based shellfish stew is a San Francisco specialty), fresh broiled salmon, or rack of lamb. ◆ Californian ◆ Daily, breakfast, lunch, and dinner. 392.8000 &

---

San Francisco's visitors total 14.4 million annually.

The San Francisco airport is the fifth busiest in the nation and the seventh busiest in the world.

"If it could be well settled like Europe, there would not be anything more beautiful in the world."

—Father Pedro Font, about the hills and bay of San Francisco, 1776

---

## 92 MONTICELLO INN

$$ Thomas Jefferson never slept here, but he might have felt at home in this country-colonial inn with 91 rooms. Complimentary breakfast and evening wine are included. ◆ 127 Ellis St (between Powell and Cyril Magnin Sts). 392.8800, 800/669.7777. www.monticelloinn.com &

Within the Monticello Inn:

### PUCCINI AND PINETTI

★★$$ This casual dining spot presents a menu that emphasizes straightforward pasta dishes, a few salads, and well-prepared panini, all at reasonable prices. Chef Adriano Paganini's menu includes angel-hair pasta with summer vegetables and basil oil, spicy *penne arrabiatta,* and grilled half-chicken with rosemary potatoes. ◆ Italian ◆ M-Sa, lunch and dinner; Su, dinner. Reservations recommended. Entrance at 88 Cyril Magnin St (at Ellis St). 392.5500

## 93 HOTEL UNION SQUARE

$$ A haunt of Dashiell Hammett's in the 1930s, this 131-room hotel has been remodeled into a modern hostelry with Art Deco influences. They opened a Dashiell Hammett Suite. The hotel includes three nonsmoking floors and complimentary coffee, tea, and croissants delivered to your floor each morning. ◆ 114 Powell St (between Ellis and O'Farrell Sts). 397.3000, 800/553.1900. www.hotelunionsquare.com &

## 94 JOHN'S GRILL

★★$$ Established in 1908 and much favored by businessmen, this place was immortalized by author Dashiell Hammett, who made it a hangout for his best-known fictional character, detective Sam Spade. The restaurant is a repository for Spade/Hammett lore. The dark-wood and brass décor is pure men's club, and meals, such as Sam Spade's favorite pork chops with a baked potato, are hearty. Steak and seafood are the specialties. Many dishes feature some Italian influence, though the menu covers a broad range of culinary tastes. ♦ American/Italian ♦ M-Sa, lunch and dinner; Su, dinner. 63 Ellis St (between Stockton and Powell Sts). 986.0069 &

## 95 THE APPLE STORE

A neon white Apple logo on this striking stainless steel-clad building can mean only one thing: the one-stop shop for award-winning desktop computers, Powerbooks, and iPods. You can easily while away an afternoon at the various computer stations, trying out the new iPods, the latest digital cameras, and the sleek G5 flat-screen computers. In the upstairs theater, an Apple pro demonstrates software on a large projection screen. Stop by the Genius Bar to huddle with a computer geek who knows the answer to every arcane question you could have about your computer. Also visit the Studio for helpful advice to the creative professional. ♦ Daily. 18 Ellis St (at Stockton and Market Sts). 392.0202. www.apple.com &

## 96 VIRGIN MEGASTORE

Modeled after its London flagship sister, this three-story megastore is stocked with more than 150,000 music titles (on CD and cassette) and 15,000 video titles, and includes a well-stocked bookstore. Listening stations with headphones allow customers to hear before they buy, and the **Citizen Cupcake and Bar** offers simple sustenance such as soups, sandwiches, and pastries. ♦ Daily. 2 Stockton St (at Market St). 397.4525 &

## 97 HOTEL BIJOU

$ This stylish 1911 hotel on the boundary between Union Square and the Tenderloin is where you'd expect to find rooms for under $100 a night. Bathrooms may be tiny and the elevator slow, but the vibrant colors in the lobby and hallways and 65 rooms named after San Francisco–based movies win you over. Bijou also has an Art Deco theater off the lobby that plays movie classics. Rates include a light continental breakfast and cheerful staff. ♦ 111 Mason St (at Eddy St). 771.1200, 800/771.1022. www.hotelbijou.com &

## 98 HALLIDIE PLAZA

As part of the **BART**/Market Street Renewal Program, this downtown plaza was created in 1973 by **Mario Ciampi, Lawrence Halprin & Associates,** and Carl-Warnecke and Associates. The subway entrance allowed the design to take the form of a terraced amphitheater. Within is a busy office of the **Convention & Visitor's Bureau,** with a wealth of material for tourists provided free or for a nominal charge. Lower level. ♦ Daily. Between Powell and Market Sts. 391.2000. Recordings about weekly events: English 391.2001, French 391.2003, German 391.2004, Japanese 391.2101, Spanish 391.2122 &

## 99 MCDONALD'S BOOKSTORE

More than one million used and out-of-print books, magazines, and records in good and questionable taste are heaped throughout this overstuffed store, in business since 1926. Management correctly describes the place as "a dirty, poorly lit place for books" (spoofing the name of "A Clean, Well-Lighted Place"—a popular bookstore on Opera Plaza in the **Civic Center** area which is now called Books Inc.). ♦ M-Sa. 48 Turk St (near Market St). 673.2235 &

## 100 WARFIELD THEATER

Originally built in 1922 by Marcus Loew to showcase the latest vaudeville and silent-screen productions, this theater now houses a full-service nightclub, restaurant, and bar. **G. Albert Lansburgh**'s conservative façade design belies its flamboyant interior. The ceiling fans out like a peacock tail, and murals can be found downstairs, where a speakeasy was reportedly operated. You can catch modern musical acts in an intimate setting that appears much as it has for over 70 years. Buy tickets at the box office to avoid service charges. ♦ 982 Market St (at Golden Gate Ave and Sixth St). 775.7722, 775.9949 &

## 101 GOLDEN GATE THEATRE

This 1922 **G. Albert Lansburgh**–designed theater is part of the Shorenstein Nederlander empire. The management put a lot of money into refurbishing the house, and it shows in the gleaming interior. Unfortunately, sight lines in the orchestra remain poor, so try the mezzanine. The 2,400-seat theater books popular musical attractions such as *Beauty and the Beast.* ♦ 25 Taylor St (between Market St and Golden Gate Ave). Call 551.2000 for current and upcoming plays. 512.7770. www.bestofbroadway.com &

---

**Restaurants/Clubs: Red | Hotels: Purple | Shops: Orange | Outdoors/Parks: Green | Sights/Culture: Blue**

# FINANCIAL DISTRICT

**O**ften called the Wall Street of the West, the Financial District, with its **Pacific Coast Stock Exchange**, several corporate headquarters, and elaborate commercial architecture, comprises an area bordered by **The Embarcadero** and **Market, Third, Kearny**, and **Washington Streets**.

When thousands of gold diggers were brought to the muddy shores of a shallow indentation known as **Yerba Buena Cove**, they began to grade the sand dunes along present-day Market Street, dumping sand into the mud flats of the cove. Before that was completed, they also started to build a seawall so ships could unload their cargo directly upon the wharves. For its time, this was a stupendous project, taking decades to complete. Meanwhile, the reclamation of the mud flats continued, with some of the city's smaller hills sacrificed to fill the area between the old waterfront and the new wall until, finally, the Financial District that's here today—everything east of **Montgomery Street**—arose from the sea. Within five years of the first news of the gold strike, Montgomery Street was lined with several bankers' offices. As the gold dust filtered down from the city of Sacramento, some means of handling it had to be found, and since the shopkeepers had scales for weighing the gold and safes for storing it, they were the first to become bankers.

Paradoxically, San Francisco was rich in gold, but poor in money. A pinch of gold subbed for one dollar, and a dollar's length of gold wire was divided into eight parts to serve as smaller coins, referred to as two bits, four bits, and so on. Coins from around the world were pressed into service at a rate of exchange based on their size. The Gold

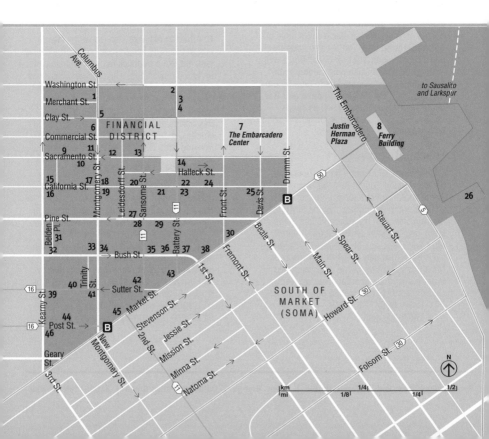

Rush boom ended in 1854, resulting in Black Friday's panic, which forced many banks to close. Not until the colossal riches began to flow from the Nevada silver mines was San Francisco firmly established as the financial center of the West. The Great Fire in 1906 precipitated the rise of another financial giant, A.P. Giannini, a food broker who had retired at age 32 to try out his banking theories with the Bank of Italy, founded by Giannini and his stepfather. Before the advancing flames reached his bank, he removed the assets and records and hauled them home in wagons from his warehouse, well camouflaged with heaps of fruit and vegetables. Consequently, the Bank of Italy—later renamed Bank of America—was the first in the city to reopen.

Imagine Montgomery Street or Kearny Street—the heart of the Financial District—paved with sticks, stones, bits of tin, and old hatch coverings. Today, Montgomery Street is sleek and imposing, with walls of stone, glass, and marble lining its sides. The street awakens before daybreak, when trading begins on the "Big Board" in New York. By 9AM, the skyscrapers are filled with thousands of brokers, bankers, executives, and clerical workers. By dark, its canyons are largely deserted, except for cleaning crews, security guards, and a smattering of restaurant-goers and barhoppers.

"Monkey Block" was the nickname for **Montgomery Block,** a four-story building that for a century stood on the present site of the **Transamerica Pyramid.** It was the first office building of any significance in San Francisco, and the first to be fireproof. Much of the city's important business was carried on here. When business moved out, American literary giants moved in: Mark Twain, Bret Harte, Robert Louis Stevenson, Rudyard Kipling, Jack London, Ambrose Bierce, and William Randolph Hearst. All either had office space in the building or regularly hung out at the Bank Exchange, the building's legendary bar. In a second-floor office, a young doctor named Sun Yat-sen plotted the successful overthrow of the Manchu dynasty and later wrote the Chinese constitution. Although they would have mourned the destruction of Monkey Block, these legendary characters probably would be somewhat cheered to know that the site is now graced by the Transamerica pyramid, one of the city's most prominent landmarks.

## 1 655 MONTGOMERY STREET

Completed in 1984, architects **Kaplan/McLaughlin/Diaz's** mixed-use tower contains condominiums above offices. ♦ At Merchant St

Within 655 Montgomery Street:

### TOMMY TOY'S

★★★$$$ The owner of this luxurious dining establishment describes the food as "haute cuisine *chinoise*"—and, indeed, it does represent an East/West melding of tastes presented in a palatial setting. The main dining room is fashioned after the 19th-century Chinese empress dowager's reading room, with ancient powder paintings framed in sandalwood. Dishes include such cross-cultural offerings as breast of duckling smoked with camphor wood and tea leaves served with a plum-wine sauce, whole fresh Maine lobster shelled and sautéed with pine nuts and mushrooms in a peppercorn sauce, and prawns in vanilla-flavored sauce with raisins and fresh melon. ♦ Chinese ♦ M-F, lunch and dinner; Sa, Su, dinner. Reservations recommended. 397.4888. www.tommytoys.com

## 2 WASHINGTON/ BATTERY STREET BUILDING

Built in 1985, **Fee and Munson**'s narrow office block is only 25 feet deep; bay windows capture additional space for tenants. The façade facing east has a large clock. ♦ Washington St (at Battery St) ♿

## 3 PUNCH LINE

They sure don't have to turn on any laugh tracks when the jokes start flying at this comedy club. Part of the Live Nation venues, it has a slick,

---

Restaurants/Clubs: Red **|** Hotels: Purple **|** Shops: Orange **|** Outdoors/Parks: Green **|** Sights/Culture: Blue

urbane look. Snacks and meals are served, but food is certainly not the reason for coming. Aspiring comedians are showcased every Sunday night. You must be 18 years of age or older to attend. Seating is on a first-come, first-served basis. ♦ Cover and two-drink minimum. Shows daily. Reservations required for dinner on weekends. Tickets available online or at the door. 444 Battery St (between Clay and Washington Sts), upstairs. 397.7573. www.punchlinecomedyclub.com &

## 4 ONE MARITIME PLAZA

**Skidmore, Owings & Merrill**'s 25-story slab block with exposed diagonal-steel bracing, built in 1967, is one of the few buildings that visually demonstrates its ability to withstand the forces of an earthquake. The entrance lobby is two floors above the street. ♦ Battery St (between Clay and Washington Sts)

## 5 TRANSAMERICA PYRAMID

**William Pereira and Associates**' 853-foot-tall building has become a landmark because of its unusual shape and location at the end of Columbus Avenue. It caused great controversy when it was built in 1972 and, until it gained acceptance, gave credence to the belief that California architecture couldn't be taken seriously. (San Franciscans always hastened to add that a Los Angeles firm designed it.) It's the head-quarters of the Transamerica Corporation, founded in 1928 by A.P. Giannini. A public observation area on the 27th floor provides excellent views of such landmarks as the Golden Gate Bridge, **Coit Tower,** and Alcatraz Island, and is open to the public weekdays. The adjoining half-acre **Transamerica Redwood Park** is a pleasant place to sit and gaze up the pyramid's walls or at the lighthearted bronze *Puddle Jumpers* sculpture. ♦ 600 Montgomery St (between Clay and Washington Sts)

## 6 BANK OF CANTON OF CALIFORNIA

The present building, designed by **Skidmore, Owings & Merrill,** was erected in 1984 to replace the bank's original headquarters, a Financial District fixture since the 1930s. The architects, who strove for a modern update of the lines and detailing of the adjacent stone buildings, commissioned the use of Texas pink granite on the façade of this 17-story structure. ♦ 555 Montgomery St (at Clay St)

Within the Bank of Canton of California:

## PACIFIC HERITAGE MUSEUM

This delightful museum, hidden on a side street on the south side of the bank, offers an impressive look at Oriental culture through art and ceremonial objects, murals, photographs, and clothing. ♦ Free. Tu-Sa, 10AM-4PM; closed on bank holidays. 608 Commercial St (off Montgomery St, between Sacramento and Clay Sts). 399.1124. www.ibankunited.com &

## 7 EMBARCADERO CENTER

This flashy eight-block complex of retail and office space stretches from Clay, Battery, and Sansome Streets to Justin Herman Plaza and the **Hyatt Regency Hotel** at the foot of Market Street. Four slender, interconnected high-rise towers by **John Portman and Associates** are staggered to allow sunlight to penetrate and to break up what might easily have been a wall-like appearance; each has a triple-level shopping area that houses a total of 125 shops and restaurants. You'll find everything here from **The Gap** (391.8826), **Banana Republic** (986.5076), and **Liz Claiborne** (283.4841) to beauty shops, bookstores, and the Embarcadero cinema—enough to keep the most avid visitor busy. Since the four original towers went up in 1982, three buildings have been added to the center: the **Embarcadero Center West** and the restored **Old Federal Reserve Bank** at Sansome and Sacramento Streets, and **Le Meridien Hotel** at Clay and Battery Streets (see the illustration below). Public areas include sculpture courts, bridges, and walkways within garden settings. The abstract *Vaillancourt Fountain* in the plaza is the center's most controversial sculpture (many think its convoluted metal shapes make it look as if it has weathered an earthquake). But the Canary Island palms swaying in the sea breeze at the new Harry Bridges Plaza give the area an appeal akin to a tropical island. Parking at the center is free with validation Monday through Friday 5PM to 3AM and all day Saturday, Sunday, and major holidays; it's discounted with validation Monday through Friday 10AM to 5PM. ♦ Bounded by The Embarcadero and Sansome St, and Sacramento and Clay Sts. 772.0700. www.embarcaderocenter.com &

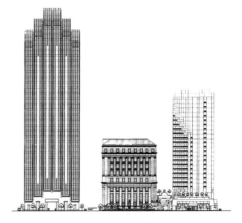

Within the Embarcadero Center:

## CHEVYS FRESH MEX

★$$ This popular restaurant has found a formula for success and repeated it many times throughout the Bay Area. Tortillas are made on the premises, along with terrific fajitas and other Mexican fare. Although the blended margaritas tend to taste more like nonalcoholic Slurpees, if you follow some patrons' remedy of ordering a shot of tequila on the side, you'll wind up with a mighty fine drink. Sun worshipers may dine on the patio except when it's reserved for happy-hour imbibing on Friday evenings. ♦ Mexican ♦ Daily, lunch and dinner. 2 Embarcadero Center, Promenade level. 391.2323. Also at 201 Third St (at Howard St). 543.8060; 3251 20th Ave (at Stonestown Galleria). 665.8705 &

## HYATT REGENCY HOTEL

$$$$ The silhouette of this quite impressive 803-room hotel is an unmistakable part of the San Francisco skyline. **John Portman and Associates'** 1973 design has received national recognition for outstanding and innovative architecture. The 17-story atrium lobby made the *Guinness Book of World Records* as the largest atrium lobby in the world. It is filled with artificial plants, trees, and greenery toppling from the tiered balconies, and the four-ton *Eclipse* sculpture by Charles Perry soars from a reflecting pool. The **Eclipse Café** serves California cuisine for breakfast, lunch, and dinner in a parklike setting, and the sweeping 60-foot-long **13 Views** watering hole is a full bar offering salads and sandwiches in the afternoon and hot appetizers in the evening. **The Equinox,** the very popular and romantic revolving-rooftop restaurant and bar, provides an incredible view of the Bay Area and serves continental cuisine for lunch and dinner daily and a Sunday brunch. **The Regency Club** offers a business center, bar, and lounge for the luxury-minded business traveler. The hotel hosts holiday events from the November tree lighting to New Year's Day buffet, and there is holiday tea service. ♦ 5 Embarcadero Center. Reservations only. 788.1234; 800/233.1234. www.sanfranciscohyattregency.com &

## LE MERIDIEN HOTEL

$$$$ This 360-room hotel is way up on the list of best places to stay in the city, especially if you are in town on business and need such standard extras as two phones and 24-hour room service. Two Mercedes are also available to shuttle you through the downtown area, and the hotel offers a full business center and 14 meeting rooms. Afternoon tea and caviar are served in the lobby lounge. Entertainment runs nonstop daily from 3PM until 11PM. ♦ 333 Battery St (at Clay St). 296.2900, 800/545.4300. www.starwood.com &

Within Le Meridien Hotel:

## PARK GRILL

★★$$$ Chef David Clawson offers American fare at this elegant restaurant adorned with rare Australian lacewood, teak, and ebony marquetry, and fantastic floral arrangements. Favorite dishes include horseradish-crusted halibut with mashed potatoes and a flurry of crispy leeks, mustard roasted chicken with whipped sweet potatoes, and grilled lamb chops accented with dates and a roasted-garlic flan. ♦ American ♦ Daily, breakfast, lunch, and dinner. 296.2933 &

## FEDERAL RESERVE BANK OF SAN FRANCISCO

Sierra-white marble covers three sides of **George Kelham**'s 1924 building, part of the Embarcadero Center complex. The Commercial Street side, which was finished later, is made of glazed terra-cotta brick. The building was renovated as law offices and retail space by **Kaplan/McLaughlin/Diaz** and reopened in 1989. The interior features both real and hand-painted faux marble. Stand across the street for a good view of the eight eagles perched above the entrance. ♦ 400 Sansome St (at Sacramento St)

## 8 FERRY BUILDING

Modeled after the Cathedral Tower in Seville, Spain, this building was designed by architect **Arthur Page Brown** in 1894. It was, in fact, known for many years as the tallest building in San Francisco with its 235-foot-high clock tower. Before the bridges were built, ferries transported as many as 50 million passengers a year from all over the bay. The **James Polshek and Partners** remodel features a center atrium opening out onto the bay.

The city's hub for California's freshest food is under one roof at the Ferry Building. Sunlight from a dramatic skylight floods the 660-foot-long **Nave,** lined with merchant stalls and specialty shops. Also explore the food boutiques, cafés, and shops of the **Market Hall** on the bay side of the building. Three restaurants—**Slanted Door, Market Bar,** and **Taylor's Refresher**—anchor the corners of the

---

## FERRY BUILDING MARKETPLACE

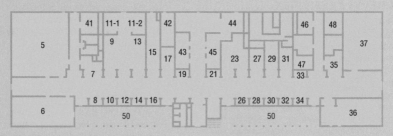

| | | | |
|---|---|---|---|
| 15 Acme Bread | 34 Far West Fungi | 19 Lulu Petite | 30 Recchiuti Confections |
| 22 Bay Crossings | 50 The Ferry Plaza Farmers' Market | 36 MarketBar | 31 San Francisco Fish Company |
| 42 Book Passage | 11-2 Ferry Plaza Seafood | 47 Mastrelli's Delicatessen | 14 Scharffen Berger |
| 48 Boulette's Larder | 23 Ferry Plaza Wine Merchant | 16 McEvoy Ranch Olive Oil | Chocolate Maker |
| 21 Capay Fruits & Vegetables | 46 Frog Hollow FarmThe Gardener | 10 Miette | 5 Slanted Door |
| 8 Ciao Bella Gelato | 13 Golden Gate Meat Company | 44 MIJITA | 28 Stonehouse California Olive Oil |
| 17 Cowgirl Creamery's | 11-1 Hog Island Oyster Company | 41 Mistral Rotisserie Provençal | 37 Sur La Table |
| Artisan Cheese Shop | 27 Imperial Tea Court | 7 Oak Hill Farm of Sonoma | 6 Taylor's Refresher |
| 35 Culinaire | 33 I Perferiti di Boriana | 43 Peet's Coffee & Tea | 26 The Gardener |
| 36 DELICA rf1 | 20 Kingdom of Herbs | 32 Prather Ranch Meat Company | 12 Tsar Nicoulai Caviar |
| 9 Farm Fresh to You | | | 29 Village Market |

building. The open-air cityside arcades bustle with shoppers every Tuesday, Thursday, Saturday, and Sunday when the **Ferry Plaza Farmers' Market** opens. ♦ Daily. One Ferry Building, The Embarcadero (at the foot of Market St). 693.0996. www.ferrybuildingmarketplace.com

Within the Ferry Building:

### TAYLOR'S REFRESHER

★★★$ Look for the red neon EAT over the kitchen and you've come to nirvana for all-natural beef burgers and fries made with roasted garlic. The Wisconsin burger is a winner, with mushrooms, bacon, cheddar cheese, and barbecue sauce on grilled sourdough bread. It's all-American diner food (hence the shiny chrome décor) but with fresh pizzazz. Try an ahi tuna burger or an espresso-bean milk shake. Daily specials like the mushroom Reuben and the duck confit taco bring the gourmet concept to fast food. In fine weather, take your feast out to a cityside picnic table. ♦ American ♦ Daily, lunch and dinner until 8PM. 328.3663. www.taylorsrefresher.com &

### THE SLANTED DOOR

★★★$$$ The cavernous glass-walled dining room of this bayside eatery boasts million-dollar bay views. It's a fitting showcase for the inventive, lively dishes that flow from chef Charles Phan's kitchen. His signature dishes, such as shaking beef (cubed filet mignon with garlic and red onions) and Florida gulf shrimp with sing qua and giant oyster mushrooms, continue to impress legions of fans. You can eat like an aristocrat on asparagus and crabmeat soup, green papaya salad, and grilled lamb with potatoes and tamarind sauce. Sample a few of the organic-vegetable side dishes. The Chinese broccoli, bok choy, and snap peas taste as

sweet as candy. Phan employs a staff of 120, including an award-winning sommelier whose wine list features old-world Riesling. Try the Selbach-Oster Riesling from Germany. Weekdays, the commuter crowd gathers at the bar and lounge area to sip elderflower martinis and raspberry vodka gimlets and nibble on spring rolls. ♦ Vietnamese ♦ Daily, lunch, afternoon tea in lounge, and dinner. Reservations recommended. 861.8032. www.slanteddoor.com &

### MARKET BAR

★$$ On special evenings when dining alfresco is possible, Market Bar on The Embarcadero is the place to be. Even in a chill, the outdoor café attracts the Friday evening crowd. Market Bar, run by Doug Biederbeck and Joseph Graham of Florida, takes advantage of its marketplace locale by buying fresh ingredients straight from the shops. The menu varies according to how the chef decides to use the bountiful seasonal products, so choose a few side dishes of heirloom tomatoes, pole beans, or forest mushrooms. There are also ahi tuna sandwiches, bouillabaisse, veal chops, steak *frites,* and charcuterie plates. The back rooms ooze romance, with intimate seating in which to sample the chef's imaginative small plates. If you are among the hungry hordes who descend on the Saturday farmers' market, stop by afterward for the weekend barbecue, which fires up at noon. ♦ Californian/French ♦ Daily, lunch and dinner. Reservations recommended. 434.1100. www.marketbar.com &

### FERRY PLAZA FARMERS' MARKET

After a 10-year effort, the Center for Urban Education about Sustainable Agriculture

(CUESA) has established a permanent outlet for hundreds of local farmers. CUESA operates the farmers' market, where farmers get top dollar for their dazzling produce. It also conducts education programs, farm tours, and cooking demonstrations. ♦ Tu, Th, Su, 10AM-2PM; Sa, 8AM-2PM. 291.3276. www.ferrybuildingmarketplace.com &

## 9 PALIO D'ASTI

★★$$ Regional Italian specialties are prepared by chef Craig Stoll in open-display kitchens at this handsome restaurant owned by Gianni Fassio. Many of the pastas are house-made; they're all dressed creatively with such flourishes as artichoke hearts, Parmesan cheese, mint, and Italian parsley. The restaurant is open for lunch and the wine bar, with murals depicting Palio pageantry and the famed Italian horse race, is open evenings. The restaurant can be rented in the evening for special functions. ♦ Italian ♦ M-F, lunch and dinner. Reservations recommended. 640 Sacramento St (between Montgomery and Kearny Sts). 395.9800. www.paliodasti.com &

## 10 JEANTY AT JACK'S

★★★$$$ Jack's is a turn-of-the-century historic room for Philippe Jeanty's authentic brasserie dishes. In 1864 a Frenchman opened Jack's and ran the kitchen. The 14-foot-high ceiling, wood paneling, plaster casts, and ornate railing on the mezzanine staircase remain untouched by time. Now Jeanty and his waiters scurry over the worn tile floor with steaming mussels, charcuterie platters, coq au vin, and tomato soup in puff pastry. The kitchen turns out perfect fried smelts and sole meunière. To go with Jeanty's excellent fare, choose a wine from Burgundy, the Rhône, or south of France. You'll also find crêpe suzettes and crème brûlée on the dessert menu. The third-floor dining room is in a garden conservatory setting. ♦ French ♦ M-F, lunch; daily, dinner. Reservations recommended. 615 Sacramento St (near Montgomery St). 693.0941 &

## 11 505 MONTGOMERY STREET

**Skidmore, Owings & Merrill**'s neo-Deco tower houses several offices and the Tokai Bank. Step inside the lobby for a look at the striking pattern of the inlaid-marble floor; the lobby is particularly pretty when it's all decked out during the Christmas season. ♦ Between Sacramento and Commercial Sts

Within 505 Montgomery Street:

### PALIO PANINOTECA

★★$ For a great panino, stop at this offshoot of the popular **Palio d'Asti** restau-rant (see this page). Assorted salads, pizzas, weekly specials, pastries, and sweets are also available to savor here or to go. ♦ Italian ♦ M-F, breakfast and lunch. 362.6900. www.paliopaninoteca.com &

## 12 RUBICON

★★★$$$ Owned by Robert De Niro, Francis Ford Coppola, and Robin Williams, this is one of the most popular new dining spots in the city. The dramatic loftlike space has huge windows crossed with earthquake-protection beams, white walls, and dark wood accents. Chef Stuart Brioza's French-inspired menu is constantly updated, but you may see such dishes as seared tuna paired with ragout of root vegetables. Inventive desserts truly satisfy, including apple tart with apple sorbet, red-wine-poached fruit tart, and satiny Black Forest cake. ♦ Californian/French ♦ W, lunch; M-Sa, dinner. Reservations required; jacket recommended. 558 Sacramento St (between Sansome and Montgomery Sts). 434.4100. www.sfrubicon.com &

## 13 LONDON WINE BAR

$$ This establishment, which opened in the mid-1980s, claims to be the oldest wine bar in California. It has a classic look, with dark wood, racks and boxes of wine lining the walls, and a clientele that likes to swirl wine, nibble on bread sticks, and discuss the day's events in relaxed surroundings. More than three dozen wines are offered by the glass and are well complemented by light lunches and snacks. ♦ Californian ♦ M-F, lunch. 415 Sansome St (between Sacramento and Commercial Sts). 788.4811. www.londonwinesf.com

## 14 353 SACRAMENTO STREET

Handsomely clad in teal- and blue-metal panels, **Skidmore, Owings & Merrill**'s low-scale corner office building is a 1984 reconstruction of a building that previously occupied this location. The result is a strange juxtaposition of styles and forms. The rotated plan of the tower ignores the grid of the street and street wall. ♦ At Battery St

## 15 580 CALIFORNIA STREET

Architects **Philip Johnson** and **John Burgee**'s pseudo-classical 1984 high-rise is topped by 12 blank-faced statues that surround the glass mansard roof; the figures allegedly represent the mayor and the 11 members of the Board of Supervisors. Classically, the design is incorrect: The front façade is divided into an equal number of bays, resulting in a column in the middle of the entry. ♦ At Kearny St

---

Restaurants/Clubs: Red | Hotels: Purple | Shops: Orange | Outdoors/Parks: Green | Sights/Culture: Blue

# San Francisco on Tap

The strong aroma wafting down city streets may signal a welcome break from sightseeing. Trace it to its source and you may arrive at a brewpub thronged with fans of local-brewed ale. To obtain its distinct aroma and characteristic bitterness, the beer is painstakingly produced following a more costly method than that used for commercial beer, in which hops is added to boiling malted barley. On tap may be the city's Anchor Brewing Company, which brews Anchor Steam; Liberty Ale; Old Foghorn Ale, a barleywine-style ale; and Anchor Porter, an old-fashioned dark brew with a smoky-toasty aroma and rich flavor.

The brewmasters handcrafting the beer are the city's current celebrities, though they were once a dying breed. In the early 1970s, San Francisco's Anchor Brewing Company wanted to distinguish its beer from the light, simple suds put out by corporate breweries. In returning to the richer, full-bodied classic beers, the company helped launch the microbrewing industry, which 15 years later has grown from 50 microbreweries to more than 1,000.

Each pub has its signature brews. You'll find British-style ales, Guinness-style stout, porter, and bitters. And since this is California, fruit-flavored beers are making a splash, with Marin Brewing Company producing some of the best. Blueberry Flavored Ale and Raspberry Trail Flavored Ale both have appealing aromas and a subtle hint of fruit.

If you have an adventurous palate, and want to try some of the city's skillfully crafted beers, here are a few places to get you started. Most are open for lunch and dinner, where you'll notice great food and beer pairings. Some welcome visitors to view their operations, though **Anchor Brewing Company** (1705 Mariposa St, 863.8350) has the best tour, offered afternoons Monday through Friday by reservation.

**Beach Chalet Brewery & Restaurant** (1000 Great Highway, Golden Gate Park at Ocean Beach, 386.8439) offers a panoramic ocean view with its signature ales.

**Gordon Biersch Brewery Restaurant** (2 Harrison St at The Embarcadero, 243.8246). Stunning views are the draw here, where you can enjoy award-winning German-style beer on the waterfront deck and tour the brewery on the premises.

**Irish Bank Bar & Restaurant** (10 Mark La off Bush St between Grant Ave and Claude La, 788.7152) is San Francisco's most authentic Irish bar, tucked away in a hidden alley. Here you can sip a Guinness or Anchor Steam in a confessional salvaged from a church.

**Magnolia Pub & Brewery** (1398 Haight St at Masonic St, 864.7468). Dave McLean brews traditional British-style ales, and features five British hand pumps for cask-conditioned beers served at cellar temperature, a common practice in England.

**San Francisco Brewing Company** (155 Columbus Ave at Pacific Ave, 434.3344) has the most historic location: inside a Barbary Coast saloon with 1907 paddle fans and a mahogany bar. Allen Paul pours his own brews (you can visit his cellar brewery) as well as those from small specialty breweries.

**ThirstyBear Brewing Company** (661 Howard St, between Second and Third Sts, 974.0905) has a two-story, state-of-the-art microbrewery on view behind glass. Seven microbrews and a seasonal ale are on tap every day, though the Spanish tapas garner as much praise as the brew.

## 16 Bank of America World Headquarters

Completed in 1969 by **Wurster, Bernardi & Emmons Inc.** and **Skidmore, Owings & Merrill,** with **Pietro Belluschi** as design consultant, this is one of the best high-rise office towers ever built—52 stories clad in dark-red carnelian marble. The faceted façade and flush glazing create a changing image depending on the season or time of day. At sunset, the reflection of the sun on the windows makes the building look like a towering inferno; at other times it disappears like a black monolith into the fog. Its asymmetrical profile at the top creates sufficient variety to prevent it from becoming boring. The large lump of abstract black marble at the entry-way has been dubbed "Banker's Heart" by irreverent locals. ♦ 555 California St (at Kearny St)

Within the Bank of America World Headquarters:

## Carnelian Room

★$$$$ The stupendous view through the floor-to-ceiling glass wall at this spot high above San Francisco is a sight you'll never forget. The food is not memorable, but stop here for a drink—especially when the sun is setting or the fog is rolling in. If you're bent on having a meal here, however, lovers and those who want to be very, very private may reserve the fabulous **Tamalpais Room,** a hideaway within the restaurant seating just two to six; waiters come only when summoned by a bell. ◆ French ◆ M-Sa, cocktails and dinner; Su, brunch and dinner. Reservations recommended. 52nd floor. 433.7500. www.carnelianroom.com &

### 17 THE OMNI SAN FRANCISCO HOTEL

$$$ Opened in 2002 after a $100 million transformation, this historic office building is a luxury hotel with Old World elegance in each of its 362 rooms. The high ceilings with crown molding, mahogany and cherry wood furniture, and textured fabrics speak to the sybarite in all of us. Bathrooms feature granite vanities and marble walls and floor. There is complimentary high-speed internet access in the lobby and all public areas. Breakfast, lunch, and dinner are served daily in **Bob's Steak and Chop House.** ◆ 500 California St (at Montgomery St). 677.9494, 800/367.6664. www.omnihotels.com

### 18 WELLS FARGO HISTORY MUSEUM

On display in a renovated and expanded 4,400-square-foot space are artifacts from the Gold Rush days, including old mining equipment, gold nuggets, early banking articles, and period photographs documenting Wells Fargo and early state and local history. The star attraction is an authentic 19th-century Concord stagecoach that was once used on old California trails. A reference library is open to the public and tours can be arranged, both by appointment only. ◆ Free. M-F; closed on bank holidays. 420 Montgomery St (between California and Sacramento Sts). 396.2619. www.wellsfargohistory.com &

### 19 SECURITY PACIFIC BANK HALL

In **George Kelham**'s impressive old banking hall, the giant granite Ionic columns outside are matched by faux-marble columns inside. Completed in 1922, the hall's spacious volume is appropriate in scale and grandeur to the traditional forms of banking. The building is currently available for lease. ◆ Montgomery and California Sts

### 20 BANK OF CALIFORNIA

Built in 1908 shortly after "The Big One," **Bliss & Faville**'s Corinthian-columned temple contains a grand main banking hall. ◆ 400 California St (at Sansome St)

### 21 345 CALIFORNIA STREET

This twin-towered building by **Skidmore, Owings & Merrill** houses a luxury hotel above offices. It was skillfully inserted into the center of the block in 1986 and has an arcade linking Sansome, Battery, and California Streets. The two towers are connected by bridges and capped by two stainless-steel-clad flagpoles. The design represents one of the best examples of modernism and is a stunning addition to the city skyline. ◆ California St (between Battery and Sansome Sts)

Within 345 California Street:

#### MANDARIN ORIENTAL SAN FRANCISCO

$$$$ Stunningly set atop the twin towers and connected by glass sky bridges, this is the Mandarin Oriental Hotel Group's first US palace. Small and beautifully furnished, it has 158 select rooms and suites with outstanding views of the city and bay; those with marble bathtubs looking out picture windows 40 floors up are incredible. The **Oriental Suite,** on the 38th floor, is a home-away-from-home in grand-luxe style, with a parlor, two bedrooms, two and a half bathrooms, a pantry, and an open-air terrace with a 180-degree view of the bay. The **Taipan Suite,** across the hall, boasts the same wide vista, as well as a luxurious bedroom, two bathrooms, and a dining room. The secret at this hostelry lies in the personalized service, with a ratio of one staff member to each guest. Particular attention is paid to visiting executives at the lobby-level **Business Center,** which is filled with the latest high-tech office equipment. The sky bridges connecting the towers are worth the admission price. Adjoining the lobby is the **Mandarin Lounge,** where cocktails and hors d'oeuvres are served. ◆ 222 Sansome St (between Pine and California Sts). 276.9888, 800/526.6566. www.mandarinoriental.com &

Within the Mandarin Oriental San Francisco:

#### SILKS

★★★★$$$ Silks's unique wall treatments and hand-painted silk chandeliers evoke the odyssey of Marco Polo and his discovery of silk. The excellent East-West fare here draws a good lunch crowd, and a growing number of evening patrons. Silks's tasting menu features dishes such as red snapper with roasted tomato bouillon of Dungeness crab and baby clams, and Hawaiian tuna and French foie gras terrine with a ruby port reduction. Other options include succulent pan-roasted squab complemented by warm cornbread cake and caramelized apples and onions. ♦ American ♦ Daily, dinner. 986.2020 ♿

## 22 TADICH GRILL

★★★$$ This is the most famous of the San Francisco fish houses that trace their lineage back for decades, and one of the first to grill fish over charcoal. Order the sand dabs, if on the menu, or the petrale sole. Better yet, ask which fresh fish they received that day; all are served with the now-legendary potato-based tartar sauce. For dessert, nothing's more soothing than the creamy rice pudding. Unless you eat in mid-afternoon, be prepared for a long but usually pleasant wait. ♦ American ♦ M-Sa, lunch and dinner. 240 California St (between Front and Battery Sts). 391.2373

## 22 AQUA

★★★$$$ Embraced by the see-and-be-seen crowd, this refined restaurant offers lovely-to-behold fish dishes that are imaginatively prepared under the direction of chef Laurent Manrique. Try the black mussel soufflé, lobster potpie, or rare tuna topped with a meltingly tender slice of foie gras. The desserts taste as spectacular as they look, and the wine list is expertly matched to the imaginative menu. ♦ Seafood ♦ M-F, lunch and dinner; Sa, dinner. Reservations recommended. 252 California St (between Front and Battery Sts). 956.9662. www.aqua-sf.com ♿

## 23 INDUSTRIAL INDEMNITY BUILDING

Formerly the **John Hancock Building**, this 1959 structure by **Skidmore, Owings & Merrill** is contemporary with the **Crown Zellerbach Building** (designed by the same architects), but demonstrates more traditional attitudes toward the street and context. It is

At 853 feet, the Transamerica Pyramid is San Francisco's tallest structure.

Use the Ferry Building at the foot of Market Street as your guide to the piers; even-numbered piers are south of the building and odd-numbered piers are to the north.

On New Year's Eve in the Financial and Downtown Districts, it's a tradition to toss calendars out of office windows. The cleanup operation is costly, but locals seem reluctant to give up the practice.

clad in polished gray granite and has a retail base with a second-level walkway above. ♦ 255 California St (at Battery St)

# PERBACCO
### ristorante + bar

## 24 PERBACCO RISTORANTE AND BAR

★★$$ After sampling chef Staffan Terje's good food and wine, you discover that the restaurant is aptly named. Perbacco is an Italian expression of pleasant surprise as well as a reference to the Roman god Bacchus. The menu covers the range of Italian flavors with roasted whole fish, milk-braised pork shoulder, and side dishes of polenta and *agnolotti* (filled pasta). House-cured meats in the Ligurian and Piedmontese style come from the kitchen's curing room. Pair these classic dishes with wines from Piedmont, Barolo, and Barbaresco. Housed in the historic 1912 Hind building, the unfinished brick wall is a handsome design element. The restaurant seats 120 in the main-floor dining room and the mezzanine. ♦ Italian ♦ M-Sa, lunch and dinner. Reservations recommended. 230 California St (between Front and Battery Sts). 955.0663. www.perbaccosf.com ♿

## 25 101 CALIFORNIA STREET

With the **Bank of America** building and the **Transamerica Pyramid**, this cylindrical structure by **Philip Johnson** and **John Burgee** acts as the third major landmark in the Financial District. Completed in 1983, its silvery reflective glass looks especially beautiful when seen from the bay at dusk. Although the entrance lobby is rather ungainly, a sloping glass wall slicing across the 90-foot-tall columns makes a dramatic sight. The north-facing plaza on California Street is flanked by two mid-rise blocks cut on the diagonal. ♦ Between Davis and Front Sts

At 101 California Street:

## THE ATRIUM

★★$$$ Off the open plaza is this sophisticated restaurant with a menu that changes daily to reflect the freshest offerings of the marketplace. Sample entrées include spicy Creole jambalaya, a grilled thick-cut pork chop with turnip gratin and Gravenstein applesauce, and *ancho* (dried *poblano*) chili-glazed breast of chicken with garlic mashed potatoes. The sleek dining room, established on several elevated levels, is decorated with black granite, pastel desert colors, and plantation shutters. On sunny days, many diners opt to lunch alfresco. ♦ Californian ♦ M-F, lunch and dinner. Entrance on Front St. 788.4101 &

## 26 FERRY BUILDING LINE

This sight-seeing boat cruises along the waterfront, under the new span of the Bay Bridge and around Treasure Island. Departure days and times for the 90-minute excursion vary seasonally. The summer season departures are at 11AM, 1PM, and 3PM. Purchase tickets online or on board. Arrive 20 minutes before departure. Gate E is at the south end of the Ferry Building. ♦ Daily, spring, summer, and fall; weekends in winter. Ferry Building, Gate E. 901.5253, 673.2900. 901.5253 www.ferrybuildingline.com &

## 27 ROYAL GLOBE INSURANCE BUILDING

Note the elaborate sculpture in **Howells and Stokes**'s 1909 white-marble building with a fine entrance and base. ♦ 201 Sansome St (at Pine St)

## 28 PACIFIC COAST STOCK EXCHANGE

This structure, once home to the US Treasury, was renovated in 1930 by **Miller & Pflueger** and features two granite sculptures by Ralph Stackpole flanking its entrance. This classically inspired structure is the heart of the Financial District and a little sister to those on Wall Street and in London. It now houses a health club. 301 Pine St (at Sansome St)

## 29 235 PINE STREET

Note the bronze work above the entrance of this impressive 25-story, limestone-clad highrise designed by **Skidmore, Owings & Merrill** in 1990. The 20 relief portrait sculptures, entitled *Called to Rise*, feature individuals who have contributed significantly to the history of San Francisco, including Juan Bautista De Anza, Phoebe Apperson Hearst, Amadeo Peter Giannini, and **Timothy Pflueger**. For more information about these bronze castings and biographies of the people portrayed, ask the person at the front desk in the lobby for a brochure. ♦ Between Battery and Sansome Sts

## 30 388 MARKET STREET

One of **Skidmore, Owings & Merrill**'s most refined buildings is this mixed-use, flatiron office tower, completed in 1987. The triangular site is occupied to the property lines, in contrast to the **Crown Zellerbach Building** two blocks away on Market Street, designed by the same firm. The building's form consists of a cylinder attached to a triangle. The apartments at the top have deeply recessed windows, while the offices below have flush windows. The façade is a dark-red polished granite, which contrasts with the green window mullions. ♦ Between Davis and Front Sts

## 31 BELDEN PLACE

The Financial District's proletarian version of Union Square's Maiden Lane (a tiny pedestrian way filled with umbrella-covered tables during the lunch hour) has a ways to go yet before it catches up to the cachet of its rival. Still, the brick-walled alley provides a welcome respite from the hustle and bustle at lunchtime. Closed to traffic from 11AM to 3PM, it offers a melting pot of kitchens to choose from, including **Plouf** (French seafood), **Café Tiramisù** (Italian), **Café Bastille** (Mediterranean), **B44** (Spanish), and **Café 52** (Mediterranean). Many have alfresco dining during the summer. ♦ Between Bush and Pine Sts

Within Belden Place:

### CAFÉ BASTILLE

★$ The first restaurant to venture out of doors on Belden, it attracts a loyal following with its simple, well-prepared brasserie fare. Choose from salads, soups, crepes, sandwiches, and entrées that range from roasted chicken breast with *pommes frites* (french fries) to *andouillette* (pork sausage) with sautéed onions. Live jazz is featured three nights a week. ♦ French ♦ M-Sa, lunch and dinner. 22 Belden Pl. 986.5673. www.belden-place.com &

### CAFÉ TIRAMISÙ

★★$$ The open kitchen at this stylish Italian restaurant turns out fresh pasta, including risotto with earthy mushrooms, osso buco with soft polenta, and roasted whole fish. Save room for the namesake dessert. The walls were decorated by the same muralists who left their mark on the city's popular **Stanford Court Hotel.** ♦ Italian ♦ M-F, lunch and dinner; Sa, dinner. Reservations recommended. 28 Belden Pl. 421.7044 &

### B44

★★$$ Spanish dining has come to this Parisian café scene. The interior is homey, with a video of a festival in the chef's hometown of Vilafranca del Penedes. Paella served in small skillets is the dish to order. Varieties include seafood, chicken, and vegetarian. Save room for the classic Spanish desserts, such as cinnamon and rice ice cream, and fresh cheese drizzled with honey, walnuts, and sherry. ♦ Catalan ♦ M-F, lunch; daily, dinner. 44 Belden Pl. 986.6287 ♿

**SAM'S Grill**

## 32 SAM'S GRILL

★★$$ This Old Guard San Francisco restaurant features polished wood, private rooms, and a menu specializing in sweetbreads served on toast points with crisp slices of bacon and roasted potatoes, minute steak, celery, and French pancakes (thin crepes drizzled with lemon juice and powdered sugar). If you've never eaten here, you've got to try it at least once, and be willing to forgive the indifferent service. Jammed for lunch, it's less crowded at dinner if you arrive early. ♦ American ♦ M-F, lunch and dinner. Reservations accepted for six or more only. 374 Bush St (between Montgomery and Kearny Sts). 421.0594 ♿

## 33 RUSS BUILDING

**George Kelham**'s 1928 Gothic high-rise was modeled after the winning entry for the Chicago Tribune Tower competition. Until 1964, it was the tallest building in the city. ♦ 235 Montgomery St (between Bush and Pine Sts)

## 34 MILLS BUILDING AND MILLS TOWER

A rare example of the Chicago School west of the Rockies, this 10-story **Burnham and Root** building, completed in 1892, suffered only interior fire damage during the 1906 earthquake. Notice the fine Richardsonian entrance archway on Montgomery Street, the subtly delineated brick planters and strong cornice, and the multifloor frieze. **Willis Polk** supervised the postfire reconstruction and also designed the adjacent Mills Tower on Bush Street. ♦ 220 Montgomery St (at Bush St). 421.1444

## 35 130 BUSH STREET

Ten stories high and just 20 feet wide, **George Applegarth**'s 1910 building is surely one of the narrowest high-rises ever built. This office building has slender Gothic lines and a defined top, middle, and bottom. ♦ Between Battery and Sansome Sts

## 36 THE SHELL BUILDING

One of the city's most beautiful Art Deco towers, **George Kelham**'s structure, built in 1929, was strongly influenced by **Eliel Saarinen**'s entry for the Chicago Tribune Tower competition. Because of its fine proportions—tripartite division of top, shaft, and base—distinctive silhouette, and contextual relationship to the urban fabric, it is now considered an important source of inspiration for the next generation of skyscrapers. The exterior is sheathed in glazed terra-cotta. ♦ 100 Bush St (between Battery and Sansome Sts)

## 37 SPECIALTY'S CAFÉ AND BAKERY

This take-out lunch spot is packed at noontime. Everything's made from scratch—even the sandwich bread comes straight from the oven—and the cookies are heavenly. Try their peanut-butter, banana, and wheat-germ sandwich for a change of pace. Catering services are available. ♦ M-F, 6AM-6PM. No credit cards accepted. 22 Battery St (at Bush St). Daily specials 896.BAKE. Also at 312 Kearny St (between Bush and Pine Sts); 150 Spear St (between Howard and Mission Sts); 1 Post St (at Market St)

## 38 444 MARKET STREET

Architects **Skidmore, Owings & Merrill**'s 38-story, aluminum-panel-clad office tower, completed in 1981, has a sawtooth profile. The building steps back on the 33rd, 34th, and 35th floors, opening out onto gardens that overlook the bay. ♦ At Front St

## 39 GALLERIA PARK HOTEL

$$$ One of the small, renovated hotels springing up around town, this has a superb location, adjacent to the **Crocker Galleria** and two blocks from Union Square and the cable cars. The 117 rooms and suites are equipped with bars and refrigerators, and the grand suite offers the comfort of a fireplace and whirlpool. Meeting rooms are available, and there's even a rooftop jogging track and a small fitness facility equipped with a few exercise machines. ♦ 191 Sutter St (at Kearny St). 781.3060, 800/792.9639 ♿

## 39 PERRY'S DOWNTOWN

★★$$ In a clubby mahogany-paneled atmosphere inspired by the original **Perry's** on Union Square, this bustling New York–style pub features hearty American fare. Two standout sandwiches are the lobster club and the New York steak with onions and mushrooms. Main dishes are just as good: Try the grilled pork chops with potato pancakes and applesauce or risotto with chicken and toasted garlic. Leave room for the creamy cheesecake or the apple brown Betty with vanilla ice cream. ♦ American ♦ Daily, lunch and dinner. Reservations recommended. 185 Sutter St (between Montgomery and Kearny Sts). 989.6895

## 39 JOHN WALKER & CO. LIQUORS

This is the largest specialty and import liquor store in the area. If you have questions or need to find that rare cognac, the staff is ready to help. Gift wrapping and shipping are available. ♦ M-Sa. 175 Sutter St (between Montgomery and Kearny Sts). 986.2707 &

## 40 HALLIDIE BUILDING

**Willis Polk and Company**'s 1917 building is an architectural favorite. Claiming to have the world's first curtain-wall glass façade, it was built for the **University of California** and named after Andrew Hallidie, the inventor of the cable car, who was also a university regent. The glass façade is projected a few feet beyond the floor edge and structure. Decorative railings integrate the fire-escape balconies and stairs and create a wonderful silhouette at the top of the building. The sixth floor is the home of the San Francisco chapter of the **American Institute of Architects,** which usually has an exhibit on display in its entryway (free and open to the public). The **US Post Office** occupies most of the ground floor. ♦ 130 Sutter St (between Montgomery and Kearny Sts)

## 41 HUNTER-DULIN BUILDING

With the revival of interest in pre-Modern architecture, this 1926 **Schultze and Weaver** building has come to be recognized as one of the finest in the Financial District. Its tripartite division of top, shaft, and base and its rich terra-cotta detailing contrast well with the banality of its more recent neighbors. The style is French château/Romanesque capped by a tile mansard roof. Medieval motifs adorn lobby walls. ♦ 111 Sutter St (at Montgomery St)

## 42 CITICORP CENTER

The best aspect of this 1984 building designed by **William Pereira and Associates** is the conversion of the old **Banking Hall** (built in 1910 by **Albert Pissis**) into an atrium space that's open to the public during the day. The **Citicorp Café** (362.6297) and a number of colorful flags help to enliven the space, which previously had an echoing, mausoleum-like quality. **Pereira**'s tower is clad in precast concrete. ♦ 1 Sansome St (at Sutter St)

## 43 CROWN ZELLERBACH BUILDING

Following the example of Lever House in New York City, this 1959 design by **Hertzka and**

**Knowles** and **Skidmore, Owings & Merrill** represented the then-current fashion for treating buildings as isolated objects withdrawn from the street by a belt of landscaping and clad in thin curtain walling. It's ironic to think that in 1981—a mere 22 years after it was constructed—a suggestion that the building might be demolished to make way for a taller building prompted discussion about listing the building as a historic landmark. ♦ Market St (between Battery and Sansome Sts)

## 44 PACIFIC TELESIS CENTER

Whereas the **Bank of America World Headquarters** represented the then-latest ideas (in 1969) about high-rise towers and their relationship to the urban fabric, **Skidmore, Owings & Merrill**'s design (completed in 1982) embodies a change in architectural thought. It rises sheer from the street without a plaza, and its surface consists of flush two-tone granite panels and mirror glazing. The corners are beveled, emphasizing the wraparound smoothness of the cladding. The matte/glossy granite and mirror glass create changing patterns at different times of the day or night. ♦ 50 Post St (at Kearny St)

Within the Pacific Telesis Center:

## CROCKER GALLERIA

This ornate, three-level, glass-barrel-vaulted shopping arcade is modeled after Milan's vast Galleria Vittorio Emanuele. Dozens of shops grace this pretty center, including **Pesaresi Ceramics, Gianni Versace,** and **Polo/Ralph Lauren.** You'll also find stores devoted to home furnishings, fresh flowers, cookies, cards, and a range of small fast-food places catering to workers and shoppers. ♦ M-Sa. Entrances are on Post St and Sutter St. 393.1505. www.shopatgalleria.com &

## 45 HOBART BUILDING

**Willis Polk and Company**'s 1914 building is part high-rise tower, part mid-rise street block. For many years it was one of the tallest structures on Market Street; now it is dwarfed by the **Wells Fargo Tower** next door. ♦ 582 Market St (at Second St)

## 46 88 KEARNY STREET (CALIFORNIA FEDERAL BANK)

Clad in white concrete and embellished with blue tiles, this 1986 **Skidmore, Owings & Merrill** building has one of the finest entrance lobbies and banking halls in the city. The detailing, materials, and lighting evoke an Art Deco flavor. Also take notice of the reconstruction of the old façade on the building located right next door. ♦ At Post St

---

# CHINATOWN

San Francisco's Chinatown is the largest Chinese community on the West Coast—and the second largest in the US next to New York City's settlement. The tourist area, bounded by **Broadway, Columbus Avenue,** and **Bush Street,** and **Kearny** and **Stockton Streets,** is home to many of the 120,000 Chinese-Americans living in the Bay Area, but the population extends to North Beach, Russian Hill, and beyond to the Sunset and Richmond Districts. Because the pulse of the community remains within the original perimeters of Chinatown—and because traditions are strong—the suburban Chinese come back on Sunday to shop and dine here.

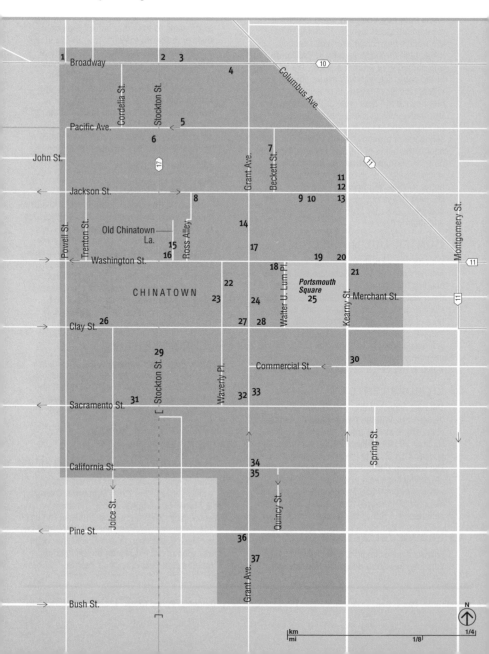

When the first Chinese immigrants arrived, they found a small community huddled around **Portsmouth Square,** which is today still the hub of Chinatown. Once the gold strike was announced, the Cantonese came by the boatload, fleeing famine and the Opium Wars. By 1850 there were more than 4,000 Chinese men (and only 7 Chinese women) in the area. Chinese "coolies," a term stemming from the word *kuli* (Chinese for "bitter toil"), were tolerated as long as they performed the tasks other groups scorned—working the mines, building the transcontinental railroad, and, later, planting the Napa vineyards. But when the work dried up in the 1880s, many Caucasian San Franciscans shared Rudyard Kipling's view of Chinatown: "A ward of the city of Canton set down in the most eligible business quarter of the City." A vicious backlash had set in. When hundreds of unemployed whites tried to run them out of town, the Chinese retaliated by organizing *tongs,* or secret associations, for protection, which soon evolved into warring gangs. These organizations turned to selling opium, running extortion rings, and promoting prostitution, with discipline maintained by squads of hatchet men. It wasn't until the 1920s that conflict was banished from Chinatown's streets.

When the area was totally destroyed by the 1906 earthquake and fire, city politicians planned to relocate the Chinese to less valuable property. Instead, the industrious Asians rebuilt with such dispatch that they reclaimed their district before City Hall could act. And the new Chinatown was just as crowded as the old. By World War II, an average of 20 people shared a bath, and there were about 12 people to a kitchen. This same area— 18 square blocks—is absorbing the newest wave of Asian immigrants.

Chinatown is so much more than the few commercial street-front blocks along **Grant Avenue,** marked by the **Chinese Gate** on Bush Street. It is the back alleys crammed with herb shops; acupressure clinics; benevolent societies that promote cultural and civic causes; upper-floor residences with balconies; fish hanging on clotheslines; garment factories; Buddhist temples; and the action on Stockton Street, which have become the true main street of Chinatown since the tourist trade usurped Grant. Here the food and tea shops are as much of an attraction as the Grant Avenue trinkets. Fish swimming in tanks, claw-snapping crabs, crate-bound chickens, hanging ducks, exotic ginseng roots, and tempting baked goods can all be found here. It doesn't matter if you can't speak any of the myriad dialects swirling around you. Sign language works very well, and shopping in Chinatown can be a remarkable adventure.

## 1 IMPERIAL TEA COURT

The first traditional teahouse in the US provides the best introduction to the art of tea. Order the authentic Gongfu tea, black tea, or pu-erh tea from the tea plantations of Yunnan province in China. When hot water is poured over the tea leaves, the leaves open up and release a heavenly aroma. The tea is resteeped two or three times, giving you time to meditate over your cup of tea in this quiet teahouse. ♦ W-M, 11AM-6:30PM. 1411 Powell St (at Broadway). 788.6080; 800/567.5898. www.imperialtea.com ♿

**YUET LEE**

## 2 YUET LEE SEAFOOD RESTAURANT

★★$ Open until 3AM, it's a refueling stop for club prowlers, and the food is always fresh

---

Restaurants/Clubs: Red | Hotels: Purple | Shops: Orange | Outdoors/Parks: Green | Sights/Culture: Blue

and plentiful. Among the best-sellers are the stir-fry combinations, but these don't show off the kitchen's talents. The salt-and-pepper squid, quickly stirred in a dry wok, is a must-order dish, as are the steamed rock cod and Dungeness crab. For a late-night snack, the shrimp with scrambled eggs will hit the spot. ◆ Chinese/seafood ◆ W-M, lunch and dinner. 1300 Stockton St (at Broadway). 982.6020 &

## 3 HING LUNG CHINESE CUISINE

★★$ Fans converge here mainly for the *congee* (a thick rice porridge offered 17 ways). The house special stirs a delicate blend of shellfish and fish into the thick, steaming mixture. Other *congee* dishes include pork liver with sliced pork; fresh clams with abalone, which has a clean, fresh flavor; and pork-blood curd, with musty nuances. Try the Chinese fried donuts. ◆ Chinese ◆ Daily, breakfast, lunch, and dinner. 674 Broadway (between Columbus Ave and Stockton St). 398.8838 &

## 4 SW HOTEL

$ This 81-room brick-front hotel has one of the best locations in town, where Chinatown meets North Beach. When the owners refurbished this four-story hotel, they hung ink-brush paintings from the Ming dynasty in the lobby and added an interesting history board of their family, featuring patriarch Sam Wong. Complimentary breakfast buffet included in-room rates. ◆ 615 Broadway (at Grant Ave). 362.2999, 888/595.9188. www.swhotel.com

## 5 NEW ASIA

★$ One of the most dramatic dim sum parlors in the city, this vast restaurant seats more than a thousand. The dim sum taste exceedingly fresh, and the *siu mai* (pork dumplings) are denser than most others, loaded with earthy-tasting cloud-ear mushrooms. One of the most interesting items is the crescent-shaped tapioca wrapper filled with coarsely chopped pork and green peas. ◆ Dim sum ◆ Daily, breakfast, lunch, and dinner. 772 Pacific Ave (between Grant Ave and Stockton St). 391.6666 &

## 6 NEW SANG SANG MARKET

If it swims and it's fresh, it's probably for sale here, and at a reasonable price too. ◆ Daily. 1145 Stockton St (between Jackson St and Pacific Ave). 433.0403

Approximately one in five San Franciscans is a Chinese immigrant.

Early morning, when shopkeepers are busy setting out their wares, is a good time to get a feel for the real (i.e., nontouristy) Chinatown.

## 7 MATSU TEMPLE

Matsu is the Taoist goddess of the sea and very popular among the Cantonese. Two 7-foot clothed statues guard the altar: one with a black face and fangs and the other with a red face. Travelers come here to light incense and ask for blessing and protection. Kwan Yin, the goddess of compassion, is in the shrine on the right of the attendant who tends the bamboo plants. The Wok Wiz Chinatown tour stops here. ◆ Daily. 30 Beckett St (between Jackson St and Pacific Ave). 986.8818 &

## 8 GOLDEN GATE FORTUNE COOKIES

In addition to the usual crunchy fortune cookies, this small factory located on a side street produces X-rated versions with declarations that would make Confucius blush. ◆ Daily. 56 Ross Alley (off Jackson St). 781.3956 &

## 9 PEARL CITY SEAFOOD

★★$$ This place looks spiffier than many restaurants in the area, with fashionable tablecloths and black-lacquer chairs. The huge fish tank on a rear wall attests to the freshness of the seafood dishes. Spiced, salted prawns, and prawns with garlic sauce, are among the tempting choices. ◆ Cantonese ◆ Daily, lunch and dinner. 641 Jackson St (between Kearny St and Grant Ave). 398.8383 &

## 10 GREAT EASTERN RESTAURANT

★$ You may be the only one in the sleek, modern dining room who doesn't speak Cantonese, but that's a tip-off for good value on lobster, abalone, duck, and quail. Dinner comes from the fish tanks that Chinese seafood restaurants like to display. Other good menu items include authentic Peking duck and dim sum. Singapore noodles and duck soup with dumplings are both tasty late-night snacks. Open until 1AM. ◆ Chinese/seafood ◆ Daily, lunch and dinner. 649 Jackson St (between Kearny St and Grant Ave). 986.2500 &

## 11 HOUSE OF NANKING

★★★$$ This is one of those hole-in-the-wall Chinese restaurants that are out of this world. Seating is in two rooms and at a counter, where you can watch the chef turn the freshest of ingredients (bright purple eggplant, fat green beans, and the like, bought daily at Chinatown markets) into delicious, spicy dishes that never miss. Expect a wait. There's also takeout. ◆ Chinese ◆ Daily, lunch and dinner. 919 Kearny St (between Jackson St and Columbus Ave). 421.1429

## 12 DPD RESTAURANT

★★$$ Some of the best Shanghai noodles in the city can be found here. The spicy, thick noodles, which turn mahogany-colored in the wok, are like manna when served with Chinese cabbage and strips of pork. The noodle soups are just as enticing, whether topped with pork chops, beef, or smoked fish. On the seafood menu try the hot braised prawns and the scallops in garlic-and-ginger sauce. ◆ Shanghai ◆ Daily, lunch and dinner. 901 Kearny St (at Jackson St). 982.0471

## 12 DAAN Chinese Herbs and Acupuncture

This shop strives to make Chinese herbs accessible to Westerners. Not only does it stock a complete selection of American ginseng and vitamins, Susan and Lois Yen, certified acupuncturists and American educated, are on hand to counsel and apply needles for a variety of ailments. DAAN (pronounced Da Ahn) means "peaceful." ◆ Daily. 614 Jackson St (at Kearny St). 433.3277. www.daan.com ᕈ

## 13 Kay Cheung Seafood Restaurant

★★$ Crowds line up outside this dim sum parlor for some of the best dumplings in the city. The fillings are simple and fresh: Try the shrimp dumplings flavored with ginger; the pork steamed buns with red vinegar sauce for dipping; and the shrimp, cilantro, and water chestnut dumplings. In the evenings, when the full dinner menu comes out, the seafood specialties are highly recommended. ◆ Chinese ◆ M, dinner; Tu-Su, lunch and dinner. 615 Jackson St (at Kearny St). 989.6838 ᕈ

## 13 Star Lunch

★$ With only 12 seats at the kitchen counter, this eatery is one of the smallest in Chinatown. Diners can feel a blast of heat as the cook turns out popular Shanghai chow mein dishes with either pork or chicken. It's a good place to sample pig's feet in noodle soup or salted cabbage and shredded pork. But stay away from the fermented tofu: Even the smell can ruin your appetite. ◆ Shanghai ◆ Tu-Su, lunch. 605 Jackson St (at Kearny St). 788.6709

## 14 Ten Ren Tea Co., Ltd.

More than 40 different teas are available here, as well as Chinese, Korean, and American varieties of ginseng. Many of the teas and ginseng roots are grown on the company's own farms. This is one of the largest such operations in existence, with 60 branches worldwide. Customers may sample whatever tea is being brewed or buy milk tea at the tapioca bar. ◆ Daily. 949 Grant Ave (between Washington and Jackson Sts). 362.0656 ᕈ

## 15 Old Chinatown Lane

This narrow street was once called the Street of Gamblers, a reference to Chinatown's mysterious history. ◆ At Washington St (between Ross Alley and Stockton St)

## 16 Jade Galore

A security officer and two gilded lions guard the entrance to this jewelry shop dealing in Burmese jade and diamonds. ◆ Daily. 1000 Stockton St (at Washington St). 982.4863. www.jadegalore.com ᕈ

## 17 Li Po

Welcome to one of San Francisco's best dive bars. From the minute you walk through the golden cave-mouth entrance, you'll know you're not in Kansas anymore. Kitschy Asian furnishings abound, streetwise waitresses move the booze, and Sinatra serenades on the jukebox. Bottoms up. ◆ Daily, 2PM-2AM. 916 Grant Ave (between Washington and Jackson Sts). 982.0072 ᕈ

## 18 Old Chinese Telephone Exchange Building

This site used to be home to the *California Star*, the first newspaper in the city and the one that started the rush in 1848 by spreading the cry of "Gold!" The present building, a three-tiered pagoda, once housed the operators for Chinatown's telephone system and later the local **Pacific Telephone and Telegraph** offices. A branch of the **Bank of Canton** is now located here. ◆ 743 Washington St (between Walter U. Lum Pl and Grant Ave)

## 19 Buddha's Universal Church

This five-story structure was built by hand using an exotic variety of polished woods. The church contains mosaic images of Buddha, bronze doors, and murals on the roof. ◆ Tours: second and fourth Sunday. 720 Washington St (between Grant Ave and Kearny St). 982.6116; 982.6117. www.bucsf.com

## 20 World Ginseng Center

This supermarket-size ginseng emporium is a good place to buy the aromatic, gnarled roots of that medicinal herb. There's ginseng from America, China, and Korea in just about every form: extract for tea, tea bags, medicinals, and candies. ◆ Daily. 801 Kearny St (at Washington St). 362.2255

## 21 Hilton San Francisco Financial District

$$$ This lodging at the crossroads of Chinatown, North Beach, Jackson Square, and the

---

Restaurants/Clubs: **Red** | Hotels: **Purple** | Shops: Orange | Outdoors/Parks: **Green** | Sights/Culture: **Blue**

Financial District is a busy gathering spot. Locals go to the spa, Chinese residents attend weddings in the ballroom, and businesspeople huddle over laptops in the lobby conservatory. Of the 549 guest rooms on 27 floors, we recommend the rooms facing Coit Tower. From the upper floors you see Mount Tamalpais and yachts skimming the bay. The hotel provides sleek workstations with ergonomic desk chairs, free Wi-Fi access, HD TVs, and a small fitness center. Club-level guests also have continental breakfast, snacks, and beverages in the concierge lounge on the 26th floor. TRU spa off the lobby is a spare modern spa that offers an excellent backstroke massage for tight muscles (www.truspa.com). **Restaurant Seven Fifty** offers a Mediterranean menu. ◆ 750 Kearny St. 433.6600, 800.HILTONS. www.sanfranciscohiltonhotel.com &

## 22 THE POT STICKER

★$$ This appealing little side-street restaurant specializes in the fried and steamed meat-filled dumplings for which it is named. ◆ Mandarin ◆ Daily, lunch and dinner. 150 Waverly Pl (between Clay and Washington Sts). 397.9985

## 23 TIEN HOU TEMPLE

Located on the fourth floor of a brightly painted building, this temple is dedicated to Tien Hou, or Tin Hau, Queen of the Heavens and Goddess of the Seven Seas. Flowers, incense, and intricately carved statues fill the small sanctuary. If you're walking past and see clouds of incense swirling down from the balcony, you may assume the temple is open. (There's no elevator, only stairs.) The street it's on—Waverly Place—is known as the Street of Painted Balconies. It's colorful, crowded, noisy, and redolent of exotic foodstuffs and incense. ◆ M-Su, 10AM-4PM. 125 Waverly Pl (between Clay and Washington Sts), fourth floor

## 24 CHINA TRADE CENTER ART GALLERY

Three floors of mall-type shops offer jewelry, linens, clothing, watches, souvenirs, and eyeglasses, among many other types of goods. Dangling from the ceiling above the staircase is a large, fierce-looking dragon. ◆ Daily. 838 Grant Ave (between Clay and Washington Sts). 837.1509 &

Within the China Trade Center:

### EMPRESS OF CHINA

★★$$$ This fancy, expensive restaurant has a celebrity clientele to match. A carved 13th-century panel stands at the entrance, which widens into a "garden pavilion" with an impressive wooden pagoda and a black-and-white marble floor laid in a starburst pattern. Three romantic and elegant dining rooms, all with beautiful views of the city, are arranged around the pagoda, where the sumptuous food reigns supreme. ◆ Chinese ◆ Daily, lunch and dinner. Reservations recommended. 434.1345. www.empressofchinasf.com &

## 25 PORTSMOUTH SQUARE

Robert Louis Stevenson spent many hours writing in this square, and his recollections of the area can be found in *The Wreckers*. ◆ Bounded by Clay and Washington Sts, and Kearny St and Walter U. Lum Pl

## 26 CHINESE HISTORICAL SOCIETY OF AMERICA

Rotating exhibitions of the society's collection of artifacts, photographs, and documents trace the history of the Chinese people in America. Displays are captioned in Chinese and English. ◆ Admission. Tu-Sa. Free first Thursday of every month. 965 Clay St (between Stockton and Powell Sts). 391.1188. www.chsa.org

## 27 RED BLOSSOM TEA COMPANY

Peter Luong travels to Taiwan's tea plantations every spring and fall to bid on the best of the harvest. He prepares tasty green tea with a hint of papaya at the tasting counter. This is a good place to stock up on white porcelain cups, and heirloom and cast-iron teapots. ◆ Daily. 831 Grant Ave (between Clay and Washington Sts). 395.0868. www.redblossomtea.com &

## 28 ORIENTAL PEARL RESTAURANT

★★$ In this place, one of the city's prettiest dim sum parlors, customers order from a menu, rather than choosing from a cart. The dumplings aren't the best choices here; instead, go for the salt-baked prawns and the Chiu Chow–style marinated duck, braised in soy sauce and served with a pungent vinegar dipping sauce. The dinner menu is even more enticing. The house special, chicken meatballs, are a mix of chicken, shrimp, water chestnuts, and ham in a delicate egg-white wrapper. Seafood in a crispy nest of taro is extraordinary in both taste and presentation. ◆ Chinese ◆ Daily, lunch and dinner. 760 Clay St (near Grant Ave). 433.1817. www.orientalpearlsf.com &

## 29 STOCKTON STREET

The street of daily life in Chinatown is no longer exclusively Chinese. Other Asian populations, including Vietnamese, Filipinos, and Koreans, have settled and opened businesses here. Chinatown residents buy goods in the grocery and butcher shops, bakeries, and quaint herb-and-spice stores along this thoroughfare and its side streets. Take note of the many handsome brick structures from the 1850s that were once plush private residences. Francis Pioche, a pioneer financier and bon vivant credited with giving San Franciscans an appreciation of fine food, lived at 806 Stockton. Pioche imported many French

chefs and cargoes of vintage wines to the city.
♦ Between Sacramento St and Broadway

## 30 HON'S WUN TUN HOUSE

★$ This tiny, bustling, downscale-looking assemblage of Formica tables and limited counter seating is where the cognoscenti gather when they want a great cheap bowl of noodles or dumpling soup. A glass of tea comes with the meal. It's usually crowded, so expect to share a table. ♦ Cantonese ♦ Daily, lunch and early dinner. 648 Kearny St (at Commercial St). 433.3966. Also at 532 Jessie St (at Mission St). 552.4933 ⅃

## 31 CAMERON HOUSE

This Presbyterian community center was named after Donaldina Cameron to honor her lifetime of work dedicated to freeing singsong slave girls. The women, mostly Chinese and some Japanese, arrived here thinking they would become brides of the mine workers, but instead were used by businessmen as prostitutes and slaves. Cameron came to be known as Lo Mo, or the mother. Inside the house are old carved cornices, calligraphy, and paintings. ♦ M-F. 920 Sacramento St (at Stockton St). 781.0408.
www.sanfraniscochinatown.com

## 32 CHINATOWN KITE SHOP

Stop here to peruse an incredible assortment of all kinds of kites, including windwheels and parafoils in cotton or nylon. Some make wonderful decorations for a child's room; all make great souvenirs. ♦ Daily. 717 Grant Ave (between Sacramento and Clay Sts). 391.8217. www.chinatownkite.com ⅃

## 33 THE WOK SHOP

Everything you need for creating your own Chinese feast, from cookbooks to utensils, can be found here. ♦ Daily. 718 Grant Ave (between Sacramento and Commercial Sts). 989.3797. www.wokshop.com ⅃

## 33 EASTERN BAKERY

At the oldest bakery in Chinatown, buy a sack of honey-coated bowties or some of the sweet Chinese cakes, such as black bean, lotus, and melon. ♦ Daily. 720 Grant Ave (between Sacramento and Commercial Sts). 392.4497 ⅃

## 34 OLD ST. MARY'S CATHEDRAL

California's first cathedral now functions as a noontime concert hall, and a neighborhood parish church, though apparently not for the Chinese Catholic community, which favors a different church offering Mass in Chinese. Built of brick in 1854, it survived both the 1906 and the 1989 earthquakes without structural damage. During wartime, it provided social refuge for soldiers on leave. It operated the first English-language school for the Chinese community. Noon concerts are often held in summer. ♦ 660 California St (at Grant Ave). 288.3800. www.oldsaintmarys.org

## 35 IMPERIAL FASHION

It's not that the hand-decorated linens and embroidered pillows are any different here than at many other Chinatown shops, but they're particularly well displayed. Prices for the ornate handiwork are less than you'd expect to pay for a lot of machine-sewn tablecloths, guest towels, or napkins. ♦ Daily. 564 Grant Ave (at California St). 362.8112 ⅃

## 36 GRANT PLAZA HOTEL

$ This is probably one of San Francisco's most outstanding values, but the beds and shower stalls are small. The lobby has glitzy accoutrements such as a crystal chandelier and leather sofas. The 72 rooms are small but well decorated. Ask for a corner room. On the sixth floor are a marvelous stained-glass dome and panels, legacies from a nightclub that existed on the premises in the 1920s. There's no restaurant, but being in the heart of Chinatown should make dining out a breeze. Internet specials available online. ♦ Reservations only. 465 Grant Ave (at Pine St). 434.3883, 800/472.6899. www.grantplaza.com

## 37 GRANT AVENUE

Chinatown's tourist shopping street is active, crowded, and fascinating. Restaurants and gift stores line the way from the ceremonial gateway located at Bush Street, down Grant Avenue, to Broadway. While many of the stores are virtually identical and most sell similar gifts and souvenirs, it's fun to stroll along and sample several of them. Many shops are open until 9PM or 10PM every day, so you can have dinner at one of the many restaurants and then browse. This part of Chinatown is best experienced on foot— don't try driving down Grant (or Stockton for that matter), as traffic is congested and slow. Leaving Grant and wandering among the short, narrow alleys and lanes will allow you to absorb the sights, sounds, and smells of Chinatown. These little passages hold a hodgepodge of businesses and organizations: travel services, temples, groceries, laundries, Chinese book and newspaper stores, and benevolent associations. The latter are protective organizations, active in the civic and cultural life of Chinese residents. Note how the brick buildings are decorated with balconies and doorways painted green, red, yellow, and orange. ♦ Between Bush St and Broadway

---

**Restaurants/Clubs: Red | Hotels: Purple | Shops: Orange | Outdoors/Parks: Green | Sights/Culture: Blue**

# Dim Sum and Then Some

If you have only one Asian experience in San Francisco, make sure it's dim sum. These delicious tidbits are a local institution; only Hong Kong has more dim sum parlors, and that's where the tradition originated.

Generally, dim sum are served for brunch; most dim sum houses open around 10AM and close in the middle or late afternoon. Typically, waiters circle the dining room pushing carts stacked with covered bamboo or stainless-steel containers filled with steamed or fried dumplings, shrimp balls, spring rolls, steamed buns, and Chinese pastries. Just point to the items that look appealing as they roll by; the dim sum won't be listed on a menu, and the waiters often speak no English, so ordering is done by gesture.

Although dim sum may appear to be exotic, most fillings are straightforward—pork, shrimp, cabbage, mushrooms, and ginger appear in many guises. Such unfamiliar delicacies as duck or chicken feet are

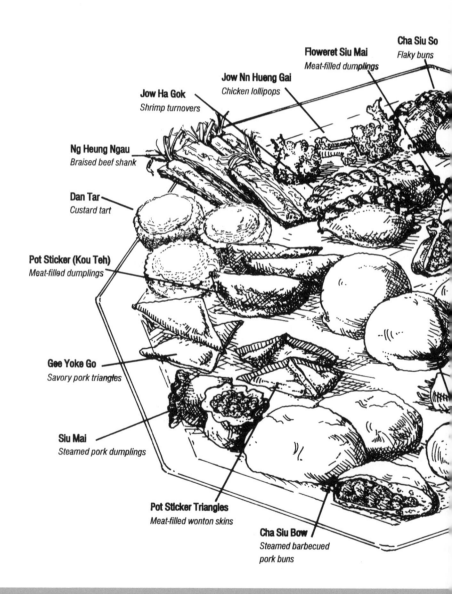

**Cha Siu So**
*Flaky buns*

**Floweret Siu Mai**
*Meat-filled dumplings*

**Jow Nn Hueng Gai**
*Chicken lollipops*

**Jow Ha Gok**
*Shrimp turnovers*

**Ng Heung Ngau**
*Braised beef shank*

**Dan Tar**
*Custard tart*

**Pot Sticker (Kou Teh)**
*Meat-filled dumplings*

**Gee Yoke Go**
*Savory pork triangles*

**Siu Mai**
*Steamed pork dumplings*

**Pot Sticker Triangles**
*Meat-filled wonton skins*

**Cha Siu Bow**
*Steamed barbecued pork buns*

sometimes offered, but they are easy to detect and reject, if you so desire. Noodle dishes may also be available, but they will be listed on a menu with English translations, rather than offered from the cart.

The carts circulate continuously, so you can order in stages, taking a few items each time they pass. In the old days, the bill was figured by the number of little plates left on the table, but today, a printed bill is updated by the servers as the meal progresses. It never adds up to much, though—you'll have to eat a lot of food to spend more than $15 a person.

Every dim sum restaurant does things a little differently, but here's a thumbnail guide to some of the most popular items.

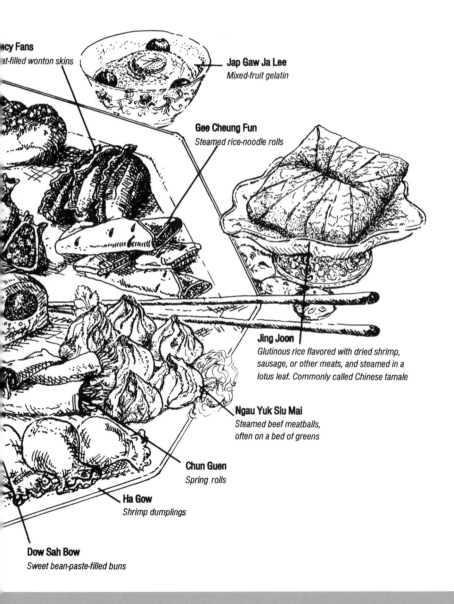

**cy Fans**
at-filled wonton skins

**Jap Gaw Ja Lee**
Mixed-fruit gelatin

**Gee Cheung Fun**
Steamed rice-noodle rolls

**Jing Joon**
Glutinous rice flavored with dried shrimp, sausage, or other meats, and steamed in a lotus leaf. Commonly called Chinese tamale

**Ngau Yuk Siu Mai**
Steamed beef meatballs, often on a bed of greens

**Chun Guen**
Spring rolls

**Ha Gow**
Shrimp dumplings

**Dow Sah Bow**
Sweet bean-paste-filled buns

# NOB HILL/ RUSSIAN HILL

**F**ormerly christened the Hill of Palaces, Nob Hill vies with Telegraph Hill for the honor of being the best known of San Francisco's many hills. The mansions of the rich are gone now, with the notable exception of James Flood's Edwardian brownstone at **1000 California Street**; they've been replaced with luxury hotels, a world-famous cathedral, several exclusive clubs and apartment houses, and upscale condominiums for millionaires.

In the late 1850s, at the site of the **Renaissance Stanford Court Hotel,** Dr. Arthur Hayne cut a trail through the chaparral to survey the land and build the first home on the hill for his bride, actress Julia Dean. Within a few years, men of means followed his trail (a steep route that even their horses found difficult to navigate) and began a mass exodus from San Francisco's Rincon Hill and South Park. The advent of the cable car in 1873 encouraged the uphill flow of money, fueling the unbridled ostentatiousness of the homes of the rich and nouveaux riches. Ironically, it was all swept away 30 years later by the massive fire following the 1906 earthquake.

In a sense, Nob Hill is still the Hill of Palaces. Fastidious men and women continue to reach their homes or clubs by cable car, though during summer months the riders are almost all tourists. But the reckless display of wealth is gone—the air is more of subdued gentility, although power brokers still make the hill their home. The generally accepted boundaries of Nob Hill are **Bush Street** and **Pacific Avenue,** and **Stockton** and **Larkin Streets.**

Russian Hill, next door, has a lot more to offer than the Powell-Hyde cable car route and the famed "crookedest" street. At the north end of **Polk Street,** a mini French quarter has emerged around **Green** and **Vallejo Streets. Little Paris** has a charming, village-like atmosphere where visitors are enticed into shops by artful displays and interiors chock-full of whimsical items. It's a great place to stop for a café au lait and brioche.

Within walking distance of Union Square, the Financial District, and North Beach, Russian Hill is full of picturesque culs-de-sac, bay views, wooded open spaces, and, of course, that wiggly part of **Lombard Street** that's better known as "the crookedest street in the world." Technically, Russian Hill extends from Pacific Avenue to **Bay Street** and from **Mason Street** to Polk Street, but its real heart is bordered by **Broadway** and **Chestnut Street,** and **Taylor** and Larkin Streets. After you've experienced downtown, slow down and savor the neighborhoods.

## 1 SAN FRANCISCO ART INSTITUTE (SFAI)

This 1871 establishment is the oldest cultural institution in the West. Home to three galleries, the institute has played a central role in the development of contemporary art in the Bay Area. Student work is displayed in the **Diego Rivera Gallery;** the **Walter/McBean Gallery** shows work by professional artists; and the **Still Lights Gallery,** adjacent to the photography studios, has photographic exhibitions. **Paffard, Keatings, Clay's** 1969 extension to the art institute, designed with great verve, is a rare example of the Corbusian *Béton brut* (concrete in the raw) style in California. It contains a lecture theater, a conference room, studios, workshops, exhibition spaces, and a café. ◆ Tu-Su during the school year. 800 Chestnut St (between Jones and Leavenworth Sts). 771.7020. www.sfai.edu &

## 2 LOMBARD STREET

Nicknamed "the crookedest street in the world," this section of Lombard was designed in the 1920s to respond to the slope's extreme steepness. Faced with brick pavers and landscaped with flowers, shrubs, and hedges, the street is a fine example of the art of road engineering integrated into the urban fabric. Cars are no longer allowed to cruise down the winding road, but it's plenty of fun just to walk down from Hyde to Leavenworth (great exercise for the legs, too). ◆ Between Leavenworth and Hyde Sts

The east end of Lombard Street is considered by most to be the crookedest street in the world, with eight turns in one block.

---

Restaurants/Clubs: Red | Hotels: Purple | Shops: Orange | Outdoors/Parks: Green | Sights/Culture: Blue

### 3 BUCA GIOVANNI

★$$$ *Buca* means "cave" in Italian, and you reach the dining room here by descending a stairway to the lower level. On any given evening, chef Vic Casanova may present ravioli stuffed with eggplant and Gorgonzola in a light basil cream sauce or linguine with fresh porcini mushrooms; the restaurant is also known for using home-smoked rabbit in many pasta dishes. ♦ Italian ♦ W-Su, dinner. Reservations recommended. 800 Greenwich St (at Mason St and Columbus Ave). 776.7766 &

### 4 ZARZUELA

★★$$ With its rough wood, stucco, and brick walls, this charming tapas place has a warm, welcoming look. Among the best hot tapas, lamb tenders are seared to a caramelized crustiness, all the better for the garlic-laced gravy that pools in the bottom of the plate. Scallops are golden outside and still silken inside and surround tender, wilted greens. The shrimp are spiced, cooked, cooled, and drizzled with a tomato-laced mayonnaise. Grilled vegetables, including eggplant and squash, get a boost from the smattering of olive oil and lemon. ♦ Spanish ♦ Tu-Sa, dinner. 2000 Hyde St (at Union St). 346.0800 &

### 5 MACONDRAY LANE

The condominiums by **Bobbie Sue Hood** fit successfully into the traditional San Francisco bay-windowed residential style on this two-block pedestrian street on the steep north face of Russian Hill. ♦ Between Taylor and Leavenworth Sts, south of Union St

### 6 LITTLE THAI RESTAURANT

★$ Beneath the spreading branches of a large (fake) coconut tree, diners are served some inexpensive and often memorable dishes. Among the many choices are coconut-milk chicken soup with chilies, lemongrass, and loads of mushrooms and vegetables; *param long srong* (a sliced-pork creation with spinach in a sweet peanut sauce); *larb pad* (ground duck with lemon sauce); and *yum plamuk* (spicy calamari with mint and lemon). ♦ Thai ♦ Daily, dinner. 2065 Polk St (between Green and Union Sts). 771.5544 &

### 7 LA FOLIE

★★★★$$$$ Without question, this is one of the top Californian/French restaurants in the city. French-born Roland Passot, his brother George (the sommelier), and his American wife, Jamie, have created a dreamy, casually elegant environment in which puffy white clouds dance across a sky-blue ceiling and rich, yellow print fabric hangs from the French windows and frames the doors. Passot's presentations are breathtaking, and the recently updated menu (which changes seasonally) is better than ever. There might be roast quail leg stuffed with foie gras, backed by a Lyonnaise salad topped with a poached quail egg; *rôti* (roast) of squab and quail; rack of lamb; or fricasseed lobster. Passot also offers an à la carte menu, a five-course Discovery Menu, and a four-course vegetarian menu. You'll enjoy the lighthearted décor: marionettes "Guignol" the owners brought from their hometown of Lyon. ♦ Californian/French ♦ M-Sa, dinner. Reservations recommended. 2316 Polk St (between Green and Union Sts). 776.5577. www.lafolie.com &

### 7 LA BOULANGE DE POLK

★$ A convivial atmosphere prevails all day at the outdoor tables with yapping dogs and chatting neighbors. The open-face sandwiches are made to order. Also good are the latte bowls, fresh-baked Parisian pastries, tartines, and quiches. ♦ French ♦ T-Su, breakfast and lunch. 2310 Polk St (near Green St). 345.1107. www.baybread.com &

### 7 LE PETIT ROBERT

★$$ This popular eatery with high ceilings and large-scale artwork is known for its authentic bistro cuisine including steak tartare, *frites* with rouille, grilled *poussin*, and fried oysters with remoulade sauce. You may order small plates of these items from the bar menu served in the afternoon. Reservations recommended. ♦ French ♦ Daily, lunch and dinner; Sa, Su, brunch. 2300 Polk St (at Green St). 922.8100. www.lepetitrobert.com &

### 8 YABBIES COASTAL KITCHEN

★★★$$$ People are flocking to Megan Smith's relaxing, unpretentious restaurant, renowned for its raw bar and grilled fish specialties. The kitchen turns out wonderful flavorsome yabbies ("crawfish" in Australian) and other seafood dishes borrowed from various cuisines. Two favorites are pepper-seared ahi with Japanese eggplant and soy-citrus juices, and grilled swordfish with Sicilian capers and green olives. A wide selection of wines by the glass keeps the bar area hopping with locals. ♦ Seafood ♦ Daily, dinner. Reservations required. 2237 Polk St (between Vallejo and Green Sts). 474.4088. www.yabbiesrestaurant.com &

## 8 GREEN'S SPORTS BAR

If you think San Francisco sports fans aren't as enthusiastic as those on the East Coast, just try getting a drink (or getting *in*, for that matter) during a 'Niners game—it's a spectacle worth checking out. Between games, however, this place transforms into a pleasant neighborhood bar. ♦ Daily. 2239 Polk St (between Vallejo and Green Sts). 775.4287 ⑤

## 8 WILLIAM CROSS WINE MERCHANTS AND WINE BAR

This venerable, much-reviewed spot (*Wine Spectator, Wine and Spirits, 7 × 7,* and *Where* have all paid tribute) in Russian Hill continues to reel in oenophiles and recreational drinkers alike with an impressive array of wines. The Wine Bar, located in the back of the store, hosts a wine-tasting event every Wednesday evening, showcasing varietals from all over the US, Italy, France, and Australia. Winemakers and importers are often on hand to inform and discuss (call for schedule). Weekends, the Wine Bar stays open and serves wines by the glass to add spark to your conversation. Check the calendar at www.localwineevents.com. ♦ Daily. 2253 Polk St (between Vallejo and Green Sts). 346.1314

## 8 TABLESPOON

★★$$ This narrow dining room is cozy but not cramped, with 18 tables and a full bar that serves half-priced appetizers during happy hour. The chef, Alvin Luna, is known for his fresh take on American dishes such as the smoked sturgeon pizza, blue lake bean salad, pork tenderloin, and a red-wine braised beef. ♦ American ♦ Daily, dinner. 2209 Polk St (between Vallejo and Green Sts). 268.0140. www.tablespoonsf.com ⑤

## 9 ANDREW ROTHSTEIN FINE FOODS

★★$$ Busy businesspeople stop by for pints of curried chicken, Cairo couscous, spicy potatoes, and leeks all set for the microwave. Complete take-away meals range from pork loin to beef bourguignonne. ♦ Daily. 2238 Polk St (between Vallejo and Green Sts). 447.4094 ⑤

## 10 RUSSIAN HILL ANTIQUES

There are two floors of pine furniture, jewelry, and gift items here; most are from early 20th-century America and Europe. ♦ Daily. 2200 Polk St (at Vallejo St). 441.5561. www.russianhillantiques.com ⑤

## 11 THE REAL FOOD COMPANY

This supermarket of organic foods (affectionately referred to by neighborhood residents as The Real Expensive Food Company) features an excellent produce section. Check the center aisle for fresh bread delivered daily by the Bay Area's best bakeries, and hidden in back is a very good meat-and-fish counter. ♦ Daily. 2140 Polk St (between Broadway and Vallejo St). 673.7420. www.realfoodco.com. Also at 3060 Fillmore St. 567.6900

## 12 PASHA

★$$$ Fine Middle Eastern fare and a sensuous, exotic ambience are the drawing cards at this Moroccan restaurant. Don't hesitate to tuck dollar bills into the belly dancer's waistband as she (or he) undulates by. Other temptations include rack of lamb with pomegranate and honey, grilled chicken brochette, or smoky prawns served with basmati rice. ♦ Moroccan/Middle Eastern ♦ Tu-Su, dinner. Reservations recommended. 1516 Broadway (near Polk St). 885.4477. www.pasharestaurant.com ⑤

## 13 1000 BLOCK OF VALLEJO STREET

One of the city's most attractive residential neighborhoods, this block consists of three narrow residential streets—Vallejo Street (which is approached from Jones Street by ramps designed by **Willis Polk**), Russian Hill Place, and Florence Street. Polk built four Mediterranean-style villas between 1915 and 1916, and **Charles F. Whittlesey** designed the three to the south on Vallejo Street. All are private residences. ♦ Vallejo St (between Taylor and Jones Sts)

## 14 ALLEGRO RISTORANTE ITALIANO

★★$$$ Tucked into an affluent residential area and a favorite of San Francisco politicos and top executives, this pretty place is owned by Angelo Quaranta, who specializes in the foods of central and southern Italy. The most popular dishes are gnocchi, cannelloni, and any of the pastas. Bruschetta (thick slices of toasted bread spread with a chopped-tomato mixture) and Cornish hen are our top choices. ♦ Italian ♦ Tu-Su, dinner. Reservations recommended. 1701 Jones St (at Broadway). 928.4002 ⑤

## 15 GLOVER STREET DUPLEX

One of the **Dan Solomon–Paulette Taggert** team's beautifully designed San Francisco houses, this consists of two units interlocked one above the other on a 25-foot-wide lot. The front façade is an interesting mixture of traditional bay-window elements and a classical portico with a severely detailed triangular pediment. The Modernist windows and gateway make the 1982 design of this private residence both Rationalist and Contextual. ♦ 15 and 17 Glover St (between Jones and Leavenworth Sts)

## 16 HARRIS' RESTAURANT

★★$$$ There's no doubt that this steak-and-prime-rib house means business—a glass refrigerator full of its stock is on prominent display to passersby and for sale to those who would rather cook at home. Mrs. Harris herself, who has a cattle-ranching background, presides over the restaurant. Top-quality meats are served in two substantial dining rooms decorated with roomy booths and wood. Lighter suppers (such as soup and salad) are served in the bar. It's reminiscent of a comfortable, old-money ranchers' club. ♦ Steak house ♦ Daily, dinner. Reservations recommended. 2100 Van Ness Ave (at Pacific Ave). 673.1888 &

## 17 VELVET DA VINCI GALLERY

A favorite haunt of globe-trotting fashionistas, this store has wearable art, contemporary jewelry, and metalwork in an impressive light-filled industrial space. ♦ Tu-Su. 2015 Polk St (at Pacific Ave). 441.0109. www.velvetdavinci.com &

## 18 RISTORANTE MILANO

★★★$$ This small, stylish restaurant serves some of the best northern Italian dishes in town at moderate prices. The waiters are polite and knowledgeable; the contemporary décor is an interesting mix of Japanese woodwork and Milanese design in charcoal gray and off-white. With plenty of repeat customers and reservations limited to parties of four or more, expect a crowd and possibly a long wait unless you dine early or very late. ♦ Italian ♦ Daily, dinner. 1448 Pacific Ave (between Hyde and Larkin Sts). 673.2961. www.milanosf.com &

## 19 HYDE STREET BISTRO

★★$$ The kitchen turns out some outstanding food in this romantic Russian Hill gem. The chef's Californian/French approach translates into a captivating vegetable strudel with layers of flaky pastry, excellent roast chicken with the barest whisper of cumin, and rustic veal fricassee with wild mushrooms and spaetzle. ♦ French ♦ W-M, dinner. Reservations recommended. 1521 Hyde St (at Jackson St). 292.4415 &

## 20 THE BELL TOWER

★★$ This handsome bar and restaurant is quickly becoming a neighborhood favorite, serving low-priced standards such as burgers, hot dogs, and chicken wings. Also on the menu are inexpensive nontraditional dishes like fried catfish sandwiches; tequila-lime-and-cilantro-marinated Chilean sea bass, served on a bed of black beans; and salmon pasta with herb cream, red onions, and capers. It's the perfect place to take a break and chat with the locals. ♦ Californian/American ♦ Daily, brunch, lunch, and dinner until midnight. 1900 Polk St (at Jackson St). 567.9596 &

## 20 FIORIDELLA

Kelly Schrock is one of San Francisco's most creative (and, yes, expensive) florists, whose designs are much favored by the socially prominent. Take a peek at her unusual gift items. ♦ M-Sa. 1920 Polk St (between Jackson St and Pacific Ave). 775.4065 &

## 21 HOUSE OF PRIME RIB

★★★$$ A favorite among beef eaters with big appetites, this grill offers handsome décor, comfortable booths, soft lighting, and generous servings of excellent prime rib that are carved at the table. There are even seconds for those who can go the distance. Good grilled salmon is offered as a non-beef alternative. ♦ American ♦ Daily, dinner. Reservations recommended. 1906 Van Ness Ave (between Washington and Jackson Sts). 885.4605. www.citysearch.com &

## 22 NAOMI'S ANTIQUES TO GO

A paradise for nostalgiaholics, this place stocks lots of American dinnerware, pottery, and china from the 1920s to the 1950s. ♦ Tu-Sa. 1817 Polk St (between Washington and Jackson Sts). 775.1207 &

## 23 VENTICELLO RISTORANTE

★★★$$$ A few years ago, this was probably the best Italian restaurant in the city; changes in the kitchen have dulled its shine a bit, but the food still can be excellent, especially pizzas and anything else from the wood oven, which is the focal point of the two-level dining room. Try the baked mussels, or venison with wild mushrooms, or pizza topped with duck breast, smoked red onions, and tangy goat cheese. ♦ Italian ♦ Daily, dinner. Reservations recommended. 1257 Taylor St (at Washington St). 922.2545. www.venticello.com &

## 24 CABLE CAR MUSEUM

The winding house for the underground cables that control the cars, known as the **Cable Car Barn,** was constructed in 1887, then rebuilt after it was badly damaged in the 1906 quake. When the cable-car system was renovated in the early 1980s, the barn was reinforced, but the exterior was left alone. The museum now has an underground viewing room where you may watch the cables work. Photographs and memorabilia are also on display, including three vintage cable cars. ◆ Free. Daily. 1201 Mason St (at Washington St). 474.1887. www.cablecarmuseum.org ᗉ

## 25 LOWER POLK STREET

The stretch between California and Geary Streets is known as Polk Gulch and was the focus of the city's gay population until most of the action moved to the Castro district. Currently, that portion of Polk is in transition, populated by many drifters and young male hustlers. Much of the gloss the street attained in the 1970s has been lost to a proliferation of shops whose wares are in questionable taste. But as strollers head north, beyond California Street, the area's appeal is alive and well, with a mix of old neighborhood food stores, antiques shops, bookstores, restaurants, and several charming specialty shops. ◆ Between Geary and Lombard Sts

## 26 NOB HILL CAFÉ

★★$ This family-run bistro, where owner Michael Deeb and his friendly staff go out of their way to make you feel at home, is tucked into a charming, quiet corner of Nob Hill. It's a neighborhood favorite, and paintings by local artists adorn the walls.

The menu offers traditional Italian cuisine and an array of California-tinged specials at prices uncommonly low for the area. Try the *crostini di polenta* (polenta topped with mozzarella and pesto), a pizza Margherita, or any of the chef's nightly creations. Be prepared to wait—there are only 14 tables and reservations are not accepted. ◆ Italian ◆ Daily, lunch and dinner. 1152 Taylor St (between Sacramento and Clay Sts). 776.6500. www.nobhillcafe.com ᗉ

## 27 ACQUERELLO

★★★★$$$ Giancarlo Paterlini, a native of Bologna, and Suzette Gresham-Tognetti operate this sophisticated restaurant, serving marvelously inventive contemporary dishes in a soothing, pastel-hued dining room decorated with original watercolors. The small menu, which changes frequently, might include salmon-and-scallop ravioli in dry vermouth, fillet of beef with balsamic vinegar and shallots, or breast of chicken rolled in pancetta with sage and Madeira sauce. They received a Michelin star in the 2007 Bay Area

Guide. ◆ Italian ◆ Tu-Sa, dinner. Reservations recommended. 1722 Sacramento St (between Polk St and Van Ness Ave). 567.5432. www.acquerello.com

## 28 SWAN OYSTER DEPOT

★★★$$ This restaurant is a favorite among knowledgeable San Franciscans, although you won't find anything fancier than a lunch counter and stools. But the cold fish dishes are fantastic and the servers among the friendliest around. There is also fish to take home. ◆ Seafood/takeout ◆ M-Sa, breakfast and lunch until 5:30PM. 1517 Polk St (between California and Sacramento Sts). 673.1101

## 29 CORDON BLEU VIETNAMESE RESTAURANT

★★$ A perfect choice before catching a movie, this is one of San Francisco's best hole-in-the-wall Vietnamese restaurants, and an unbelievably fine value. Five-spice chicken, a Vietnamese staple, is sumptuous here. ◆ Vietnamese ◆ Tu-Sa, lunch and dinner; Su, dinner. 1574 California St (at Polk St). 673.5637

## 30 CRUSTACEAN

★★$$ Part of the An family restaurant dynasty, the kitchen turns out flavorful Euro-Asian seafood dishes in this sleek restaurant with its witty, under-the-sea décor. Popular menu picks include Vietnamese crepes, roast Dungeness crab, and royal tiger prawns served over garlic noodles. ◆ Seafood ◆ Daily, dinner. Reservations recommended. 1475 Polk St (at California St), third floor. 776.2722. www.restaurants.com ᗉ

## 31 SHALIMAR

★★$ In the quest for delicious curry, true aficionados wait on line. They know when they get to the counter, they can order like maharajahs on very little money. Curries usually start with a slow-simmered broth of onion, ginger, garlic, and fresh tomatoes. Lamb curry comes with fresh spinach, coriander, and herbs, while the chicken curry is a stew of yogurt, saffron, and other spices. Skewers of marinated chicken, lamb, or beef acquire an exquisite taste baked over charcoal in the tandoor. For all of the above, the best accompaniment is Shalimar's basmati rice, cooked in a stock of spices, onions, and saffron. ♦ Indian/Pakistani ♦ Daily, lunch and dinner. No credit cards accepted. 1409 Polk St (at Pine St). 776.4642. www.shalimarsf.com &. Also at 532 Jones St (at Geary St). 928.0333

## 31 FIELDS BOOK STORE

This shop full of spiritual and esoteric books has been helping its readers solve life's deepest mysteries since 1932. Check online for in-store events. ♦ Daily. 1419 Polk St (between Pine and California Sts). 673.2027. www.fieldsbooks.com &

## 32 ACORN BOOKS

Used books are bought, sold, and exchanged here. The roughly 30,000 volumes range from rare first editions to paperback mystery thrillers. ♦ Daily. 1436 Polk St (at California St). 563.1736. www.acornbooks.com &

## 33 GRACE CATHEDRAL

**Lewis P. Hobart**'s fine neo-Gothic cathedral, modeled after Notre Dame in Paris, took 53 years to build and was finally consecrated in 1964. Notice the beautiful rose window, completed by Gabriel Loire in Chartres, and the spectacular entry, with its *Doors of Paradise*, taken from the same mold used for the entrance to Ghiberti's Baptistry in Florence. There is also an outdoor labyrinth, a magnificent organ, and a not-to-be-missed boys' and men's choir. World-renowned vocalists and musicians perform throughout the year. Site of a full round of holiday events. Parking available. ♦ 1051 Taylor St (bounded by Taylor and Jones Sts, and California and Sacramento Sts). 749.6300; concert event line 749.6350. www.gracecathedral.org &

## 34 HUNTINGTON PARK

This delightful oasis atop Nob Hill has a central fountain that replicates Rome's 16th-century Tartarughe Fountain. ♦ Taylor St (between California and Sacramento Sts)

## 35 THE PACIFIC-UNION CLUB

Remodeled by **Willis Polk** in 1908 after the quake and fire, this Edwardian brownstone was originally built in 1886 for James C. Flood, one of the city's railroad kings. He reputedly spent $1.5 million on the house alone, an enormous sum for the times. Polk added the attic story and the entrance tower, which somewhat mar the original classical lines. The building is now used as a very, very private social retreat for male members of "the Establishment." ♦ 1000 California St (at Mason St)

## 36 THE FAIRMONT

$$$$ This hotel was constructed on the property of Senator James "Bonanza Jim" Fair, and the foundations of the palace he had planned to build were later incorporated into the hotel. Son-in-law Hermann Oeirichs planned and began construction of the hotel, to the consternation of the city fathers, who could not understand placing any hotel so far from the center of town. New owners took over before the building was completed, hoping to open it in 1906. Although the frame withstood the earthquake, the subsequent fire ate up the interior and work had to begin all over again. When Senator Fair's daughter offered to take the property back, the disheartened owners jumped at the chance. On 18 April 1907, Mrs. Hermann Oeirichs kicked off the opening of the hotel with a magnificent banquet symbolizing the rebirth of the city one year after the earthquake.

The restoration of the Italian marble floor in the grand lobby, where the **Laurel Court** restaurant is now located, bring back the hotel's original splendor. With the original building and a 22-story tower, this grand hotel has 600 rooms and suites. ♦ 950 Mason St (at California St). 772.5000, 800/527.4727. www.fairmont.com

Within The Fairmont:

## TONGA RESTAURANT AND HURRICANE BAR

$$ Disneyland meets the South Pacific at this funky restaurant on the terrace level; hourly thunderstorms are staged here, with water pouring down over a central pool, the hotel's old indoor swimming pool. A band plays on a float in the middle of the old pool. A waterfall behind the low-lit bar and artificial orchids and other plants evoke the tropics, as do the drinks (such as the Bora-Bora Horror, a mixture of rum, banana liqueur, Grand Marnier, and pineapple juice). Happy hour is still a San Francisco experience with all-you-can-eat appetizers. ♦ Polynesian ♦ M-F, happy hour; daily, dinner. 772.5278 &

## 37 NOB HILL MASONIC CENTER

This 3,165-seat auditorium is large, but the sight lines are terrible. Orchestras, dance groups, and lecturers appear on the thrust stage. Check the online calendar. ♦ 1111 California St (between Taylor and Jones Sts). 292.9190. www.masonicauditorium.com &

## 38 THE HUNTINGTON HOTEL

$$$ Small, elegant, impeccably groomed, and located on the peak of Nob Hill, this 140-room hotel is the kind of place that has such a loyal following that advertising is unnecessary. This is partly due to the permanency of its

staff, which does much to preserve the Huntington brand of personal hospitality. No two rooms are alike; they all look as if they might well belong in a private residence, and all have a view of either the city or the bay. Suites are equipped with a complete kitchen or a wet bar. Hotel guests can access an indoor pool, fitness classes, health equipment, and the **Nob Hill Spa,** which is the only spa outside New York to offer European photo-modulation facials. Three of the ten luxurious treatment rooms have fireplaces. For day-use visitors, the spa is complimentary with the purchase of a treatment. Complimentary Town Car service to the financial and shopping districts and tea or sherry served upon your arrival are among the amenities. ♦ 1075 California St (between Mason and Taylor Sts). 474.5400, 800/227.4683. www.huntingtonhotel.com

Within The Huntington Hotel:

## BIG 4 RESTAURANT

★$$$ Named in tribute to four railroad magnates of San Francisco—Collins P. Huntington, Charles Crocker, Mark Hopkins, and Leland Stanford—this restaurant features décor that brilliantly evokes the late 1800s with such touches as etched beveled-glass panels and polished woods. Chef Gloria Ciccarone-Nehls prepares a combination of French and nouvelle Californian cuisine. Try the pan-fried Dungeness crab cakes or garlic mashed potatoes. ♦ Californian/French ♦ M-F, breakfast, lunch, and dinner; Sa, Su, breakfast and dinner. Reservations recommended. 771.1140

THE
*Mark Hopkins*

**39 MARK HOPKINS INTER-CONTINENTAL SAN FRANCISCO**

$$$$ Ever since its opening in 1926, this 392-room hotel (familiarly known as The Mark) and the **Top of the Mark** cocktail lounge have been well regarded internationally. The Mark was host to officials during the formation of the United Nations, and a vacation site for Presidents Hoover and Eisenhower and countless other celebrities. Major renovations of the famous **Peacock Court** and **Room of the Dons** have restored the ballrooms' historic murals and elegant ambience, and the rooms have once again become favored for society weddings, debuts, and charity parties. Amenities include 24-hour room service, one-day laundry and valet services, terry-cloth robes, in-room movies, video messages posted on the TV screen, minibars, baby-sitting and concierge services, and a health club. Executive-floor guests have access to a street-level lounge with an entertainment center; business center with computers, fax machine, and Internet access; and food and beverage service throughout the day. Use of the lounge is available to hotel guests for a surcharge. ♦ 1 Nob Hill (at California and Mason Sts). 392.3434, 800/972.3124. www.san-francisco.intercontinental.com

Within the Mark Hopkins Inter-Continental San Francisco:

## TOP OF THE MARK

Dating from 1939, this renowned sky-high lounge, which boasts glorious views from its 19th-floor perch, set the standard for those that came after it. It's an elegant, charming place to watch the sun set or to take in the twinkling lights of the city. On Sundays, when an elaborate, expensive buffet brunch is offered, cocktails are served all day, and afternoon tea from 2:30PM to 5:30PM. ♦ M-Th, 2:30PM-1AM; F, Sa, 3PM-2AM; Su, brunch 10AM-2:30PM. 392.3434 ♿

## NOB HILL RESTAURANT

★★$$$$ The atmosphere is formal at this handsome, oak-paneled restaurant, which is largely patronized by hotel guests. The menu changes often and might include consommé of pheasant with poached quail egg and chives, sea bass steamed with fennel and served with a parsnip-caviar mousse and grilled Portobello mushrooms, or roast loin of veal with sun-dried-cherry sauce. One of the best deals is a prix-fixe, three-course dinner offered nightly. ♦ Californian/French ♦ Daily, breakfast, lunch, and dinner. Reservations recommended. 392.3434 ♿

**40 THE STANFORD COURT, A RENAISSANCE HOTEL**

$$$$ America's top executives often rank this hotel (part of Marriott) as their favorite in San Francisco. The attractive décor is combined with the amenities of a European-style hostelry. Each of the 402 rooms and suites has individually controlled air conditioning, a marble bath with a dressing room, a color TV well hidden in an armoire, and heated towel racks. Many have canopied beds. Coffee, newspapers, and overnight shoe shines are among the complimentary services. Mercedes and Rolls-Royce limousines are available for hire from 7AM to 8PM. It was built on the site of railroad magnate Leland Stanford's mansion, later the location of a 1912 apartment building, which was gutted to

---

Restaurants/Clubs: Red | Hotels: Purple | Shops: Orange | Outdoors/Parks: Green | Sights/Culture: Blue

create the hotel. The only remainder from the Stanford days is a 30-foot-high wall surrounding the property, although the design borrows something from the original house. For example, the Stanfords had a circular vestibule illuminated by an amber glass dome three stories above. A similar effect has been achieved in the hotel by covering the central courtyard and fountain with a lofty stained-glass canopy; tea and cocktails are served here. There's also indoor valet parking and a multilingual staff. ◆ 905 California St (at Powell St). 989.3500. www.marriott.com &

Within the Stanford Court:

## FOURNOU'S OVENS

★★★$$$$ The most distinctive places to dine in this multilevel restaurant are in the glass-enclosed conservatory area, which is pleasant for breakfast and lunch, or at the "oven" level, which boasts a magnificent open hearth decorated with Portuguese tiles and a floor-to-ceiling wine cellar. Chef Werner Albrecht's creative menu includes gnocchi with vegetables in a truffle broth, and pasta with rock shrimp and sun-dried tomatoes. The filet mignon, served on a bed of corn-kernel-studded mashed potatoes, is topped with a Parmesan-cheese wafer and a square of foie gras with fried leeks and smoky tomato vinaigrette. One of the best bargains around is the two- or three-course Twilight Supper, served from 5:30PM to 6:30PM. There is two-hour complimentary valet parking for breakfast and lunch. ◆ American ◆ Daily, breakfast, lunch, and dinner. Reservations recommended. 989.1910. www.fournoursovens.com &

## 41 THE RITZ-CARLTON SAN FRANCISCO

$$$$ This hostelry occupies a full city block in a renovated 1909 neoclassical building that used to house Metropolitan Life Insurance. Throughout the public areas are fine collections of 18th- and 19th-century artwork and antiques, as well as Aubusson tapestries and Persian carpets. It has 336 beautifully furnished rooms and suites, including a Club Floor with such amenities as private concierge and complimentary continental breakfast and afternoon tea. The multilingual staff offers impeccable, old-fashioned service, and guests have use of an indoor lap pool and fitness center. An elegant afternoon tea is available daily in the lobby lounge from 2:30PM to 5PM. ◆ 600 Stockton St (between Pine and California Sts). 364.3450, 800/241.3333. www.ritzcarlton.com

Within the Ritz-Carlton San Francisco:

## THE DINING ROOM

★★★★$$$$ Chef Ron Siegel presides over the kitchen and turns out the city's most

creative Californian/French cuisine. The setting is formal and luxurious, ideal for romance and celebration. The chef's tasting menu is a series of memorable dishes including the light and fresh sea-urchin panna cotta and the roasted Maine lobster, which has a pungent sweet-and-sour sauce. Other seasonal specialties are glazed oysters with leek fondue; duck breast with crisp potato croutons, rhubarb, lavender, and cracked almonds; and roast squab, the best in town, with sage and pancetta, paired with foie gras and Yellow Finn potatoes. Stephan Lacroix has put together a 1,200-bottle wine list featuring boutique wineries. Desserts are heavenly: Leave room for either the blackberry soufflé or the chocolate-hazelnut *croustillant*, crackling with praline. ◆ Californian/French ◆ Tu, Sa, dinner. Reservations recommended. 773.6198 &

## THE TERRACE

★★$$$ Under the guidance of chef Bradley Bennick, the Italian-inspired menu offers such interesting selections as a plate of delicate greens with squares of puff pastry filled with caramelized onions and artichoke hearts, and Tuscan-style chicken with zucchini and roasted potatoes. This spot is perfect for a leisurely lunch; select one of the 15 wines served by the glass to complement your entrée. Located on the courtyard level. ◆ Mediterranean ◆ M-Sa, breakfast, lunch, and dinner; Su, brunch and dinner. 296.7465 &

## 42 O'REILLY'S HOLY GRAIL BAR AND RESTAURANT

★$$ The restaurant retains the 15-foot-high stained-glass windows, antiques, and Renaissance art of the historic Mays Oyster House. Chef Sean Canavan has also kept the raw oyster bar. Seafood reigns on the menu! Try the wild salmon, whole petrale sole, or Monterey Bay calamari. The chef's Irish side comes through in the crispy smoked cod and potato cakes, the beef, and the Guinness and barley soup with Irish cheddar. Live jazz, blues, and Irish music are played every Monday from 9PM. ◆ Seafood/European ◆ M-F lunch; daily, dinner; Sa, Su, brunch. 1233 Polk St (between Fern and Bush Sts). 923.1233. www.oreillysholygrail.com &

## 43 ALLIANCE FRANÇAISE

Here's the educational heart of San Francisco's sizable French-speaking community, and an ideal place to learn to *parle français*. **La Cave Bistro Restaurant** (923.1375), below Alliance Française, is open Tuesday through Saturday for lunch, Thursday through Saturday for dinner, and Saturday morning for espresso and pastries. ◆ M-Sa. 1345 Bush St (between Larkin and Polk Sts). 775.7755. www.afsf.com &

## 44 CAFÉ MOZART

★★★★$$$$ One of Nob Hill's best restaurants, this refined establishment with intimate dining on three levels produces food that arrives so beautifully arranged on the plate, it's hard to decide whether it should be photographed or eaten. Gourmets who can't make up their minds should choose the *menu dégustation,* which provides samplings of many different dishes that change regularly to reflect the freshest products in the market. Other notable options include tiger prawns, champignons, and roast duck de Provence. The ambience here is cozy and traditional, with Corots and Monets gracing the walls. A fireplace glows in the main dining room, and only Mozart is played in the background. The wine list is pricey. ♦ French ♦ Tu-Su, dinner. Reservations recommended. 708 Bush St (between Powell and Mason Sts). 391.8480. www.cafemozartsf.com &

## 45 HOTEL CARLTON

$ This lower Nob Hill hotel, a Joie de Vivre property, provides value and comfort in 165 remodeled rooms, a boon for travelers on a budget. Colorful bed linens and pillows brighten up the otherwise spartan furnishings. In the pillared, high-ceiling lobby, guests can mingle over the evening complimentary wine reception. Also take advantage of the high-speed Internet access, which is a great amenity to travelers. Exotic travel photography enlivens the lobby, hallways, and guest rooms. The adjacent **Saha** restaurant (345.9547) serves Arabic-fusion cuisine. ♦ 1075 Sutter St (between Hyde and Larkin Sts). 673.0242, 800/922.7586. www.carltonhotel.com &

## 46 YORK HOTEL

$$ Moderately priced and centrally located, this is one of the many small hostelries that have been spiffed up. The 96 rooms are attractive, and there are trendy extras such as a complimentary wine hour, a complimentary breakfast, and an executive gym. There is no on-premises restaurant. ♦ 940 Sutter St (between Leavenworth and Hyde Sts). 885.6800, 800/808.9675. www.yorkhotel.com &

Within the York Hotel:

## THE EMPIRE PLUSH ROOM

Big-name as well as up-and-coming entertainers play at this unique, aptly named cabaret. Among those who've performed here are Michael Feinstein, Charles Pierce, Jim Bailey, Margaret Whiting, and Andrea Marcovicci. Note the spectacular stained-glass ceiling. ♦ Cover. Hours vary according to show times. Box office Tu-Sa. 885.2800. www.empireplushroom.com &

## 47 CANTEEN

★★$$ Canteen has quite a following, since Michael Bauer, the *San Francisco Chronicle* restaurant critic, named it one of San Francisco's top ten. Chef Dennis Leary personally prepares each dish. He serves a classic salmon à la barigoule, with artichokes and Provençal sauce. The calamari salad is full of zesty citrus and earthy garbanzo beans. More and more locals are dining downtown, since many of the city's most refreshing restaurants are there. At press time, Leary was looking to move out of this tiny space, so check online. ♦ American ♦ 817 Sutter St (near Jones St). 928.8870. www.canteensf.com &

## 48 HOTEL BERESFORD ARMS

$ One of the finest small hotels in the theater district provides a friendly atmosphere and personal service. Many of the 95 rooms have whirlpool baths and wet bars. Senior citizens get discounts and children under 12 may stay free. There is an unusually attractive lobby for entertaining your guests, but no restaurant. ♦ 701 Post St (at Jones St). 673.2600, 800/533.6533. www.beresford.com &

# FISHERMAN'S WHARF/ TELEGRAPH HILL/NORTH BEACH

The North Beach district was named after a beach that once extended from Telegraph Hill to Russian Hill, but has long since been built up by landfill. Although North Beach is synonymous with "Little Italy," Italians were not the first nor the last to arrive. Chilean prostitutes came first, in the 1850s, attracted by the Gold Rush, only to be chased out by the Irish, who were eventually replaced by more Latin Americans. On a site first occupied by a Russian Serbian Greek Orthodox Church, the **Washington Square Theater** presented Enrico Caruso in concert. North Beach was home to Italian immigrants in the 1880s. Joe DiMaggio, son of an immigrant fisherman, played in the North Beach playground on Lombard and Powell while growing up in the city. It is said he learned baseball skills by hitting balls with a broken oar. Beatniks turned North Beach into an international scene in the 1950s. The Beats took their name from Jack Kerouac, who called his contemporaries a "beaten generation." Local columnist Herb Caen began writing about the "beatniks" flocking there from the East. During this era, jazz clubs and coffeehouses on Grant and Columbus Avenues held nightly poetry readings. "Howl," which Allen Ginsberg wrote when he lived at 1010 Montgomery Street, scandalized the nation and drew more attention to this San Francisco neighborhood. Traces of the Beat legacy live on at jazz clubs, coffeehouses, and Lawrence Ferlinghetti's City Lights bookstore. In the 1960s, the Chinese began crossing Broadway from Chinatown. Today the North Beach population is approximately 50 percent Chinese—and growing—although new Italian immigrants are also settling here once again. The perfect place to sample the tempo of this neighborhood is **Washington Square**. Relax on a park bench here and let the gossip in Chinese and Italian swirl around you while old men and women practice tai chi and kids and shop workers hang out on the grass.

Bordering North Beach is Telegraph Hill, with its quaint cottages and vine-covered lanes, flowering gardens, stunning views, and impossible parking. Artists and writers once lived here, but now it's mostly the affluent and established who've made it home. The "Hill," as

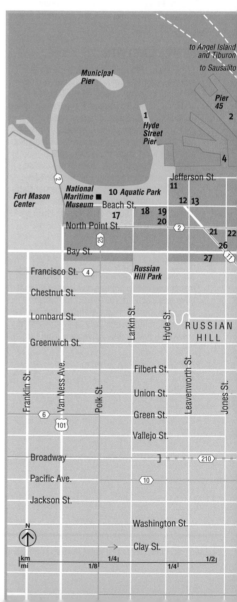

residents call it, looked quite different in the days of the Gold Rush. Although its height is the same (284 feet), the east slope used to be smooth and round and covered with grazing goats. The barren, jagged cliff you see today was created by sailors digging out ballast for their empty ship holds back when water lapped at the hill's base. The area went through several names, but after the Morse Code Signal Station was set up in 1853, the current name stuck. Although most of North Beach burned in the post-earthquake fire of 1906, the Italians managed to save a number of the old wooden cottages on the hill with a bucket brigade, using barrels of homemade red wine. The tiny shacks, built by early fishermen, now sell for hundreds of thousands of dollars. Crowning the hill is **Coit Tower,** named for Lillie Hitchcock Coit, who provided the funds to build it.

**Fisherman's Wharf,** also bordering North Beach, is one of the city's most popular tourist attractions. Seafood houses stand where crab fishers once hauled in their catch, and there are enough souvenir shops to keep the locals away. It's best to get to the area on the streetcar. An extension of the Muni F-line starts at the top of Market Street, travels the palm-tree-

lined Embarcadero, and ends at Fisherman's Wharf: a total distance of 10.2 miles that provides riders with dramatic waterfront views.

Not much more than a legend remains of the **Barbary Coast,** the once-notorious neighborhood extending between **Washington Street** and **Pacific Avenue,** and **Montgomery** and **Kearny Streets.** Named after the unsavory pirate headquarters in North Africa, this was where the term *shanghaied* originated, describing the practice of drugging a hapless seaman and shipping him out as a crew member for an understaffed ship. The Barbary Coast was a gathering place for *hoodlums*—a word coined here during the early 1900s, when the city had a worldwide reputation for viciousness. The area was finally shut down after World War I. In the 1950s it was renamed **Jackson Square** by the decorators who renovated the old buildings, exposing handsome brick walls and restoring the mid-19th-century structures. As a result, these blocks became the city's first designated historic site.

## 1 HYDE STREET PIER

As San Francisco is first and foremost a seaport, no visit to the area would be complete without a tour along the waterfront. Several vessels are docked at this pier (where ferries once carried passengers to Sausalito and Berkeley), which is part of the **San Francisco Maritime National Historic Park System.** The three that are open to the public, the *C.A. Thayer,* the *Eureka,* and the *Balclutha,* hold artifacts, photography collections, and displays that help bring their exciting pasts alive. Stop at the new visitors' center for the San Francisco Maritime National Historic Park. ♦ Daily. 447.5000. ♦ Admission; seniors and children under 12 free. Daily. Hyde St (at Jefferson St, at the west end of Fisherman's Wharf). www.nps.gov/safr &

At Hyde Street Pier:

### C.A. THAYER

Built in 1895, this schooner (pictured above) was the Pacific Coast's last commercial sailing ship. It transported lumber, served in two wars, and was most recently employed by the fishing industry. It has been fully restored.

### EUREKA

This was the last diesel-powered ferry to operate in the US. Built in 1890, this vessel hauled freight and passengers for the **San Francisco** and **Northern Pacific Railroads.**

### HERCULES

Berthed beside the *Eureka,* this frigate (pictured above) is under restoration and not open to the public. Built in 1907, the ocean-going tug hauled cargo, crippled ships, barges, and even materials for the Panama Canal.

### BALCLUTHA

A favorite city landmark, this is a classic square-rigged, three-masted sailing ship. Built in Scotland in 1883, it sailed the Cape Horn route for many years, bringing European goods to the West Coast and taking California grains back home. After the turn of the century, it served as a lumber ship, a salmon cannery in Alaskan waters, and finally a carnival ship and Hollywood movie prop.

## 2 FISHERMEN'S AND SEAMEN'S MEMORIAL CHAPEL

Saint John the Apostle Oratory sings Gregorian chant on selected Sundays. Missa Cantata or High Mass is the ancient music of the Roman liturgy named after Pope Gregory. This chapel is also unique as the only place to hear Latin mass. The award-winning Society of Saint John Schola produces a series of Gregorian chant CDs. Download a schedule online. ♦ Su, 9:30AM. Jefferson and Taylor Sts, Pier 45B. www.traditio.com/stjohn &

Angel Island, also known as the Ellis Island of the West, served as an immigration and quarantine station until November 1940. It's the largest island in the bay.

### 3 BLAZING SADDLES

The city's oldest bike rental shop began the famous Bike the Bridge tour. They have the latest-model mountain bikes, hybrids, road-racing bikes, and tandems. Choose one of five locations for pick-up and drop-off. ♦ Daily from 8AM. Jefferson and Powell Sts, Pier 41, Blue & Gold Ferry Terminal. Also at Pier 43½, Jefferson and Taylor Sts (at the Red and White Ferry Terminal); 2715 Hyde St (at Bay St); 1095 Columbus Ave (at Francisco St). 202.8888. www.blazingsaddles.com ৬

### 4 SCOMA'S

★★$$ Believe it or not, this venerable but run-down seafood house is the highest-grossing restaurant in San Francisco, packing people in just about every day of the year. It's the kind of joint where disinterested waiters sling your food at you on the run and present the check before dessert even arrives. Much of the charm of the place is its dockside location. As for the food, the fish is generally very fresh and portions are generous, but the presentation is fatally flawed.

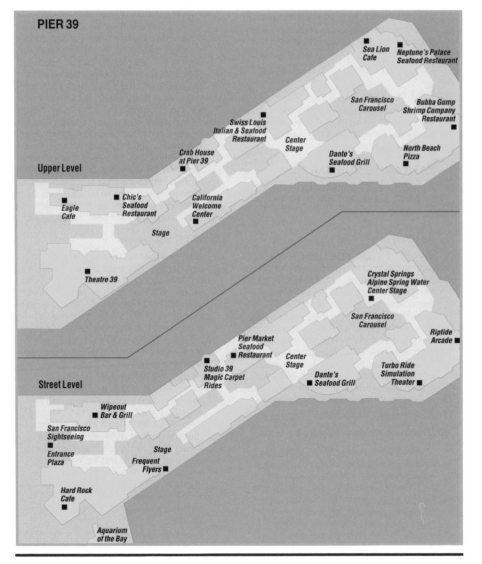

Restaurants/Clubs: Red | Hotels: Purple | Shops: Orange | Outdoors/Parks: Green | Sights/Culture: Blue

Oysters on the half shell, for instance, are mishandled, buried in ice, and sloppily served. Best bets are the grilled fish steaks with simple sauces. ◆ Seafood ◆ Daily, lunch and dinner. Pier 47 (at Jones and Jefferson Sts). 771.4383 ₺

## 5 FISHERMAN'S WHARF

The wharf was once the center of San Francisco's commercial fishing fleet, and while the boats are still here, this is now heavy tourist territory. The Silver Dollar man stands on a silver-painted milk carton near the entrance to Boudin Bakery, moving like the Tin Man in time to the music from his boom box. Tourists come by to take their picture with him. The Escape Man's act also draws a crowd. His assistant ties him into a straightjacket and he wiggles on the ground until he frees himself. Also watch for the Bush Man, who conceals himself behind foliage, then pops out to scare visitors. ◆ Taylor St (at The Embarcadero). www.fishermanswharf.org

At Fisherman's Wharf:

### RED & WHITE FLEET

Sightseeing bay cruises circle Alcatraz and point out the sights of the bay. ◆ Admission. Daily. At pier 43$^1/_3$. 447.0591. www.redandwhite.com

### PAMPANITO SUBMARINE

This World War II original is docked at the pier. ◆ Admission. Daily. At pier 45. 567.4653

### ALIOTO'S

★★$$$ This is the oldest restaurant in the area, known for the spectacular views from the upstairs dining room. The streetside stand offers cracked crab, while the eatery below, **Nonna Rose** (359.1200), serves Sicilian home-style seafood dishes. The upstairs dining room is washed in a quiet brown color scheme that lets the colorful view of gently rocking boats stand out. Sicilian specialties are mixed in with such standard Cal/Ital dishes as ziti with pine nuts, raisins, tomatoes, and flakes of fresh-tasting fish. ◆ Seafood ◆ Daily, lunch and dinner. 8 Fisherman's Wharf (at Taylor St). 673.0183. www.aliotos.com

## 6 BOUDIN AT THE WHARF

After 150 years, Boudin Bakery knows how to make French sourdough bread. The Boudins' fortunes rose with the city's, as you learn on the Boudin Museum & Bakery Tour. You also hear about the mysterious alchemy between the San Francisco fog and Boudin yeast. A glass-walled catwalk traverses the large demonstration bakery. The tour concludes in the tasting room, with the heavenly scent of oven-fresh bread. The complex includes the **Bakers Hall** market, **Boudin Café** with the ubiquitous sourdough bread bowl, and the upscale **Bistro Boudin**, which has a stone-hearth pizza oven that turns out delicious sweet fennel sausage pizza. ◆ Daily. 160 Jefferson St (at Taylor St). 928.1849. www.boudinbakery.com ₺

## 7 RIPLEY'S BELIEVE IT OR NOT! MUSEUM

Tour two floors of oddities collected by sports cartoonist, author, and radio broadcaster Robert L. Ripley, who was born in 1893 in Santa Rosa, California. ◆ Admission. Daily. 175 Jefferson St (at Taylor St). 771.6188. www.ripleysf.com ₺

## 8 HERB CAEN WAY...

Punctuated with historical plaques and pylons recalling events and people of the past, this boardwalk on the bay side of The Embarcadero is named in honor of the late Herb Caen. For more than a half century, the *San Francisco Chronicle*'s Caen was the city's premier columnist, the expert on the city's finest offerings and most titillating gossip. His first column on San Francisco appeared 5 July 1938. It soon evolved into an upbeat blend of news, scandals, vignettes, and thought-provoking dramas, spiced with schmaltz and an occasional thorn in the side of those in power. His wit and flair with words made him one of the most quoted columnists in *Reader's Digest*. The three dots were made part of the promenade's name because Caen always used them to separate items in his column. The Embarcadero (between Berry and Taylor Sts).

## 9 PIER 39

America's third-most-visited amusement attraction (Disney takes the top spots), this two-level shopping street, particularly popular with families, runs along the north waterfront near Fisherman's Wharf (see the map on page 91). It's the northernmost point of the San Francisco peninsula, thus providing superb views of Alcatraz, the Golden Gate Bridge, the bay, and the city skyline. It opened in 1978 after being transformed from a cargo pier into a fictional image of a turn-of-the-century San Francisco street scene, although it resembles a village on Martha's Vineyard more than a West Coast site. It includes shops, waterfront restaurants serving a variety of cuisines (including more than 20 specialty restaurants for families on a budget), the **Blue & Gold Fleet** (sightseeing boats), a waterfront park, a 350-berth marina, a double-deck carousel, an amusement area, and an aquarium.

Among the pier's stores are those specializing in kites, music boxes, and teddy bears. Other attractions include the wildly popular sea lions that have taken over part of the marina on the west side of the pier, and the street performers who play daily free of charge at **Stage I**, at **Center Stage**, or by the carousel. The **Pier 39 Cable Car Company** operates a fleet of motorized trolleys—replicas of cable cars—for city tours and charters.

Restaurants include **Chic's Place** (421.2442), with its Art Nouveau décor; the **Eagle Café** (433.3689), a San Francisco landmark that has been in business since 1928 (it was once a longshoremen's hangout on the site of what is now the garage, until it was lifted and moved to its present location); **Neptune's Palace** (434.2260), a seafood restaurant; **The Crab House,** one of the better places to eat on the pier, with a great view (434.0432); and the **Swiss Louis Italian Restaurant** (421.2913), which was long established in North Beach before relocating here. A parking garage is located across from the pier on Beach Street (the entrance is on Powell Street). ♦ Beach St (at The Embarcadero). 981.8030. Recorded information line 981.7437 &

Within Pier 39:

## BLUE & GOLD FLEET

Sightseeing bay cruises depart daily from the pier; call 705.5444 or 750.5555 for the schedule. Tickets can also be purchased online at www.telesails.com. The Blue & Gold Fleet Bay Cruise is included in the CityPass booklet.

## HARD ROCK CAFÉ

★$$ Even if you didn't notice the life-size black-and-white cow outside, you couldn't miss this link in the popular chain because of the continuous line of people waiting to get in. This is where the younger set wants to hang out, scarf down burgers, and then take home a T-shirt bearing the famous logo. ♦ American ♦ Daily, lunch and dinner. 956.2013 &

## AQUARIUM OF THE BAY

This 707,000-gallon marine attraction transports visitors along a 400-foot-long "journey through the sea" tunnel where they view nearly 200 species of marine life—including sharks and stingrays—in a 12,000-square-foot aquarium. Visitors may step off the moving footpath at any time during the journey onto a stationary platform to get a closer look. A new exhibit features marine life of San Francisco Bay. ♦ Admission. Daily. 623.5300

## 9 CALIFORNIA WELCOME CENTER

Stop here for discounts to local attractions, itinerary planning, Internet service, and car rentals. ♦ Pier 39, Building P, 2nd level. 981.1280. E-mail: sfconcierge@aol.com; www.visitcwc.com &

## 9 CRAB HOUSE

★$$ Windows span the dining room in this traditional New England fish house with weathered wooden beams and fishing nets. While diners ogle the view of **Alcatraz** and the **Golden Gate Bridge,** waiters swing through the room with two-pound Dungeness crabs nesting on platters. The sweet, tender, butter-dipped morsels melt in your mouth. On a second visit, you may want to branch out and try the skillet-roasted mussels. ♦ Seafood ♦ Daily, lunch and dinner. Pier 39, 2nd floor. 434.2722. www.crabhouse39.com &

## 10 AQUATIC PARK

This terraced park overlooking the bay sits adjacent to **Ghirardelli Square.** Historic ships managed by the **San Francisco Maritime National Historic Park System** are docked at nearby piers. There is swimming for hardy types, fishing off the scenic **Municipal Pier,** a small beach for wading, and plenty of grass for picnicking with a view. ♦ Beach St (at Polk St)

Within Aquatic Park:

## NATIONAL MARITIME MUSEUM

Part of the **San Francisco Maritime National Historic Park System,** this museum documents maritime history through displays of ship models, photographs, and memorabilia. It's housed in an old bathhouse building. The fascinating miniatures include passenger liners, freighters, US Navy ships, and a model of the *Preussen,* the largest sail-powered ship ever built. Tours by rangers are available daily. ♦ Free. Daily. Aquatic Park (at Polk St). 561.7100 (closed until summer 2009) &

## 11 ARGONAUT HOTEL

$$ Another boutique hotel from the Kimpton Group, the Argonaut used to be a warehouse at the Cannery. The Maritime National Historic Park had stored equipment in the 198,000-square-foot Haslett Warehouse before Kimpton converted it into a 268-room boutique hotel. Guests experience the luxury and personal service of a Kimpton property plus breathtaking waterfront views. Stop by the **Blue Mermaid Chowder House & Bar** (771.2222) for a bowl of Dungeness crab and corn chowder. On the lobby level is the Maritime Park Visitors Center. ♦ Located in The Cannery at Fisherman's Wharf. 495 Jefferson St (at

---

Restaurants/Clubs: Red | Hotels: Purple | Shops: Orange | Outdoors/Parks: Green | Sights/Culture: Blue

Hyde St). 563.0800, 866/415.0704.
www.argonauthotel.com

## 12 THE CANNERY

Constructed in 1909 as the Del Monte Fruit Company's peach-canning plant, this building was remodeled in 1968 by **Joseph Esherick & Associates** following the successful redevelopment of **Ghirardelli Square**. The three-story complex contains shops, restaurants, a comedy club, galleries, and a movie theater. Its sunken courtyard filled with flowers and century-old olive trees hosts mimes, musicians, and other talented street performers. Treasures from the estate of newspaper tycoon William Randolph Hearst have been installed in some of the facilities. The interior of **Jacks Cannery Bar**, for example, has a 90-foot-long hall, a carved fireplace, and a Jacobean staircase originally built in the early 1600s by **Inigo Jones**—England's first true Renaissance architect—for Queen Elizabeth I's ambassador to France. ♦ 2801 Leavenworth St (at Jefferson St). 771.3112. www.delmontesquare.com &

Within The Cannery:

### GREEN ROOM

Belly laughs are induced here nightly. Patrons get three hours of validated parking at the nearby **Anchorage Garage**. ♦ Cover. Shows nightly. S bldg, courtyard entrance. 673.9333. www.greenroomcomedy.com &

### OAKVILLE GROCERY

Shelves of gourmet products include mustards, jams, olive oils, and chocolate, and there's a fresh-food bar and brick-oven pizza counter. There is also a good collection of California wines that you can taste at the wine bar. ♦ Daily. N bldg, first floor. 614.1600 &

### BASIC BROWN BEARS

This small stuffed-animal factory has taken Elvis's advice and chosen the teddy bear as its official mascot. Don't miss the free 30-minute tour; at the end of the tour the staff will help you stuff your own teddy bear. Children love it. ♦ Daily. Tours: daily, 1PM; also Sa, 11AM. 409.2806 &

### LARK IN THE MORNING

Here you can shop for musical instruments and recordings from 50 cultures. You'll find alpenhorns, zithers, bagpipes, and bodhrans, as well as one-of-a-kind instruments. They also stock artwork of musical subjects, books, videos, and instruction books. Ground level. ♦ Daily. 922.4277

## 13 THE ANCHORAGE

Heavy on souvenir shops, this complex is downstream from **Ghirardelli Square** and **The Cannery**. ♦ Daily. 2800 Leavenworth St

(between Beach and Jefferson Sts). 775.6000 &

## 14 WAX MUSEUM

This new $15 million museum includes Leonardo DiCaprio and Kate Winslet on the bow of the *Titanic*, and former San Francisco mayor Willie Brown. Old favorites have been spruced up. The Chamber of Horrors is back in all its gory detail. ♦ Admission. Daily. 145 Jefferson St (between Mason and Taylor Sts). 202.0400. www.waxmuseum.com

Within the Wax Museum:

### RAINFOREST CAFÉ

★★$ With its 15,000-gallon aquarium, live birds, and two-story waterfall, this entertainment eatery dazzles kids and adults. Amid thunder, lightning, animatronic gorillas, and live macaws, you dine on fresh California pastas, salads, and sandwiches themed to Asian, Caribbean, Southwest, Mexican, and Cajun cuisine (with names like Rasta Pasta and Rumble in the Jungle). You can also enjoy the fun from a giraffe-leg stool under the giant mushroom while sipping organic vegetable juice. ♦ Daily, lunch and dinner. 440.5610

## 15 THE WHARF INN

$ Granted, it's not the Ritz (and there's no restaurant), but for its location (a block from Fisherman's Wharf) and price (most of the 51 rooms are under $100 a night off-season), this utilitarian hotel is an understated bargain. Add to this free parking and the "no extra person charge," and suddenly one can learn to live with the green-and-mustard décor. ♦ 2601 Mason St (at Beach St). 673.7411, 800/548.9918

## 16 RADISSON HOTEL FISHERMAN'S WHARF

$$ If you're looking for clean, tastefully decorated rooms at a reasonable price, this above-average chain hotel with 355 rooms is right on the money. Amenities include a pool, restaurant, and lounge, free parking, and, for a few dollars more, a balcony overlooking Alcatraz Island. It's also within just a few steps of Fisherman's Wharf. ♦ 250 Beach St (at Mason St). 392.6700, 800/333.3333. www.radisson.com &

## 17 GHIRARDELLI SQUARE

During the Civil War this was the site of a woolen mill, but it was the famous chocolate factory built here by Domenico Ghirardelli that gave the square its name. The factory was converted into the most attractive commercial complex in the city by **Wurster, Bernardi & Emmons Inc.** and **Lawrence Halprin & Associates** from 1962 to 1967. Their innovative renovation set the stage for retail conversions of Faneuil Hall Market Place in Boston and New York's South Street Seaport, as well as other adaptive-reuse architectural projects around the nation. The location is blessed with views of the bay, and at night the buildings are illuminated with strings of lights. The *Mermaid Fountain* in the central plaza, designed by local artist Ruth Asawa, is a good resting and meeting place. There is usually free entertainment somewhere within the square, which contains dozens of specialty shops, galleries, and restaurants. Among the many interesting places to browse are **Aardvark to Zebra** (346.1044); **Operetta** (928.4676), which carries Italian ceramics and tapestries; and **Something/Anything** (441.8003), which is a good place to find interesting jewelry and California crafts. The **Information Booth** has a detailed guide to shops and restaurants. ◆ 900 N Point St (across from Aquatic Park). 775.5500. www.ghirardellisq.com &

Within Ghirardelli Square:

### McCormick & Kuleto's

★★$$$ Famed restaurant designer Pat Kuleto has put his distinctive stamp on this fish restaurant. The décor is tasteful and plush, the views are astounding, and the seafood menu is one of the most extensive in the city. The food can be excellent, but with 400 seats plus private receptions and banquets, consistency is a problem. Dozens of fish are featured each day. ◆ Seafood ◆ Daily, lunch and dinner. Reservations recommended. 929.1730 &

### The Mandarin

★★★$$$ This pricey, pretty restaurant with a view of the bay has exceptional Chinese cuisine. The smoked tea duck is excellent, as is the Beggar's Chicken, which you must order 24 hours in advance. The pot stickers are also of the highest quality. ◆ Chinese ◆ Daily, lunch and dinner. Reservations recommended. 673.8812 &

### Ghirardelli Chocolate Manufactory and Soda Fountain

This old-fashioned ice-cream parlor and candy store sells luscious hot-fudge sundaes and five-pound chocolate bars. Take a look at the display of some original chocolate-making machinery in the back. ◆ Daily. 474.3938 &

### Wattle Creek Winery

Sample limited releases of this exciting Alexander Valley winery. The Sonoma County winery produces an excellent Shiraz and Yorkville Highlands rosé. In November the tasting room hosts the "Golden Oyster Party" and in December, a holiday party. The web site lists special events at the Ghirardelli Square tasting room. ◆ Daily. 359.1206. www.wattlecreek.com &

### 18 The Electric Tour Company

Imagine a motorized skateboard that you stand on and steer with handlebars. Tourists zip along The Embarcadero and the Marina Green on Segways, which are becoming popular. You can travel 24 miles on a single charge on lithium ion batteries. Guided Segway tours start at 9AM in the summer, 10:30AM in winter, and last 3 hours, including a 40-minute training session. The rear parking lot near Hyde Street serves as the training area. Riders wear helmuts and safety vests. No individual rentals. ◆ Daily. 757 Beach St (between Hyde and Larkin Sts). 474.3130; 474.9855. www.sfelectrictour.com &

### 19 The Buena Vista

$$ Always jammed with tourists and locals, this is the place where Irish coffee got started, and it's still a specialty. There's food too (American fare, such as burgers and chicken), but do a snack tour of nearby **Ghirardelli Square** instead, and have Irish coffee as the finale. ◆ American ◆ Daily, breakfast, lunch, and dinner. 2765 Hyde St (at Beach St). 474.5044. www.thebuenavista.com

### 20 Restaurant Gary Danko

★★★★$$$$ Having received 6 five-star Mobil awards, Gary Danko is *the* place to go for a meal that you'll remember long after you leave. The two dining rooms are wood-paneled and sleek. Try the lobster salad, the roast lobster or scallop mousse, or the guinea hen with cabbage, apples, and fresh chestnuts. Don't pass up the cheese course. The wine cellar holds over 1,500 wines, including some coveted vintages that sommelier Renee-Nicole Kubin helped to locate. ◆ French/Asian ◆ Daily, dinner. Reservations required. 800 North Point St (at Hyde St). 749.2060. www.garydanko.com ⑂

## 21 MAHARISHI AYURVEDA HEALTH SPA

Authentic Ayurvedic treatments from India leave your skin feeling soft and sensually charged. Abhyanga is an oil massage with two therapists working in synchrony on either side of the body. Shirodhara is a warm, herbal oil treatment poured on the forehead producing a paroxysm of bliss. The Swedena heat chamber envelops the body from the neck down while cooling coconut oil is lavished on your hair and forehead. The serene setting with shimmering drapes and mirrored cabinets appeals to one's post-treatment mood. A potent antioxidant worth trying is Amrit Nectar, a paste of herbs and fruit including the amia berry, a concentrated source of vitamin C. ◆ Daily. 685 North Point St (at Columbus Ave). 441.0685. www.maharishispa-SF.net. ⑂ Also at 1777 Union St (at Octavia St). 922.1777

## 22 HOLIDAY INN EXPRESS AND SUITES

$$ This new five-story hotel, now an InterContinental brand, has 240 guest rooms and 20 suites and ample underground parking. No pool, but more intimate than the 585-room Holiday Inn–Fisherman's Wharf next door. ◆ 550 North Point St (between Taylor and Jones Sts). 409.4600. 800/972.3124. www.hiexpress.com

## 23 COST PLUS WORLD MARKET

This warehouse-size store offers reasonably priced imports from all over the world, including baskets, glassware, pottery, tables, specialty foods, and wines. ◆ Daily. 2552 Taylor St (at Bay St). 928.6200. www.worldmarket.com ⑂

## 24 THE BEST WESTERN TUSCAN INN

$$$ This 220-room inn, follows the successful Kimpton formula, offering style and personal service. Complimentary services include wine every evening and daily coffee or tea by the fireplace in the lobby, and limousines to the Financial District

weekday mornings. There's in-house parking, room service, same-day valet/laundry service, and programs for children. ◆ 425 North Point St (at Mason St). 561.1100, 800/648.4626. www.tuscaninn.com

Adjoining the Best Western Tuscan Inn:

## CAFÉ PESCATORE

★★$$ Modeled after a classic Italian trattoria, this attractive, informal restaurant may be the best dining choice in the Fisherman's Wharf area, where pickings are plentiful but culinary excitement is scarce. Diners enjoy fresh pizza from the wood-burning oven and *tonna saltimbocca* (seared tuna wrapped in prosciutto) with garlic mashed potatoes and *brodetto,* a hearty fish stew. ◆ Italian ◆ Daily, breakfast, lunch, and dinner. Reservations recommended. 2455 Mason St (at North Point St). 561.1111. www.cafepescatore.com ⑂

## 25 SHERATON AT FISHERMAN'S WHARF

$$$ This handsome complex of redwood, brick, and greenery has 525 guest rooms interspersed with courtyards. ◆ 2500 Mason St (at Beach St). 362.5500, 800/325.3535. www.sheratonatthewharf.com

## 26 SAN FRANCISCO MARRIOTT FISHERMAN'S WHARF

$$$$ One of the most elegant hotels in the wharf area blends apricot marble, comfortable leather, and an abundance of greenery. There are 285 rooms and suites complete with writing desks, cable TV, and quilted-top foam mattresses. **Spada's,** the hotel restaurant, specializes in Angus beef and fresh seafood. The lobby lounge features a complimentary buffet. ◆ 1250 Columbus Ave (at Bay St). 775.7555, 800/228.9290. www.marriott.com ⑂

## 27 635 BAY STREET

This apartment building boasts a charming trompe l'oeil exterior that includes painted-on moldings and a giant "keyhole." It's a private residence. ◆ At Jones St

## 28 VANDEWATER STREET

In this short, narrow alley between Powell and Mason Streets are several architectural firms and some interesting housing examples—notably **No. 55,** a condominium development designed by **Daniel Solomon & Associates** in 1981. Its beautifully proportioned façade is adorned with a gently curved arch at the top and a palette of pinks and beiges. **No. 33** next door, designed in 1981 by **Donald**

**MacDonald & Associates,** is a simpler version, painted white. **No. 22** is an apartment block that the architecture firm **Esherick, Homsey, Dodge & Davis** designed in 1976.

## 29 210 FRANCISCO STREET

This 25-foot-wide structure is a modern re-interpretation of the traditional San Francisco row house. **Backen, Arrigoni & Ross**'s 1985 design has all the essential elements—the curved bay window, the false façade—but is constructed out of contemporary materials, including white porcelain enamel panels, glass blocks, and poured-in-place concrete. It's a private residence. ◆ At Grant Ave

## 30 TELEGRAPH TERRACE

**Backen, Arrigoni & Ross**'s award-winning group of expensive Spanish-style condominiums climbs the steep hillside and looks out over ornamental details that make it fit into its context. The private residences were built in 1984. ◆ Francisco St (at Grant Ave)

## 31 ALBONA

★★$$ This is the West Coast's only restaurant serving food of the Istrian Peninsula, the body of land that pokes out below Trieste and is across the Adriatic Sea from Venice. The restaurant is named after a city on the peninsula that was once Italian, then Yugoslav, and now belongs to Croatia, and the food reflects the Italian and Central European influences of that region. This may be the only establishment in the country that makes cheese-and-nut-filled *crafi Albonesi* (Albonese ravioli). All the desserts, including a knockout apple strudel, are made on the premises. ◆ Italian/Croatian ◆ Tu-Sa, dinner. Reservations recommended. Complimentary valet parking. 545 Francisco St (at Taylor St). 441.1040. www.albonarestaurant.com &

## 32 SAN REMO HOTEL

$ The only budget-priced hotel in North Beach, this lovingly restored Italianate Victorian building was constructed in 1906 by A.P. Giannini, Bank of America's founder. With the exception of the penthouse, a cottage on the roof with a brass bed and bay views, the hotel's 64 rooms all share immaculate baths with charming Victorian fixtures. Each of the guest rooms is furnished with antiques or would-be antiques, and some have sinks. There are no telephones or TVs, but there is abundant charm. The penthouse books months in advance. ◆ 2237 Mason St (at Chestnut St). 776.8688, 800/352.7365

Within the San Remo Hotel:

### FIOR D'ITALIA

★$$$ Opened in 1886, this place claims to be the oldest Italian restaurant in America. Specialties, including risotto, homemade pastas, and veal dishes, can be eaten at the bar or in the more formal dining room. ◆ Northern Italian ◆ Daily, lunch and dinner. Reservations recommended. 986.1886. www.fior.com &

## 33 CHARLES CAMPBELL GALLERY

This gallery specializes in contemporary Bay Area artists. ◆ Tu-Sa. 647 Chestnut St (at Columbus Ave). 441.8680. www.charlescampbellgallery.com

## 34 TEATRO ZINZANNI

★★★★$$ What goes on under the colorful tent on The Embarcadero? Love, chaos, and dinner...each in appropriate measure. Enter the opulent spiegeltent, handcrafted in Europe in the 1920s, where the sultry Madame ZinZanni coos love songs. Over a leisurely, four-course dinner the commedia dell'arte entertainment never stops, from aerialists, a high-stepping boxer, and a hula-hoop swinger to a talented tango dancer. Hats off to Norman Langill for creating a winning spectacle. ◆ Californian ◆ W-Su, dinner and show. Reservations required. Pier 29 on The Embarcadero (at the end of Sansome St and Lombard St). 438.2668. www.zinzanni.org &

## 35 JULIUS' CASTLE

★$$$$ This romantic, elegant restaurant perched on the hills near **Coit Tower** has reopened after a complete renovation. Check next edition of Access for a review. Please consult their web site for information and new details. ◆ French/Italian ◆ Daily, dinner. Reservations required. 1541 Montgomery St (at Lombard St). 392.2222. www.juliuscastle.com

## 36 COIT MEMORIAL TOWER

Located at the top of Telegraph Hill, this 1934 tower (pictured here) by **Arthur Brown Jr.** marks the point where the first West Coast telegraph sent messages notifying the arrival of ships from the Pacific. Messages were then signaled downtown by a semaphore tower.

---

Restaurants/Clubs: Red | Hotels: Purple | Shops: Orange | Outdoors/Parks: Green | Sights/Culture: Blue

Lillie Hitchcock Coit, who as a girl of 15 had been the mascot of the crack firefighter company Knickerbocker No. 5, left funds to beautify the city in 1929. An incorrect story persists that the tower was shaped to look like a firehose nozzle to commemorate her interest in the fire department. Inside are restored murals depicting California workers. Painted as a Public Works of Art Project during the Depression, the murals, some leaning politically to the left, created a stir when first unveiled. Take the elevator to the top for a spectacular view of the city and bay. The tower's base, from which there are panoramic views, is accessible all day. ♦ Admission for elevator ride. Daily. At the end of Telegraph Hill Blvd

## 37 LEVI'S PLAZA

In 1982 **Hellmuth, Obata & Kassabaum** built this enormous three-building development for the Levi Strauss Company. The architects reduced the vast scale by stepping back the profiles of the buildings so that they would blend into the shape of Telegraph Hill. All the buildings are clad in brick tiles that match the adjoining **Ice House,** a converted office complex. Wander among the Monterey pine and waterfalls, and hop the stepping-stones across the creek. Any spot is good for a picnic. ♦ Sansome and Battery Sts (between Union and Greenwich Sts)

Within Levi's Plaza:

### IL FORNAIO

★★$$ This enormously popular restaurant is the last word in trendy décor and dining, and though not each dish the kitchen produces is a roaring success, most are—especially at breakfast, with Italian adaptations of oatmeal and French toast and a knockout fruit-filled calzone. The premises include a pastry shop, pizzeria, *rosticceria* (rotisserie), café (986.0646), and bar, all incorporated into what the management calls *gastronomia Italiana.* Sandwiches at lunch are made with delicious herb breads. ♦ Italian ♦ Daily, breakfast, lunch, and dinner. Reservations recommended. 1265 Battery St (at Greenwich St). 986.0100, 927.4400. www.ilfornaio.com &

### FOG CITY DINER

★★$$ The diner concept merely served as design inspiration for this ultrasleek restaurant filled with polished stainless steel, chrome, and neon. A creative, eclectic menu of Californian cuisine offers something for everyone, from crab cakes and grilled sesame chicken to quesadillas and Asian prawns to homemade pickles. It's operated by the same restaurateurs who own the popular **Mustards Grill** in Napa Valley and **Buckeye Roadhouse** in Mill Valley. ♦ Californian ♦ Daily, lunch and dinner; Sa, Su,

brunch. Reservations recommended. 1300 Battery St (off The Embarcadero). 982.2000. www.fogcitydiner.com &

## 38 PIER 23 CAFÉ

★★$$ "Excuse me, do you mambo?" Well, after a few pitchers of sangria at this bayside restaurant and dance club, you probably will. It's great fun even for people who can't dance (and you know who you are). The food's good too: Come early and try the spicy meat loaf with mashed potatoes or the crab-and-shrimp quesadilla before squeezing onto the dance floor. When the weather's nice, the alfresco dining is unbeatable. Friday is salsa night, and Saturday is reggae. ♦ Californian ♦ Tu-Sa, lunch and dinner; Su, brunch. Closed Mondays and Tuesdays in winter. Reservations recommended. Pier 23 (near the end of Lombard St). 362.5125. www.pier23cafe.com &

## 39 GRAFFEO COFFEE ROASTING CO.

You can smell the dark beans roasting several blocks away at this long-established firm, which turns out a daily grind. There's no brewed coffee, however. ♦ M-Sa. 735 Columbus Ave (at Filbert St). 986.2429, 800/222.6250. www.graffeo.com

## 40 PAUL THIEBAUD GALLERY

American painter Wayne Thiebaud is known for his Laguna Beach scenes and Californian images of burgers, hot dogs, and dogs at the beach. On view at the gallery, run by his son, Paul, is his dreamy landscape *Riverscape.* Browse the online catalog. ♦ Tu-Sa. 718 Columbus Ave (between Filbert and Greenwich Sts). 434.1350. www.paulthiebaudgallery.com

## 41 MAYBECK BUILDING

This office building was constructed in 1909 around a courtyard with apartments on the upper floors. It was once the **Old Telegraph Hill Neighborhood Center Building** (the oldest neighborhood center in the city). ♦ 1736 Stockton St (between Filbert and Greenwich Sts)

## 42 1360 MONTGOMERY STREET

Featured in the Humphrey Bogart movie *Dark Passage,* this 1937 apartment house is designed in the moderne style, with exterior murals and a fine glass-block façade leading to the entrance lobby. It's a private residence. ♦ At Filbert St

## 42 FILBERT STEPS

Down the east side of Telegraph Hill, the terrain is so steep that Filbert Street becomes Filbert Steps—a series of precariously perched platforms and walkways with some of the city's oldest and most varied housing. A beautifully landscaped walkway climbs down the hill and gives access to the lanes on either side—Darrell Place, Napier Lane. **No. 228** Filbert Steps, built in the 1870s, is a fine example of Carpenter Gothic style. These are private residences. ◆ Between Sansome and Montgomery Sts

### 43 KAHN HOUSE

Similar to his Lovell House in Los Angeles, this 1939 building by **Richard Neutra** steps down the hill and offers its occupants superb views over the bay. Walk to the end of the lane and look over the stone wall. It's a private residence. ◆ 66 Calhoun Terr (between Green and Union Sts)

### 44 REMODELED WAREHOUSES

Some old warehouses in this neighborhood, most built in the 1930s, have been turned into offices for architects, graphic artists, and TV companies. Of particular note are **855 Battery Street,** for **Channel 5/Westinghouse TV,** remodeled by **Gensler & Associates** (1980-1981); **243 Vallejo,** by **Marquis Associates** (1972); **220 Vallejo,** by **Kaplan/McLaughlin/Diaz** (1978); and **101 Lombard Street,** by **Hellmuth, Obata & Kassabaum,** completed in 1979. There are fine old brick warehouses on Battery between Union and Green Streets, plus the old **Ice House,** which is now an office complex, on Union Street between Sansome and Battery Streets. ◆ From Broadway to Lombard St (between Battery and Sansome Sts)

### 45 PIPERADE

★★★$$ Come here for food that you just may dream about for days afterward. Chef Gerald Hirigoyen, who has delighted the Bay Area with his culinary creations at **Fringale,** returns to his culinary heritage at Piperade and **Bocadillos.** He created a gorgeous rustic room with oak floors, wine barrels, and a large square communal table. Start with the mussel and bread salad with red wine vinaigrette, or the prawns with garlic, parsley, and lemon. The chef goes for absolute authenticity with the Basque specials served Monday through Friday. Piperade—a classic Basque dish made by slow-cooking onions, peppers, tomatoes, and garlic—is served with Serrano ham and a poached egg. Large glass doors open onto a heated patio for year-round alfresco dining. ◆ Basque ◆ M-Sa, dinner. Reservations recommended. 1015 Battery St (at Green St). 391.2555, www.piperade.com. ♿ Also Bocadillos at 710 Montgomery St (at Washington St). 982.2622

### 46 CAFE DE STIJL

★★$ Started by Assyrian architect **Nilus de Matran** in an old brick warehouse, this hip restaurant serves up Middle Eastern fare

including tabbouleh salad with fresh mint and sun-dried tomatoes; Turkish lamb salad with toasted almonds, cranberry, and lemon vinaigrette; and a four-spice chicken sandwich with orange-cayenne sauce. ◆ Middle Eastern/ Californian ◆ M-W, F, Sa, breakfast and lunch. 1 Union St (at Front St). 291.0808. www.destijl.com ♿

### 47 WASHINGTON SQUARE

Located halfway along Columbus Avenue, this plaza is the center of the Italian North Beach community. On the north side is the **Church of Saints Peter and Paul;** on the east, next to the post office, is the **Italian Athletic Club.** Lunching at **Caffè Malvina** (391.1290) on the corner of Stockton and Filbert Streets is a pleasant way to watch the world go by. ◆ Bounded by Union and Filbert Sts, and Stockton and Powell Sts

### 48 THE WASHINGTON SQUARE INN

$$ Each of the 16 large, luxurious rooms at this European-style hostelry, located in the heart of North Beach midway between Fisherman's Wharf and Union Square, is individually decorated and furnished with English and French antiques. Two of the rooms have bathrooms across the hall. The hotel overlooks Washington Square and the **Church of Saints Peter and Paul.** Continental breakfast, afternoon tea and cookies, and wine are included in the price of a room, but there's no restaurant. ◆ 1660 Stockton St (at Filbert St). 981.4220, 800/388.0220. www.wsisf.com

### 48 MOOSE'S

★★★$$$ Popular with movers and shakers for power lunches and dinners, it's modern and airy, with windows overlooking the street, an expansive open kitchen, arches separating the bar from the dining area, and live jazz at dinnertime. Try the roasted tomato Gruyère soup and gnocchi with smoked salmon, pistou (basil, garlic, and olive oil) sauce, crème fraîche, and caviar. The desserts are heavenly. ◆ American ◆ Daily, lunch and dinner; Su, brunch. Reservations recommended. 1652 Stockton St (between Union and Filbert Sts). 989.7800, 800/28-Moose. www.mooses.com

### 49 GIRA POLLI

★★$ No one does chicken better than this stylish 8-table restaurant, with 18 spits whirling in the wood-fired rotisserie. The Sicilian menu is small, simple, and to the point. Chicken is served with luscious Palermo-style potatoes (boiled in chicken

---

Restaurants/Clubs: **Red** | Hotels: **Purple** | Shops: Orange | Outdoors/Parks: **Green** | Sights/Culture: **Blue**

stock and baked with white wine and herbs). The homemade pasta is also richly rewarding, as is the sensational lemony cheesecake. The place does a brisk take-out and delivery business. ♦ Italian/takeout ♦ Daily, dinner. Reservations recommended. 659 Union St (at Powell St). 434.4472. Also at 590 E Blithedale Ave, Mill Valley, Marin County. 383.6040 ♿

## 50 PASTA POMODORO

★★$ This pasta house offers incredible deals and generous portions. Plus the gnocchi, coated in Gorgonzola sauce and spiked with diced tomato, are better than preparations that cost twice as much. The dozen or so pasta dishes include *penne puttanesca* (with black and green olives and a slightly spicy tomato sauce); rigatoni with roast chicken, cream, mushrooms, and sun-dried tomatoes; and spaghetti with calamari, mussels, and scallops in a light tomato sauce. ♦ Italian ♦ Daily, lunch and dinner. 655 Union St (between Columbus Ave and Powell St). 399.0300 ♿ Seven locations in San Francisco including 2027 Chestnut St (at Fillmore St). 474.3400. www.pastapomodoro.com ♿

## 51 VOLARE TRATTORIA

★★$$ Homemade pastas and carefully grilled meats draw enthusiastic diners to this pleasant, tiled trattoria. ♦ Sicilian ♦ Daily, dinner. 561 Columbus Ave (between Green and Union Sts). 362.2774. www.volarecafe.com ♿

## 51 IL POLLAIO

$ Grilled chicken (hence the name, which means "chicken coop") doesn't come any better than at this pie-shaped wedge of a café. Other entrées—lamb chops, pork chops, and rabbit—are spiced and grilled in the richly flavored and heavily spiced Argentine manner. Soup, a couple of salads, and two desserts round out the short menu. ♦ Italian/Argentine ♦ M-Sa, lunch and dinner. 555 Columbus Ave (between Green and Union Sts). 362.7727 ♿

## 52 MARIO'S BOHEMIAN CIGAR STORE

★$ You'll hear lots of Italian spoken at this tiny, friendly spot, where the clientele hunkers down over a few tables. It's smaller and plainer than other coffeehouses in the area, but many swear it has the best espresso and focaccia sandwiches. It was a cigar store in the 1960s, but you won't find any stogies here anymore. ♦ Coffeehouse ♦ Daily. 566 Columbus Ave (at Union St). 362.0536 ♿

## 53 ITALIAN FRENCH BAKERY

This bakery's breads and breadsticks have won top awards in North Beach culinary competitions. ♦ Daily. 1501 Grant Ave (at Union St). 421.3796 ♿

## 54 YONÉ

Sift through a veritable gold mine of beads, buttons, and jewelry; you could even make yourself a necklace or a pair of earrings with what's available here. ♦ M, Tu, Th-Sa. 478 Union St (at Grant Ave). 986.1424

## 55 NORTH BEACH PIZZA

★★$ The variety of toppings at this jam-packed pizza parlor is impressive: Ten combinations are offered, including one with pepperoni, mushrooms, and cheese, and another with clams, garlic, and cheese—all smoothed over the slightly doughy crust. You may order your food to go or have it delivered. ♦ Pizza ♦ Daily, lunch and dinner. 1499 Grant Ave (at Union St). 433.2444. Also at 1310 Grant Ave (at Green St). 433.2444

## 56 CAFÉ JACQUELINE

★★$$ Soufflé's the thing at this cozy, romantic restaurant. Owner Jacqueline Margulis serves savory—albeit costly—selections that might include crab and lobster, salmon and asparagus, shiitake mushrooms, or white corn with ginger and garlic. The dessert soufflés are all irresistible. ♦ French ♦ W-Su, dinner. 1454 Grant Ave (at Union St). 981.5565

## 57 SAVOY TIVOLI

$ This long-established, charmingly decrepit North Beach hangout with a sidewalk café and recreation room is a great place for meeting the locals. ♦ Bar ♦ Tu-Sa. 1434 Grant Ave (between Green and Union Sts). 362.7023

## 58 CLUB FUGAZI

The popular cabaret-style show *Beach Blanket Babylon* has been playing here in various incarnations for years. The show's theme changes annually, but it invariably features outrageous costumes, zany hats, and an earnest, high-energy, talented cast bent on making the lowbrow material seem funny. No one under 21 is admitted except for the Sunday matinee. ♦ Admission. Shows daily. Reservations required three to four weeks in advance. 678 Green St (between Columbus Ave and Powell St). 421.4222. www.beachblanketbabylon.com ♿

## 58 CAPP'S CORNER

★$$ If you have a hungry family or group with not-so-discriminating tastes and not-so-unlimited funds, head for the corner that's belonged to Capp since who knows when. Here you'll learn what Italian "family dining" is all about: back-to-back Sinatra tunes, endless glasses of headache-quality Chianti, and brusque but cheery service. Granted, the food isn't tops, but if you order the mussels marinara, you'll at least leave pleasantly stuffed. ♦ Italian ♦ Daily, lunch and dinner. 1600 Powell St (at Green St). 989.2589. www.cappscorner.com ⅊

## 59 L'OSTERIA DEL FORNO

★★★$ This hole in the wall is what you'd expect in North Beach—tables wedged together by the front windows, and friendly and casual service. The kitchen turns out the best focaccia sandwiches, pizza, excellent pasta, and a roast of the day, usually beef or a delectable pork that has been marinated and braised in milk. All this for what amounts to small change. ♦ Italian ♦ M, W-Su, lunch and dinner. No credit cards accepted. 519 Columbus Ave (between Green and Union Sts). 982.1124

## 59 LA RACCOLTA

Victoria Doggett's shop could easily tempt you to fill every room of your house with old world pottery. From multi-tiered chandeliers to tiny espresso cups, these hand-painted Italian ceramics are a treasure. The Limoncello sets from the Amalfi coast are dainty cups and a carafe for the Italian liqueur. ♦ Tu-Sa. 521 Columbus Ave (between Green and Union Sts). 693.0199

## 60 CAFFÈ SPORT

$$ Although the wait may be long, and the service could be a little friendlier, this neighborhood stalwart has lots of charm and character—starting with its roomful of kitschy décor. Popular dishes include cioppino and any of the pastas, which may be paired with lobster, pesto, calamari, shrimp, scallops, or four kinds of cheese. ♦ Italian ♦ Tu-Sa, lunch and dinner. 574 Green St (at Columbus Ave). 981.1251 ⅊

## 61 DANILO ITALIAN BAKERY

An all-purpose bakery specializing in Tuscan recipes, this shop makes a lot of things very well, among them breads, breadsticks, biscotti, focaccia, and *panettone* (including the very special anise-flavored *buccelatto*). One of the unique treats is a *torta di verdura*, a dense pie made with Swiss chard, liqueur, raisins, and pine nuts. ♦ Daily. No credit cards accepted. 516 Green St (near Grant Ave). 989.1806 ⅊

## 62 BOCCE CAFÉ

★$$ One of the better bargains in North Beach, this spacious Italian restaurant at the end of a trellised walkway serves respectable cuisine at competitive prices. Try its best dish, the *linguine pescatore* (with a seafood sauce), wash it down with some cheap Chianti, and try not to fall asleep on the sinfully comfortable pillowed booths. Avoid Friday night, when the band shows up and ruins everyone's meal. ♦ Italian ♦ Daily, lunch and dinner. 478 Green St (at Grant Ave). 981.2044. www.boccecafe.com

## 62 MAYKADEH

★★$$ Very popular and very good, this attractive restaurant serves exotic Persian cuisine in a mauve, California-like setting. The lamb dishes are a delight. ♦ Persian ♦ Daily, lunch and dinner. Reservations recommended. 470 Green St (at Grant Ave). 362.8286 ⅊

## 63 STELLA PASTRY & CAFFÈ

Try the famous *sacrapantina*, layers of sponge cake brushed with maraschino liqueur and zabaglione. Other noteworthy selections include tiramisù, biscotti, Sicilian cannoli, and *panettone*. ♦ Café ♦ Daily. 446 Columbus Ave (between Vallejo and Green Sts). 986.2914 ⅊

## 63 HOTEL BOHÈME

$$ Formerly the **Millefiore Inn,** this once-Victorian place has been transformed by interior designer Candra Scott into a hotel that captures the true spirit of North Beach. Look for such touches as handmade light fixtures (some fashioned from parasols found in Chinatown) and bohemian-style furnishings. Along the staircase and hallways, Terry Stoll's black-and-white photographs capture the parties and mayhem of the Beat era. Each of the 15 guest rooms has a private bath and a queen-size bed. If you're looking for quiet, be sure to request a room away from Columbus Avenue. ♦ 444 Columbus Ave (between Vallejo and Green Sts). 433.9111. www.hotelboheme.com

---

Restaurants/Clubs: Red | Hotels: Purple | Shops: Orange | Outdoors/Parks: Green | Sights/Culture: Blue

## 64 NORTH BEACH MUSEUM

The history of North Beach, Chinatown, and Fisherman's Wharf is presented in old photos and artifacts. ♦ Free. M-F. 1435 Stockton St (between Vallejo and Green Sts), mezzanine. 566.4497

## 65 CAFFÈ GRECO

★$ Ultrafriendly owners Sandy and Hanna Suleiman and their family quickly made this North Beach coffeehouse popular. It's always crowded, and on warm days and evenings conversation spills onto the street through open picture windows. The desserts, including tiramisù and cappuccino cake, are worth every sinful bite. There are also focaccia sandwiches and salads. ♦ Coffeehouse ♦ Daily. 423 Columbus Ave (between Vallejo and Green Sts). 397.6261. www.caffegreco.com

## 66 CALZONE'S

★$$ Savor trendy pizzas from a wood-burning brick oven while people-watching through the large picture windows. For a real winner, try chicken-liver pasta. The management dispatches a free limousine to the Financial District to pick up lunchtime customers. ♦ Italian ♦ Daily, lunch and dinner. 430 Columbus Ave (between Vallejo and Green Sts). 397.3600 ♿

## 67 LA BODEGA

★$ Decorated in bright, bold colors, this Spanish restaurant features a lovely abstract brush painting of flamenco dancers. Try the thinly sliced *chorizo*, and follow it with the paella or the chicken served over vegetable-studded rice. There's live entertainment nightly (after 8PM). ♦ Spanish ♦ Daily, dinner. 1337 Grant Ave (between Vallejo and Green Sts). 433.0439 ♿

## 68 CAFFÈ PUCCINI

★$ Minimal operatic-themed décor graces this invariably full coffeehouse favored by local residents, who love the Lucca-style biscotti, or Italian sandwiches and antipasto specials. ♦ Coffeehouse ♦ Daily. 411 Columbus Ave (between Vallejo and Green Sts). 989.7033

## 69 RISTORANTE IDEALE

★★★$$ True Roman cooking is showcased in Maurizio Bruschi's restaurant, made warm and friendly by the terra-cotta-toned décor and the satisfying pasta dishes such as crab ravioli, pappardelle in tomato-based lamb sauce, and penne with fresh and smoked salmon in a creamy tomato sauce. ♦ Italian ♦ Tu-Su, dinner. Reservations recommended. 1309 Grant Ave (at Vallejo St). 391.4129 ♿

## 70 VICTORIA PASTRY CO.

Try the delicious Saint Honoré cake here, as well as the biscotti, *corcini* (chocolate cake), and other types of pastries. ♦ Daily. 1362 Stockton St (at Vallejo St). 781.2015 ♿

## 71 MOLINARI'S

This landmark Italian deli has been a local monument since 1896 and offers a huge selection of Italian sandwiches and sausages, among other imported specialty food. ♦ M-Sa. 373 Columbus Ave (at Vallejo St). 421.2337 ♿

## 72 CAFFÈ TRIESTE

★$ This quintessential San Francisco coffeehouse is a haven for artists, writers, and gawkers. There are live opera performances and slightly higher drink prices Saturday afternoons. ♦ Coffeehouse ♦ Daily. 609 Vallejo St (at Grant Ave). 392.6739

## 73 THE STINKING ROSE

★$$ You won't find a vampire in sight at this popular restaurant and bar, where *everything—* from the eggs in the morning to the cocktails at night—contains traces of the stinking rose (a nickname for garlic). There's a small store hawking garlic paraphernalia too. ♦ Italian/American ♦ Daily, lunch and dinner. Reservations recommended. 325 Columbus Ave (between Broadway and Vallejo St). 781.7673 ♿

## 74 HOUSE

★★$$ This North Beach industrial space revels in the urbanity that some diners avoid. If you don't like the décor, let Larry Tse's inventive menu win you over. Diners love the organic products and bright flavors of dishes such as Tomales Bay oysters with spicy cilantro mignonette and crispy blue-lake bean tempura with pickled ginger soy. Hong Kong–born Tse pairs angus flatiron steak with addictive warm wasabi house noodles. He enhances Niman Ranch pork chops with a sensual pomegranate-currant sauce. ♦ Asian/Californian ♦ M-Sa, lunch; daily, dinner. Reservations recommended. 1230 Grant Ave (between Columbus Ave and Vallejo St). 986.8612. www.thehse.com ♿

## 75 CONDOR LOUNGE

$$ San Francisco's moral minority let out a cheer in 1991 when the **Condor Club**'s Carol Doda sign (a larger-than-life rendering of the city's most famous stripper) was torn down and the landmark topless bar became a bistro. It has since been transformed into a sports bar, serving your typical "pub grub." ♦ American ♦ Daily, lunch and dinner. 300 Columbus Ave (at Broadway). 781.8222 ♿

## 76 BROADWAY

This brash strip has been a monument to man's mammary fascination since 1964, when Carol Doda first performed her topless act at the **Condor Club.** Once a family street with Italian grocery stores, it became a center

## THE BEST

**Barbara Stauffacher Solomon**

Artist/Writer (author of *Green Architecture and the Agrarian Garden*)

In San Francisco, the edge of the city is the center of the city. That line—where the land meets the water—is the domain of seagulls, fishermen, and frail strongmen, athletes and aesthetes, dreamers, dolphins, drunks, and me. I was born here.

**The Embarcadero:** Walk the piers stretched straight out onto the bay; scan the streets and skyscrapers shooting straight up Teleg... down San Fran... Delight in pelic... along the Rib... "utopia" des... Saitowitz).

**The Marina:** Walk... over the Palace of Fine Ar... Yacht Harbor, and go to the Safew... Marina Green.

**The Waterfront:** As you pass Fisherman's Wharf watch crabs cooked in champagne.

for bootlegging in the 1930s, and in the 1940s was dotted with brothels and pool halls. Then, in the 1950s, the strip began to clean up its act when the likes of Lenny Bruce and Barbra Streisand played here at the **Hungry i,** Johnny Mathis sang at **Ann's 448,** and folk musicians strummed at **On Broadway.** The entertainment boom went bust as high-paying Vegas clubs wooed the big names, and by the mid-1960s the street had turned raunchy again. Loud barkers lured leering tourists into the 20 topless clubs, which featured expensive cover charges, lightly liquored drinks, and a parade of breasts. The strip is more subdued now. Most of the surviving topless clubs do not have liquor licenses, and many of the new businesses are restaurants. ◆ Between Sansome St and Grant Ave

## 76 BLACK OAK BOOKSTORE

Browse through new and used books at discount prices. ◆ M-Th, Su; F, Sa, until midnight. 540 Broadway (near Columbus Ave). 986.3872 &

## 77 HELMAND RESTAURANT

★★★$$ San Francisco's premier Afghan restaurant has an exotic menu that includes such intriguing choices as *kabuli* (rice baked with lamb tenderloin and raisins), *mourgh challow* (chicken sautéed with spices and yellow split peas), and *theeka kabob* (char-broiled beef tenderloin marinated in yogurt, baby grapes, and herbs). All dishes are deftly prepared and complex in their spicing, but not fiery hot. ◆ Afghan ◆ Tu-F, lunch buffet; daily, dinner. Reservations recommended. 430 Broadway (between Montgomery and Kearny Sts). 362.0641 &

## 78 HUNAN

★$$ When San Francisco first fell in love with fiery Hunanese food, this restaurant was here to heat up willing palates. Devotees keep coming back for Diana's specials, a deep-fried pie filled with pork, cheese, and onions; the house-smoked duck; and smoked ham with bell peppers and onions. ◆ Chinese ◆ Daily, lunch and dinner. Reservations recommended. 924 Sansome St (off Broadway). 956.7727 &

## 79 CITY LIGHTS BOOKSELLERS & PUBLISHERS

More than any other bookstore, this one, especially beloved by night owls, evokes the atmosphere and accomplishments of literary San Francisco. Owned by poet Lawrence Ferlinghetti, the shop's heyday was the Beat era of the 1950s. Many of the writers who immortalized that time—Allen Ginsberg, Gregory Corso, Michael McClure, Jack Kerouac, and Ken Kesey—are featured, and there's a marvelous poetry section. ◆ Daily until midnight. 261 Columbus Ave (between Pacific Ave and Broadway). 362.8193

## 79 VESUVIO

If it's bohemian atmosphere you're after, this is the place. This landmark North Beach bar is still frequented by artists and poets from the Beat era, in addition to more current representatives of the arts scene. The walls are covered with objets d'art. ◆ Daily. 255 Columbus Ave (between Pacific Ave and Broadway). 362.3370. www.vesuvio.com &

## 80 TOSCA CAFÉ

★$ Media types, socialites, and a cross section of the city's creative community all love to hang out at this unassuming café. Visiting celebrities have been known to pop up as impromptu bartenders. A coffeeless cappuccino made with steamed milk, brandy, and chocolate is the specialty drink. Put a quarter in the jukebox. Cash only. ◆ Café ◆ Tu-Su. 242 Columbus Ave (between Pacific Ave and Broadway). 986.9651 &

Restaurants/Clubs: Red | Hotels: Purple | Shops: Orange | Outdoors/Parks: Green | Sights/Culture: Blue

## ...S THE LIMIT

...rea, especially San Francisco, is ...or its sweeping views. Here are a few ...y best:

...Square Victorian row houses on **Hayes** ...Steiner Streets are backdropped by downtown ...scrapers.

**Gateway to Chinatown** Capture the sights and smells in this historic area at **Grant Avenue** and **Bush Street.**

**Golden Gate Bridge Vista Point** From the south end of the bridge at the toll plaza, you can see the islands in the bay, the bridge, and the north waterfront.

**Mount Tamalpais** On a very clear day, the summit views extend to the **Farallon Islands,** east to **Mount Diablo** and the east bay, and

sometimes as far as the Sierra Nevada, 200 miles away.

**Nob Hill** Easily reached by any of the three cable-car lines, this affords a spectacular view down **California Street** (at Powell St) straight to the bay.

**Ocean Beach** Sunset at this beach, on San Francisco's westernmost edge, affords beautiful views of the city.

**Strawberry Point** Catch a glimpse of San Francisco's skyline from the point just off **Highway 101** at the end of **Seminary Drive.** Look down on the bay, the bridge, and the north waterfront.

**Twin Peaks** From the top of **Market Street** you can scan the best of the Bay Area in every direction— the city, the bay and its islands, the bridges, and the mountains to the north and south.

## 81 TOMMASO'S RESTORANTE ITALIANO

★★$$ *People* magazine proclaimed it one of the country's top three pizza places, but success hasn't spoiled this little spot, which is credited with producing San Francisco's first brick-oven pizza some 60 years ago. All the crisp, thin-crust pizzas are superb. So is the pasta, served with sensible, traditional sauces. ◆ Italian ◆ Tu-Su, dinner. 1042 Kearny St (between Pacific Ave and Broadway). 398.9696

## 82 PACIFIC AVENUE

Interesting shops on this street include **Thomas Cara Ltd.** (517 Pacific at Sansome St, 781.0383), an old establishment selling coffee, espresso machines, and kitchenware. ◆ Between Sansome and Montgomery Sts

## 82 MYTH

★★★$$$ Myth has several dining areas, and the staff welcomes you as if to a private home. The bar and lounge have the contemporary furnishings favored by San Franciscans. The 120-year-old brick building is a handsome survivor, now resplendent in dark hardwood floors, exotic woods, and halogen lighting that draws attentions to the food. After years at **Gary Danko's,** chef Sean O'Brien strikes out on his own with roasted cauliflower soup with curry, duck confit, and black trumpet mushrooms. Another starter is wild Burgundy escargots with baby octopus, garlic, Pernod, and fennel salad. The risotto is offered as an appetizer or entrée and priced accordingly. Wine is also offered in two-ounce pours. Try the spiced pumpkin soufflé with

crème anglaise or flourless chocolate cake in a warm butterscotch sauce for dessert. **Myth Café** next door is open for breakfast and lunch. ◆ French/California ◆ Dinner. 470 Pacific Ave (at Montgomery St). 677.8986. www.mythsf.com &

## 83 BRANDY HO'S

★★$ This is one of the best Hunan restaurants in the city, especially for those whose palates are up to the challenge of lots of chili peppers and garlic. The deep-fried dumplings with garlic sauce, onion cakes, smoked ham with garlic, and lamb with crispy rice noodles are but a few of the many pungent temptations available. ◆ Hunan ◆ Daily, lunch and dinner. 217 Columbus Ave (between Pacific Ave and Broadway). 788.7527 &

## 84 NIEBAUM-COPPOLA CAFÉ

★★$$ This store, café, and wine bar is an extension of Francis Ford Coppola's Napa Valley winery. You can sample the Coppola reds and whites in low-priced wine flights. Try the thick grilled vegetable sandwiches for lunch and a hearty risotto for dinner. Caesar salad was first created at this location when it was Caesar's Grill. Coppola has revived the original recipe and serves it fresh with egg yolk. ◆ Italian ◆ Tu-Su, lunch and dinner. 916 Kearny St (at Columbus Ave). 291.1700

## 85 SAN FRANCISCO BREWING COMPANY

$ Allen Paul's brewery, the last of the Barbary Coast saloons, now gets customers who mine their gold in the nearby Financial District. By law, food is served here, but the attraction is the 20 types of domestic and imported beers from small specialty breweries, along with several brewed by the owner on the premises. The interior, dating from 1907, is graced by a solid mahogany bar trimmed with brass, as well as a tile spittoon. Babyface Nelson was captured in what is now the women's room, and Jack Dempsey was a bouncer here for a short time. The management organizes beer tastings and brewpub crawls sporadically. There's live blues Wednesday and Thursday, and jazz on Monday and Saturday. ♦ American ♦ Daily, lunch and dinner. 155 Columbus Ave (at Pacific Ave). 434.3344 ఈ

### 86 THOMAS BROTHERS MAPS

Browse through an extraordinary selection of maps, from pocket- to wall-size, as well as globes, atlases, and guides, in this shop that's also known as the Map House. The hanging brass lamps complement the Victorian premises. ♦ M-F. 550 Jackson St (at Columbus Ave). 981.7520 ఈ

### 87 BIX

★★★$$$ The location on quiet Gold Street, tucked away in the shadow of the **Transamerica Pyramid,** sets the mood for a visit to this posh 1920s-style supper club, where people sip martinis at the elegant bar backed by a bigger-than-life mural, and a torch singer croons in the corner. The menu changes seasonally, but always includes such standbys as Waldorf salad, updated with Roquefort cheese, and chicken hash. Other homey dishes might include grilled pork chops with mashed potatoes, grilled lamb chops with mustard and mint, duck confit, and sturgeon with roast vegetables. In these drop-dead surroundings, you might be inclined to splurge on the Russian *osetra* caviar with crème fraîche and toast points. ♦ American ♦ F, lunch; daily, dinner. Reservations required. 56 Gold St (between Sansome and Montgomery Sts). 433.6300. www.bixrestaurant.com ఈ

### 88 WILLIAM STOUT ARCHITECTURAL BOOKS

One of the few great architectural bookstores in America, this shop has grown from a handful of books available at Bill's apartment to a collection of more than 10,000 volumes of rare books, magazines, and portfolios. ♦ M-Sa. 804 Montgomery St (at Jackson St). 391.6757

### 89 CAFFÈ MACARONI

★★$$ This very small, very good, very Italian restaurant has a menu that changes daily to accommodate the market's freshest selections; choices can range from baked stingray to classic pasta dishes. *Note:* Lunch is served across the street at **Macaroni Sciue Sciue,** 124 Columbus (between Jackson and Kearny Sts.). 217.8400. ♦ Italian ♦ Daily, dinner. Reservations recommended. 59 Columbus Ave (at Jackson St). 956.9737

### 90 JACKSON SQUARE HISTORIC DISTRICT

Designated the city's first historic district, this area contains the only group of downtown business buildings to survive the 1906 earthquake and fire; most date back to the 1850s. Some buildings sustained additional damage in the 1989 quake, but all survived. Most are brick and have been carefully restored and remodeled to become the city's antique showroom center for the prestigious Challiss House, Antonio's Antiques, and others. ♦ Bounded by Sansome and Montgomery Sts, and Washington and Jackson Sts

### 90 HOTALING PLACE

This block-long alley leads from Jackson Street, between Montgomery and Sansome Streets, right into the base of the **Transamerica Pyramid.** There are two old warehouses that were distilleries in the Barbary Coast days.

### 91 W. GRAHAM ARADER III GALLERY

Aficionados of rare maps, hand-colored prints, and engravings should stop here and have a chat with director Gregory McIntosh. An expert on pre-20th-century fine art, McIntosh will guide you through his treasures whether your interest is natural history, florals, botanicals, or rare books of California. The gallery is housed in San Francisco's oldest building, an 1850s whiskey warehouse that survived the 1906 earthquake and fire because firefighters wanted to protect the whiskey. ♦ M-Sa; Su, by appointment. 435 Jackson St (at Hotaling Pl). 788.5115. www.aradergalleries.com

The fortune cookie was invented in San Francisco during the turn of the century by Makoto Hagiwara, chief gardener of the Japanese Tea Garden in Golden Gate Park.

The first buffalo born in San Francisco was delivered in Golden Gate Park on 21 April 1892.

## 92 US APPRAISER'S BUILDING

This government building occupies the same block as the **US Custom House,** and both represent contrasting attitudes toward federal architecture. Erected by **Gilbert Stanley Underwood** in 1941, this building represents the aesthetics of the WPA era with its stripped-down Moderne styling. It was reclad in 1988 by **Kaplan/McLaughlin/Diaz** with precast concrete and a new polished-granite base. The same firm redid the windows in 1992. ◆ Battery and Jackson Sts

## 93 KOKKARI

★★$$$ Mark this spot on your culinary journeys for contemporary Hellenic cuisine. Kokkari also brightens one's dining options around Jackson Square. Entering the restaurant is like coming into a secluded hilltop retreat on Rhodes. A fire blazes in the hearth and makes the old wood gleam. A silver-haired Greek waiter brings a bowl of penne with braised lamb. But the supreme lamb experience is *arnisia paidakia,* three grilled chops with oregano and lemon. For dessert try the poached pear over rice pudding. ◆ Greek ◆ M-Sa, lunch and dinner. Reservations recommended. 200 Jackson St (at Front St). 981.0983.

## 94 722 MONTGOMERY STREET

This three-story brick building is registered as a historic landmark. The first meeting of Freemasons in California was held here on 17 October 1849. ◆ At Washington St

## 95 US CUSTOM HOUSE

Older than the **US Appraiser's Building** on the same block, this classical Baroque building has a massive rusticated base, an elaborate cornice line, and a generously proportioned entrance hall. It was constructed from 1906 to 1911 by **Eames & Young. Room 504** on the fifth floor houses the US Geological Survey offices, which sell maps of the US and Apollo 11 maps of the moon. ◆ 555 Battery St (at Jackson St)

# SAN FRANCISCO'S ISLANDS

The rocky islands in **San Francisco Bay** are home to a once-notorious prison, naval training stations, and wildlife refuges teeming with sea lions and birds. Tours of **Alcatraz, Angel,** and **Treasure Islands** can be arranged, or you may cruise by them on one of the ferries that dock at **Fisherman's Wharf.**

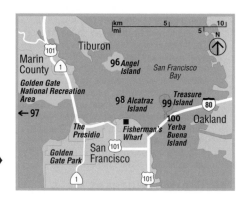

## 96 ANGEL ISLAND

This square mile of rocky land rising to a summit of 781 feet is the largest island in the bay. It was also the place Lieutenant Juan Manuel de Ayala initially anchored in 1775 during the first European expedition to sail through the Golden Gate. Between 1860 and 1890, the island's **Camp Reynolds** operated as a Civil War outpost and later as a staging area for soldiers engaged in fighting Indians. It is the only remaining garrison of its type from the Civil War. During the Spanish-American War and World Wars I and II, the island served as a debarkation and discharge point for troops. From 1910 to 1940 it was regarded as the "Ellis Island of the West," serving mostly Asian immigrants. It became an internment camp for Italian and German prisoners during World War II.

Today the State Park Service maintains the island, and it's a perfect spot for a day of hiking, bicycling, or beachcombing. Trails meander along rugged slopes on a five-mile route. There are nine environmental campsites on the island. For reservations, call 800/444.7275. There are also picnic and barbecue facilities, a snack bar during the summer months, and a souvenir kiosk. The **Visitors' Center** offers 20-minute video tours year-round and guided tours of historic sites from April through October. For more information, call 435.1915. ◆ Park: Daily, 8AM to sunset. Ferries: Daily in summer, weekends only in winter. The island is accessible by two routes: The Red & White Fleet runs ferries from San Francisco (447.0591, www.redandwhite.com), and the Angel Island/Tiburon Ferry Company departs from Tiburon (435.2131)

## 97 FARALLON ISLANDS

In 1872, this chain of craggy islands located 32 miles from Point Lobos was incorporated into the city and county of San Francisco. The name Farallon is derived from the Spanish expression for small, rocky, pointed islands. Inhospitable to humans, these islands today are closed to the public. There is, however, a Coast Guard station on **South Farallon** (the island most visible from San Francisco's shores), and until 1968, a handful of stoic families lived there. Lighthouse keepers had to climb a steep zigzag path 320 feet up to the light, sometimes crawling on their hands and knees during the onslaught of a gale or storm. Today an automated lighthouse and foghorn warn ships to stay away from the treacherous rocks. To many San Franciscans, the significance of the Farallon Islands is meteorological, demonstrated by the expression "On a clear day you can see the Farallon Islands." They are best viewed from Ocean Beach or Point Reyes in Marin County. ♦ You can board a day cruise to the Farallons June through November by calling Oceanic Society Expeditions, 441.1104. www.oceanic-society.org

## 98 ALCATRAZ ISLAND

When Lieutenant Juan Manuel de Ayala discovered the island in 1775, he named it Isla de los Alcatraces (Island of the Pelicans) after the colony of pelicans roosting here. The first lighthouse on the West Coast was installed here in 1854. The island's strategic and isolated position made it ideal for use as a defensive and disciplinary installation. The first cell block was built by the US Army, and from that time on, the island was fated to be a prison facility. Crude stockades held unruly soldiers convicted of crimes in the 1860s, and Indians who proved troublesome were detained here in the 1870s. The island served as a quarantine post for soldiers returning from the Spanish-American War, and after the 1906 earthquake and fire, prisoners from the crumbled San Francisco jails were temporarily held here. In 1934 it became a federal maximum-security prison. The fame of the "Rock" spread as it became home to such notorious criminals as Al Capone, Machine Gun Kelly, and Robert Stroud, who was also known as the Birdman of Alcatraz. A new section has opened to the public so you can see exactly where the Anglin brothers made their famous escape into the water in 1962. The prison was closed in 1963. Between 1969 and 1971 a political protest and occupation by about a hundred Native Americans put the island in the headlines. Today it is part of the **Golden Gate National Recreation Area** (although some San

Franciscans are lobbying hard to turn it into a casino, albeit without much luck so far). An excellent cell-house audio tour (recorded by former inmates and wardens), ranger-led programs, and a slide show are available daily. Dress warmly and plan to stay about two hours. ♦ Fee for ferry. Daily ferry departures from The Hornblower pier at the foot of Bay St. Reservations required. 981.7625. www.nps.gov/alcatraz; www.alcatrazcruises.com

## 99 TREASURE ISLAND

This artificial island was created to serve as the site of the Golden Gate International Exposition of 1939-1940. After the awe-inspiring effort to simultaneously construct two of the largest bridges in the world (the Golden Gate and Bay Bridges, completed within a few months of each other), it seemed fitting to celebrate by building an artificial 400-acre island for the fair. Later it was slated to become the **San Francisco Airport.** Of course, it was found to be too small and much too close to the Bay Bridge, and with the outbreak of World War II, the navy closed the island as a base in 1997. The city of San Francisco acquired this hotly contested property, and it's worth a visit for the spectacular views of the city skyline and both bridges. ♦ To reach the island, take the Bay Bridge to the Treasure Island exit or take an AC Transit T bus

## 100 YERBA BUENA ISLAND

This island connects and anchors the cantilever and suspension sections of the Bay Bridge. Known in early days as Wood Island to seafarers, it was officially named Yerba Buena (good herb) after the wild mint that grew here. Historically, Indians used to paddle from the shore in barges made of bundles of reeds and use the island as a fishing station. Remains of an Indian village and cremation pits have been dug up, along with buried contraband from smugglers, portions of a shipwrecked Spanish galleon, and graves of soldiers, pioneers, and goatherds. Today, the island is a **Coast Guard Reservation and Naval Training Station.** It is connected to Treasure Island by a 900-foot causeway.

---

Restaurants/Clubs: Red | Hotels: Purple | Shops: Orange | Outdoors/Parks: Green | Sights/Culture: Blue

# UPPER FILLMORE/ PACIFIC HEIGHTS/MARINA

**W**hen a cable-car line was built in the Pacific Heights District in 1878, this area quickly became an enclave of San Francisco's nouveaux riches. They moved into huge, gray Victorians, monuments to the bonanza era, and attempted to outdo the wooden castles on Nob Hill with Gothic arches, Corinthian pillars, Norman turrets, Byzantine domes, mansard roofs, and enough stained glass to outfit several cathedrals. Their houses lined **Van Ness Avenue,** which was five feet wider than Market Street and considered the Champs-Elysées of San Francisco.

But the magnificence on **Van Ness Avenue** was short-lived. The earthquake of 1906 reduced the exquisite homes to shambles, and the area never fully recovered. However, eastern Pacific Heights, like Russian and Nob Hills, was rebuilt with luxury apartment houses, and a substantial number of the original Victorians still remain. Today the Pacific Heights and Marina areas, along with **Cow Hollow** and **Presidio Heights,** hold more college graduates, professionals, and families earning upper-middle and higher incomes than any other city district. There are more

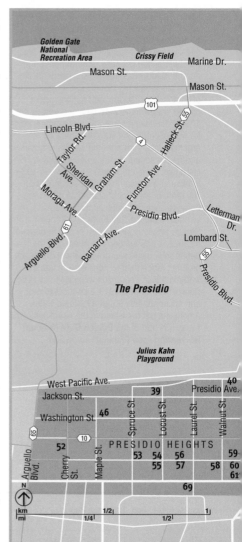

mansions per city block as well, with handsome examples of the work of architects **Bernard Maybeck, Willis Polk, Ernest Coxhead,** and **William Knowles** on the streets feeding into **Broadway.** One of the oldest is at **2727 Pierce Street.** The city's most photographed group of dainty Victorians is along the south side of **Alta Plaza Park.** The fine collection of Victorian houses on **Union Street** has been turned into a shopper's dream, with more than 300 boutiques, restaurants, antiques stores, and coffeehouses. A drive on Broadway to the **Presidio Gate** will give you a capsule glimpse into the privileged lives of years past and present. Private ownership of such enormous buildings was destined to die out, and many of the more impressive mansions now house schools, consulates, and religious orders, or have been converted into apartments.

Although technically part of the Richmond District, Presidio Heights is philosophically, socially, and economically akin to its neighbor, Pacific Heights. It's a low-density area, filled with elegant private houses. **Sacramento Street,** which starts at **The Embarcadero,** turns into a chic commercial enclave between **Divisadero** and **Spruce Streets.** In this restrained, exclusive neighborhood, more than a whiff of affluence wafts across the few blocks of expensive specialty shops and antiques stores, some of which are open by appointment only.

Cow Hollow, the area north of Pacific Heights, was named for the 30 dairy farms established there in 1861. A tiny lagoon, **Laguna Pequeña** (also known as **Washerman's Lagoon**), was used as a communal washbasin for the city's laundry. In the late 1800s, tanneries, slaughterhouses, and sausage factories appeared because of the dairies and fresh water from the lake and springs. But pollution from open sewage, industry, and the cows forced the city to banish livestock forever and to fill the putrid lagoon with sand from the dunes on **Lombard Street.**

After the devastating 1906 earthquake and fire, to show the world it was a city that refused to die, San Francisco proceeded to stage one of the most spectacular fairs of all time—the Panama-Pacific International Exposition of 1915. The excuse was the opening of the Panama Canal, and the exposition was the springboard for a citywide open house that drew more than 18 million visitors. On the bay north of Cow Hollow, 600 acres of marshland were filled in, a seawall was built running parallel to the shoreline, and sand was pumped up from the ocean bottom to serve as fill. The dredging produced enough

deep water to build the **San Francisco Yacht Harbor,** the present site of the **Saint Francis Yacht Club,** and enough land to create the Marina District. **Crissy Field** has been returned to marshland and has a good swimming beach. One of the exhibition's buildings, the monumental **Palace of Fine Arts,** is now home to the **Exploratorium,** a very popular family science museum and auditorium. However, the landfill proved to be a dangerously shaky foundation during the 7.1 quake that rocked the city in October 1989.

The Marina reflects the Mediterranean-revival architecture popular in the 1920s, with mostly pastel, single-family dwellings and large, well-maintained flats along the curving streets. Although **Chestnut Street** offers fine neighborhood restaurants and interesting shops, Lombard Street is "Motel Row." The **Marina Green,** which borders the harbor, is often full of kite flyers, volleyball players, sunbathers, joggers, and boaters. Nearby **Fort Mason,** planned by the Spanish in 1797 as a gun battery for the protection of **La Yerba Buena** anchorage, now functions as a giant community center offering theaters, including **Magic Theatre;** workshops; exhibition space; galleries; classes; and **Greens,** the best-known vegetarian restaurant in San Francisco.

## 1 St. Francis Yacht Club

This Spanish-style building overlooks the bay and the Marina yacht harbor. Badly damaged by a fire on Christmas day in 1976, the private club was completely remodeled by **Marquis Associates,** only to once again sustain heavy losses after the 1989 quake. ♦ Marina Blvd (at Baker St)

## 2 Wave Organ

Located at the tip of the Marina jetty is this often described "very peculiar musical instrument" built by scientists from the **Exploratorium.** The "organ" is nothing more than a series of underwater tubes echoing the sounds of the changing tide, which visitors can hear in a miniature amphitheater. Although chances are that what you hear will sound more like a gurgling toilet than organ music, the city and bay views here make this a worthwhile destination. ♦ Near Marina Green and Marina Blvd at the end of Yacht Rd

## 3 Marina Green

Area residents jog, bike, skate, fly kites, and sun-worship along this green swath of park that runs from the yacht harbor to **Fort Mason.** On a sunny day, it's a glorious place to drink in the magnificent bay. ♦ Marina Blvd (between Webster and Scott Sts)

## 4 Palace of Fine Arts

Originally built in 1915 for the Panama-Pacific Exposition, the palace houses the **Exploratorium,** a science museum for kids and adults, and an auditorium used for lectures and film presentations. Architect **Bernard Maybeck's** building was the pièce de résistance of his career as well as of the exposition. It has a great stage set consisting of a classical Roman rotunda with two curved colonnades, behind which is the curved exhibition shed. The setting is in the midst of a small park, complete with an artificial lake and waterfowl (including two swans). The palace became so popular that the buildings were retained and completely rebuilt after the exposition ended. For the **Palace of Fine Arts Theater,** call 567.6642. 3601 Lyon St (between Bay and Jefferson Sts)

Within the Palace of Fine Arts:

### Exploratorium

Restoration was completed in 1969, the year the **Exploratorium** opened as a science museum.

The museum was conceived on the premise that one learns by doing, and the more than 650 exhibits require visitor participation. You can pull, push, and manipulate various objects to demonstrate principles of prisms, sound, electricity, lasers, plant behavior, and more. At the **Listening Walks** exhibit, visitors can put on blindfolds and explore a rich dynamic soundscape. The special **Tactile Dome,** which some private groups have explored in the nude, has a separate admission charge and requires reservations (call 561.0362). ♦ Admission; children three and under free; free the first Wednesday of each month (excluding some special exhibitions). Daily, Memorial Day to Labor Day; Tu-Su, Labor Day to Memorial Day. Exploratorium events 563.7337. www.exploratorium.edu &

## 5 Fort Mason Center

Dating from the mid-1800s, when it served as a command post for the army that tamed the West, this proud reserve was added to by

WPA workers in the 1930s. Today the area is part of the **Golden Gate National Recreational Area (GGNRA)** and houses theaters, classes, workshops, a restaurant, and art galleries, as well as trade shows and special exhibitions. **SF Bay Whale Watching** (www.sfbaywhalewatching.com) runs expeditions to the Farallons from Gaslamp Cove. Humpback whales sometimes pop up so close to the boat, you can count the barnacles on their backs. ♦ Marina Blvd (entrance at Buchanan St). 441.3400. www.fortmason.org ♿

Within Fort Mason Center:

## SAN FRANCISCO MUSEUM OF MODERN ART GALLERY

An arm of the **San Francisco Museum of Modern Art,** this gallery focuses on works of lesser-known, emerging northern California artists. It has frequently changing exhibitions. Artwork is offered for sale and/or rent. ♦ Free. Tu-Sa. Bldg A. 441.4777

## SAN FRANCISCO CRAFT & FOLK ART MUSEUM

Exhibitions of contemporary crafts, American folk art, and traditional ethnic art from home and abroad are on display. ♦ Nominal admission; free Saturday, 10AM-noon and the first Wednesday of each month. Tu-Su. Bldg A. 775.0990 ♿

## YOUNG PERFORMERS THEATRE

This theater produces children's classics, adaptations, and new works, with children working alongside professional adult actors. The theater school offers classes for children preschool age and up. Parties are held after weekend shows (it's a perfect place for birthday celebrations). ♦ Bldg C, third floor. 346.5550 ♿

## THE MAGIC THEATRE

This experimental playhouse (founded in 1967) has achieved international recognition for its contribution to American theater. New plays by such writers as Pulitzer Prize–winner Sam Shepard, poet/playwright Michael McClure, and Pulitzer Prize nominee Rebecca Gilman have been produced here, as well as innovative works by emerging playwrights. The season runs from September through June. ♦ Bldg D. 441.8822. www.magictheatre.org ♿

## BAYFRONT THEATER

This theater hosts the best works of local and national theater groups, and it's the site of a variety of music and dance concerts. ♦ Bldg B. 441.5706 ♿

## COWELL THEATER

One of the Bay Area's most exciting performance spaces, its elegant design takes advantage of the architectural character of the more-than-75-year-old pier. Held here Saturday mornings is *West Coast Live,* San Francisco's radio show to the world. For tickets, call 664.9500. ♦ Pier 2. 441.3687 ♿

## MUSEO ITALO-AMERICANO

Dedicated to researching, preserving, and displaying the works of Italian and Italian-American artists, this museum also strives to foster the appreciation of Italian art and culture. ♦ Admission. W-Su. Bldg C. 673.2200 ♿

## GREENS

★★★$$$ San Francisco's finest vegetarian restaurant, under chef Annie Somerville, is affiliated with the S.F. Zen Center. Its opening in 1979 made vegetarianism stylish, and it's easy to see why. You won't find any ordinary vegetables-stirred-in-a-wok here, only tasty culinary creations so interesting you'll forget you're not eating meat. The soups, homemade breads, and salads can't be matched. The black-bean chili, herb-flavored potatoes baked in parchment, and Green Gulch salad with lettuces, Sonoma goat cheese, pecans, and oranges are all excellent. Large windows overlook the bay and the Golden Gate Bridge. Also visit the take-out counter if the weather puts you in the mood for an impromptu picnic. ♦ Californian/vegetarian ♦ M, dinner; Tu-Sa, lunch and dinner; Su, brunch. Reservations recommended. Bldg A. 771.6222. www.greensrestaurant.com ♿

## 6 SAN FRANCISCO GAS LIGHT COMPANY BUILDING

This fine late-19th-century building, which originally held storage tanks for the San Francisco Gas Light Company, has been converted into offices. Notice the corner turret and consistent brick and stone detailing throughout. ♦ 3600 Buchanan St (at North Point St)

## 7 A16

★★★$$ Follow the long, narrow passageway back to the dining room and you'll see why the restaurant was named for the Autostrada 16 that traverses the Naples region. The open kitchen in the dining room has two wood-burning ovens blazing away for crisp, tasty Neapolitan pizza. One

---

offering is topped with escarole, black olives, and anchovies; another with mushrooms, smoked provolone, and Pecorino. Entrées such as quail with prosciutto, braised pork with olives and chestnuts, and tuna with chicory and cannelini beans also simmer in the wood-burning ovens. For dessert, the ricotta sformatino with walnuts, dried fruit, and blood oranges is a quick trip to a Neapolitan bakery. Handsome large-scale paintings of Neapolitan characters—one of the sirens of the Bay of Naples; another of Princess Margherita, for whom pizza was created—grace the dining room walls. ◆ Italian ◆ W-F, lunch; daily, dinner. Reservations recommended. 2355 Chestnut St (between Scott and Divisadero Sts). 771.2216. www.a16sf.com &

## 8 BECHELLI'S COFFEE SHOP

★★$ Homemade desserts and more than 25 varieties of omelettes, along with traditional coffeehouse chow, are the draw at this charming little restaurant. The hamburger and thick french fries are a delight, and the all-American, house-made apple pie, cherry pie, and chocolate cake are classic. ◆ American ◆ Daily, breakfast and lunch. 2346 Chestnut St (between Scott and Divisadero Sts). 346.1801 &

## 9 JUDY'S CAFÉ

★★$ This country-cute café features a dozen omelettes with a twist: taco style, with ground chuck and salsa; Italian, with sausage, mushrooms, and marinara sauce; Russian, with black caviar and cream cheese; and Nordic, with smoked salmon. The Texas version is filled with chili, and the farm-style omelette comes with ham, onions, and home fries. ◆ American ◆ Daily, breakfast and lunch. 2268 Chestnut St (between Pierce and Scott Sts). 922.4588 &

## 10 E'ANGELO

★★$$ Ignore the meat dishes and try the really fine pasta in this bustling, family-run place. The fettuccine carbonara, tortellini papalina (stuffed with veal in a cream sauce with prosciutto and peas), and lasagna draw raves. ◆ Italian ◆ Tu-Su, dinner. No credit cards accepted. 2234 Chestnut St (between Pierce and Scott Sts). 567.6164 &

## 11 JOHNNY ROCKETS

★$ A nostalgic re-creation of a 1950s diner with countertop jukeboxes (they're cheap to play too), this fountain makes the best milk shake in town and is a good place for a late bite. ◆ American ◆ Daily, lunch and dinner. 2201 Chestnut St (at Pierce St). 931.6258. Also at Fisherman's Wharf, 81 Jefferson St (at Mason St). 693.9120; 1946 Fillmore St (at Pine St). 776.9878 &

**Andalé**
**TAQUERÍA**

## 12 ANDALÉ TAQUERÍA

★★$ Only in the Marina District would a taco place be as nattily put together as this architectural gem. A profusion of tables clutters an outdoor patio in front, all warmed by a corner fireplace. Inside, a copper pot of lacy palms, stippled walls, and wrought-iron fixtures gussy up what is really a fast-food restaurant. Traditional dinners feature chiles rellenos (stuffed chili pepper), tacos, and tamales, although the best choices here are the tacos and burritos filled with rotisserie-roasted chicken or mesquite-grilled beef. The agua fresca (freshly made fruit juices) and sangria are excellent. ◆ Mexican ◆ M-F, lunch and dinner; Sa, Su, breakfast, lunch, and dinner. 2150 Chestnut St (between Steiner and Pierce Sts). 749.0506 &

## 13 THE BODY SHOP

Satin-smooth celebrities, as well as regular folk, are rumored to stock up on body and bath products from this London-based firm. Try the peppermint foot lotion—it's heavenly on tired feet. ◆ Daily. 2106 Chestnut St (between Steiner and Pierce Sts). 202.0112 &

## 13 LUCCA DELICATESSEN

One of the city's many fabulous Italian delis, this place sells fresh cheese, cold cuts, pasta, salads, and frittatas, plus imported canned goods. The staff also makes savory sandwiches on delicious bread. ◆ Daily. 2120 Chestnut St (between Steiner and Pierce Sts). 921.7873 &

## 14 IZZY'S STEAKS & CHOPS

★★$$$ The memorabilia-covered walls and the dark wainscoting—topped with a shelf that's lined with every steak sauce and condiment ever made—add considerable charm to this first-rate steak house. Entrée accompaniments—potatoes, roasted carrots and onions, steamed broccoli, and especially creamed spinach—are excellent too. ◆ Steak/seafood ◆ Daily, dinner. Reservations recommended. 3349 Steiner St (between Lombard and Chestnut Sts). 563.0487 &

## 15 BARNEY'S GOURMET HAMBURGERS

★$ For a quick, cheap bite to eat, nothing beats this joint, which offers all kinds of burgers—from big and beefy to turkey to vegetarian, chicken sandwiches, and a variety of salads. ♦ **American** ♦ Daily, lunch and dinner. 3344 Steiner St (between Lombard and Chestnut Sts). 563.0307. Also at 4138 24th St (between Castro and Diamond Sts). 282.7770 &

## 15 BISTRO AIX

★★$$ Reserve a table on the heated patio and enjoy the skillfully executed dishes of this popular Mediterranean dining spot. All the appetizers prepared by Jonathan Beard are superb. Try the grilled pear salad with endive, radicchio, arugula, Gorgonzola, and walnuts; or the mussels steamed in white wine with shallots and parsley. Top choices among the entrées include seared, black-pepper–crusted ahi tuna, roasted half-chicken with tarragon butter, mashed potatoes and ratatouille, and curried eggplant risotto with caramelized carrots and balsamic vinegar reduction. Organic vegetables are used whenever possible. ♦ **Mediterranean** ♦ Tu-Su, dinner. Reservations recommended. 3340 Steiner St (between Lombard and Chestnut Sts). 202.0100 &

## 15 HAHN'S HIBACHI

★$ You'll find good Korean-style barbecued pork, chicken, and beef to go at this small take-out place, which also has a delivery service and five small tables for those who want to eat on the spot. ♦ **Korean/takeout** ♦ M-Sa, lunch; daily, dinner. 3318 Steiner St (between Lombard and Chestnut Sts). 931.6284. Also at 1710 Polk St (at Clay St). 776.1095; 1305 Castro (at 24th St). 642.8151

## 16 CHESTNUT STREET

Between Fillmore and Divisadero Streets, Chestnut becomes a main shopping artery for Marina residents. In marked contrast to trendy Union Street just a few blocks away, it is characterized by ordinary groceries, drugstores, small restaurants, and bars. However, several chichi shops and cafés have sneaked in recently, making this a street definitely worth a stroll. ♦ Between Fillmore and Divisadero Sts

## 17 LIVERPOOL LIL'S

★$ The cozy, publike atmosphere and reasonably priced food bring locals and enlisted folks from the Presidio back again and again. A hearty specialty for the hungry is the Manchester Wellington—ground round wrapped in ham and a flaky crust. This is a great place for a late supper. ♦ **English** ♦ Daily, lunch and dinner. Reservations recommended. 2942 Lyon St (at Lombard St). 921.6664 &

## 18 LA LUNA INN

$ If you are looking for an affordable inn on the motel strip, try this one. A high-tech update of the 1950s motor inns, all 62 rooms have flat-screen TVs, pillow-top mattresses, wireless Internet, and plenty of motor-inn kitsch. Rates include basic continental breakfast and—how wonderful—complimentary parking. ♦ 2599 Lombard St (at Broderick St). 346.4664. www.lalunainn.com &

## 19 HOTEL DEL SOL

$$ A lively remodel of a 1950s motor lodge, the hotel's exuberant colors, artwork, and furnishings bring the pizzazz of the California beach scene to the Marina District. The hotel's 57 rooms overlook a courtyard with a heated pool. Three of the suites have kitchenettes and the family suite features bunk beds. The reasonable rates include parking and a light continental breakfast. ♦ 3100 Webster St (at Lombard St). 921.5520, 877/433.5765. www.thehoteldelsol.com

## 20 MARINA INN

$$ Ideally located for family sightseeing, this attractive 40-room inn is decked out in an Early American theme. **Fort Mason** and Fisherman's Wharf are both nearby. Continental breakfast is included, although there is no restaurant. ♦ 3110 Octavia St (at Lombard St). 928.1000, 800/274.1420. www.marinainn.com &

## 21 L'AMOUR DANS LE FOUR

★★$$ When Blaise Bourdais and Adrienne Fair opened this tiny restaurant on busy Lombard Street, Francophiles quickly found out and began coming for escargots, duck confit roulé, and coquilles Saint Jacques. Nor does chef Laurent Bornier stray far from the Seine with entrées, offering beef tenderloin with mushroom cream sauce and salmon quenelles. For dessert, try the cheese platter or the apple tart. The owners know their clientele and always provide a selection of hard-to-find French wines by the glass. They offer a bargain three-course prix-fixe menu before 7PM. ♦ **French** ♦ Daily, dinner. Reservations recommended. 1602 Lombard St (at Gough St). 775.2134. www.amoursf.biz &

## 22 PLUMPJACK WINES

This wine store, owned by the **PlumpJack Cafe** gang, has quickly become one of the best in the city. There is a large selection of California vintages, including hard-to-find small-vineyard wines. The bottles are beautifully displayed and fairly priced. PlumpJack

---

**Restaurants/Clubs: Red** | **Hotels: Purple** | Shops: Orange | **Outdoors/Parks: Green** | Sights/Culture: Blue

Wines has an interesting web site with information on tasting notes, recipes, and food and wine pairings. ◆ Daily. 3201 Fillmore St (at Greenwich St). 346.9870. www.plumpjackwines.com &

### 23 BALBOA CAFE

★$$ What used to be a hamburger place in the back room of a bar has been turned into an adventure in American cooking. But the elongated, juicy "Balboa Burger," tucked into a baguette, is still around, and is the one memorable item on the frequently changing menu. Run by the owners of **PlumpJack Cafe,** the place is usually filled with socialites by day and lovelorn singles in the evening. ◆ Californian ◆ Daily, lunch and dinner; Sa, Su, brunch. 3199 Fillmore St (at Greenwich St). 921.3944. www.balboacafe.com &

### 24 MATRIXFILLMORE

In 1965 Marty Balin chose this historic location to play with his new band, Jefferson Airplane. Until 1972 famous bands of the "Summer of Love" rocked the place. The cool industrial interior suits today's hip dance tribe. Local bands play every Tuesday, and salsa music is heard every Wednesday. ◆ Daily, 5:30PM-2AM. 3138 Fillmore St (near Greenwich St). 563.4180. www.plumpjack.com &

### 25 PLUMPJACK CAFE

★★$$$ An overpriced but pleasant neighborhood restaurant and a good place to enjoy chef James Syhabout's appetizers, including bruschetta topped with roasted beets, baby lettuces, goat cheese, and roasted garlic; gravlax with blini on the side; and a salad made from lettuce, Gorgonzola, beets, and walnuts. Entrées range from $19 to $34. ◆ Californian ◆ Daily, dinner. 3127 Fillmore St (between Filbert and Greenwich Sts). 563.4755. www.plumpjackcafe.com &

### 26 LA CANASTA

★★★$ The only seating is on a bench outside, but the food is so tasty that fans don't mind sitting there and trying to balance their *chalupas* (tortillas layered with beans, meat, cheese, and guacamole), burritos, and tamales—and inevitably splattering their clothes. The burritos are outstanding. ◆ Mexican/takeout ◆ Daily, lunch and dinner. 2219 Filbert St (at Fillmore St). 921.3003. Also at 3006 Buchanan St (between Union and Filbert Sts). 474.2627 &

### 27 ROSE'S CAFE

★★★$$ With Venetian glass chandeliers and glazed-tile bread ovens, this bakery–café serves rustic Italian fare. For dinner try the vegetable pastas *en papillote* or pan-roasted mussels, and for lunch the delicious stuffed *focaccia,* plump round rolls, and salads. Whenever the sun shines, tables spill out onto the sidewalk where people congregate and while away the afternoon in neighborly conversation, like any other day in Venice. Check out **Terzo** (3011 Steiner St, 441.3200), their sister restaurant across the street. ◆ Italian ◆ Daily, breakfast, lunch, and dinner. 2298 Union St (at Steiner St). 775.2200. www.rosescafesf.com &

### 28 UNION STREET INN

$$$ The elegance of a 19th-century Edwardian home is combined with personal attention typical of a fine European pensione. This six-room inn has a small but exquisite garden where breakfast, tea, and coffee are served, plus a parlor well stocked with books and magazines. The carriage house on the far side of the garden has a suite with a Jacuzzi. Other rooms have private vanities, but share baths. ◆ 2229 Union St (between Fillmore and Steiner Sts). 346.0424. www.unionstreetinn.com

### 29 BETELNUT

★★★$$ Named for a seed found only in Asia, this comfortable yet exotic restaurant is so popular it's nearly impossible to get a reservation! Chef Alexander Ong's pan-Asian menu includes delicious Singapore chili crab, spicy coconut chicken from Thailand, and a wonderful appetizer of sun-dried anchovies, peanuts, and chili from Taipei. All the food goes well with the Asian and American brews on tap and by the bottle. ◆ Pan-Asian ◆ Daily, lunch and dinner. Reservations recommended. 2030 Union St (at Buchanan St). 929.8855. www.betelnutrestaurant.com &

### 29 ORIGINAL COW HOLLOW FARMHOUSE

Marked by a big palm tree in front, this Victorian former farmhouse contains a complex of shops. In the rear is what was once the barn (the hayloft is still obvious); it's now a gallery. ◆ 2040 Union St (between Buchanan and Webster Sts)

### 30 BLUE LIGHT CAFE

★★$$ This café offers Cajun cuisine in a modern interior gussied up with galvanized-metal walls and glass panels etched with bayou scenes. The place is invariably crowded with young singles. The kitchen turns out a hearty, spicy meat loaf with mashed potatoes, a commendable pot roast, and tasty barbecued ribs. ◆ Cajun ◆ Daily, dinner. 1979 Union St (between Laguna and Buchanan Sts). 922.5510 &

### 31 PERRY'S

★$$ Perry Butler escaped from Manhattan back in 1969, bringing with him the idea for this typical Upper East Side New York saloon. Originally popular as a singles' place, it has retained a fiercely loyal clientele over the years, but now the old regulars bring their kids. A smattering of singles can still be found at the traditional bar, which is reminiscent of the 1970s. Offerings include veal chops, steaks, calves' liver, ahi tuna, and such bar favorites as chicken fajitas, quesadillas, and excellent burgers and fries. ◆ American ◆ Daily, breakfast, lunch, and dinner. 1944 Union St (between Laguna and Buchanan Sts). 922.9022. Also at 185 Sutter St (between Montgomery and Kearny Sts). 989.6895 ♿

### 32 UNION STREET

In the 19th century this district was known as Cow Hollow because it was used as grazing land for the city's dairy cows. Since the 1950s the six-block stretch from Gough to Steiner Streets has undergone a dramatic metamorphosis, from neighborhood stores to chic shops and swinging bars. Its streets are lined with cleverly remodeled Victorian houses transformed into boutiques, art galleries, and cafés. Not all nearby residents are happy with the change, however; crowds can make parking difficult. (There is a parking garage at Buchanan and Union Streets, and buses run frequently along here.) ◆ Between Gough and Steiner Sts

### 32 BUS STOP

In business since 1900, this plain neighborhood bar provides an inkling of what the street was like before it was gentrified. The place draws a lot of local sports fans who just want an honest drink without having to come up with clever, sociable conversation. ◆ Daily. 1901 Union St (at Laguna St). 567.6905

### 32 JOJI'S HOUSE OF TERIYAKI

★$ Established in 1972, this unpretentious 20-seat restaurant has a faithful following of local people who like the low prices, French toast, and tasty teriyaki dishes. It's probably the best food value in the area. ◆ Japanese/American ◆ Daily, breakfast, lunch, and dinner. 1919 Union St (between Laguna and Buchanan Sts). 563.7808 ♿

### 33 OCTAGON HOUSE

Home of the National Society of Colonial Dames, this beautifully preserved 19th-century house is now a museum, built on the strength of the once popular belief that eight-sided houses were lucky. It has been moved

**Octagon House**

across the street from its original location and the lower-floor plan has been changed, but the upper floor displays the original layout, with square bedrooms on the major axes and bathrooms and service areas in the remaining triangular spaces. ◆ Admission. Second Su, second and fourth Th of every month; closed in January. 2645 Gough St (at Union St). 441.7512 ♿

### 33 PANE E VINO

★★★$$ This spot is so popular that even those with reservations may have to wait to be seated, but the food is worth it. All the pastas are superb, and if it's on the menu, try the braised rabbit (or any other long-simmered meat), the whole roasted fish, or daily specials from the rotisserie. Curbside delivery available on take-home orders. ◆ Italian ◆ M-Sa, lunch and dinner; Su, dinner. Reservations recommended. 1715 Union St (at Gough St). 346.2111 ♿

### 34 MUDPIE

Shop here for casual upscale clothing for children and newborns, including lots of European designer wear for the budding fashion-conscious. ◆ Daily. 1694 Union St (at Gough St). 771.9262 ♿

### 35 CASEBOLT HOUSE

Built in the mid-1860s, this noteworthy Italianate house is one of the oldest in Pacific Heights. It's also a private residence. ◆ 2727 Pierce St (between Vallejo and Green Sts)

### 36 PACIFIC HEIGHTS MANSIONS

Some of the finest Victorian mansions grace the tree-lined streets that run along the crest of the hill, offering spectacular views north across the bay and to Golden Gate Bridge. The 1700 to 2900 blocks of Broadway have houses in Italianate, Stick, Georgian, Queen Anne, and Dutch Colonial styles. Look for Queen Anne houses on the 1600 to 2900 blocks of Vallejo Street, and mansions on

# Lights, Camera, Action: SF On-Screen

San Francisco has always been a director's dream. If you count the early silent days, when the city was a major filmmaking center, literally hundreds of movies have been filmed here. What follows is a selective roster of important films shot entirely (or partially) in this city by the bay.

*The Barbary Coast* (1935) Howard Hawks's brawling, period adventure film stars Edward G. Robinson and Miriam Hopkins.

*Basic Instinct* (1992) Michael Douglas and Sharon Stone tangle in a tense thriller. Obsessed with cracking the case, tough but vulnerable Douglas descends into San Francisco's forbidden underground, where he finds within himself an instinct more basic even than that for survival.

*The Birdman of Alcatraz* (1962) Burt Lancaster portrayed the island prison's famous inmate as a mild-mannered and humane individual, winning an Academy Award for best actor.

*Bullitt* (1968) Cars go flying in the definitive San Francisco chase sequence. Steve McQueen plays a police detective; Peter Yates directs.

*The Conversation* (1974) Gene Hackman stars in Francis Ford Coppola's masterpiece of paranoia, probably the director's best film.

*Dark Passage* (1947) Humphrey Bogart and Lauren Bacall court and spark in an atmospheric thriller set in the foggiest Frisco you ever saw.

*Days of Wine and Roses* (1962) Under Blake Edwards's direction, Jack Lemmon and Lee Remick give memorable performances as they battle with the bottle.

*Dirty Harry* (1971) This action masterpiece from director Don Siegel stars Clint Eastwood as mean Inspector Callahan. Siegel's brilliant visuals show San Francisco to fine advantage.

*Fearless* (1993) Jeff Bridges plays a San Francisco architect who is more wildly alive and taking more risks than ever since he stared death in the face and discovered he was unafraid.

*48 Hours* (1982) Cop Nick Nolte and prisoner Eddie Murphy team up to solve a crime, incidentally wreaking havoc with a **Muni** bus and provoking much violence.

*Freebie and the Bean* (1973) This comic cops-and-robbers movie stars James Caan and Alan Arkin, plus flying cars—all directed by Richard Rush.

*Golden Gate* (1994) Joan Chen and Matt Dillon star in this yarn about a 1950s FBI agent fighting the "Red menace" in San Francisco's **Chinatown.**

*Guess Who's Coming to Dinner* (1967) This socially conscious interracial comedy was directed by Stanley Kramer, with Spencer Tracy, Sidney Poitier, and Katharine Hepburn. Katharine won an Oscar.

*Harold and Maude* (1972) A swinging septuagenarian (Ruth Gordon) and suicidal youngster (Bud Cort) fall in love in Hal Ashby's popular black comedy.

*Invasion of the Body Snatchers* (1978) Bay Area filmmaker Philip Kaufman concocted this stylish remake of Don Siegel's scary original.

*I Remember Mama* (1948) Irene Dunne gives a memorable performance in this sentimental favorite.

*The Joy Luck Club* (1993) This uplifting story is set in San Francisco, where four remarkable lifelong

Divisadero and Jackson Streets and Clay Street at Steiner Street. At **2776 Broadway** is a very contemporary home dramatically different from its neighbors; it was the first custom-designed solar home in San Francisco. All are private residences. ♦ Bounded by Fillmore and Steiner Sts, and Pacific Ave and Broadway

## 36 Apartment Towers

Pacific Heights has many splendid towers in many different styles. Most of the apartments, built in the 1920s, have elaborate marble-faced entrance lobbies complete with doormen. The penthouses create interesting silhouettes along the skyline. ♦ Broadway

(between Fillmore and Steiner Sts). Also at Washington and Steiner Sts

## 37 Convent of the Sacred Heart

The former **Flood Mansion,** built in the Spanish Renaissance style by **Bliss & Faville** in 1916, is now an exclusive private school for girls. The building may be rented for private functions. ♦ 2222 Broadway (between Webster and Fillmore Sts). 563.2900 ♿

## 38 2000 Broadway

**Backen, Arrigoni & Ross**'s 1973 design is a modern version of the great apartment towers built along Broadway during the 1920s. This is a private residence. ♦ At Buchanan St

friends paint a tapestry of startling events that have shaped their lives.

**The Lady from Shanghai** (1949) See Orson Welles and Rita Hayworth stroll through **Steinhart Aquarium**! This pyrotechnic thriller was mostly shot in studios, but sharp-eyed viewers will spot several fascinating location sequences.

**Magnum Force** (1973) This *Dirty Harry* sequel feels the loss of director Siegel, but has amusing moments.

**The Maltese Falcon** (1941) So popular is this P.I. classic that a Dashiell Hammett walking tour has been put together following Humphrey Bogart's footsteps. For information, call 707/939.1214.

**Mrs. Doubtfire** (1993) Robin Williams is no ordinary father as he disguises himself, hires on as a nanny in his ex-wife's home so he can spend more time with his children, and creates a new life with his family.

**Murder in the First** (1994) Christian Slater, as a prisoner sentenced to life in the dungeons of **Alcatraz** for stealing $5 for his starving sister, launches an attack on San Francisco attorneys.

**Out of the Past** (1947) Arguably the greatest film noir ever made, this features Robert Mitchum as a cynical detective and Jane Greer as the lethally attractive woman who proves his cynicism inadequate.

**Pacific Heights** (1990) Melanie Griffith, Matthew Modine, and Michael Keaton star in this powerful psychological thriller about two young San Francisco homeowners battling a pathological tenant.

**Pal Joey** (1957) This cleaned-up screen version of Rodgers and Hart's great musical features Frank Sinatra and Kim Novak.

**Petulia** (1968) Julie Christie, George C. Scott, and Shirley Knight star in Richard Lester's sad, moving love story about life in the 1960s. It's highly regarded by critics.

**The Presidio** (1988) Sean Connery and Mark Harmon team up to solve a murder at **The Presidio** military compound.

**The Princess Diaries** (2001) Filmed in **Russian Hill**. A gangly teenager (Anne Hathaway) discovers she is the only surviving member of a European royal family. Her grandmother (Julie Andrews) oversees Anne's catastrophe-ridden transformation into a princess.

**The Rock** (1996) Sean Connery stars in this thrilling rescue at Alcatraz. The penthouse at the **Fairmont** is also in the movie.

**San Francisco** (1936) Clark Gable, Jeanette MacDonald, and Spencer Tracy find plenty of adventure in turn-of-the-century San Francisco. The Great Quake provides a shattering climax and a terrific special-effects scene.

**Star Trek IV** (1986) William Shatner, Leonard Nimoy, and the *Enterprise* crew drop into **Golden Gate Park** in the 1980s. There are fantastic shots of 23rd-century San Francisco.

**Vertigo** (1958) James Stewart stars as an obsessed lover trying to remake Kim Novak into the dead Madeleine in this Hitchcock classic. It was shot at some of the city's most popular locales.

**A View to a Kill** (1985) Roger Moore, in his last James Bond role, must save **Silicon Valley** from destruction by villain Christopher Walken.

## 39 ROOS HOUSE

This 1909 structure by **Bernard Maybeck** is a highly personalized example of English Tudor with typical Maybeck window and eaves detailing. It is a private residence. ♦ 3500 Jackson St (between Locust and Spruce Sts)

## 40 3200 BLOCK OF PACIFIC AVENUE

One of the most unusual groups of houses in the city, this complex is located on a wedge-shaped lot that steps downhill. The entire block is clad in brown shingles and contains some of the city's best turn-of-the-century domestic architecture. Each house retains its own special identity with distinct window or doorway detailing while maintaining the unity of the entire block. **Nos. 3203** and **3277** are by **Willis Polk; No. 3233** is by **Bernard Maybeck;** and **Nos. 3232** and **3234** are by **Ernest Coxhead. No. 3232** is of particular interest for its fine doorways and bizarre balcony. All of the homes are private residences. ♦ Between Presidio Ave and Walnut St

Restaurants/Clubs: Red | Hotels: Purple | Shops: Orange | Outdoors/Parks: Green | Sights/Culture: Blue

# Union Street Shopping

## GOUGH STREET

*holistic health* **Chiromedica**
*monogramming/giftware* **Promotions Store**
**Union French Cleaners**
*clothing* **Canyon Beachwear**
*bridal accessories* **Forget-Me-Knots**
*flowers* **Mandy Scott**
*pet store* **Bella & Daisy's**
**Union Street Apothecary**
*Italian clothing* **Porto**
*housewares* **Mömen Futon**
**Chic Nails Salon**
*antique furniture* **Ever Arts**
**Psychic Tarot Reading**
*shoes/clothing* **Dantone**

**Octagon House**
**Pane e Vino** *Italian restaurant*
**Thread Lounge** *designer samples*
**Brownie's** *tanning/fitness*
**T. C. Jeweler** *jewelry*
**Moxa** *handbags*
**Cow Hollow Shoe Repair**
**Sean's** *menswear*
**Union Street Chiropractic**
**Marina Dental Care**
**Wonders of Tibet** *gifts*
**Jean Marie** *childrenswear*
**Maharishi Ayurvedic** *health spa*
**Skipjack** *Japanese restaurant*
**Bayside** *sports bar/restaurant*
**Twenty-one Tango** *clothing*

## OCTAVIA STREET

**Wolf Camera Photo Lab**
*salon* **The Red Chair**
*mens-/womenswear* **Croll Sport**
*womenswear* **CaraMia**
*hair salon* **Salon di Moda**
*womenswear* **Girlfriends**
*Asian housewares* **City Joon's**
*restaurant* **Caffè Union**
*jewelry* **Silver Moon**
*wine cafè* **Ottinista**
*womenswear* **Bryan Lee**
*soap/perfume* **L'Occitane**
*lingerie* **Carol Doda's**
*clothing* **Ambiance**
*clothing* **LF**
**David Clay Jewelers**
**Serge Matt Antiques**
*art classes* **Susan Miller Gallery**
*greeting cards* **Papyrus**
*jewelry* **Stuart Moore**

**UNION STREET**

**Fenzi Uomo** *menswear*
**B & A Estate** *jewelry*
**Campannina** *Italian restaurant*
**Mingle** *clothing*
**BCBG Maxazria** *womenswear*
**The Blue Jean Bar** *clothing*
**Mac** *cosmetics*
**Pavillon de Paris** *crystal/glass*
**Hourian Galleries** *art*
**Bianca Luna** *clothing*
**Luisa's** *Italian restaurant*
**El** *Eurasian interiors*
**Jest Jewels** *jewelry/gifts*
**Pasta Pomodoro** *Italian restaurant*
**Indulge Yourself** *eyewear*
**Dava Dava** *hair salon*
**The Enchanted Crystal** *gifts*
**Starbucks Coffee**

## LAGUNA STREET

**Wells Fargo Bank**
*garage* **Public Parking**
*jewelry* **Simayof**
*American restaurant/bar* **Perry's**
*eyewear* **bjorn**
*womenswear* **PeLuche**
**Artisans Picture Framing**
*clothing* **Lucy**
*restaurant* **Extreme Pizza**
*salon* **Moxi**
*bar* **Bar None**
*teenwear* **Entrance**
*childrenswear* **Thursday's Child**
*beauty/therapy center* **Rezvan**
*juice bar* **Jamba Juice**

**Bus Stop** *bar*
**Union St. Goldsmith**
**La Boulange** *cafè*
**Joji's** *Japanese/American restaurant*
**Helene René** *hair salon*
**Glamour** *jewelry*
**John Wheatman Interior Design**
**Dreamy Angels Boutique** *womenswear*
**Puffins** *jewelry*
**Beleza** *children's clothing*
**Patronik Designs** *jewelry*
**Trendy Moda** *clothing*

## CHARLTON COURT

**John Atencio** *jewelry*
**Kozo** *handmade paper*
**Sporting Company** *clothing*
**Vie Vie** *clothing*
**Blue Light Café** *Cajun restaurant*
**Lululemon Athletica** *athletic clothing*
**Bank of America**

*Map continues on next page*

## BUCHANAN STREET

| | |
|---|---|
| Asian restaurant **Betelnut** | **Comerica Bank** |
| jewelry **Marcello** | |
| pottery studio **Color Me Mine** | **Shaw Shoes** women's shoes |
| clothing **Red Lantern** | **Union Street Plaza** shops |
| restaurant **Home** | **Firuzé** womenswear |
| shops **Victorian Court** | **Samsara** Tibetan goods |
| gifts **Tate Kennedy** | **The Ocularium** optician |
| clothing **Fog City Leather** | **Sunhee Moon** womenswear |
| bridal **Jinza Boutique** | **Z Gallerie** gifts/posters |
| jewelry **Max Kyle** | **Sephora** cosmetics |
| Japanese fashions **UKO** | **Hermes** acupuncture |
| comic books/memorabilia **Collector's Cave** | |
| shoes **Kenneth Cole** | |
| shoes **Nine West** | |
| clothing **Armani Exchange** | **Bebe** womenswear |

## WEBSTER STREET

| | |
|---|---|
| eyewear **See** | **Gallery of Jewels** |
| soap, cosmetics **Lush** | **Primadona** skin care |
| chocolates **Cocoa Bella** | **Hill & Co.** real estate |
| **Wine Styles** | **Kenneth Wingard** housewares |
| womenswear **Vivo** | **Mimi's** clothing |
| alterations **Reid's** | **Cingular** cell phone store |
| restaurant **La Cucina** | **ATYS** gifts |
| Southwestern restaurant **Left at Albuquerque** | **Tampico** womenswear |
| | **Nail Today** nail salon |
| accessories **Excessorize** | **Berniece** salon |
| upholstery **Van Galen** | **Lorenzini** menswear |
| furnishings **Z Gallerie** | **Persimma** womenswear |
| **Secret Flower Garden** | **Crepes a go-go** restaurant |
| stationery **Union Street Papery** | **Sumbody** bath products |
| | **Dianne's Old & New Estates Jewelry** |
| crafts **Twig** | **Three Bags Full** womenswear |
| clothing **American Apparel** | **Nice Cuts** hair salon |
| rugs **Krimsa** | **Eyes in Disguise** optician |
| liquor **Michaelis** | **Coffee Roastery** coffee house |

## FILLMORE STREET

| | |
|---|---|
| **Prudential** | **The Humidor** gourmet cigars |
| florist **The Bud Stop** | **Images For Hair** hair salon |
| womenswear **Capezio** | **Le Bouquet** florist |
| antiqued recycled goods **Past Perfect** | **Nails 2001** nail salon |
| day spa **Novella** | **City Pantry** market |
| clothing **Union B** | **Cafe Chez Mama** Italian restaurant |
| clothing **Workshop** | **Union Street Inn** hotel |
| children's clothing **Wee Scotty** | **D'Lynne's** dancewear |
| nail salon **Two Sisters** | **Light Me Up** lighting |
| homewear **Modica** | |
| kids/maternity **Minis** | **Mona Lisa** womenswear |
| **Sun Days Tanning Salon** | **Jeanie's Dream** hair salon |
| skincare/manicures **Bamboo** | **Marina Submarine** deli |
| Italian restaurant **Rose's Café** | |

(center vertical label: UNION STREET)

## STEINER STREET

## 41 HOTEL DRISCO

$$ This San Francisco landmark, now a Joie de Vivre property, opened in 1903 has hosted many distinguished guests—including Presidents Eisenhower, Truman, and Nixon—because of its discreet ambience and unique location (it was Pacific Heights's only hotel for decades). Some of the 48 elegant rooms have spectacular views, and the English Victorian interiors favor the light colors of the bay.

There's no restaurant, but continental breakfast is included in the room rate. ♦ 2901 Pacific Ave (at Broderick St). 346.2880, 800/634.7277. www.hoteldrisco.com

## 42 FILLMORE STREET

Cosmopolitan upper Fillmore Street has attracted many of the city's talented chefs, designers, and retailers. As you explore this unique shopping district, your options range from trendy boutiques to resale shops and restaurants that feature the home-style cooking of Tokyo, Tuscany, or Thailand. Stately homes from a bygone era line the adjacent streets. Especially beautiful is the grand Victorian neighborhood that escaped the great fire that leveled much of San Francisco 100 years ago. Wander the streets around **Lafayette Park** to the east and **Alta Plaza Park** to the west. The stately Italianate and Queen Anne homes were built between 1875 and 1895 for affluent businessmen and civic leaders. The working class bought the Victorian row houses, originally mass-produced and placed on tiny 25-by-100-foot lots. They now sell for more than $1 million.

## 42 JUICY NEWS

This newsstand carries fashion magazines and newspapers. ♦ Daily. 2453 Fillmore St (at Jackson St). 441.3051 &

## JACKSON FILLMORE

## 43 JACKSON FILLMORE TRATTORIA

★★★$$ There's almost always a wait, especially for tables; many customers choose to sit at the diner-style counter overlooking the antipasto selections. Few appetizers are better than the grilled Portobello mushrooms: Roughly the size of a saucer, they are sliced, drizzled with olive oil, sprinkled with herbs and garlic, and arranged on a bed of arugula. The gnocchi, if on the menu, are as light as a feather and worth the wait. Sure bets among the entrées are such braised dishes as woodsman-style chicken with sausage, mushrooms, and beans. ♦ Italian ♦ Daily, dinner. Reservations required for three or more. 2506 Fillmore St (between Jackson St and Pacific Ave). 346.5288

## 44 JACKSON COURT

$$ On a quiet residential street, Jackson Court is an elegant three-story brownstone mansion with antiques and tasteful contemporary furniture. It's a surprising bargain for those who love the quiet atmosphere of a private home. Each of the 10 rooms has a private bath, and the rate includes breakfast in the dining room and afternoon refreshments in the front parlor. ♦ 2190 Jackson St (at Buchanan St). 929.7670. www.jacksoncourt.com

## 45 WHITTIER MANSION

This red-brown sandstone mansion was completed in 1896 for William Whittier, a prosperous paint manufacturer. It's a private residence. ♦ 2090 Jackson St (at Laguna St)

## 46 3778 WASHINGTON STREET

A mixture of Bay Area and International styles, this house was built in 1952 by **Eric Mendelsohn,** whose trademark details such as the rounded corner bay and the porthole windows characterize this private residence. ♦ At Maple St

## 47 SWEDENBORGIAN CHURCH

**Arthur Page Brown** built this church in 1884, and **Bernard Maybeck** and **A.C. Sweinfurth,** who were in Brown's office, worked on the designs, as you can see by the beautiful Craftsman-style detailing. The church is adjacent to a fine walled garden that is raised up above the surrounding street and contains trees, flowers, and shrubs from every continent on earth. Inside the church, where services are still held, is a large fireplace, as well as stained-glass windows by Bruce Porter and furniture by Gustav Stickley. ♦ 2107 Lyon St (at Washington St)

## 48 ALTA PLAZA PARK

One of a series of urban parks laid out when Pacific Heights was first developed, this green space is set on the top of the hill with terraces stepping down to Clay Street. The park offers superb views south and east to **Saint Mary's Cathedral** and the **Civic Center.** Around it is an interesting mixture of mansions, apartment towers, and false-front Italianate row houses. ♦ Bounded by Steiner and Scott Sts, and Clay and Jackson Sts

## 49 REPEAT PERFORMANCE RESALE SHOP

This thrift shop is run by volunteers, with proceeds benefiting the **San Francisco Symphony.** There's often a good supply of evening wear. ♦ M-Sa. 2436 Fillmore St (between Washington and Jackson Sts). 563.3123 &

## 49 YOUNTVILLE—CLOTHES FOR CHILDREN

Look here for sophisticated sportswear for children. ◆ Daily. 2416 Fillmore St (at Washington St). 922.5050 &

## 50 SPRECKELS MANSION

Called the Parthenon of the West, this is the grandest home in San Francisco. Architect **George Applegarth** built the limestone mansion in 1913 for German immigrant Claus Spreckels, a sugar czar in the Gold Rush era. Years later, moviegoers saw the mansion as the nightclub **Chez Joey** in the 1957 film *Pal Joey*, and again in the 1969 movie *The Eye of the Cat*. Writer Danielle Steel purchased the mansion in 1990, reportedly for $8 million. The garden was sold separately. ◆ 2080 Washington St (between Gough and Octavia Sts)

## 51 HAAS-LILIENTHAL HOUSE

One of the most grandiose Stick-style houses in the city, this 1886 confection is a great Romantic pile of forms with elaborate wooden gables and a splendid Queen Anne–style circular corner tower. Inside, it has a series of finely preserved Victorian rooms complete with authentic period furniture. Walking tours of surviving pre–World War I mansions in Pacific Heights take place every Sunday, sponsored by the **Foundation for San Francisco's Architectural Heritage.** The group departs from here at 12:30PM; call 441.3000 for details. Docent-led tours of the house are given on Wednesday and Sunday. It may also be rented for private functions (call 441.3011). ◆ Admission. W, Su. 2007 Franklin St (between Washington and Jackson Sts). 441.3004. www.sfheritage.org

## 52 LEM HOUSE

**Daniel Solomon & Associates** built this stucco-clad row house with an imposing Palladian window and rusticated base in 1986. It is a private residence. ◆ Cherry St (between Sacramento and Clay Sts)

## 53 SACRAMENTO STREET

A mixture of auto garages, movie theaters, ice cream parlors, gift and antiques shops, boutiques, and a store that is open only two months each year to present an incredible selection of Christmas ornaments are located along this less overwhelming, less touristy version of Union Street. ◆ Between Baker and Spruce Sts

## 53 DOTTIE DOOLITTLE

If you've got plenty of money to spend on little clotheshounds, you'll like these fine kids' clothes, mainly European imports. ◆ M-Sa; daily in December. 3680 Sacramento St (between Locust and Spruce Sts). 563.3244 &

## 54 BATH SENSE

This shop stocks all kinds of soothing, fragrant products for bath and body, including gift items created by local artists. ◆ M-Sa. 3600 Sacramento St (at Locust St). 567.2638

## 55 BEYOND EXPECTATIONS

★★★$ This is everything a café should be. The food, served cafeteria-style, is excellent, with most of it made on the premises (the morning cheese pie with blueberries is to die for). The coffee is terrific, as are the sandwiches, fluffy quiches, fresh salads, soups, and homemade baked goods. There are periodicals for reading, and a view of a pretty little garden from the back dining area. ◆ American ◆ M-Sa, breakfast and lunch. 3613 Sacramento St (between Locust and Spruce Sts). 567.8640 &

## 56 JONATHAN-KAYE BY COUNTRY LIVING

Cluttered and dedicated to quality, this shop offers a charming selection of children's furnishings and toys. ◆ Daily. 3548 Sacramento St (between Laurel and Locust Sts). 563.0773. www.jonathankaye.com &

## 57 THE DESIGNER CONSIGNER

Owners Brenda Alessandria and Cheryl Lund receive new merchandise daily, they say, from the city's best-dressed women. Browse the racks for bargains on Chanel, Gucci, Hermès, and Versace womenswear. ◆ Daily. 3525 Sacramento St (between Laurel and Locust Sts). 440.8664

## 58 THE URBAN PET

Everything from basic collars to Burberry raincoats for the pampered dog, cat, or bird is on display at this well-stocked shop. ◆ M-Sa. 3429 Sacramento St (between Walnut and Laurel Sts). 673.7708 &

## 59 ELAINE MAGNIN NEEDLEPOINT

All the needlework accoutrements are sold here, including patterns for pillows that carry the words "Living Well Is the Best Revenge."

---

**Restaurants/Clubs: Red | Hotels: Purple | Shops: Orange | Outdoors/Parks: Green | Sights/Culture: Blue**

# Fillmore Street Shopping

## JACKSON STREET

Tully's Coffee Company
newsstand/juice bar **Juicy News**
**UPS Store**
**Pacific Heights Cleaners**
**L.P. Nail Care**



restaurant **Chouquet's**

**Mayflower Market** grocery store
**Fillmore Estate** antique jewelry
**S.F. Boot and Shoe Repair**
**Posh** hair salon
**Bond Cleaners**
**Repeat Performance** thrift shop
**Heidi Says** womenswear
**Eric Trabert** gallery
**GJ Mureta's Antiques**
**Yountville-Clothes for Children**
**Twenty Four Twelve** hair salon
**Erica Tanov** clothing
**Margaret O'Leary** womenswear

## WASHINGTON STREET

**Pets Unlimited**



restaurant **Crepevine**

**Kiehl's** beauty products
**Gimme** shoes
**Cottage Industry** exotic imports
**Aneu** skincare/laser clinic
**Bank of America**
**Supercuts** haircutters
**Nest** antiques

## CLAY STREET

European womenswear **Blù**
**Clay Theater**
day spa **Relax Now**
**diPietro Todd Salon**
womenswear **Jim-Elle**
Japanese restaurant **Ten-Ichi**
clothing **Cielo**
housewares **Simon Pearce**
**Noah's Bagels**
**Pacific Heights Travel Service**
Provence body products **L'Occitane**
**The Coffee Bean & Tea Leaf**

**Fillmore Grill** restaurant
**Seconds To Go** thrift shop
**Via Veneto** Italian restaurant
**Aumakua** handmade gifts/collectibles


**Next-to-New Shop** thrift shop
**Starbucks Coffee**
**Eileen Fisher** womenswear
**La Mediterranée** Lebanese restaurant
**Olivers & Co.** specialty food
**D&M Liquors**

*FILLMORE STREET*

## SACRAMENTO STREET

**Pete's Coffee & Tea**
**Browser Books**
housewares/furniture **Shabby Chic**
housewares **Jonathan Adler**
Italian deli/restaurant **VIVANDE Porta Via**
emporium **Bittersweet Chocolate Café**
clothing **Jigsaw**
gifts **Winterbranch Gallery**
beauty products **BeneFit**
**Gallery of Jewels**
greeting cards **Papyrus**
**Dino's Pizza**

**Marc Jacobs** clothing
**Jurlique** skincare
**In Water** florist
**Jet Mail** mail service
**Pure Beauty Salon**
**Crosswalk** shoes
**Metro 200** womenswear

**Fresca** Peruvian restaurant

**Wells Fargo Bank**

## CALIFORNIA STREET

fast food restaurant **La Salsa**
clothing **Her**
Cajun/Creole restaurant **Elite Cafe**
health/vitamins **Vitamin Express**
café, bakery **La Boulange**
womenswear **Mio**
thrift shop **Victorian House**
womenswear **Betsey Johnson**
lingerie **My Boudoir**
**Walter Adams Gallery**
ice cream **Tango Gelato**
cosmetics **MAC**
Thai restaurant **2001 Thai Stick**

**Royal Ground** coffee
**Wash 'n Royal** laundromat
**GNC Vitamins**
**Mrs. Dewson's Hats**
**10 International Orange** yoga studio/day spa
**Smith & Hawken** garden supplies

**Harry's Bar** restaurant
**The Grove** restaurant
**Paolo** shoes

## PINE STREET

Map continues on next page

| | |
|---|---|
| *cosmetics* **Shu uemura** | **Johnny Rockets** *American restaurant* |
| *craft supplies* **Paper Source** | **Starlet** *womenswear* |
| *Japanese restaurant* **Osaka** | **Flicka** *clothing* |
| **Hydra Soaps** | **Fillmore Glass and Hardware** |
| *bistro* **Florio** | **Aveda** *skincare/body products* |

**WILMOT STREET**

| | |
|---|---|
| *furniture* **Design Within Reach** | **Toraya's** *sushi* |
| *mediterranean* **Chez Nous** | **Linco & Co.** *jewelry* |
| **Perfect Cleaners** | **Baxter Hull** *outdoor clothing and gear* |
| *optician* **Invision** | **Maruya Sushi** |
| *furniture/housewares* **Zinc Details** | **Narumi Antiques** |
| *used clothing* **Crossroads Trading Company** | **Beads & Clasps Craftshop** |
| | **Vogue Nails** |

*(FILLMORE STREET)*

**BUSH STREET**

| | |
|---|---|
| **Walgreens** | **Patisserie Delange** *bakery* |
| **Pacific Heights Optical** | **Fillmore Florist** |
| *womenswear* **Sunhee Moon** | **Trio Cafe** |
| *bedding* **Duxiana** | **Lotte Beauty Salon** |
| *real estate* **Keynote Properties** | **Neja** *cosmetics* |
| | **J.T.** *nails* |
| | **Barry for Pets** |
| | **Muse Ten** *handbags* |
| | **Pizza Inferno** |

**SUTTER STREET**

Lessons are available too. ♦ Daily. 3310 Sacramento St (between Presidio Ave and Walnut St). 931.3063. www.elainemagnin.com &

## 60 KOUCHAK'S RUGS OF YESTERDAY

This shop carries imported handicraft and decorative items, and specializes in Persian tribal rugs. ♦ Daily. 3369 Sacramento St (between Presidio Ave and Walnut St). 928.7378 &

## 61 RETURN TO TRADITION

These naturally dyed carpets are woven in a Turkish cooperative. ♦ Tu-Sa. 3319 Sacramento St (between Presidio Ave and Walnut St). 921.4180

## 62 FORREST JONES

Check out the culinary ware and piles of exotic-looking baskets here. ♦ Daily. 3274 Sacramento St (between Lyon St and Presidio Ave). 567.2483

## 63 OSTERIA

★★★$$ The kitchen at this popular neighborhood restaurant owned by Vahid Ghorbani knows how to please its clientele. Green tagliatelle pasta with shrimp and garlic, and linguine with tomatoes and clams, are two of the excellent pasta possibilities. Veal and fish are also featured among its extensive menu in grilled and simmered delightfully subtle flavorings. ♦ Italian ♦ Tu-Su, dinner. 3277 Sacramento St (at Presidio Ave). 771.5030. www.osteriasf.com &

## 64 SUE FISHER KING

Chic tableware and home accessories that are aimed at upmarket households are sold at this elegant shop. ♦ Daily. 3067 Sacramento St (between Broderick and Baker Sts). 922.7276 &

## 65 EILEEN FISHER

This shop is nirvana for devotees of the soft sweater look. Browse the racks of cozy cardigans, wraps, and shrugs matched with knitted wool skirts and trousers. Manager Beate Sykes exudes feminine grace in the various Eileen Fisher ensembles she wears every day. It's not for everyone, but who can resist the tactile sensation of light-as-air yarns? ♦ Daily. 2216 Fillmore St (between Sacramento and Clay Sts). 346.2133. &

## 66 NEXT-TO-NEW SHOP

Mostly women's clothing, along with some household items and menswear, is sold at this resale shop run by the Junior League of San Francisco and stocked principally by its enthusiastic members. Proceeds benefit community programs. ♦ M-Sa. 2226 Fillmore St (between Sacramento and Clay Sts). 567.1628 &

---

Restaurants/Clubs: Red | Hotels: Purple | Shops: Orange | Outdoors/Parks: Green | Sights/Culture: Blue

## 66 D&M LIQUORS

You'll find an incredible selection of California wines here. The specialties are champagne and sparkling wines—250 different varieties. ♦ Daily. 2200 Fillmore St (at Sacramento St). 346.1325 ♿

## 67 MARC BY MARC JACOBS

The New York designer shows his fun and funky side with men's and women's clothing. Also check out the pig-shaped erasers, red-heart compacts, and political buttons. ♦ Daily. 2142 Fillmore St (at Sacramento St). 447.9322. www.marcjacobs.com ♿

## 68 PACIFIC HEIGHTS CONFERENCE CENTER & CULINARY ARTS INSTITUTE

This landmark building is the only private residence built by the renowned architect **Arthur Page Brown,** whose other projects include the **Ferry Building.** The 1895 structure's interior incorporates 17 different woods. It is now used for private functions. ♦ 2212 Sacramento St (at Laguna St)

## 69 LAUREL VILLAGE CAFÉ

★$ Stop here for a sandwich and a frozen yogurt. ♦ Café ♦ M-Sa, breakfast and lunch. 3415 California St (at Laurel St). 751.4242 ♿

## 69 PEET'S COFFEE & TEA

One of the Bay Area's best-regarded coffee chains features beans and brews for coffee and tea connoisseurs. ♦ Daily. 3419 California St (at Laurel St). 221.8506 ♿. Also at numerous locations throughout the city.

## 70 ELLA'S

★★★$ Line up here on weekends for one of the best brunches in San Francisco. It's a comfortable place with an open kitchen, a dining counter bedecked with fresh flowers, and simply set, closely placed tables. The house-made sticky buns alone are worth a visit. Other noteworthy items include chicken hash, buttermilk pancakes, and the fresh punch of ginger and orange juice. The lunch menu ranges from grilled fish and chicken potpie to a warm spinach salad with bacon, mushrooms, and a sherry vinaigrette. ♦ American ♦ Daily, breakfast, lunch, and dinner. 500 Presidio Ave (at California St). 441.5669 (press 2 for the recorded daily menu) ♿

## 71 VIVANDE PORTA VIA

★★★$$ There is no doubt that owner/chef Carlo Middione makes the best pasta in the city, as well as some marvelous desserts. His bustling trattoria specializes in southern Italian fare; it also houses a deli that showcases prepared foods and high-quality specialty products to take out. All the dishes are simply prepared and rich in flavor from start to finish. ♦ Italian ♦ Restaurant: daily, lunch and dinner. Deli: daily. 2125 Fillmore St (between California and Sacramento Sts). 346.4430 ♿

## 72 ELITE CAFÉ

★★$$ One of the few New Orleans–style restaurants in the city, it dishes up authentic Cajun and Creole fare. You'll find great-tasting raw oysters, seafood chowder, soft-shell crabs, baby back ribs, and pecan pie. The dark wood appointments, oyster bar in the window, and tall booths along the wall give the place a clubby ambience. Most of the time the service is professional and friendly, although occasionally, when they're jammed, it can be a bit curt. ♦ Cajun/Creole ♦ Daily, dinner; Su, brunch. 2049 Fillmore St (between Pine and California Sts). 346.8668 ♿

## 72 VICTORIAN HOUSE

Used clothing and bric-a-brac are sold by volunteers to benefit the nearby **California Pacific Medical Center.** ♦ M-Sa. 2033 Fillmore St (between Pine and California Sts). 567.3149 ♿

## 72 MY BOUDOIR

Shop here for unique designs and fabrics from Europe. Geraldine Moreno Nuval is passionate about feminine lingerie, custom-fitted bras, and custom corsets. Check their web site for fashion shows and artist parties. Lingerie by Cosabella (of *Sex and the City* fame) ♦ Daily. 2029 Fillmore St (between Pine and California Sts). 346.1502. www.myboudoir.net ♿

## 73 HARRY'S BAR

★★$ Renowned for its social scene, this establishment features lots of dark mahogany and brass, a white-tile floor, a grand piano, and great hamburgers. ♦ American ♦ Daily, dinner. 2020 Fillmore St (between Pine and California Sts). 921.1000 ♿

## 73 THE GROVE-FILLMORE

★$ This homey coffeehouse appears just when you're feeling footsore and hungry and need a place to settle in for an hour. Head for a sofa by the fireplace with a latte and fresh fruit pie, or a bowl of vegetarian chili. Adding to the homey atmosphere is a large communal table, plank flooring from a Penn-sylvania barn, and Danish stained glass. From eggs Florentine and waffles in the morning right through to shepherd's pie and chicken enchiladas in the evening, the kitchen keeps cranking out satisfying, good-tasting food. The hot-pressed Reuben sandwich is made with Brooklyn pastrami, and the apple chicken salad is made with free-range chicken. The owner's primo music collection ranges from Billie Holiday to the Stones. All of the above set the Grove a notch above most coffeehouses. ◆ Café ◆ Daily, breakfast, lunch, and dinner. 2016 Fillmore St (between Pine and California Sts). 474.1419. Also at 2250 Chestnut St (at Avila St). 474.4843 &

### 73 STARLET

Shop here for sexy cocktail dresses and make an entrance like a starlet. The shop carries a full line of special-occasion and holiday dresses and gowns by Musani Collezioni, Dolce Jovani, Nicole Miller, and Tadashi. ◆ Daily. 1942 Fillmore St (near Pine St). 440.3550 &

### 74 FLORIO

★★$$ If you can recall a favorite corner bistro in Paris, Florio can transport you there as fast as you can say *bon appétit.* You may want to start with the creamy chicken liver pâté, and follow with steak frites or halibut meunière. Other house specialties include a garden radish selection with butter and salt, and roasted organic chicken. ◆ French/Italian ◆ Daily, dinner. 1915 Fillmore St (between Bush and Pine Sts). 775.4300. www.floriosf.com

### 74 OSAKA JAPANESE RESTAURANT

★★★$$ For years this place has maintained its reputation as one of the top sushi bars and Japanese restaurants in San Francisco. The impeccably prepared food is served in a comfortable, unpretentious setting of Formica-topped tables and blond-wood chairs with rush seats. *Yousenabe* (a seafood stew) and *ton katsu* (pork cutlet) are among the many highly recommended dishes served here. ◆ Japanese ◆ W-F, lunch; daily, dinner. 1923 Fillmore St (between Bush and Pine Sts). 346.6788 &

### 75 FLICKA

Shop here for clean lines, fresh colors, and trendy prints of Scandinavian designers such as Bruuns Bazaar of Denmark. Flicka carries the narrow-leg jeans by Denimbirds. The store is like a designer's studio with comfortable seating and a coffee table strewn with Scandinavian design books and magazines.

◆ Daily. 1932 Fillmore St (between Bush and Pine Sts). 292.2315. www.flickaboutique.com &

### 75 THOMAS REYNOLDS GALLERY

A good place to buy California landscapes, still-life oil paintings, and San Francisco images. Reynolds is an expert on paintings from the Arts & Crafts period. ◆ Th-Sa, noon-6PM and by appointment. ◆ 2291 Pine St (at Fillmore St). 441.4093. www.thomasreynolds.com &

### 76 CHEZ NOUS

★★★$ Chef Manuel Vera has taken over the small tapas bistro on Fillmore where patrons wait on the sidewalk for one of the 45 seats. The authentic Mediterranean dishes include lamb chops with lavender sea salt, *pommes frites* with harissa aioli, Mediterranean fish soup, and braised rabbit with mushrooms and celery root purée. Other tasty treats include sautéed spinach with golden raisins and pine nuts, phyllo turnovers, and Moroccan-spiced duck confit. For dessert try the *canneles de Bordeaux.* ◆ Mediterranean (small plates) ◆ W-Su, lunch; daily, dinner. 1911 Fillmore St (between Bush and Pine Sts). 441.8044

### 77 ZINC DETAILS

The store stocks Marimekko and Knoll home furnishings and accessories as well as locally designed housewares. Owner Vasilios Kiniris believes in well-designed everyday objects. Check out the cool "plynyl" placemats and Miam-Miam coffee mugs. There are two stores within two blocks. Check the web site for fun store events. ◆ Daily. 1905 Fillmore St (at Bush St). Also at 2410 California St (at Fillmore St). 776.2100. www.zincdetails.com &

### 77 NARUMI JAPANESE ANTIQUES

This intriguing shop specializes in Japanese antiques, particularly 18th- and 19th-century dolls and stained glass. ◆ Daily. 1902B Fillmore St (between Bush and Pine Sts). 346.8629 &

Restaurants/Clubs: Red | Hotels: Purple | Shops: Orange | Outdoors/Parks: Green | Sights/Culture: Blue

# THE HAIGHT/ JAPANTOWN

he Haight is a district of extremes, an amalgam of subcultures that includes **Golden Gate Park, Buena Vista Hill, Ashbury Heights, Edgewood,** and the celebrated neighborhood of **Haight-Ashbury.** There are villas and ghetto flats, new developments and Baroque mansions, as well as what is probably the oldest house in San Francisco (at **329 Divisadero Street**), which was shipped around the Horn in sections as a gift for a homesick bride.

All this was once part of a 4,000-acre land grant to a man named José de Jesus Noe, the last alcalde (mayor) of San Francisco when the city was still known as Yerba Buena

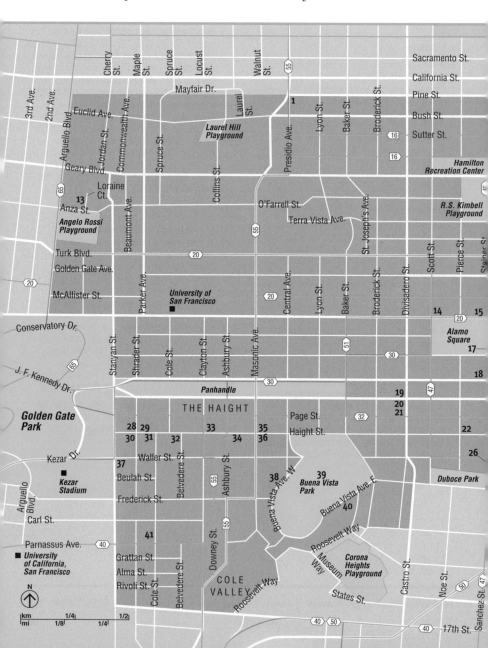

and belonged to Mexico. The area was developed somewhat later than the one around Alamo Square just to the east (traditionally known as the Western Addition), so the houses have more of the ornate character of the 1890s. The Haight (as Haight-Ashbury is often known) was everything a proper 19th-century neighborhood should be, with more than a thousand Victorian houses (many still standing), the beginnings of an enormous park, and a landscaped strip for promenading called the **Panhandle**, which looked something like Boston's Commonwealth Avenue, except for the difference in the architecture of the homes.

The names of other nearby streets honor the men who worked to make **Golden Gate Park** possible: **Cole, Clayton, Shrader, Stanyan,** and **Ashbury.** The neighborhood's decline began in 1917, when the Twin Peaks tunnel encouraged people to move out toward the Sunset District, and it continued through the 1950s. The big houses were divided into flats and then divided again. Then there was "the Happening" and 1967's "Summer of Love"—the blossoming of the flower children and the hippie movement, which brought the psychedelic sounds of Jefferson Airplane and the Grateful Dead. The flower children disseminated the values of their counterculture all around **Haight Street,** but idealism mixed with drugs and unemployment ultimately proved an ineffective formula for social improvement. The area fell into a state of marked decay and became a place where only the streetwise could walk comfortably. But with the rise in real-estate values around the city, a gentrification trend soon reached the Haight. The neighborhood has become home to middle-class and upper-middle-class professionals. These days at coffeehouses, laptops are more common than guitars.

From **Masonic Avenue** to Stanyan Street, Haight Street is lined with some of the city's most interesting shops, bookstores, nightclubs, and cafés. It's a haven for vintage-clothing aficionados, tattoo artists, and anarchists. And the rebellious spirit hasn't been silenced completely. In 1988 a chain drugstore was burned to the ground during the construction stage. Since then, upscale retailers like The Gap have opened without a quarrel. Farther east, Hayes Street, popular with patrons of the performing arts, is also experiencing a renaissance with many unique boutiques and restaurants.

Japantown, *Nihonmachi* to its residents,

is a surprising oasis—a pristine village located within the approximate boundaries of **Geary Boulevard** and **Bush Street,** and **Octavia** and **Fillmore Streets.** Ever since the end of World War II, when the city's Japanese-Americans returned from internment camps to find their former homes occupied, the greatest proportion have lived in other neighborhoods. Only about 4% of San Francisco's Japanese-Americans actually live in Japantown now, but most return here regularly for shopping and for social and religious activities. The construction of the **Japan Center** in 1968 inspired a community-renewal program, with residents and merchants of Nihonmachi working together to beautify the surrounding blocks. As you approach the center's main entrance from the north, the block-long **Buchanan Mall,** landscaped with flowering trees, resembles a meandering stream, with fountains by noted sculptor Ruth Asawa. On many weekends, especially during the spring Cherry Blossom Festival and the summer months, you can see a variety of Japanese cultural activities, from tea ceremonies and martial-arts presentations to flower arranging and musical performances. Robert Redford's Sundance Group plays independent and documentary films at the Japantown theaters (**Sundance Kabuki Sundance**). In the gardens along the neat rows of Victorians, you will see shrubs crafted into exotic shapes and a stone lantern here or there in well-tended grounds, planned with obvious respect for the tea-garden tradition. Set aside time for shopping, eating, and soaking up the atmosphere.

## 1 MONTE CRISTO BED AND BREAKFAST

$ Located in a building that dates back to 1875, the inn's 14 rooms (3 with shared bath) are simply but tastefully furnished with authentic period pieces. Better yet, it's just two blocks from bustling Sacramento Street and near transportation to downtown. A buffet breakfast is served in the private dining room. ♦ 600 Presidio Ave (at Pine St). 931.1875. www.montecristoinn.com

## 2 RESTORED VICTORIAN ROW HOUSES

These painted ladies were moved from their former sites when the Western Addition was being destroyed in the name of urban renewal. They have been carefully restored and given front gardens, in contrast to their previous condition, when the houses were located on the street front. ♦ Bush St (between Buchanan and Webster Sts)

## 3 PATISSERIE DELANGE

You'll find fine French pastry at this friendly shop. Perfect for a light snack. ♦ Tu-Su. 1890 Fillmore St (at Bush St). 923.0711 &

## 4 DUXIANA

Swedish bedding and linen are the specialties here, as well as the Dux bed, which has two sets of inner springs, and adapts to the contours of your body to help keep your spine straight while sleeping. ♦ Daily. 1803 Fillmore St (at Sutter St). 673.7134 &

## 5 CAFÉ KATI

★★★$$$ Chef Kirk Webber's monthly-changing menu offers a host of intriguing combinations: steamed mussels and Thai salmon sausage with red curry; chicken breast stuffed with Roquefort and walnuts and moistened with sage brown butter; crispy salmon fillet with Chinese five spices and a light oxtail broth; and filet mignon with house-dried tomatoes and a frothy herbed zabaglione. This is not the place to grab a bite and run; it's designed for an evening's entertainment, in cozy surroundings. Check the web site for a current menu, winemaker dinners, and BYOB Tuesdays. ♦ Californian/Pacific Rim ♦ M-Sa, dinner. Reservations recommended. 1963 Sutter St (between Webster and Fillmore Sts). 775.7313. www.cafekati.com &

## 6 BEST WESTERN MIYAKO INN

$$ This eight-story, 125-room hotel comfortable and reasonably priced, is now under Joie de Vivre management. Sixty of the rooms are equipped with steam baths, and the café offers Eastern and Western cuisine. ♦ 1800 Sutter St (at Buchanan St). 921.4000. www.bestwestern.com/MiyakoInn &

## 7 BENKYODO CONFECTIONERS

★$ The social hub of Japantown, this place specializes in homemade mochi and other Japanese confections and light lunches served at a counter. ♦ Japanese ♦ M-Sa, breakfast and lunch. 1747 Buchanan St (at Sutter St). 922.1244

## 8 QUEEN ANNE HOTEL

**$$** Although this is one of the largest bed-and-breakfasts in town, no two of the 49 rooms or suites are decorated alike. Each has a private bath, telephone, color TV, and king- or queen-size bed. Ten have fireplaces, and all are furnished with English and American antiques. Although there's no restaurant, a continental breakfast is served in the salon, and tea and sherry are offered every afternoon. Of architectural interest are the oak paneling in the hall, the carved Spanish-cedar staircase, and the fine inlaid floors. The structure was originally built by Senator James Fair, one of the Comstock silver kings, to house a girls' school. It served in turn as an elite gentlemen's club, a home for young working women, and finally a hotel. ◆ 1590 Sutter St (at Octavia St). 441.2828, 800/227.3970. www.queenanne.com ♿

## 9 HOTEL MAJESTIC

**$$$** This hostelry has a long history, and, according to an 1888 document, it just might be the city's oldest surviving hotel. Today, its 58 rooms (including 9 luxurious suites) are replete with furniture from the French Empire and English manor houses, fine paintings, hand-painted four-poster beds, and many fireplaces. It runs a very high occupancy year-round and is often unavailable. ◆ 1500 Sutter St (at Gough St). 441.1100, 800/869.8966. www.thehotelmajestic.com ♿

## 10 SANPPO

**★★$$** Elegant Japanese food is served in a setting that's better than most. Offerings include yakitori (grilled skewered meat and vegetables), nabemono (clay-pot dishes), udon and soba noodles, donburi (rice with meat and vegetables), a particularly delicate and delicious tempura, and many other specialties, mostly seafood. ◆ Japanese ◆ Daily, lunch and dinner. 1702 Post St (at Buchanan St); 346.3486 ♿

## 11 SOKO HARDWARE

This is a great place to find rice cookers, Japanese garden tools, kitchen utensils, and even a state-of-the-art toilet. ◆ Daily. 1698 Post St (at Buchanan St). 931.5510 ♿

## 12 JAPAN CENTER

You step onto authentic Japanese turf at Japan Center. The area around Post and Buchanan Streets has been called Nihonmachi, or Japantown, since the early 1900s. Begin at the Peace Plaza, the center-piece of the three buildings that constitute Japan Center. Studios inside the center are devoted to taiko drumming, sumi brush painting, and ikebana (flower arranging). Zen Buddhism, which informs the Japanese aesthetic, extends beyond gardens and deco-rative arts to health-conscious cuisine. Try the yakitori (grilled skewered meat and vegetables), nabemono (clay-pot stew), or donburi (rice with meat or seafood and vegetables) and see how healthy you feel. Finish off your visit with a Japanese-style shiatsu and amma massage at Mount Fuji massage parlor on the Buchanan Street mall, a quaint cobblestone replica of a village square. The Cherry Blossom Festival in April and the Nihonmachi street fair in August are wonderful times to immerse yourself in Japanese culture. ◆ Bounded by Geary Blvd and Post St, and Laguna and Fillmore Sts ♿

Within Japan Center:

## KABUKI SPRINGS & SPA

Japanese-style communal baths—including a giant hot tub, large cold tub, walk-in sauna, steam room, Japanese-style washing area, and Western-style showers—leave customers feeling relaxed and squeaky-clean. Towels, bathrobes, sea salts, and tea are provided. Shiatsu (Japanese pressure-point massage) is the specialty. ◆ Daily. Men only in the communal baths M, Th, Sa; women only W, F, Su; co-ed Tu. 1750 Geary Blvd (at Fillmore St). 922.6000. www.kabukisprings.com ♿

## MIYAKO HOTEL

**$$$** Eastern and Western traditions merge in the 218 rooms and suites of this Joie de Vivre hotel. Most rooms are furnished in Western style with a few Japanese touches, such as authentic shoji and hand-painted and lacquered fusuma screens, and niches for flowers and art objects. There is a variety of deluxe accommodations here. Ten luxury suites have private saunas. Two rooms and one suite combine American and Japanese accommodations and are ideal for families. One area has a king-size bed, while a second partitioned space is carpeted with heavy tatami mats and traditional down-filled futon bedding. The **Club Floor** has a private entryway and includes 14 deluxe rooms and suites, a whirlpool in every room, and a spacious lounge. Within the hotel are conven-tion and meeting facilities. **Dot** restaurant serves an expanded breakfast buffet and cooked-to-order American and Japanese breakfasts until 10:30AM. Dot cocktail lounge and restaurant reopens Monday through Saturday at 5PM. Children 18 years old and under may stay free in their parents' room. ◆

---

Restaurants/Clubs: Red | Hotels: Purple | Shops: Orange | Outdoors/Parks: Green | Sights/Culture: Blue

**Peace Pagoda**

1625 Post St (at Laguna St). 922.3200, 800/533.4567. www.miyakohotel.com &

## THE PEACE PAGODA

The focal point of the center, the pagoda rises 100 feet in five tiers from the reflecting pool in the middle of the **Peace Plaza.** It was designed by **Yoshiro Taniguchi** of Tokyo, an authority on ancient Japanese structures.

## KINOKUNIYA BOOK STORE

Books about Japan in English and Japanese, as well as Japanese publications and recordings, are this store's focus. ♦ Daily. Kinokuniya Bldg, 1581 Webster St (at Post St). 567.7625 &

## MIFUNE

★★$ The Japanese version of fast food is served here, with every sort of noodle dish you could think of—and then some. ♦ Japanese ♦ Daily, lunch and dinner. Restaurant Mall, Kintetsu Bldg, 1737 Post St (at Webster St). 922.0337 &

## MIKADO

Look here for an impressive collection of items that accessorize a kimono, from obis to tassels to footwear. There are also Japanese dolls, toys, and chinaware. ♦ Daily. Restaurant Mall, Kintetsu Bldg, 1737 Post St (at Webster St). 922.9450 &

## ISOBUNE SUSHI

★★$$ Sushi boats float past customers seated around an oblong bar as chefs launch their creations from the center. If you don't see what you want right away, wait until another boat sails by. ♦ Japanese ♦ Daily,

lunch and dinner. Restaurant Mall, Kintetsu Bldg, 1737 Post St (at Webster St). 563.1030 &

## KOJI OSAKAYA

★★$$ Japanese curry is among the specialties of this small eatery, which has a pleasant Asian ambience. ♦ Japanese ♦ Daily, lunch and dinner. Kintetsu Bldg, 1737 Post St (at Webster St). 922.2728 &

## ASAKICHI

This shop offers a good selection of antique *tansu* chests and decorative objects. ♦ Daily. Kinokuniya Bldg, first floor. 1730 Geary Blvd (at Fillmore St). 921.2147 &

## SHIGE KIMONO

The excellent selection here makes this store great for browsing as well as for buying vintage kimonos. ♦ Daily. Kinokuniya Bldg, 1581 Webster St (at Post St). 346.5567 &

## KINOKUNIYA STATIONERY & GIFTS

This shop stocks lovely Japanese greeting cards and imported paper. ♦ Daily. Kinokuniya Bldg, 1581 Webster St (at Post St). 567.8901 &

## MISEKI JEWELRY

You'll find a huge selection of pearls at attractive prices. ♦ Daily. Kintetsu Bldg, 1737 Post St (at Webster St). 567.2400 &

# THE LONG AND WINDING ROADS

**Lombard Street** has long laid claim to being the crookedest street in the world, but it seems the famed San Francisco roadway has a little competition. The good citizens of Burlington, Iowa, insist the honor belongs to their own Snake Alley, a brick-laid street that was constructed in 1894 and consists of seven curves on a 16 percent grade. They say that although Lombard boasts more switchbacks and an 18.2 percent grade, it is broken up into a series of short increments, whereas Snake Alley maintains a sinuous stretch of continuous curves. Then again, some San Franciscans claim that the crookedest-street title may really belong to yet another curvaceous roadway: **Vermont Street,** in San Francisco's **Potrero Hill District.** The street has only six curves and a measly 14.3 percent grade, but its muscle-straining, hair-raising turns are much sharper than those of the other contenders.

San Francisco has other winding ways worth exploring, including the following favorites:

**Twin Peaks** Drive up the hill at the intersection of **Clarendon Avenue** and **Twin Peaks Boulevard,** then wind down the 12 curves (in a 9,000-foot stretch) to **Portola Drive.** The view, 910 feet above sea level, is spectacular.

**O'Shaughnessy** and **Teresita Boulevards** Begin at the intersection of Portola Drive and O'Shaughnessy Boulevard, heading southeast. Arrows shaped like C's warn you of the curves—20 of them in 12,000 feet. Turn right on **Brompton Avenue** and again on **Joost Avenue.** Then turn right on **Foerster Street** for two blocks and again at Teresita Boulevard. The following block—which alone has nine curves—is lined with charming, colorful houses.

**Telegraph Hill** Four curves—and, unfortunately, a passel of traffic jams—in 2,400 feet lead to the landmark **Coit Tower.** On a clear day, the view of **Alcatraz** and the city is tremendous and worth the effort.

## IKENOBO IKEBANA SOCIETY

This branch of Japan's largest flower-arranging school is its North American headquarters. On Saturday, from about 10AM to noon, you might be able to see the experts creating the weekly floral window displays. Call for a class schedule. ◆ Kintetsu Bldg, 1737 Post St (at Webster St). 567.1011 &

## MIKI BOUTIQUE

This shop carries handbags, accessories, and giftware that appeal to its Japanese customers. ◆ Daily. Kintetsu Bldg, 1737 Post St (at Webster St). 781.3208

## MAKI

★★★$$ In this small restaurant you can dine on beautifully prepared Japanese dishes. Beef sukiyaki, sushi, *donburi,* and various *udon* and *soba* dishes are a notch above other Japan Center restaurants. The elegant service and attention will leave you feeling pampered and restored for more shopping. ◆ Japanese ◆ Tu-Su, lunch and dinner. 1825 Post St (at Fillmore St). 921.5215

## 13 NEPTUNE SOCIETY COLUMBARIUM

ⓟ This domed mausoleum, which holds the ashes of 10,000 early San Franciscans, is one of the hidden secrets of the city. It was originally built for the **Oddfellows Cemetery** by **B.J.**

**Cahill** in 1897, and has been restored to its original splendor, with stained glass, artwork, and silver and gold urns. Names of prominent families, many of whom have streets named after them, are everywhere. ◆ Daily, mornings. 1 Loraine Ct (off Anza St, between Stanyan St and Arguello Blvd). 221.1838 &

## 14 1198 FULTON STREET

Stop here to ogle one of the grandest and most beautiful Victorian mansions in the city. It's a private residence. ◆ At Scott St

## 15 THE ARCHBISHOP'S MANSION INN

$$$ This has to be one of the most spectacular bed-and-breakfast inns in San Francisco. Built for an archbishop in 1904, the handsome building has been lovingly restored by its present owners. It features a three-story open staircase covered by a 16-foot-tall stained-glass dome, 18 fireplaces with magnificently carved mantelpieces, and belle epoque furnishings with Victorian and Louis XIV chandeliers. There are 15 guest rooms in all, each with a private bath; 10 rooms have fireplaces and several are suites. A continental breakfast is included, and there is a private dining room available for catered functions. ◆ 1000 Fulton St (at Steiner St). 563.7872, 800/543.5820. www.thearchbishopsmansion.com. (The

---

Restaurants/Clubs: Red | Hotels: Purple | Shops: Orange | Outdoors/Parks: Green | Sights/Culture: Blue

# SEVEN HILLS OF SAN FRANCISCO

As the Honorable James Bryce, onetime British ambassador to the US, once said, "The city itself is full of bold hills, rising steeply from the deep blue . . . one involuntarily looks up to the tops of those hills for the feudal castle, or the ruins of the Acropolis, that must crown them." San Francisco's topography boasts as many as 43 hills, but here are the famous 7, which, like the hills of Rome, have long been favorites of visitors to the city. Each hilltop offers its own breathtaking view.

**1. Telegraph Hill** Named for the signal station erected on its summit that informed the citizenry of the arrival of ships back in the early days, Telegraph Hill offers a wide panorama of northeast San Francisco and the bay. Because parking is all but impossible, public transportation is highly recommended. Board the No. 39 bus at **Washington Square** for easiest access to the hill.

**2. Nob Hill** The home of palatial mansions built by the city's early mining and railroad tycoons (its name is derived from *nabob,* meaning Indian prince), this is the best known of San Francisco's hills. Robert Louis Stevenson described it as "the hill of palaces." In addition to its present-day luxury hotels, you'll find **Grace Cathedral** and many apart-ment houses and condos for those millionaires among us. The generally accepted boundaries of Nob Hill are **Bush, Larkin, Pacific,** and **Stockton Streets.** The hill is easily reached by any of the city's three cable-car lines.

**3. Rincon Hill** Located close to the southern portion of **The Embarcadero,** this hill (which literally means "corner" in Spanish) is only one and a half blocks long. Approach it from The Embarcadero on **Bryant Street** just south of **I-80.**

**4. Twin Peaks** From here, some 910 feet above sea level, you can partake of sweeping panoramic views of the city and Bay Area. Drive up the hill at the intersection of **Clarendon Avenue** and **Twin Peaks Boulevard;** then weave your way around the 12 curves to **Portola Drive.**

**5. Russian Hill** Named to honor the early Russians who settled here, today it is a mix of exclusive and bohemian cultures. It is within walking distance of **Downtown,** the **Financial District,** and **North Beach** and is noted for its colorful culs-de-sac and lovely bay views. This is the hill where you'll find **Lombard Street,** the crookedest street in the world. Russian Hill extends from **Pacific** to **Bay Streets** and from **Polk** to **Mason,** but its core is bounded by **Broadway, Chestnut, Larkin,** and **Taylor Streets.** The Hyde Street cable car takes you right to it.

**6. Lone Mountain** Once surrounded by graveyards, legend has it that **Richmond** district landscapers engaged in planting shrubbery dug up some unexpected remains. Lone Mountain is crowned by a tower that is part of the **University of San Francisco. The Presidio** and **Lincoln Park** are on its north side, **Golden Gate Park** on the south. From downtown, take **Geary Boulevard** west, turning left on **Parker Avenue.** Go two blocks to **Lone Mountain Terrace** at the edge of the campus.

**7. Mount Davidson** At 938 feet, this is the highest spot in San Francisco. At its summit is a concrete-and-steel cross, rising another 103 feet above the hill's summit. Easter sunrise services have been held here annually since 1923. From downtown, take **Market Street** southwest to where it becomes Portola Drive. Portola passes within one block of **Mount Davidson Park** and any exit to the left will get you to **Juanita Way,** which is the park's periph-eral road.

Archbishop's Mansion Inn is temporarily closed for major renovations. It will reopen in late 2007.)

## 16 AFRICAN AMERICAN ART AND CULTURAL CENTER

At the center is the **African American Histor-ical & Cultural Society,** the **African American Shakespeare Company,** AfroSolo **Theatre Company,** and **Cultural Odyssey.** Check online for exhibits, performances, and special events in the 210-seat **Buriel Clay Memorial Theater.** ♦ M-Sa, noon-5PM. 763 Fulton St (between Buchanan and Webster Sts). 922.2049. www.aaacc.org ♿

## 17 700 BLOCK OF STEINER STREET

The six almost identical houses by **Matthew Kavanaugh** have been carefully restored and painted. With the backdrop of the city's Financial District skyline, this late-19th-century row is often featured in tourist photographs. All are private residences. ♦ Between Hayes and Grove Sts

## 18 601 STEINER STREET

Constructed in 1891, this Queen Anne house, a private residence, boasts elaborate carving and a fine turret. ♦ At Fell St

### 19 COUNTRY CHEESE

You'll find excellent buys on dried fruit, cheeses, grains, and nuts—great for party givers. ♦ M-Sa. 415 Divisadero St (between Oak and Fell Sts). 621.8130 ♿

### 20 1111 OAK STREET

Completed in 1860, this is one of the oldest houses in San Francisco. It has been beautifully restored, and is now used for office space. Nearby buildings from the same era have also been converted for commercial use. ♦ Between Divisadero and Broderick Sts

### 20 COOKIN'

The recycled gourmet kitchen gear sold here has been a subculture secret. Cooks will be thrilled by the variety of wares, including oodles of cookie cutters, molds, vintage cherry pitters, grinders, and the like. ♦ Tu-Su. 339 Divisadero St (between Page and Oak Sts). 861.1854

### 20 GAMESCAPE

The only serious game store in town carries everything from board games to fantasy games. You can find used games too. ♦ Daily. 333 Divisadero St (between Page and Oak Sts). 621.4263 ♿

### 20 329 DIVISADERO STREET

The oldest house in San Francisco is well hidden in the middle of the block. Built in 1850, it has been moved twice, and a glimpse of it can be caught on Oak Street at Divisadero. It is a private residence. ♦ Between Page and Oak Sts

### 21 THE METRO HOTEL

$ This 23-room Victorian hotel is a well-kept secret, but known by some visiting Europeans. In the past, it was a residential hotel that was reputedly a home to shady ladies; in its current incarnation, the high-ceilinged rooms are full of innocent charm. There's a pleasant garden in the back that guests may use, a nice little adjoining coffee shop called **The Metro Café,** and off-street parking. ♦ 319 Divisadero St (between Page and Oak Sts). 861.5364. www.metrohotelsf.com

### 21 COMIX EXPERIENCE

Fans of the genre will enjoy perusing this collection of new and used comic books. ♦ Daily. 305 Divisadero St (at Page St). 863.9258 ♿

### 22 AXUM CAFE

★$ If your quest for dining adventures leads you to Axum's, you will become adept at using spongy Ethiopian bread to scoop up stew. Their spicy chicken stew and vegetarian lentil stew are served on a single family-sized platter. A pitcher of beer adds to the fun and pairs well with the food. ♦ Ethiopian ♦ Daily, dinner. 698 Haight St (at Pierce St). 252.7912. www.axumcafe.com ♿

### 23 294 PAGE STREET

Designed by architect **Henry Geilfuss,** this 1885 Victorian Stick-style house, a private residence, has been beautifully preserved. ♦ At Laguna St

### 24 THE MAD DOG IN THE FOG

★$ This brewpub is a comfortable place to knock back a few pints of bitter, throw some darts, and indulge in a genuine shepherd's pie. Fans of British football watch the matches on live satellite. ♦ English/Irish ♦ Daily, lunch and dinner. 530 Haight St (between Fillmore and Steiner Sts). 626.7279 ♿

### 25 TORONADO

Belly up to the bar and ask for your favorite brew—they're bound to have it at this friendly watering hole that proudly boasts 53 top-notch draft beers, one of the largest selections in the city. ♦ Daily until 2AM. 547 Haight St (between Fillmore and Steiner Sts). 863.2276 ♿

### 26 GERMANIA STREET HOUSES

**Donald MacDonald** built these two minuscule dwellings in 1984. Each occupies a 20-by-20-foot footprint and proves that it is possible to build affordable housing in San Francisco. They have basic detailing and an almost cartoonlike form. ♦ At Steiner St

### 27 THEP-PHANOM

★★$ This intimate, attractively decorated restaurant serves a great combination of bright tastes and striking textures. Particularly good is the *tom kha ghi* (chicken soup with coconut milk and ginger). Other entrées include *kiew warm ghi* (green curry chicken) and *sam kasatr* (a fiery pork curry). Every dish is a wonderful bargain. ♦ Thai ♦ Daily, dinner. 400 Waller St (at Fillmore St). 431.2526 ♿

### 28 SKATES ON HAIGHT

This is one of the few places near **Golden Gate Park** to rent (or buy) skateboards, in-line skates, roller skates, and all the pads you

---

need to help cushion you against those inevitable tumbles. ♦ Daily. 1818 Haight St (between Shrader and Stanyan Sts). 752.8375. www.skates.com &

## 28 MILK BAR

Another hip Haight Street hangout, this DJ bar and lounge is a smoky, dark dancin' and drinkin' club. Check online for the latest lineup of live tunes. ♦ Cover. Daily. 1840 Haight St (between Shrader and Stanyan Sts). 387.6455. www.milksf.com &

## 29 THE CITRUS CLUB

★★★$ News of this restaurant passed among friends like wildfire and despite the line at the door, they continue to come. Order a Citrus punch, sake martini, or one of the microbrews on tap and decide what to order. Get ready to slurp and swirl an amazing variety of Asian noodles. They come in salads and soups, and tossed in the wok with meat, seafood, and vegetables. Sauces and spices draw on the cuisine of China, Malaysia, Thailand, Indonesia, and Vietnam. Try the garlic beef and shiitake mushroom chow fun or the curry shrimp rice noodles. ♦ Asian ♦ Daily, dinner. 1790 Haight St (between Cole and Shrader Sts). 387.6366 &

## 30 CHA CHA CHA

★★★$$ Most people come for tapas and the spicy grilled meats, washed down by excellent sangria. The food here reflects Spanish, Cajun, and Caribbean influences, including traditional dishes such as black-bean soup, Cajun shrimp, and fried calamari. Bright décor (including a collection of Santeria altars), friendly service, and reasonable prices make this restaurant one of Haight Street's best bets. Be prepared to wait for a table, although it has recently doubled its seating capacity. ♦ Latin ♦ Daily, lunch and dinner. 1801 Haight St (at Shrader St). 386.5758 &

## 30 AMOEBA MUSIC

If your CD collection is valued in the thousands of dollars, you probably already know about Amoeba. Housed in a former bowling alley, Amoeba is *the* mecca for CDs. There are miles of CD shelves to browse before making

a purchase. Flag down a staff member if you need help—many of them have encyclopedic knowledge of various bands and love to talk music. ♦ Daily. 1855 Haight St (between Shrader and Stanyon Sts). 831.1200. Also at 2455 Telegraph Ave, Berkeley. 510/549.1125

## 31 LA ROSA

Vintage tuxedos and dresses from the 1920s and 1930s are sold or rented to those who want to make a deliberate out-of-style statement. ♦ Daily. 1711 Haight St (at Cole St). 668.3744 &

## 31 RED VIC MOVIE HOUSE

A worker-owned-and-operated haven for art-film lovers. ♦ 1727 Haight St (between Cole and Shrader Sts). 668.3994 &

## 32 THE RED VICTORIAN BED & BREAKFAST INN

$$ The only surviving hotel on Haight Street was purchased in 1977 by artist Sami Sunchild, who strives to preserve the unique history and character of the building (circa 1904) in the form of an art gallery and bed-and-breakfast. The 18 guest rooms are quite nice—and each one is decorated in its own fanciful (sometimes eccentric) way. A continental breakfast is included, served in a private dining room. ♦ 1665 Haight St (between Belvedere and Cole Sts). 864.1978. www.redvic.com

## 33 MENDEL'S ART SUPPLIES AND STATIONERY/FAR-OUT FABRICS

An incongruous assortment of fascinating fabrics, feathers, buttons, and a vast variety of art supplies share retail space with office supplies. ♦ Daily. 1556 Haight St (between Ashbury and Clayton Sts). 621.1287 &

## 34 THE PORK STORE CAFÉ

★$ Once a butcher shop, with a porker immortalized in a stained-glass window to prove it, this place now draws locals to its counter for breakfast and burgers. ♦ American ♦ Daily, breakfast and lunch. 1451 Haight St (between Masonic Ave and Ashbury St). 864.6981 &

## 35 PIPE DREAMS

*The* smoke shop of the 1960s, it offers an eclectic assortment of nontraditional smoking accoutrements such as water pipes, in addition to Egyptian jewelry, and T-shirts. ♦ Daily. 1376 Haight St (between Central and Masonic Aves). 431.3553. www.pipesinthecity.com &

## 35 MAGNOLIA PUB & BREWERY

★★$$ This appealing brewery and restaurant is on the site of what was one of

Of the city's 32,866 hotel rooms, 20,000 are within walking distance of Moscone Center.

---

The flamboyant green-and-ochre Gateway to Chinatown at Grant Avenue and Bush Street serves as the symbolic entrance to the Chinese capital of the Western world. Dragons and lions adorn the gateway, which was erected in 1970.

Haight-Ashbury's most notorious businesses in the 1960s. In those psychedelic times, it was a café called the **Drugstore,** and well-tended marijuana plants were on view in its window boxes. Dave McLean brews traditional British-style ales, and features five British hand pumps for cask-conditioned beers served at cellar temperature, a common practice in England. ♦ Brewpub ♦ M-F, lunch and dinner; Sa, Su, brunch and dinner. 1398 Haight St (at Masonic Ave). 864.7468. www.magnoliapub.com ♿

## 36 BOUND TOGETHER

The volunteers who operate this anarchist bookstore and meeting place have been keeping the faith for 30 years. Check out the anarchist T-shirts. ♦ Daily. 1369 Haight St (between Central and Masonic Aves). 431.8355

## 36 RECYCLED RECORDS

Rare and hard-to-get tapes, CDs, and records are bought, sold, and traded here. ♦ Daily. 1377 Haight St (between Central and Masonic Aves). 626.4075 ♿

## 37 STANYAN PARK HOTEL

$$ Another stylish establishment near **Golden Gate Park,** this building exhibits the designers' elegant style of transition from Queen Anne to Beaux Arts classicism. The hotel has 30 rooms and 6 suites; the suites have fireplaces and bay windows overlooking the park. A continental breakfast, and tea and cookies in the afternoon, are served in a private dining room. The two-bedroom suite rents for $335 a night. ♦ 750 Stanyan St (at Waller St). 751.1000. www.stanyanpark.com ♿

## 38 SPRECKELS MANSION

Not to be confused with the other, grander **Spreckels Mansion** on Washington Street, this elegant edifice was built in 1887 and is situated on a hill next to **Buena Vista Park.** Formerly a bed-and-breakfast (Ambrose Bierce and Jack London were celebrated guests), it has been converted into a private residence. ♦ 737 Buena Vista Ave W (between Frederick St and Central Ave)

## 39 BUENA VISTA PARK

The park affords a wonderful view of the Coast Range Mountains as far as Mount Tamalpais to the north, Mount Hamilton to the south, and Mount Diablo to the east. Avoid this park after dark, however, as it can be a dangerous spot. ♦ Haight St (between Buena Vista Ave E and Buena Vista Ave W)

## 40 PARK HILL CONDOMINIUMS

Architects **Kaplan/McLaughlin/Diaz** converted the **Saint Joseph's Hospital** building into residences in 1986. The former chapel is now a recreation center and the whole scheme has been repainted in warm, pastel shades. ♦ 355 Buena Vista Ave E (off Duboce Ave)

## 41 ZAZIE

★★$$ This tiny French bistro makes up for its size with impressive food. At breakfast, the Belgian waffles with caramelized pecans and the omelette specials win raves; lunch selections include a large variety of sandwiches. The dinner menu offers such hearty dishes as a bone-warming daube (a marinated beef stew), free-range chicken with garlic and herbs, and trout prepared a different way each day. ♦ French ♦ M-Sa, breakfast, lunch, and dinner; Su, breakfast and lunch. 941 Cole St (between Parnassus Ave and Carl St). 564.5332. www.zaziesf.com ♿

## THE BEST

### Kimberly Fishman
Group Coordinator/The Phoenix Hotel

It's hard not to have a good time in San Francisco. The architecture, landscape, weather, food, people, etc., are just great! Stop by **The Phoenix Hotel** for their complimentary City Guide devised by their staff—full of great suggestions on all kinds of sights, sounds, and tastes of the city.

If you have a car, the best view of the city and the entire Bay Area is from **Mount Tamalpais** in **Marin County.** Only a 30-minute drive from downtown.

**Haight Street** is a great place to go for some shopping at the city's most modern clothing stores, thrift shops, and record stores. Enjoy **Ben & Jerry's Ice Cream** on the infamous corner of Haight and **Ashbury.**

If you're looking for a great coffeebuzz and think you can handle it, try a "depth charge" at the **Coffee Zone** on Haight and **Masonic.**

For breakfast try **The Patio Cafe** in the **Castro District.** It's intimate, pretty, and the food is great!

Restaurants/Clubs: Red | Hotels: Purple | Shops: Orange | Outdoors/Parks: Green | Sights/Culture: Blue

# THE MISSION/POTRERO HILL/BERNAL HEIGHTS

**E**arly in the 1800s, the sunny, fog-free valley that is part of today's Mission District became a rural locale for San Francisco's resort activities. When a private franchise was granted permission to construct a 40-foot-wide planked toll road from present-day **Third Street** to **16th Street**, gambling houses, saloons, dance halls, pleasure parks, and racetracks sprang up among the farmhouses and country homes to take advantage of the increased traffic. Over the next 30 years, the number of people here grew from 23,000 to 36,000, and except for the adobe **Mission Dolores,** founded in 1776, not a trace of the area's previous Spanish influence remained. Instead, colorful Victorian row houses were built everywhere. Yankees, Germans, and Scandinavians moved in, and after the 1906 earthquake and fire ravaged the North Beach and South of Market areas, the homeless Italians and Irish followed. It was then that the residents began cultivating a kind of Spanish revival. Palm trees were planted along **Dolores Street,** turning it into a handsome boulevard; the mission's stucco was repaired; a pseudo-Spanish church was built alongside it; and red-tiled roofs appeared on buildings. Latinos began to pour into the area, and today the Hispanic population continues to expand, and restaurants and markets catering to their tastes thrive here.

You'll find heavy traffic, palms, and a few parks in this area. When *Vanity Fair* named the Mission District the hippest neighborhood in America, the article referred to the Valencia Street corridor (Valencia St between 16th and 25th Sts), where you'll find restaurants serving Vietnamese, Indian, Mexican, and Middle Eastern food, along with great bars and shopping. The district is the haunt of iPod-wearing, creative professionals. Many art groups have also made their homes in the area. There are many clubs in the district; most open in early afternoon and the beat goes on until 2AM.

The Spanish dubbed the land stretching south from the Mission *Potrero Nuevo* (new grazing ground). When industry expanded here from the Mission, marshlands were bridged to provide additional access and a five-mile streetcar line was added, making this area the city's first suburb. Today Potrero Hill is a community of small and colorful houses, with a few contemporary apartments basking in the sun while the rest of the city shivers—a place where some of the cottages have *banyas* (Russian steambaths) in the backyard. This is not tourist country. Instead of chic boutiques, you'll see utilitarian shops. At the foot of the hill are early-19th-century warehouses, including **Showplace Square,** which houses one of the largest wholesale furnishing centers in the West. The working-class neighborhood is giving way to gentrification. The agreeable climate and

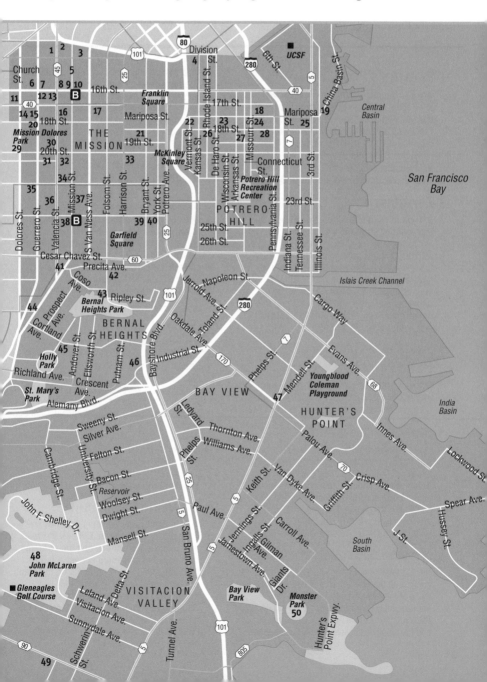

sweeping views have attracted artists and professionals whose lifestyles range from bohemian to deluxe. The thriving community gardens adjoining **McKinley Square**, where neighbors work side by side, are proof of Potrero Hill's ability to assimilate many different ethnic groups.

The less congested **Outer Mission** is dotted with single-family homes. The land here was originally part of a Spanish land grant. In the Excelsior District, many of the original farmhouses rub shoulders with 1930s-style homes. **Bay View/Hunter's Point,** the southeast corner of San Francisco, represents the largest concentration of African-Americans in the city. It has been in a state of flux since the **Third Street Railway** began running in April 2007, connecting Bay View to downtown. Nearby is **Monster Park** (formerly **Candlestick Park Stadium**), home to the **San Francisco 49ers**.

## 1 PAULINE'S PIZZA

★★$$ Gourmet pizza is served in a variety of eclectic, eccentric expressions, from pesto pizza to a little number covered with chèvre. There's no atmosphere to speak of—just great pizza few Italians would recognize as their native food. Takeout is available. ♦ Pizza ♦ Tu-Sa, dinner. 260 Valencia St (between 14th St and Duboce Ave). 552.2050 &

## 2 ZEITGEIST

$ If you roll into town on a motorbike, make this your first stop. You'll find kindred folk at this legendary biker bar. Shoot the breeze with the Zeitgeist bartenders. Order fresh-off-the-grill burgers and fries at the kitchen, then have a seat at any of the picnic tables in the huge backyard. The Tamale Lady will take your tamale order for the soft cornmeal treats. ♦ American ♦ Daily, 9AM-2AM. 199 Valencia St (at Duboce Ave). 255.7505 &

## 3 SAN FRANCISCO HERB COMPANY

Spice up your life; buy herbs by the pound, wholesale. ♦ M-Sa. 250 14th St (between S Van Ness Ave and Mission St). 861.7174

## 4 SHOWPLACE SQUARE

In these restored brick warehouses are whole-sale furniture and design showrooms, open to the trade. The Design Center consists of two warehouses linked by a modern, glass-faced atrium building used for exhibitions and conferences. A restaurant on the ground floor serves mediocre food in a very chic setting. ♦ M-F. 2 Henry Adams St (at Division St). 864.1500 &

## 5 MISSION STREET

This is the Mission District's great commercial artery, with the heaviest concentration of activity that's of interest to strollers stretching from approximately Cesar Chavez to 15th Streets. The street buzzes with entrepreneurial energy, and the small businesses supply the neighborhood with produce (much of it geared toward Hispanic recipes). There are clothing shops for budget-minded buyers; furniture stores with some of the most garish, overwrought designs imaginable; and small restaurants reflecting the area's diverse Hispanic populations. ♦ Between Cesar Chavez and 15th Sts

## 6 BODY MANIPULATIONS

At this place (possibly the weirdest entrepreneurial effort in San Francisco), customers who like a primitive look may be pierced anywhere they want to be (yes, anywhere), ears being the tamest option. Currently nostril and navel piercings are the most popular. There's a tattoo studio upstairs, and the owners say that a professional medical consultant advises them. ♦ Daily. 3234 16th St (between Guerrero and Dolores Sts). 621.0408 &

## 7 ANDALU

★★★$$ Andalu is a tapas-style bar and restaurant located in the heart of San Francisco's Mission District. The ceiling is painted with voluminous clouds and the walls hung with rust velveteen drapes. The Amy Wilson mural in vibrant colors behind the bar lends a high-style glamour to Andalu. Chef Ben deVries offers a seasonal menu of international small plates complemented by an extensive list of wines by the glass and half bottles. The crab tacos melt in your mouth. ♦ Californian/inter-national ♦ Daily, dinner; Sa, Su, lunch. 3198 16th St (at Guerrero St). 621.2211

## 8 TAQUERÍA LA CUMBRE

★$ In its heyday, 20 years ago, this was the best *taquería* in town. But over the years, it grew into a large chain, and the style and food have become more impersonal. But there are still some good items on the menu: The *carne asada* (marinated beef) is a winner. The business recently passed to the younger generation of the family and the menu has changed slightly. ♦ Mexican ♦ Daily, lunch and dinner. No credit cards accepted. 515 Valencia St (at 16th St). 863.8205 &

## 9 ESTA NOCHE

At San Francisco's first Latin drag-queen bar, some think the "ladies" are good looking. There's disco dancing to a salsa beat in the evenings. ♦ Cover. Daily. 3079 16th St (at Mission St). 861.5757 &

## 10 THEATRE RHINOCEROS

Gay and lesbian issues are explored in the offbeat productions staged at this 112-seat theater. ♦ 2926 16th St (between S Van Ness Ave and Mission St). 861.5079

## 11 MISSION DOLORES

Spanish settlers led by Captain José Moraga founded San Francisco's first mission in 1776, on the site of an Indian village, just five days before the signing of the Declaration of Independence. Formally called the **Mission San Francisco de Assisi,** this is the sixth of the 21 missions built by Franciscans along El Camino Real, the Spanish road linking the missions from Mexico to Sonoma, California. Though the mission was dedicated to Saint Francis de Assisi, it became better known by its current name after a nearby lagoon called Lake of Our Lady of Sorrows (*dolores* is Spanish for "sorrow"). The city's oldest building, its structure has withstood four major earthquakes and is the only one of the original missions that has not been rebuilt. Its four-foot-thick adobe walls have survived the years without serious decay or extensive restoration. **Mission Dolores Basílica,** the larger church next door, was rebuilt in 1918 and was declared a basilica in 1952 by Pope Pius XII. In addition to several historical figures, more than 5,000 native Costanoan Indians are buried in the cemetery garden (most died from diseases transmitted by white settlers). Scenes from Alfred Hitchcock's *Vertigo* were filmed in the chapel and cemetery. ♦ Daily. Dolores St (at 16th St). 621.8203, ext. 30 &

## 12 THE ROXIE

This vintage movie house (with seating for about 280) specializing in classic and esoteric movies is film-buff heaven. ♦ 3117 16th St (between Valencia and Guerrero Sts). 863.1087 &

## 13 VALENCIA STREET

From 16th Street south toward 30th Street, this thoroughfare is a microcosm of the Mission District's diverse flavors, including some Asian restaurants, Hispanic influences, and offbeat bookstores, cafés, and clubs for the young and hip. ♦ Between 30th and 16th Sts

## 13 TI COUZ

★★$ The focus in this cozy Breton creperie is the counter, where cooks make crepes with dozens of fillings: Savory choices include sausage, mushroom, and ratatouille, while sweet options might be apples, chocolate, or caramel. Sparkling hard cider, the traditional accompaniment to crepes, is served. ♦ French ♦ M-F, lunch; daily, dinner. 3108 16th St (at Valencia St). 252.7373 &

## 13 LIMÒN

★★$$ Love ceviche? Come to the Castillo brothers' lime-green-and-tangerine dining room for heaping bowls of the house specialty. Ceviche Limòn is made with halibut, fresh lime, yams, Peruvian corn, and mussels. The bounty of the Pacific also goes into the Peruvian-style paella and Peruvian fish stew. Other dishes to love are *lomo saltado* (beef, onions, tomatoes, and a side of fries) and empanadas made with beef, eggs, and raisins. To complete the taste-bud submersion, for dessert order the fruit ice cream, which is flown in from Peru. ♦ Peruvian/Californian ♦ Daily, lunch and dinner. Reservations recommended. 524 Valencia St (between 17th and 16th Sts). 252.0918. www.limon-sf.com &

## 14 DELFINA

★★★★$$$ Delfina's dining room sports the industrial-chic look that fits its Mission District location, but the food is what garners the raves. The food elite all around the country seem to know about Delfina. For such a small, moderately priced restaurant, the word has spread. A few of the dishes that people crave are the grilled calamari with warm white beans, grilled sardines on *crostini*, roast chicken, flatiron steak, and spaghetti with tomatoes and chili flakes. For dessert try the profiteroles with coffee ice cream. ♦ Italian ♦ Daily, dinner. 3621 18th St (between Guerrero and Dolores Sts). 552.4055

## 15 TARTINE BAKERY

One of the country's better-known artisan bakeries has found a home in San Francisco's Mission District. Husband-and-wife team Elisabeth Prueitt and Chad Robertson serve batches of French-style pastries and naturally leavened breads every day. The new bakery–café also has a menu of fresh open-face sandwiches, savory pastries, and light breakfast items. ♦ Daily; Tu-Su, dinner. 600 Guerrero St (at 18th St). 487.2600

## 16 ELBO ROOM

This is the Mission District's version of upper Market Street's popular **Cafe Du Nord,** filled with an eclectic, alternative crowd and a suitably cool atmosphere. Wear lots of black or vintage clothing, order an imported beer, and you'll fit right in. ♦ Daily. 647 Valencia St (between 18th and 17th Sts). 552.7788 &

### 17 ODT THEATRE

Experimental music, theater, and dance are presented at this 187-seat theater. ♦ Daily. 3153 17th St (at Shotwell St, east of S Van Ness Ave). 863.9834 &

### 18 BOTTOM OF THE HILL

One of the best places to hear live music. The playbill spans the spectrum of musical tastes from rockabilly to funk and pop. The kitchen stays open late and the patio gives you a breather from the enthusiastic crowd. Musicians play nightly. ♦ Daily. 1233 17th St (at Missouri St). 621.4455. www.bottomofthehill.com &

### 19 THE RAMP

★★$$ Although hidden away in a boatyard, this place's reputation has spread by word of mouth, and an eclectic crowd of suits, gays, and boat workers gathers here for a good time. Hamburgers, salads, daily specials, and creative stews are the culinary attractions. There's also live music in the summer—jazz, salsa, rock—Thursday through Sunday, as well as an outdoor weekend barbecue. ♦ American ♦ Daily, dinner; M-F, lunch, but hours may vary with the season and weather. 855 China Basin St (at the end of Mariposa St). 621.2378 &

### 20 PIZZERIA DELFINA

★★$$ Craig and Anne Stoll fire up the pizza ovens nightly and turn out perfectly blistered Margheritas (roma tomatoes, cheese, and basil). Put your name on the board and order a glass of Montepulciano. There's always a wait, but use the time to visit with friends. ♦ Pizza ♦ Daily, dinner; Tu-F, lunch. 3611 18th St (between Guerrero and Dolores Sts). 437.6800. www.pizzeriadelfina.com &

### 21 UNIVERSAL CAFÉ

★★★$$ Small, sunny, smartly designed, and a favorite with locals and serious foodies alike, this café is worth a visit just for its pan-seared filet mignon with whipped Gorgonzola potatoes. Other specialties might include roast chicken with tomato coulis (thick purée) and braised greens, or roast salmon with avocado-leek salad. ♦ American ♦ Daily, dinner; M-Sa, breakfast and lunch; Sa, Su, brunch and dinner. 2814 19th St (at Bryant St). 821.4608. www.universalcafe.net &

### 22 VERMONT STREET

The view is nice and the absence of mobs even nicer at southern San Francisco's answer to Lombard Street. ♦ South of 20th St to Mariposa St

### 23 ANCHOR BREWING CO.

It's San Francisco's version of a Dickens tale: Fritz Maytag, a young, carefree college student who also happens to be heir to a washing-machine company, stops into his local beer hall, orders his first pint of Anchor Steam, and instantly becomes smitten with the rich amber brew, forgetting all about the family business. Meanwhile, Lawrence Steese is struggling to keep his old Anchor brewery out of bankruptcy and is desperately in need of a deep-pocketed partner. This is where our hero Fritz steps in and saves the day, much to the delight of beer aficionados around the world. Take a tour of the delightfully anachronistic brewery and a tasting of what many consider one of the few *real* beers left. ♦ Free. M-F. One tour each afternoon by reservation only. Due to high demand, call a month ahead of time to arrange a tour. 1705 Mariposa St (at De Haro St). 863.8350 &

### 24 SAN FRANCISCO BAR-B-QUE

★★$ Despite its limited menu and simple presentation, this restaurant always comes through with tasty, honest, addictive Thai-style barbecue dishes at modest prices. The chicken and pork ribs are the most popular, cooked to lean succulence and flavored with a medium-hot sweet-sour Thai sauce. ♦ Thai ♦ Tu-F, lunch and dinner; Sa, Su, dinner. 1328 18th St (between Pennsylvania and Missouri Sts). 431.8956

### 25 MOSHI MOSHI

★★$ Tucked into a wasteland of warehouses, this place serves good Japanese food at prices that are more than fair. The décor is simple—almost spare—with bleached-wood tables and chairs and pale-green walls. The menu offers all the classic favorites: chicken and steak teriyaki (served quite rare, as it should be), shrimp tempura and yakitori, as well as excellent sushi. The quality and value are hard to beat. ♦ Japanese ♦ Daily, dinner; M-F, lunch. Reservations required for six or more. 2092 Third St (at 18th St). 861.8285

### 26 610 RHODE ISLAND STREET

Designed for **Kronos Quartet** members Pat Gleeson and Joan Jeanrenaud, this contemporary home amid rows of traditional 19th-century houses became an object of controversy. Critics maintained that its industrial look was out of context in the neighborhood. The 24-foot-high living space covered in black asphalt shingles is visible to passersby. This private residence was built in 1989 by **Daniel Solomon**. ♦ At 18th St

### 27 GOAT HILL PIZZA

★★$ The view of downtown is spectacular, and the food homey and filling. Family-style pastas and classic pizza such as pesto with feta and pepperoni are the favorites here. Monday is all-you-can-eat night. ♦ Pizza ♦ M-F, lunch and dinner; Sa, dinner; Su, brunch and dinner. 300 Connecticut St (at 18th St). 641.1440 &

## 28 300 PENNSYLVANIA STREET

Situated on top of Potrero Hill, this was one of a series of mansions built as the city grew south of Market Street. A private residence, it was constructed in 1868. ♦ At 18th St

## 29 MISSION DOLORES PARK

This green oasis on the fringes of the Mission District is where tennis players, dog walkers, and sun worshipers gather for neighborhood recreation. In the summer, locals gather to watch performances of the **San Francisco Mime Troupe,** enjoy outdoor movies, and to hear the **San Francisco Symphony.** ♦ Bounded by Dolores and Church Sts, and 20th and 18th Sts

## 30 RANGE

★★★Cooking with only a range, chef Phil West creates small masterpieces of flavor, texture, and color. When you enter the spare yet inviting dining room, feast on the aroma of good cooking. As you will see from the menu, West cuts a wide swathe across California's culinary territory. Seasonal highlights include white bean soup, albacore confit, pan-roasted steak with baby turnips, pork loin with butter beans, and coffee-rubbed pork shoulder. Pastry chef Michelle Polzine, a punk-rocker in another life, now makes music with a whisk and mixing bowl. Try the plum upside-down cake with cardamom ice cream and blackberries, or the tart with caramel-coriander ice cream. There is an excellent wine list and creative cocktails. ♦ Californian ♦ Daily, dinner. 842 Valencia St (between 20th and 19th Sts). 282.8283. www.rangesf.com &

## 31 LIBERTY HILL HISTORIC DISTRICT

The blocks from Castro to Valencia Streets contain some of the best Italianate houses in San Francisco, unspoiled since the last century. **No. 159,** built in 1878, is where Susan B. Anthony—whose dollar coin we now seem to have forgotten—used to visit her fellow suffragists. **No. 109** was built in 1870. ♦ Between Valencia and Castro Sts

## 32 LA RONDALLA

★★$$ It's nothing to look at, but this is a hugely popular, extremely lively Mexican restaurant known for mariachi music, good margaritas, and year-round Christmas décor. The menu goes far beyond the usual tacos and enchiladas. You can get interesting grilled-pork creations and Mexican egg dishes for a fine late-night snack. And if you hanker for goat meat, this place has it. ♦ Mexican ♦ Tu-Su, lunch and dinner. 901 Valencia St (at 20th St). 647.7474 &

## 33 CAFÉ GRATITUDE

★★$ Rub elbows with yoga instructors, Reiki masters, and earth-loving pagans at this colorful café. The menu reads like a medicine cabinet of restorative ingredients, so prepare for a healthy makeover. I Am Grateful is a salad bowl brimming with organic greens and raw vegetables to which you can add scoops of hummus, nut-seed falafel, or carrot-almond pâté. I Am Passionate is buckwheat pizza and nut cheese; and I Am Giving is a plate of butternut-squash noodles with a zippy topping of ginger, garlic, lemon, tomatoes, cucumber, and cilantro. The artwork and the names of the dishes come from the "Abounding River" board game, which you can play over lunch or dinner with a few pals. Even the wine list is organic. ♦ Vegetarian ♦ M-Sa, breakfast, lunch, and dinner; Su, brunch. 2400 Harrison St (at 20th St). 824.4652. www.withthecurrent.com &

## 34 DOSA RESTAURANT

★★$$ Fans of contemporary Indian cuisine favor this ethnic spot. If a maharaja moved to Valencia Street, this is how the palace would be decorated: in shades of coral and crimson. A *dosa* is something similar to a crepe that's served in South India with a variety of tantalizing fillings such as spiced lamb. The samosas and *saag paneer* (spinach with cheese cubes) are right on the rupee, if you like spicy food. Also excellent are tandoori prawns, chicken biryani (rice with meat or seafood), and South Indian curries. ♦ Indian ♦ Tu-Su, dinner; Sa, Su, lunch. 995 Valencia St (at 21st St). 642.3672. www.dosasf.com &

## 35 PAO CAFÉ

★★$$ This ordinary-looking little storefront restaurant is short on ambience but big on culinary satisfaction. The menu changes every six weeks and reflects "world-beat cuisine"—unusual cross-cultural combinations and dramatic presentations such as rack of lamb coated with pecans and served with wild rice and a tart mint-fig compote, or salmon blackened and served

---

Restaurants/Clubs: Red | Hotels: Purple | Shops: Orange | Outdoors/Parks: Green | Sights/Culture: Blue

with spicy shrimp bread pudding. ◆ French/Vietnamese ◆ Daily, dinner. Reservations recommended. 1000 Guerrero St (at 22nd St). 641.9955 ♿

## 36 BUFFALO EXCHANGE

The young crowd loves the new and recycled clothing stocked here, and many keep their wardrobes going by regularly exchanging what they have for something they like better. ◆ Daily. 1210 Valencia St (at 23rd St). 647.8332

## 37 FOREIGN CINEMA

★★★$$ Dinner and a movie in one spot: The idea appeals to many people. The foreign films are outside on the heated patio projected onto a whitewashed wall. The adjoining room is an art gallery. Inside is a roaring fire in a giant fireplace and an open kitchen. Seasonal specialties include endive salad with smoked trout; house-cured sardines with roasted peppers; grilled duck breast with fresh cranberry beans; and rack of lamb with Moroccan spices. For dessert try the chocolate pot de crème. ◆ Mediterranean ◆ Tu-Su, dinner. 2534 Mission St (near 22nd St). 648.7600

## 38 LA TRAVIATA

★★★$$ Although the Italian population has declined here, this restaurant remains (along with **Dianda's Italian Bakery** across the street) after more than 30 years in the Mission District. This one is so good that it draws not only customers from across town but world-famous opera stars as well. Pictures of divas and great tenors line the walls, and opera plays constantly. The pastas are marvelous, and the chicken and veal dishes are first-rate. ◆ Italian ◆ Tu-Su, dinner. Reservations recommended. 2854 Mission St (between 25th and 24th Sts). 282.0500 ♿

## 39 LA VICTORIA MEXICAN BAKERY AND GROCERY

For more than 30 years, this place has been turning out Mexican specialties, including sugary wedding confections and custardy cones. ◆ Daily. 2937 24th St (at Alabama St). 642.7120

## 39 GALERIA DE LA RAZA/ STUDIO 24

Since its founding in 1970, this nonprofit gallery exhibiting works of Latino artists has gained worldwide renown. The adjoining studio supports the work of the gallery with sales of crafts representing contemporary and traditional arts of Latin American countries. ◆ W-Su. 2857 24th St (at Bryant St). 826.8009 ♿

## 40 ROOSEVELT TAMALE PARLOR

★★$ This place built its reputation around its crowd-pleasing tamales, which have drawn customers since 1922. Other traditional Mexican dishes are offered as well. Customers are an enthusiastic mix of gringos from north-of-Market neighborhoods and locals who share a common interest in good food in a spruced-up dining room. ◆ Mexican ◆ Tu-Su, lunch and dinner. 2817 24th St (between York and Bryant Sts). 648.2690 ♿

## 40 SAINT FRANCIS FOUNTAIN

★★$ Not much has changed in this soda fountain since it opened its doors in 1918. It sells Mitchell's homemade ice cream and peanut brittle and has cases filled with candies that will take you back to your childhood. More substantial fare includes grilled cheese sandwiches and a daily blue-plate special. Weekend brunch is a popular time to go. ◆ American ◆ Daily, lunch and dinner. No credit cards accepted. 2801 24th St (at Bryant St). 826.4200 ♿

## 41 EL RÍO

Dance to the beat of Latin, Cuban, and Brazilian salsa and African world music. A mixed crowd dances to the live shows on Thursday, Saturday, and Sunday. A wonderful courtyard awaits out back. ◆ Cover. Daily. 3158A Mission St (at Cesar Chavez St). 282.3325. Show schedule available online: www.elriosf.com ♿

## 42 MISSION DISTRICT MURALS

Painted by Mexican-American artists and other residents, these murals are a colorful example of community spirit. The artists have brightened and humanized their urban environment with vivid wall paintings dispersed throughout the neighborhood between Mission and York Streets and 14th and Army Streets, adorning banks, restaurants, schools, housing projects, and community centers. Some of the murals are inside buildings. Sightseers may take a self-guided walk or a two-hour, eight-block walking tour given by the **Precita Eyes Mural Arts Center** every Saturday at 1:30PM. Group tours can be arranged at other times with advance notice. Forty murals are covered on the tour. Maps are available from the center, in addition to a checklist of all Mission District murals. ◆ Nominal fee; discount for seniors, students, and children. Arts Center: 348 Precita Ave (at Folsom St). 285.2287

## 43 170-80 MANCHESTER STREET

Built on the slopes of Bernal Heights in 1986 by **William Stout,** these modern, stucco-clad houses capture the spirit of the white architecture of the modern movement. They are private residences. ♦ At Bernal Heights Park (south end of Folsom St)

## 44 JASMINE TEA HOUSE

★★$ In an attractive dining room hung with Chinese brush paintings and decorated with ceramic teapots, you can dine on Shanghai fish, Mongolian beef, Peking duck, and shrimp rolls with mango. Another house special is noodle soup with chicken, shrimp, and scallops. Every dish has an appealing twist that puts Jasmine Tea House a notch above most Chinese restaurants. ♦ Chinese ♦ Daily, lunch and dinner. 3253 Mission St (near 30th St). 826.6288

## 45 THE LIBERTY CAFÉ & BAKERY

★★$$ The menu of this charming café features only four appetizers and four main courses, but each is perfectly prepared. The Caesar salad is excellent; the chicken potpie has a burnished puff-pastry crust and a lightly thickened filling of roasted pearl onions, carrots, and big chunks of potatoes and chicken; the trout is coated in cornmeal, pan-seared, and served with lemony spinach and sautéed baby artichokes; and the banana cream pie is rich and creamy. They sell fresh bread from the bakery in the rear garden, 695.1311. ♦ American ♦ Tu-F, lunch and dinner; Sa, brunch and dinner; Su, brunch. 410 Cortland Ave (at Bennington St). 695.8777 ♿

## 46 ALEMANY FARMERS' MARKET

Saturday is the big shopping day at this open-air market where California farmers sell their seasonal produce at prices lower than those in most supermarkets. Sunday is flea market day, although the collectibles are overpriced. ♦ Sa, Su. 100 Alemany Blvd (between Crescent Ave and Putnam St). 647.9423

## 47 THE BAYVIEW OPERA HOUSE

The city's oldest theater opened its doors in 1888. Seating 300, it has been renovated and provides the community with a variety of plays, dance concerts, and musical theater. ♦ Call for information on shows. 4705 Third St (at Oakdale Ave). 824.0386 ♿

## 48 JOHN MCLAREN PARK

🅿 The city's second-largest park was named for the man who created its biggest one, **Golden Gate Park.** Several residential districts make use of the rugged, wooded tract: the Portola, Bay View, Visitación Valley, Excelsior, and Crocker Amazon. The steep slopes offer good views of Visitación Valley and the San Bruno Mountains. ♦ Bounded by Moscow and Delta Sts, and Felton St and Geneva Ave

Within McLaren Park:

## GLENEAGLES GOLF COURSE

This challenging par 36 course, designed by John Fleming, is forested and located on rolling and sometimes steep hills. The 9-hole course can be played as 18 holes from different tee and pin locations. Call the golf shop to reserve tee times. ♦ Daily. 2100 Sunnydale Ave (off Persia Ave). 587.2425. www.parks.sfgov.org

## 49 COW PALACE

This place hosts everything from livestock shows to the Exotic Erotic Ball and the Dickens Faire. With a seating capacity of 10,300 to 14,300, it offers an ever-changing series of events. ♦ Geneva Ave (at Santos St), Daly City. 469.6000 ♿

## 50 MONSTER PARK

🅿 The former **Candlestick Park Stadium** and former **3Com Park** is home to the **San Francisco 49ers** with seating for up to 70,000 people. Built in 1960 by **John S. Bolles and Associates**, it is situated on a rocky promontory overlooking the bay. The site suffers from exposure to bitter cold winds and occasional flooding, and it is widely regarded as one of the most uncomfortable places in which to watch—or play—a game. It was the first major-league baseball stadium to be constructed entirely of reinforced concrete, and there is movable seating for the switch between baseball and football. The park sold its name (for a sizable fee) to Monster Cable Company, although most fans have refused to adopt the new name. ♦ Take Candlestick Park Exit off Hwy 101 S, to Giants Dr at Gilman Ave. 49ers tickets 656.4900. Single tickets available online: www.49ers.com ♿

# NOE VALLEY/CASTRO/ UPPER MARKET

**T**he Noe and **Eureka Valleys** snuggle below **Twin Peaks** and share much of the same history, climate, and architecture. Both also underwent dramatic population shifts in the 1970s, as escalating real-estate prices in fashionable, white-collar neighborhoods north of **Market Street** drove hordes of young professionals to the more affordable southern reaches of San Francisco. Both valleys are quaint neighborhoods of Victorian

storefronts and homes, and were originally called Horners' Addition after Mormon Gold Rush pioneers Robert and John Horner, who made their fortune selling food to gold diggers. (A street named Horner was renamed 23rd Street in 1861.)

Noe Valley, separated from Eureka Valley by the ridge of 22nd Street, was historically part of the 4,000-plus-acre land grant given to the last Mexican mayor of San Francisco, José de Jesus Noé, by California governor Pio Pico in the 1840s. Noé's ranch house was one of the first buildings in the district and stood at the corner of 22nd and Eureka Streets. The area was once filled with blue-collar German and Irish families. More recently, Noe Valley has been called "Mommy Valley" because of the proliferation of baby strollers. In 2006, an environmentally friendly "green house" brought in a lot of green: the four-bedroom home sold for $2,150,000. In this relaxed urban village, residents frequently spot raccoons in their backyards, gather for an annual picnic and a local history day at the library, and spend Saturday morning at the farmers' market in a converted parking lot. Between Dolores and Diamond Streets, 24th Street is a lively shopping area dispensing the stuff of everyday life, with supermarkets, coffeehouses, and ethnic delis where you can buy a burrito, a knish, and a quiche, all within a four-block range. Church Street, named for the many houses of worship that once stood there, is fast developing as another commercial thoroughfare, with most of the shops concentrated between 24th and 30th Streets. To preserve the small-town atmosphere, with people shopping and chatting together, one residential group has promoted a hard stance against establishments selling liquor. In Upper Noe Valley, steep streets and hills create truly spectacular housing sites.

At the same time that double-income heterosexual couples were flocking to Noe Valley, Eureka Valley was becoming a magnet for gays from everywhere in the country. Castro Street is the main thoroughfare, and so strong is its impact that the area is commonly known as the Castro District rather than Eureka Valley. This center of San Francisco's gay social life is a crowded collection of unique shops, bars that stay open until 2AM, and restaurants, mostly concentrated on Castro between Market and 20th Streets. The gay influence extends to the Upper Market area, which was also part of Noe's land grant in the early 1800s. San Francisco's gay and lesbian population is well organized, and it has been said that no politician can win an election in the city without gay support. Gilbert Baker designed the first rainbow flag, a 20- by 30-foot-long flag billowing over Harvey Milk Plaza at the corner of Market and Castro. It has become an icon for the gay rights movement. Although the scourge of AIDS has caused more than 18,000 deaths here, it also has united the gay community, focusing its political spokespeople on gay rights, including single-sex marriages. The Pride parade draws 500,000 people each June, making it the largest pride parade in the world. On any given day in the Castro District, rainbow flags fly in support of the GLBT (Gay, Lesbian, Bisexual, Transgender) community.

Restaurants/Clubs: Red | Hotels: Purple | Shops: Orange | Outdoors/Parks: Green | Sights/Culture: Blue

# ATHS FOR PEDAL PUSHERS IN THE CITY BY THE BAY

There's no better way to get a feel for San Francisco than to ride through it on a bicycle. Don't be put off by the city's famous hills—just rent a bike with many gears, and follow the numbered bicycle-route signs erected by the Department of Parking and Traffic. These placards help cyclists find the most direct and least hilly routes to a variety of places. They also have the advantage of letting drivers know that they are sharing the road with two-wheelers. Not all the routes are on city streets; some veer off onto bike paths and lanes, as in **Golden Gate Park.** Sunday morning is a good time to hit the road—car traffic is minimal and the bike paths have fewer cyclists. Be sure to carry a map of the routes within the city as well as those in the park, water, and extra clothing. The weather can change dramatically: foggy and cold one minute on the **Golden Gate Bridge,** blistering hot the next in **Sausalito.** Whatever your destination, you're sure to have a fun time seeing the sights of San Francisco by bike. For information on rentals, see "Bicycles" in the Orientation chapter.

## 1 THE WILLOWS INN

$ Popular with the gay and lesbian community, this quiet, 12-room bed-and-breakfast inn in a 1904 Edwardian is central to the Castro, the Mission, and downtown and near easy connections to **BART** and **Muni.** The graceful California Gypsy Willow furniture was designed specifically for each room, and the place has a restful, European-country look. There is a telephone, washbasin (guests share the bathrooms), and kimono in each room, and a continental breakfast is served with a morning paper. Complimentary sherry and truffles are left in each room in the evening. ♦ 710 14th St (at Church St). 431.4770

## 2 MECCA

★★★$$$ Start off a meal here with chef Lynn Sheehan's herbed flatbread that's served with different toppings—the hummus-and-pickled-spring-onions variety is a particular favorite. Other wonderful appetizers include goat cheese wrapped in grape leaves with beets, and Caesar salad. Mediterranean flavors come through on grilled tuna accompanied by a ragout of artichokes and sun-dried tomatoes. Gourmet pizzas are a hit,

topped with house-made venison sausage and goat cheese, or wild mushrooms and Roquefort. The circular zinc bar is the restaurant's action hub, while velvet drapes lend a sensual style to the dining room. ♦ American/Mediterranean ♦ Tu-Su, dinner. Reservations required. 2029 Market St (between Dolores and 14th Sts). 621.7000. www.sfmecca.com

## 3 CAFÉ DU NORD

★★$$ For those in the know, this basement-level, windowless club/café is the place to see and be seen. Moody lighting, a gilt-edged ceiling, dark wood paneling, musty oil paintings, and a stylish crowd combine to give this place the decadent air of a speakeasy. Jazz is the main theme for entertainment here and it varies from night to night; straight jazz, bebop, acid jazz, big band, vintage blues, and salsa are all featured. The small American-style dinner menu with a Mediterranean twist offers soup and pasta of the day; arugula salad; filet mignon; and garlic roasted chicken breast four nights a week. ♦ Californian/Mediterranean ♦ Cover. W-Sa, dinner; music nightly. Reservations recommended. 2170 Market St (at Sanchez St). Café 861.5016. Entertainment schedule available online: www.cafedunord.com

## 4 THE RANDALL MUSEUM

The emphasis at this nature and history museum is on participation, with live animals and a petting corral, a ceramics room, a woodworking shop, a seismograph, and biology classes and an environmental learning garden. Many special workshops and events are offered, especially during the summer. ♦ Free. Tu-Sa. 199 Museum Way (at Roosevelt Way between 17th and 14th Sts). 554.9600 &

Once a year a fire hydrant at 20th and Church Streets is painted gold. It's believed to be the only hydrant in the city that continued to function during the 1906 earthquake and fire, and is credited with saving the area. A memorial plaque in the sidewalk next to the hydrant reads: "Though the water mains were broken and dry on April 18, 1906, yet from this Greenberg hydrant on the following night there came a stream of water allowing the firemen to save the Mission District."

la Méditerranee

## 5 LA MÉDITERRANÉE

★★★$ This Middle Eastern–inspired restaurant offers good food in intimate surroundings at excellent prices. The lemony hummus with fresh herbs is a good starter. Among the popular main courses are the "Levant" sandwiches, pinwheels of cream cheese and other ingredients, which change daily; ground lamb kabob served with rice; and chicken drumsticks marinated in pomegranate sauce and baked. Main courses come with salad or a cup of soup. They provide sidewalk tables for smoking patrons. ♦ Middle Eastern ♦ Tu-F, lunch and dinner; Sa, Su, brunch and dinner. 288 Noe St (at Market St). 431.7210. Also at 2210 Fillmore St (between Sacramento and Clay Sts). 921.2956; 2936 College Ave (between Ashby Ave and Russell St), Berkeley. 510/540.7773 ♿

## 6 JOSEPH SCHMIDT CONFECTIONS

This small shop is where chocoholics go to worship. Joseph Schmidt, who has mastered chocolate sculpture, creates bowls, flowers, sports equipment, animals, bottles, and auto-mobiles in his edible medium. He also makes the best chocolate truffles in town—maybe anywhere. ♦ M-Sa. 3489 16th St (between Church and Sanchez Sts). 861.8682 ♿

## 7 INN ON CASTRO

$$ One of the smaller guest houses in the city (eight rooms, each with private bath), this inn's intimate surroundings make it truly a home away from home. Although located in an Edwardian town house, its interiors are contemporary: white walls, track lighting, classic modern furniture, brilliant flowers, and the original art of one of the owners. Upstairs, breakfast is served every morning on an extensive and ever-changing collection of imported china and stoneware dishes. ♦ 321 Castro St (at Market St). 861.0321 ♿

## 8 IXIA

When daisies just won't do, this unusual florist specializes in exotic, esoteric plants and flowers. ♦ M-Sa. 2331 Market St (between Noe and Castro Sts). 431.3134

The San Francisco Ballet Company, founded in 1933 by Adolphe Bolm, is the oldest resident classical ballet company in America.

## 9 TWIN PEAKS

Always lively, always friendly, this was the first gay drinking establishment in San Francisco to come out of the closet by having large picture windows where clients could see and be seen. ♦ Daily. 401 Castro St (off Market St). 864.9470 ♿

## 9 THE BEAD STORE

All kinds of nifty beads and unique pieces of jewelry are displayed for those who want to do things themselves, or have their adornment done by someone else with lots of talent. ♦ Daily. 417 Castro St (off Market St). 861.7332 ♿

MARCELLO'S PIZZA

## 10 MARCELLO'S PIZZA

★★$ In San Francisco, this is as close as you're likely to come to a New York–style pizza. There's a smattering of small, crowded tables, but most customers grab a slice to go. It's one of the few places nearby where you can find sustenance late at night. ♦ Pizza/takeout ♦ Daily, lunch and dinner; M-Th, Su until 1AM; F, Sa until 2AM. 420 Castro St (off Market St). 863.3900 ♿

## 11 CASTRO THEATRE

San Francisco officialdom dubbed this structure the finest example of a 1930s movie palace in the city. Designed by **Timothy Pflueger** in 1922, the 1,600-seat theater has earned its reputation because of its remarkable Spanish colonial architecture. The auditorium ceiling is probably the most noteworthy feature, an extraordinary affair cast in plaster to resemble a giant cloth canopy tent, complete with swags, ropes, and tassels. And in what better setting could you enjoy an ever-changing series of movies from Hollywood's heyday? Anybody who swoons over *Camille* or drools over the exquisite timing in *Bringing Up Baby* will want to take in a flick at this classic theater. ♦ 429 Castro St (off Market St). 621.6120 ♿

Restaurants/Clubs: Red | Hotels: Purple | Shops: Orange | Outdoors/Parks: Green | Sights/Culture: Blue

## Castro Street Shopping

### 17th STREET

| | CASTRO STREET | |
|---|---|---|
| casualwear **Diesel** | | **Twin Peaks** bar |
| cell phone store **Sprint** | | **Hot Cookie** |
| **Marcello's Pizza** | | **Castro Smoke House** cigarettes/magazines |
| **Louie's Barber Shop** | | **Quickly** tapioca bar |
| **Rossi's Deli** | | **The Bead Store** |
| casualwear **In-Jean-ious Lounge** | | **Bare Necessities** |
| **Cove Cafe** | | **The Castro Cheesery** cheese/coffee/chocolate |
| **Thailand Restaurant** | | **Castro Theatre** |
| bar **440 Castro** | | **Castro Nail Station** |
| **Citibank** | | **U.S. Bank** |
| menswear **Body** | | **Pharmacare** pharmacy |
| **The Bar on Castro** | | **Sliders Diner** |
| **Osaka Sushi** | | **Naia-Castro** gelateria |
| American restaurant **Welcome Home** | | **All American Boy** menswear |
| take-out **A. G. Ferrari Foods** | | **Fuzio** restaurant |
| DVD rentals **Superstar** | | **Cliff's Variety** hardware/fabrics |
| **Likewise Cafe** | | **A Different Light** bookstore |
| | | **Posh Bagel** |
| | | **La Tortilla** fresh-mex |
| **Walgreens** | | **Ritz Camera** |

### 18th STREET

| | |
|---|---|
| bar **Harvey's** | **Bank of America** |
| **Tully's Coffee Co.** | **The Sunglass Hut** |
| toiletries **The Body Shop** | **The Sausage Factory** Italian restaurant |
| pizza **Escape from New York** | **Castro Video** |
| gifts **Phantom** | |
| gifts **Planet Weavers** | **Best in Show** pet store |
| erotic art **Rock Hard** | **Benefiting the AIDS Community** gifts |
| sushi bar **All Season** | **Under One Roof** charity/gift store |
| menswear **Citizen** | **Herth** real estate |
| clothing **In-jean-ious** | |
| Japanese restaurant **Nirvana** | **Wells Fargo** bank |
| **Always Tan and Trim** | **Notorious for Hair** salon |
| **Castro Day Spa** | |
| French skincare products **L'Occitane** | **First American Title Company** |
| Italian restaurant **Luna** | **Anchor Oyster Bar & Seafood Market** |
| bakery/café **Castro Tarts** | |
| florist/nursery **Hortica** | |
| **Brand X Antiques** | **Clobba** clothing |
| liquor **Swirl on Castro** | |
| menswear **Worn Out West** | |
| mailbox services **PO Plus** | |
| optician **Eye Gotcha** | |
| **Buffalo Whole Food & Grain Company** | |
| health food | **Thai House** restaurant |

### 19th STREET

retail, gifts **HRC Action Center and Store**

### 12 CLIFF'S VARIETY

This Castro Street institution is actually two shops side by side. One carries all manner of fabrics, spangles, and feathers for making costumes or embellishing a smashing drag getup; the other sells straightforward household needs, such as hardware and paint. It's beloved for its folksy merchandising approach and cordial staff. ♦ M-Sa. 471-479 Castro St (between 18th and Market Sts). 431.5365 &

### 13 FIREWOOD CAFÉ

★★$ At peak hours the line extends to the sidewalk, but it moves fast. Specialties are the rotisserie chicken, gourmet pizza, and grilled marinated vegetables. Skip dessert. ♦ Californian/Italian ♦ Daily, lunch and dinner. 4248 18th St (at Diamond St). 252.0999

### 14 LIKEWISE CAFE

★★$ Velvet sofas in intimate living-room arrangements make this an elegant respite from busy Castro Street. Over a morning croissant and latte or late-night wine and cheese, you can sample the bon-vivant life on a budget. The lunch menu has hot sandwiches on foccacia bread that are filled with ratatouille, grilled chicken with Portobello mushrooms and vegetables, and other French-inspired combinations. Try the excellent salade Niçoise. The dessert case is full of Alain Benoit's mouth-watering fruit tarts and confections. ♦ Californian ♦ Daily, breakfast, lunch, dinner, and late-night menu. 476 Castro St (between 18th and Market Sts). 863.2725 &

### 15 A DIFFERENT LIGHT

The only store in San Francisco devoted to both gay and lesbian literature. ♦ Daily until midnight. 489 Castro St (at 18th St). 431.0891 &

### 16 THE MIDNIGHT SUN

Boy meets boy at this popular gay video bar, sleekly designed with a galvanized-metal exterior. ♦ Daily to 2AM. 4067 18th St (between Noe and Castro Sts). 861.4186 &

### 16 BODY

Rather revealing men's sportswear for the let-it-all-hang-out crowd is in this shop. ♦ Daily. 4071 18th St (between Noe and Castro Sts). 861.6111

### 17 EUREKA RESTAURANT AND LOUNGE

★$$ You could eat a satisfying meal here every night of the week and not grow tired of the menu. The grilled pork chops come with roasted potatoes and sautéed escarole.

Smoked bacon adds an earthy flavor to the seafood gumbo. For starters, try the butternut squash soup spiked with bourbon. The bar serves excellent wines and aperitifs by the glass. Reservations recommended. ♦ American ♦ Tu-Su, dinner. 4063 18th St (at Castro St). 431.6000 &

### 18 NOBBY CLARKE'S FOLLY

This attractive, eclectic construction was built in 1892 by Alfred Clarke, who worked as a clerk in the police department. It was alleged to have cost $100,000—a fortune then—and originally included a 17-acre estate. Today it is an apartment house. ♦ 250 Douglass St (at Caselli Ave)

### 19 HORTICA

When your rooms look empty but you don't have the money for furniture, try plants instead. The horticultural accomplishments here are quite artful. ♦ Daily. 566 Castro St (between 19th and 18th Sts). 863.4697 &

### 19 BRAND X ANTIQUES

A lovely selection of antique and estate jewelry and collectibles is on display. It's not cheap, but it's awfully nice. ♦ Daily. 570 Castro St (between 19th and 18th Sts). 626.8908 &

### 20 BUFFALO WHOLE FOODS & GRAIN COMPANY

This health-food store is packed with select organic produce, plentiful breads, packaged convenience foods, and lots of vitamins. ♦ Daily. 598 Castro St (at 19th St). 626.7038 &

### 20 DOES YOUR MOTHER KNOW?

We won't tell her if you shop here for unusual, outrageous, and funny greeting cards. ♦ Daily. 4141 18th St (between Castro and Collingwood Sts). 864.3160 &

### 21 ANCHOR OYSTER BAR & SEAFOOD MARKET

★★$$ When you have a yen for chowder and shellfish, this neat little place, with a counter and a few tables, satisfies it nicely. And if you get a hankering for an "oyster shooter" (an oyster in a shot glass with Bloody Mary mix, Worcestershire sauce, a touch of Tabasco, and a squeeze of lemon), you'll find that here too. ◆ Seafood ◆ M-Sa, lunch and dinner; Su, dinner. 579 Castro St (between 19th and 18th Sts). 431.3990 &

## 21 THAI HOUSE

★★$ With an astonishing 104 Thai dishes on the menu, all under $10, you have plenty of reasons to come back. Locals favor the coconut-milk curries and spicy noodle dishes topped with Asian vegetables. Try the pan-fried rice noodles with chicken, egg, dried squid, bean sprouts, and ground peanuts. $10 credit card minimum. ◆ Thai ◆ Daily, lunch and dinner. 599 Castro St (at 19th St). 864.5000 &

## 22 SPIKE'S COFFEES AND TEAS

They carry about 30 varieties of well-displayed coffees here, plus chocolates for those who want to indulge all their minor vices at once. ◆ Daily. 4117 19th St (between Castro and Collingwood Sts). 626.5573

## 22 CASTRO VILLAGE WINE COMPANY

More than 400 California wines are stocked here. The shop offers wine tastings, and shipping is available. ◆ Daily. 4121 19th St (between Castro and Collingwood Sts). 864.4411 &

## 23 3733-3777 AND 3817-3871 22ND STREET

The panels framing the plaster floral arrangements and the banded laurel (which looks like the letter *X*) are trademarks of builder **John Anderson.** These private residences were built in 1905 and 1906. ◆ Between Noe and Castro Sts

## 24 3780 23RD STREET

Constructed in 1865, this white Italianate Victorian is believed to be the oldest house in Noe Valley. It's a private residence. ◆ At Church St

## 25 NOE VALLEY

The last alcalde (mayor) of San Francisco under Mexican rule, José de Jesús Noé was one of many Spanish-Mexican notables to have a street named after him. Now his name defines a pretty neighborhood bordering the Castro and the Mission that appeals to families who favor the small-town ambience, abundant gardens, and period architecture. Its main shopping district is 24th Street, where boutiques, bookstores, and cafés proliferate. ◆ 24th St (between Dolores and Douglass Sts)

## 25 FIREFLY

★★★$$ You might miss this small place were it not for the bright yellow door and the glowing firefly above the entrance. The ambience here is comfortable and eclectic with mismatched flea market furniture and food that owner Brad Levy characterizes as home cooking from around the world. That might include appetizers of pot stickers with shrimp and scallops, chopped chicken livers, or latkes with apple sauce. Main-course choices may be barbecued chicken with mashed potatoes, grilled tuna with buckwheat noodles, or beef brisket. For dessert, try the chocolate chip cake. ◆ Californian ◆ Daily, dinner. 4288 24th St (at Douglass St). 821.7652. www.fireflyrestaurant.com &

## 26 BACCO RISTORANTE ITALIANO

★★$$ At first glance the menu might seem ordinary, but the preparations are anything but. Try the gnocchi, tender and light, or the simply sauced pastas, cooked exactly as they should be with just a little bite. The main courses are equally outstanding, especially the lamb chops and any veal dish. For dessert the warm chocolate cake, with a slightly runny center, is a real winner. To top it all off, the consummate Italian waiters are efficient yet friendly, with a good sense of humor. ◆ Italian ◆ Daily, dinner. Reservations recommended. 737 Diamond St (between 24th and Elizabeth Sts). 282.4969 &

## 27 PEEK-A-BOOTIQUE

New and lots of used clothing and toys for infants and children line the shelves of this pleasant shop. ◆ Daily. 1306 Castro St (at 24th St). 641.6192 &

## 28 OCEAN FRONT WALKER

Whimsical 100% cotton clothing for adults is this store's specialty. ◆ Daily. 4069 24th St (between Noe and Castro Sts). 550.1980. Also at 1458 Grant Ave (between Union and Green Sts). 550.1980 &

## 28 COVER TO COVER BOOKSELLERS

This spacious neighborhood bookstore is known for its excellent children's section and knowledgeable staff. Your kids will love it. ◆ Daily. 1307 Castro St (at 24th St). 282.8080 &

## 29 THE VALLEY TAVERN

This friendly neighborhood bar carries just about every brand of beer imaginable. There's a pool table and a dartboard. ◆ Daily. 4054 24th St (between Noe and Castro Sts). 285.0674 &

# TEA TIME

After exploring this exciting city, what could be more soothing to the spirit than a relaxing afternoon tea? Coffee-crazed San Franciscans can find their favorite brew on nearly every corner, but finding a good cup of tea and a pleasant place at which to enjoy it may prove more of a challenge.

In recent years, afternoon tea has replaced cocktails as a nonalcoholic alternative to happy hour with friends or as an informal setting for business meetings. But a bit of linguistic confusion prevails. Perhaps because the experience can be so uplifting, it often is called high tea. But any English person knows that high tea is a light supper of cold meats, fish, salads, and tea, usually served Sunday night.

Afternoon tea, by contrast, is a snack served late in the day that consists of tea, finger sandwiches, scones, and pastries. The Duchess of Bedford is said to have originated the tradition (partly to show off her beautiful tea services) in 1830. Since dinner was served quite late in those days, she decreed that tea be served at 5PM, and the late-afternoon restorative became all the rage.

Here are some of the many spots in San Francisco where you can indulge in afternoon tea. They afford a pleasant alternative to the city's ubiquitous coffeehouses—even the duchess would approve.

**King George Hotel** (334 Mason St, between O'Farrell and Geary Sts, 781.5050) is steeped in all the charm of a small European hotel. Afternoon tea is served on the mezzanine, along with assorted finger sandwiches, biscuits, and trifle.

Tea is served Monday through Saturday from 3PM to 6PM.

**Mark Hopkins Inter-Continental San Francisco** (1 Nob Hill, California and Mason Sts, 392.3434) The **Top of the Mark** makes a fine setting for afternoon tea, which is served daily from 2:30PM to 5:30PM. The tea consists of assorted sandwiches (perhaps Scottish smoked salmon, or a combination of English cheddar, cucumber, and York ham), scones and fancy pastries, and a choice of Darjeeling, Earl Grey, English breakfast, jasmine, or orange pekoe tea.

**Ritz-Carlton San Francisco Lobby Lounge** (600 Stockton St, at Pine St, 296.7465) serves a traditional English tea in formal surroundings—marble, French décor, and towering floral arrangements. Fourteen varieties of tea, plus sandwiches, cookies, scones, and all the trimmings, are available. Special events include fashion-show teas, etiquette teas, and even Teddy Bear teas for children at Yuletide. Tea is served daily from 2:30PM to 4:30PM.

**Teahouse at the Japanese Tea Garden** (Golden Gate Park, 752.1171) offers a truly unique setting to enjoy Japanese tea and a plate of simple cookies served by a staff wearing traditional costume. A reflective stroll along the manicured paths winding past flowers, shrines, and pools adds to the experience. The teahouse is located on the northwest side of the **Music Concourse.** Tea is served daily from 10AM to 5:30PM.

## 30 ELISA'S BEAUTY & HEALTH SPA

Here's a legitimate place to get the knots worked out of your body. Massage, an outdoor hot tub, a sauna, and a steam room are offered. Prices are discounted from noon to 4PM. ♦ Daily. 4028A 24th St (between Noe and Castro Sts). 821.6727

## 31 1051 NOE STREET

Constructed in 1891, this home is one of the 387 tower houses built in San Francisco. The tower was generally unconstructed within and is there just for show, although it's in dire need of a paint job. This is a private residence. ♦ At Elizabeth St (between 24th and 23rd Sts)

## 32 TULLY'S COFFEE CO.

Serious coffee for caffeine addicts is poured daily. The store does its own roasting too. ♦ Daily. 3966 24th St (between Sanchez and Noe Sts). 550.7416.

## 33 AMBIANCE

Womenswear in romantic retro styles fill the racks and store windows of two locations. The selection changes seasonally. Secondhand treasures from vintage stores and garage sales add to the ambience. ♦ Daily. 3985 and 3989 24th St (between Sanchez and Noe Sts). 647.5800. www.ambiancesf.com.

Restaurants/Clubs: Red | Hotels: Purple | Shops: Orange | Outdoors/Parks: Green | Sights/Culture: Blue

**Restored Victorians off 24th Street**

Also at 1458 Haight St. 552.5095; and 1864 Union St. 923.9797 &

### 33 STREETLIGHT

One of the largest selections of used CDs in the Bay Area can be found here. The store also carries a wide array of mainstream and unconventional music from classical to Cajun, used videos, and out-of-print and collectible 45s and LPs. The staff is notably helpful. ♦ Daily. 3979 24th St (between Sanchez and Noe Sts). 282.3550 &

### 34 HIDDEN COTTAGE

$$ Longtime Noe Valley residents Dave and Ginger Cannata rent charming guest apartments in Victorian-style buildings in this historic section of San Francisco. Each apartment has a full kitchen and stocked pantry. Rates are $175 a night with a two-night minimum. View apartments online. ♦ 1186 Noe Street. 282.4492. www.hiddencottage.com &

### 35 24TH ST. CHEESE CO.

Three hundred different cheeses are offered along with excellent pâtés, fine wines, and specialty food items. ♦ Daily. 3893 24th St (at Sanchez St). 821.6658

### 35 TUGGEY'S

Noe Valley's beloved hardware store offers personal service to do-it-yourselfers. It's been in the neighborhood since the early 1900s and hasn't changed much since.

♦ Daily. 3885 24th St (between Church and Sanchez Sts). 282.5081 &

### 36 HOLEY BAGEL

Ex–New Yorkers rejoiced when this business opened in San Francisco. Here's the place to find those foods dear to a Jewish-food lover's heart: bagels made daily, smoked fish, pickled tomatoes, and knishes. ♦ Daily, breakfast and lunch. 3872 24th St (between Church and Sanchez Sts). 647.3334

### 37 NOE'S SPORTS BAR & GRILL

A neighborhood tavern with a vaguely publike appearance, this place specializes in Irish coffee. It opens pretty early for those who hanker for a drink along with their sunshine. ♦ Daily, 10AM-2AM. 1199 Church St (at 24th St). 282.4007 &

### 38 NOE'S NEST B&B

$$ Each guest room in this stately 19th-century Victorian has a private bath and a queen- or king-size bed. Visitors appreciate the TVs, DVD players, and free local phone calls. Rates are $119 to $169 and include what owner Sheila Ash calls a Brooklyn breakfast: quiche, fresh fruit, bagels, lox, cream cheese, cereal, and juice. ♦ 1257 Guerrero St (between 25th and 24th Sts). 821.0751. www.noesnest.com &

### 39 LOVEJOY'S TEA ROOM

★★$$ Leave it to the English to impress upon us the importance of teatime with

The variable weather of San Francisco is often more noticeable in Pacific Heights, with the fog funneling through the Golden Gate Bridge and flowing around the shoreline and hills. At almost any time of year, you can climb up a gray hillside to the sound of foghorns and stare down onto a sun-drenched view of the other side.

---

For a walk that will literally take your breath away, head over to Filbert Street, the steepest street in San Francisco. It boasts a whopping 31.5 percent grade between Hyde and Leavenworth Streets—enough to make even the most shipshape soul sweat.

In 1907, famous escape artist Harry Houdini put on a show at San Francisco's Aquatic Park. While submerged deep in the frigid waters of the bay, he unshackled himself from chains in just 57 seconds.

---

"It's an odd thing, but anyone who disappears is said to be seen in San Francisco. It must be a delightful city and possess all the attractions of the next world."

Oscar Wilde

---

San Francisco has about 3,200 restaurants and bars, or one for every 230 residents.

friends. You'll feel at home on a plump sofa or in front of the window at a lace-draped table. Yorkshire Gold is the house tea, which you sip from dainty china cups. High tea comes with salad, sandwiches, a scone with Devonshire cream, shortbread, and biscuits. Aside from high tea you can have ploughman's lunch, shepherd's pie, or Cornish pasties. ♦ English ♦ W-Su, 11AM-6PM. 1351 Church St (at Clipper St). 648.5895

## 40 ERIC'S

★★$ In a converted store in a Victorian apartment building, Eric's has large picture windows, hardwood floors, and a comforting ambience. Noe Valley residents have adopted Eric's as their neighborhood restaurant and show up weekly for tiger prawns, bird's nest soup, or fiery *kung pao* chicken. ♦ Hunan and Mandarin ♦ M-Sa, lunch; daily, dinner. 1500 Church St (at 27th St). 282.0919

## 41 ONE STOP PARTY SHOP

Stock up on cards, glitter, gift bags, banners, balloons, and all the other stuff that makes a party fun. It's the only store of its kind in Noe Valley. ♦ Tu-Su. 1600 Church St (at 28th St). 824.0414 &

## 42 DREWES MEATS

This friendly meat-and-fish market was established as the **Fairmount Market** in 1888 by German immigrant Frederick Drewes and his partner, Otto Dierks. It has had only two names and three owners since it opened. ♦ Daily. 1706 Church St (at 29th St). 821.0515 &

## 43 PESCHERIA

★★$$ Italian-inspired pasta, soup, and calamari. The garden at Pescheria blooms year-round and the brick patio is the best in the valley for alfresco dining. ♦ Italian seafood ♦ Tu-Su, dinner; Sa, Su, brunch. 1708 Church St (between 30th and 29th Sts). 647.3200

---

Restaurants/Clubs: Red | Hotels: Purple | Shops: Orange | Outdoors/Parks: Green | Sights/Culture: Blue

# SUNSET/TWIN PEAKS

The heart of San Francisco's fog belt encompasses a large expanse lined with row after row of single-family, pastel-colored, look-alike houses.

During the 1920s and 1930s, the Sunset emerged as a residential neighborhood, with most of the houses financed by the Federal Housing Administration (FHA). Developer Henry Doelger paved over the sand dunes and built two houses a day throughout the Depression, selling them for $5,000 each. The general image of the district is of conservative, white, middle-class families, although international stirrings are gradually

being felt with the advent of a number of Asians around Noriega Street and a young Irish colony. The **Ingleside** area, the site of one of San Francisco's early racetracks, is another residential enclave. And on **Irving Street** in the so-called **Inner Sunset,** cafés and clubs offer restaurants and shops with an international flavor. Craig Newmark runs Craigslist from a Victorian at 1381 Ninth Avenue. The Sunset is home to **Stonestown Galleria** and **San Francisco State University.** Also here is **Lake Merced,** originally named **Lake of Our Lady of Mercy** and part of a surrounding ranchero granted by José Castro to José Antonio Galino in 1835. Today it is a standby reservoir for the city, as well as its "backyard fishin' hole."

**Stern Grove** comes alive on Sunday during the summer, when thousands settle in for picnics and free jazz and classical-music concerts. Beautiful **Saint Francis Wood** is an expensive development of large homes with gates and fountains designed by Beaux Arts architect **John Galen Howard.** Nearby is sedate, middle-class **West Portal,** whose diagonal and curving streets make it look somewhat like a Swiss village. It lies at the foot of three hills: **Mount Davidson, Forest Hill,** and **Edgehill Heights.** Land here was originally part of a Spanish land grant.

Twin Peaks, an area containing the second- and third-highest hills in the city, offers wonderful 360-degree panoramas of the Bay Area. Even view-crazy San Franciscans left the area alone until World War II, but today it is a very popular neighborhood, with spectacular houses the size of great villas and many apartment complexes. On the south side, single-family homes face the **San Bruno Mountains** and the ocean. The upscale neighborhood known as **Forest Hill,** which was planned in 1913 and had racially restrictive covenants until the 1950s, remains a generally conservative and stable family bastion, full of handsome houses and lush landscaping. Tucked away in **Glen Park,** a neighborhood with the feeling of a small village, lies **Glen Canyon,** where, according to old-timers, Russian smugglers once hid their contraband.

# The Yeast Also Rises

San Franciscans lay such possessive claim to sourdough bread that many visitors assume it originated here. But the truth is the ancient Egyptians actually whipped up the first batch of sourdough more than 4,000 years ago. Columbus supposedly carried a sour starter on his voyage to America, and the Pilgrims routinely used sour starters in bread making.

When commercially available yeasts and baking powders began to be produced in the 19th century, sour starter fell out of favor. (The starter, a combination of fermented flour, water, and sugar that makes the dough rise, had to be sustained from batch to batch, with the baker replenishing the ingredients weekly.) Once cooks could readily purchase yeast and baking powder, the use of sour starters was largely limited to folks who lived far from settlements. During the Alaskan Gold Rush in the 1890s, for instance, prospectors used sour starters so extensively they earned the nickname "sourdoughs." And since many set sail for the Yukon gold fields from San Francisco, the bread became inexorably linked with the city.

Although it is, of course, possible to bake sourdough bread anywhere, San Franciscans maintain that the flavor of their loaves cannot be duplicated. Chef and cookbook author Bernard Clayton, determined to test this chauvinistic assertion, imported samples of San Francisco sourdough starter to his home in Bloomington, Indiana. Each time, however, no matter how carefully he tried to preserve the integrity of the starter, the batch metamorphosed into what he called "Bloomington sourdough bread," which had a distinctly different flavor. "I came to appreciate," he finally lamented, "that to bake San Francisco sourdough bread consistently I would probably have to live there."

Clayton and other aficionados claim that the unique flavor of the local bread can be attributed to the spores, fungi, and bacteria that waft through the San Francisco air. So popular is this theory, in fact, that one of the chefs at a top **Nob Hill** hostelry is rumored to have maintained the same batch of sourdough starter for years in a box on the hotel's roof so it may absorb all those atmospheric San Francisco treats.

## 1 Marnee Thai

★★$ Although it's one of the most popular Thai restaurants in the city, the food has lost a bit of its edge recently. The signature dish is a fresh, thin corn-and-ginger cake that is deep-fried to a honey brown. Other top choices are raw spinach leaves filled with dried shrimp and ginger, and spicy green papaya salad with wedges of tomatoes and whole green beans. ♦ Thai ♦ M, W-Su, lunch and dinner. Reservations recommended. 2225 Irving St (at 23rd Ave). 665.9500 &

## 1 Yum Yum Fish

★★$ A sushi bar in a fish market on this stretch of Irving Street means top-quality selections. The sashimi and fancy sushi rolls are a deal at this small restaurant and fish market. Try the dragon roll or sushi combo, which is served with complimentary hot tea. Last call for sushi is at 7:15PM. ♦ Japanese ♦ Tu-Su, lunch and early dinner. 2181 Irving St (at 23rd Ave). 566.6433 &

## 2 Ebisu

★★$$ Before sushi became trendy, Ebisu had been serving some of the best raw fish in the city for 25 years. The surroundings are plain, but people will wait for a seat at the sushi bar or in the dining room. The prime spot is at the bar, where diners can talk to the sushi chef, who advises them on what's best that night. Other than the excellent sushi and sashimi, which includes live scallops and toro, you can order seafood salad with seaweed or chicken teriyaki. ♦ Japanese ♦ Daily, lunch and dinner. 1283 Ninth Ave (between Irving St and Lincoln Way). 566.1770

## 3 Irving Street

This is a main shopping thoroughfare for residents of the Sunset District. Stores, cafés, and small restaurants (with a heavy emphasis on Asian cuisines) are concentrated between 5th and 26th Avenues. The area is not chic, but serves the day-to-day needs of the locals.

## 3 Naan 'n' Curry

★★$ The name of the restaurant sums up just what you need on a foggy night in the Sunset. Tandoori lamb chops with fresh naan and a mango lassi make a great trio. The Pakistani owners whip up tasty curries, as well as chana masala with garbanzos and aloo ghobi with potato and cauliflower. Order at the counter, get your own tableware, then pay afterward. ♦ Indian ♦ Daily, lunch and dinner. 642 Irving St (near Eighth Ave). 664.7225. & Also at 478 O'Farrell St (at Jones St). 775.1349; and 533 Jackson St (at Columbus Ave). 693.0499

## 4 University of California, San Francisco

Adolph Sutro contributed the land that became the 107-acre **Parnassus Campus** of one of the world's great centers for biomedical research. Professional schools of medicine, pharmacy, nursing, and dentistry, as well as a separate graduate studies division, are here. The campus also includes the **Langley Porter Psychiatric Institute and Hospital,** which was the city's first psychiatric hospital and training center, and the **Medical Center,** composed of **Moffitt/Long Hospitals** and the **Ambulatory Care Center.** In addition, the campus contains two of the country's major social- and public-policy institutes, and at least 600 community outreach programs, some of which operate statewide. The medical center pioneered the study and treatment of infant respiratory distress syndrome. On campus, the **Cole Hall Cinema** presents weekly movies and stages lectures and entertainment for the general public. ♦ Entrance at 513 Parnassus Ave (bounded by Parnassus Ave, Fourth Ave, Crestmont Dr, Clarendon Ave, and Stanyan St). Weekly campus tours 476.9000 Ꮺ

Within the Parnassus Campus:

### Sutro TV Tower

In 1968 this tower was built on top of Mount Sutro; it supports TV antennae for several of San Francisco's stations. Once a controversial design because of its tripod form and size, it is now an accepted part of the landscape. ♦ Off Warren Dr

## 5 Polly Ann Ice Cream

This parlor dishes up 400 flavors (50 on any given day), including passion fruit, lychee, guava, jackfruit, and taro. For less exotic tastes, owner Charles Wu offers Bumpy Road (his answer to Rocky Road) and coffee rum fudge. If it's too hard to decide what to order, spin the flavor wheel and hope you like what it lands on. Oh, and bring your pooch—they'll give the lucky pup a free Doggie Cone. ♦ Daily. No credit cards accepted. 3142 Noriega St (between 38th and 39th Aves). 664.2472 Ꮺ

## 6 Forest Hill

This upscale community, planned in 1913 by **Mark Daniels,** who also designed Sea Cliff (a well-to-do neighborhood near The Presidio), follows the contours of a hill and is favored by those who like big homes and don't mind a lot of fog. A triangular piece of manicured lawn and a huge urn, located before Magellan Avenue, suggest a sense of formality for the area. ♦ Main entrance is on Pacheco St (off Dewey Blvd)

Within Forest Hill:

### Forest Hill Association Clubhouse

Rented out for weddings and other events, this Tudor-inspired building was built, along with the gardens, by neighborhood volunteers in 1919. **Bernard Maybeck** was the architect. ♦ 381 Magellan Ave (at Montalvo Ave). 664.0542 Ꮺ

## 7 Twin Peaks

The Costanoan Indians believed that these peaks were created when the Great Spirit separated a quarreling couple with a clap of thunder in order to have peace. Spanish explorers named them Breasts of the Indian Girl. Then unimaginative Americans changed the name to Twin Peaks. The steep, grassy slopes are a wonderful, if windy, lookout point, providing a 360-degree view of the entire bay—the best vista in San Francisco. At night, the crest is surrounded by a sea of twinkling lights spreading in every direction. It was from this spot that **Daniel Burnham** conceived his city plan in 1905. Today the view provides cause for reflection on civilization and the effects of "progress;" too often the panorama is marred by smog from polluted air, and you can see how the hills have been carved up and nearly obliterated by stacks of housing developments. Take a sweater; the winds here are chilly even in the summer. ♦ Off Twin Peaks Blvd

## 8 Taraval Street

Another of the Sunset's main shopping streets, this one is less lively than Irving Street. Most of the activity is concentrated between 14th and 23rd Avenues.

## 9 West Portal Avenue

In this shopping area that serves neighborhood residents, most of the small businesses are concentrated between Ulloa Street and 15th Avenue.

On West Portal Avenue:

### Café for All Seasons

★★$$ The food at this trendy, attractive Forest Hill establishment is tasty and fresh with creative pastas always on the menu. It's worth a visit if you're in the area. ♦ Californian ♦ M-F, lunch and dinner; Sa, Su, brunch and dinner. 150 West Portal Ave (at 14th Ave). 665.0900. www.cafeforallseasons.com Ꮺ

---

Restaurants/Clubs: Red  |  Hotels: Purple  |  Shops: Orange  |  Outdoors/Parks: Green  |  Sights/Culture: Blue

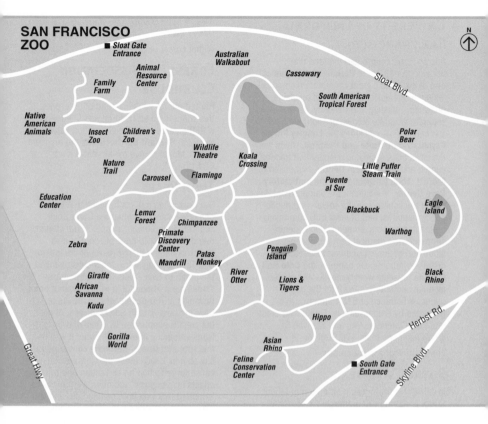

**SAN FRANCISCO ZOO**

■ Sloat Gate Entrance
Australian Walkabout
Animal Resource Center
Family Farm
Cassowary
Sloat Blvd.
South American Tropical Forest
Native American Animals
Insect Zoo
Children's Zoo
Polar Bear
Wildlife Theatre
Koala Crossing
Nature Trail
Carousel
Flamingo
Little Puffer Steam Train
Puente al Sur
Education Center
Lemur Forest
Chimpanzee
Blackbuck
Eagle Island
Warthog
Zebra
Primate Discovery Center
Mandrill
Patas Monkey
Penguin Island
Giraffe
African Savanna
Kudu
River Otter
Lions & Tigers
Black Rhino
Hippo
Herbst Rd.
Gorilla World
Asian Rhino
Feline Conservation Center
■ South Gate Entrance
Great Hwy.
Skyline Blvd.

## 10 MOUNT DAVIDSON

Part of Adolph Sutro's 12,000-acre estate, this is the highest spot in San Francisco, rising 938 feet. A great white concrete-and-steel cross looms 103 feet above the summit. George Davidson, surveyor for the US Coast and Geodetic Survey, originally surveyed the mountain in 1852 and dubbed it Blue Mountain. It was later renamed in his honor. Easter sunrise services have been held at the base of the cross since 1923. ♦ Off Portola Dr

## 11 SAN FRANCISCO ZOO

In recent years, the zoo (see the map above) has had its share of woes, including the 1989 earthquake, which damaged a few exhibits; scandals regarding some zookeepers' treatment of the elephants; and design flaws in the much-heralded primate center. Still, millions of dollars have been spent on innovative exhibitions, and management is dedicated to transforming this 73-year-old institution into a world-class zoo. They recently added a new entry, village, and outdoor café. It attracts more than a million visitors annually. Natural habitats are gradually taking the place of cramped, fenced enclosures, with nearly a thousand exotic animals hanging from treetops, roaming through fields, and lounging on foggy islands.

These settings enable visitors to see the animals behaving more naturally. The **Thelma and Henry Doelger Primate Discovery Center** highlights this philosophy. Here, from multi-level walkways, you can watch many species of monkeys and apes leap from tree to tree. **Gorilla World** is one of the planet's largest naturalistic gorilla exhibits, with two young and five adult gorillas.

This is also one of only a handful of zoos in the country that have koalas. The cuddly, eucalyptus-eating marsupials, native to Brisbane, Australia, live on a grassy knoll in **Koala Crossing.** When the weather is bad, they move to an indoor thicket of eucalyptus boughs. Black tie is always required on **Penguin Island,** where a colony of more than 54 Magellanic penguins with names such as Anne Arctica, Popsicle, and Oreo nestle in specially landscaped burrows. The **Lion House** is home to African lions and Siberian, Sumatran, and Bengal tigers. A crowd always shows up at 2PM (except on Monday) to watch the feeding of the big cats. The **Children's Zoo** features a **Barnyard** where you may pet and feed the assorted menagerie of domestic animals, as well as an **Insect Zoo,** featuring everything from a working beehive to the hissing cockroach. The *Zebra Zephyr Train* takes you on an informative 20-minute safari tour, daily during the spring, summer, and fall, and on weekends in the winter.

The zoo opened in 1929, and now takes up 65 of its allocated 125 acres of land. New attractions include the **Feline Conservation Center,** where rare and endangered small cats such as snow leopards and pumas are bred and researched, and the **Australian WalkAbout,** featuring wallabies and kangaroos. ♦ Admission. Free the first Wednesday of every month. Daily. Tours weekends. Sloat Blvd (at 45th Ave). 753.7080. www.sfzoo.org &

## 12 SIGMUND STERN MEMORIAL GROVE

Ⓟ A 63-acre grove of eucalyptus, redwood, and fir trees shelters a sunken natural amphitheater. This is a favorite spot among city dwellers for its free Sunday-afternoon summer concerts, which showcase a variety of programs from opera to jazz to dance. Reserve a picnic table in advance (call 666.7027 the Monday morning preceding the concert) to make the most of the day. Most of the park's benches are reserved for senior citizens and people with disabilities, on a first-come, first-served basis. The gingerbread **Trocadero Clubhouse** in the grove was once a gambling house and hideout for Abe Rueff, a political shyster. It was renovated by **Bernard Maybeck,** who left the two bullet holes in the door as souvenirs of the shootout that led to Rueff's capture, and was spruced up again in the 1980s. ♦ Sloat Blvd (at 19th Ave). &

## 13 ST. FRANCIS WOOD

Beautifully landscaped, this development of large, expensive homes has gates and a fountain designed by **John Galen Howard,** noted Beaux Arts architect. It is rich in Spanish Revival structures. Although a well-established, affluent neighborhood, it is bourgeois and located in the less-than-fashionable southern fog belt (the cream of San Francisco's society lives on the north side of the city). The entry gate—marked by gardens and a central fountain—is an impressive site. ♦ Portola Dr (at St. Francis Blvd)

## 14 COMMODORE SLOAT SCHOOL

This renovation of an existing public grammar school, together with a new extension by **Marquis Associates,** has been designed as a series of courtyards. It is faced in stucco and sports a nautical look, with large portholes that have become a feature of the school's design. ♦ Ocean Ave (at Junipero Serra Blvd)

## 15 STONESTOWN GALLERIA

California's first regional shopping center, and the third in the entire US, was built and owned by the Stoneson family in 1951, then sold to a Chicago realty firm in 1990. Shops are located beneath skylit vaulted ceilings in a neoclassical setting with bubbling fountains. It was originally conceived as a city-within-the-city, and although much of the merchandising has gone upscale, the original concept still remains. There is a medical building, a supermarket, a movie theater, a drugstore, two main department stores **(Nordstrom** and **Macy's),** and 120 other shops selling everything from specialty foods to music boxes. The free parking gives this mall an edge over downtown stores. ♦ Daily. 19th Ave (at Winston Dr). 564.8848 &

## 16 SAN FRANCISCO STATE UNIVERSITY

This 100-acre campus, part of the California state university system, provides undergraduate and graduate programs for approximately 26,000 students. Celebrated graduates have included actor Danny Glover, singer Johnny Mathis, authors Anne Rice and Ernest Gaines, Congressman Ron Dellum, and San Francisco's mayor, Willie Brown. The university's **McKenna Theatre** often has programs that are open to the public including a monthly chamber music series. ♦ 1600 Holloway Ave (at 19th Ave). 338.1111 &

## 17 INGLESIDE

One of the city's first racetracks opened here to a crowd of 8,000 people on Thanksgiving Day in 1885. Twenty years later the track was closed, and Ingleside Terrace was built in its place. Development was slow until the Twin Peaks Tunnel was completed in 1917 and large-scale residential construction began. The loop of the racetrack is now Urbano Drive. ♦ Bounded by Junipero Serra Blvd, Holloway Ave, Ashton Ave, Ocean Ave, and Cerritos Ave

## 18 LAKE MERCED

Ⓟ Once part of a rancho, this large, tree-lined freshwater lake is one of San Francisco's standby reservoirs. It is also a popular trout-fishing hole, with good catches available year-round. Small craft for trips around the lake can be rented at a boathouse run by the **Recreation and Parks Department.** Rowboats, canoes, and paddleboats are available every day (weather permitting). ♦ Boat rentals: daily from an hour before sunrise to an hour after sunset. Off Harding Blvd (adjacent to the zoo). 681.3310

---

Restaurants/Clubs: Red | Hotels: Purple | Shops: Orange | Outdoors/Parks: Green | Sights/Culture: Blue

# GOLDEN GATE PARK

**B**y the middle of the 1800s, the relatively new city of San Francisco was determined to shape itself along the grandiose lines of the well-established East Coast and European metropolises. Civic pride, fueled by a desire to have a public park comparable to New York City's Central Park, launched **Golden Gate Park,** a 1,017-acre oasis of greenery, museums, and recreational facilities stretching from the Haight to the Pacific Ocean. The project's beginnings were tempestuous and mired in difficulties. Squatters, who claimed ownership by right of possession, slowed progress for years after the city originally petitioned the board of land commissioners for the property in 1852.

Renowned landscape architect Frederick Law Olmsted, who had designed New York City's Central Park, paid a visit to the proposed park site, laughingly called "the great sand bank," at the invitation of the Board of Supervisors. He took one look at the seemingly inhospitable tract of land, declared the project impossible, and advised that another location be chosen. But William Hammond Hall took up the gauntlet, and designed a layout for a park that respected the land's natural contours. By 1866 plans were under way to transform the barren, windswept, shifting sand dunes into a verdant oasis that would function as the lungs of the city.

Work began in 1871 with reclamation and development of the **Panhandle,** the block-wide strip of land between **Fell** and **Oak Streets** that leads into the park from **Baker** to **Stanyan Streets.** Public-spirited citizens donated funds for most of the buildings and statues in the park.

A dour, determined young Scot named John McLaren was the gardening wizard whose expertise and vision shaped the park that many naysayers had regarded as a white elephant. When he took on the formidable task in 1890 as superintendent of gardening, his formula was to plant grass to "tack down the sand," and then plant trees. Though many of his initial efforts were buried underneath mounds of sand, his crews persistently coaxed and coddled the struggling plants with manure and humus. Through perseverance that continued for more than half a century, until his death at age 96, McLaren lovingly tended his "white elephant;" trees grew and thrived, and the park evolved into a forest enhanced by lakes and meadows.

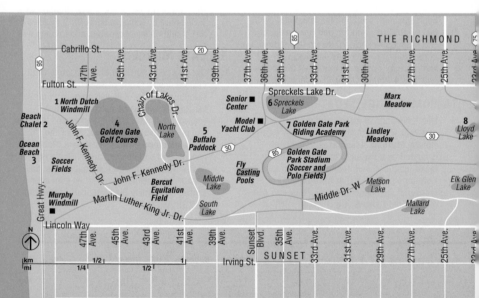

Affectionately known as Uncle John, McLaren developed a correspondence with horticulturists all over the world that paid off with a rich bounty of plants and trees. He planted about a million trees and introduced 700 new species of trees and shrubs to California in 1931 alone. His germinated seeds grew into gigantic trees up to 80 feet tall.

The feisty Scotsman battled regularly with City Hall to prevent the encroachment of non-park-related enterprises into *his* empire. One time, he thwarted construction of a streetcar line through the park by arguing that some of his precious trees would have to be uprooted to accommodate it. In turn, the engineers explained that they had planned the route through unplanted areas, but McLaren insisted they were wrong. When the supervisors arrived at the site the following morning to mediate the argument, they were greeted by shrubbery, small trees, and rhododendrons, which resulted in their veto of the streetcar proposal. What they didn't know was that 300 of Uncle John's employees had been busy planting all those shrubs only the night before. McLaren continued to shape the park until the end of his life, firmly rooted in his conviction that it was a place to be used and enjoyed, rather than a look-but-don't-touch showplace. He forbade "keep off the grass" signs, and tucked pompous-looking statues into corners where they would soon be hidden by rapidly growing shrubs. After the city's 1906 earthquake and fire McLaren had to rebuild many of the landscaped areas because thousands of displaced residents had set up camp in the park. At age 90, still superintendent of the park, he was asked what he wanted for a birthday gift; his response was "10,000 yards of good manure." When he died, Uncle John took one last ride through his beloved park on 14 January 1943 with 400 grieving gardeners and foremen standing at attention. His statue stands at the entrance of the **Rhododendron Dell**.

In the 1970s it was discovered that much of the park was dying, as trees planted when the park was first born had reached maturity. A reforestation program was instituted, and thousands of new trees were planted.

**Golden Gate Park** today is a countryside of flower beds, meadows, lakes, gardens, waterfalls, rolling hills, and forests. You could spend days in it and be unaware of the surrounding metropolis. The park offers something for everyone: recreational facilities for baseball, soccer, horseshoe pitching, fly casting, golf, horseback riding, tennis, and

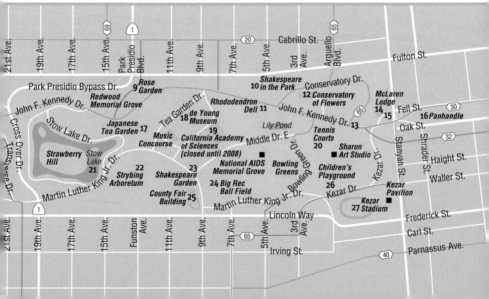

picnicking. And it has a huge network of walking paths and bicycle tracks, more than 6,000 varieties of flowers, dozens of species of trees, bowling greens, boccie courts, a football field, stables, and checker pavilions.

Over the years, the park has been the site of many events. Thousands of hippies tuned in, turned on, and dropped out during the Human Be-In of 1967. The famous annual Bay to Breakers race still takes place and features more than 100,000 runners, joggers, and walkers (many of them dressed in costumes—or wearing nothing at all) panting their way to the finish line at **Ocean Beach;** the summer Shakespeare in the Park festival; the free Opera in the Park concert in September; and Comedy Celebration Day in July.

The park is well used by residents and visitors by day (especially on Sunday, when a large section of **JFK Drive,** which traverses the park, is closed), but city-sense is advised. Neither parking (unless authorized for special events) nor sleeping is permitted in the park after dusk. Rain or shine, several free guided walking tours take place on the weekends from May through October. Lasting an hour and a half to two hours, these tours operate under the auspices of the **Friends of Recreation and Parks.** For information on meeting places and itineraries, call 221.1311. The **Panhandle** and **Golden Gate Park** also have beautiful—albeit unmarked and obscure—bicycle trails, including the seven-and-a-half-mile route from the Panhandle through the park out to **Lake Merced.** To find out more about bike, bus, or special-interest tours, call 263.0991, or San Francisco Parks Trust at 750.5105. For information, visit the park online: www.parks.sfgov.org.

## 1 NORTH DUTCH WINDMILL

Built in 1902, this windmill was rededicated in 1981 after its restoration. Surrounding it is the **Queen Wilhelmina Tulip Garden,** a rainbow of color in the spring. ♦ Near 47th Ave and JFK Dr

## 2 BEACH CHALET

Built in 1925, and restored in 1996, this visitors' center has exhibits on park history while the surrounding 1930s murals depict scenes of the era. The **Beach Chalet Brewery and Restaurant** upstairs (1000 Great Highway, 386.8439) offers microbrew on tap, good food, and panoramic views of Ocean Beach. ♦ Near JFK Dr, off Great Hwy

## 3 OCEAN BEACH

When San Franciscans say "the beach," they are referring to this one, which stretches the length of the Great Highway. The undertow is extremely dangerous, swimming is prohibited, and wading is inadvisable, but it's fun for sunning, strolling, and beach games. ♦ Off the Great Hwy

## 4 GOLDEN GATE GOLF COURSE

This nine-hole course is open to the public. ♦ Daily. Off 47th Ave (between JFK Dr and Fulton St). 751.8987

## 5 BUFFALO PADDOCK

Strictly speaking, the shaggy creatures that roam this 35-acre enclosure are American bison. The park is home to 14 of them (1 male and 13 females), many brought here in 1984 to replace descendants of the original herd, which was genetically weakened from years of inbreeding. ♦ West end of JFK Dr (east of Chain of Lakes Dr)

## 6 SPRECKELS LAKE

This small lake is the setting for operating and watching model motorboats and sailboats. It is also a way station for a variety of migratory birds. ♦ 36th Ave (off Fulton St)

## 7 GOLDEN GATE PARK RIDING ACADEMY

A great way to see the park is on one of the guided trail rides offered here. The jaunts last about an hour (they're all walking, no cantering or trotting) and must be scheduled two or three days in advance. Riders must be at least eight years old. (They are not currently offering trail rides.) ♦ 36th Ave (at JFK Dr). 831.2773

## 8 PORTALS OF THE PAST

These two columns once graced the porch of a Nob Hill home, and were all that remained

# CHILD'S PLAY

A trip with your children in tow doesn't usually provide much in the way of rest and relaxation . . . but if you come to San Francisco, your vacation doesn't have to be as comically disastrous as *National Lampoon's Vacation* implies (remember Chevy Chase and his pack on their way to Wally World?). This city bends over backward to please everyone, even the most inquisitive toddlers and easily bored teenagers, so here's a guide to San Francisco's most amusing (and even educational) family-oriented sights, shops, and restaurants.

**1 Alcatraz** Both the ferry ride and the spooky atmosphere at the "Rock" make this excursion a favorite with youngsters. Rent the excellent audio-tour headset on the island; it will help your kids imagine what this former federal prison was like back in the days when Al Capone and the Birdman roamed its halls. The steep walk up to the prison and the somber nature of the tour make this an activity best suited to older children.

**2 Cable Cars** These quaint conveyances never fail to delight the kiddies, especially if you sit in the open-air section of the car on a hilly route. The wait to climb aboard can be long (see the cable-car routes on the inside back cover of this guide), but street performers are usually around to keep children and their parents amused.

**3 The Cannery, Ghirardelli Square, and Pier 39** All three of these lively tourist meccas at Fisherman's Wharf are replete with interesting shops, informal restaurants, and free performances by jugglers, mimes, musicians, and dancers. Kids will especially enjoy the **Ghirardelli Chocolate Manufactory;** nobody can resist indulging in a luscious sundae, float, or a steaming cup of chocolate with whipped cream at this ice-cream parlor-cum-choco-

late factory. At the Cannery, take the little ones to the **Basic Brown Bear Factory,** where they can stuff their own teddies, then dress them up as a witch, pumpkin, musketeer, or astronaut.

**4 Exploratorium** Located within the **Palace of Fine Arts,** this dynamic, hands-on science museum will keep school-age kids (and their parents) busy for hours. The museum store has a great selection of educational and science-related toys and the grounds include a lovely duck pond.

**5 Golden Gate Park** The **Children's Playground,** with its carousel, is great fun for toddlers on up. There are all kinds of boats for rent on **Stow Lake,** and remote-control craft to watch at **Spreckels Lake.** Bicycles, in-line skates, and roller skates are available to rent too. Other kid-pleasing attractions include the **Buffalo Paddock,** the **Japanese Tea Garden,** and the **Strybing Arboretum.**

**6 National Maritime Museum** Give little landlubbers a taste of life at sea. This museum employs photographs, memorabilia, and models to evoke the nautical history of the region, while the nearby **Hyde Street Pier** boasts three wonderful old sailing ships open to the public.

**7 The Randall Museum** Young nature fanciers will enjoy the animals at the **Petting Corral,** the gigantic whale skull, and other exhibits at this wildlife and California-history museum.

**8 San Francisco Zoo** There's a lot more to this zoo than lions and tigers and bears, oh my! Highlights include the **Primate Discovery Center** (with a family of seven gorillas), the **Children's Zoo,** a gorgeous old carousel, **Koala Crossing,** the **Zebra Zephyr Train** tour, an energy-expending playground, and feeding time at the **Lion House.**

after the 1906 earthquake. They suffered some damage in the quake of October 1989. ♦ North side of Lloyd Lake (off JFK Dr)

## 9 ROSE GARDEN

Ⓟ Fifty-three beds of award-winning roses bloom here in great variety. ♦ South end of Park Presidio Blvd (between JFK Dr and Fulton St)

## 10 SHAKESPEARE IN THE PARK

A temporary outdoor theater is erected annually in **Liberty Tree Meadow** for

professional performances of the Bard's work. ♦ Free. Sa, Su, Labor Day through 30 Sept. Off JFK Dr (west of The Conservatory). 831.5500 &

## 11 RHODODENDRON DELL

Ⓟ This memorial to John McLaren honors him with his favorite flower. There are more than 3,000 plants and 500 species here. ♦ Between Middle Dr E, JFK Dr, and the California Academy of Sciences

**Restaurants/Clubs: Red | Hotels: Purple | Shops: Orange | Outdoors/Parks: Green | Sights/Culture: Blue**

## 12 THE CONSERVATORY OF FLOWERS

The oldest existing building in the park, The Conservatory was modeled after the Palm House at Kew Gardens in London and erected by **Lord and Burnham** in 1878 for eccentric millionaire James Lick. The structure was shipped from Ireland around Cape Horn and survived both the 1906 earthquake and a major fire. This masterpiece of Victorian architecture is the oldest and only glass-and-wood conservatory in the US. It contains 10,000 specimens of rare and endangered species, including carnivorous plants and a world-famous collection of orchids. The Conservatory of Flowers reopened after the catastrophic winter of 1995. Winds up to 100 mph shattered over 3,000 panes of glass and destroyed thousands of plants. ♦ 100 JFK Dr (in the eastern end of Golden Gate Park). Free the first Tuesday of every month. 666.7001. ♿. www.conservatoryofflowers.org

## 13 JFK DRIVE

On Sunday, this street is closed to auto traffic from Kezar to Transverse Drives, and open to roller skaters, in-line skaters, skateboarders, and joggers, many of them locomoting to private rhythms emanating from their headphones. Skate-rental facilities are located nearby on both Fulton and Haight Streets. ♦ Between Kezar and Transverse Drs

## 14 MCLAREN LODGE

The home of John McLaren throughout his long term as superintendent of the park now serves as the headquarters of San Francisco's Recreation and Parks Department. Park information and maps are available in this Richardsonian Romanesque pile of sandstone. ♦ M-F. Fell St (at Stanyan St). 831.2700 ♿

## 15 GOLDEN GATE PARK SHUTTLE

Ride the free Golden Gate Park Shuttle to all park attractions on weekends and holidays from May to October. Look for Park Shuttle Stops from McLaren Lodge to Ocean Beach. The shuttle also stops near the Conservatory of Flowers, Academy of Sciences, National AIDS Memorial Grove, Japanese Tea Garden, Strybing Arboretum, Stow Lake, Buffalo Paddock, the Polo Fields, and the Beach Chalet. ♦ JFK Drive (near Fell St)

## 16 PANHANDLE

🅟 The trees here are the oldest in the park. Beginning with barley, then sand grass, then blue gum and live oak trees, park engineer William Hammond Hall gradually worked up the botanical chain as the hardier plants took root and more diversified shrubs could be planted. ♦ Bounded by Baker and Stanyan Sts, and Oak and Fell Sts

## 17 JAPANESE TEA GARDEN

This and the **Music Concourse**—both built for the California Midwinter International Exposition of 1894—are the only structures gardener McLaren did not have torn down after the fair ended. In 1895 the tea garden became the charge of the Hagiwara family, who tended it with loving devotion. Makoto Hagiwara is credited with inventing the fortune cookie here. Ironically, the cookies have come to be called Chinese fortune cookies and are a favorite item of the tourist trade in Chinatown. The Hagiwara family maintained the garden until World War II, when they, along with 110,000 other Japanese-Americans, were sent to internment camps. This jewel of **Golden Gate Park** is so artfully designed that even the hordes of visitors cannot mar the tranquil experience.

Architecture, landscape, and humans blend subtly and beautifully in a harmonious pattern of bridges, footpaths, pools, flowers, trees, statuary, shrines, and gates. It is especially breathtaking in April when the cherry trees are in bloom. The *Bronze Buddha,* donated by the Gump brothers in 1949, was cast in Japan in 1790. The **Shinto Pagoda** is a five-tiered wooden shrine. The **Moon Bridge,** also called the **Wishing Bridge,** casts its semicircular reflection in the pool below, making a full circle.

The piles of old stones in a clearing behind the tea garden are the disassembled remains of a medieval Cistercian monastery from Spain. In 1932 William Randolph Hearst bought the monastery, had it dismantled and shipped over here, and later donated it to the **M.H. de Young Memorial Museum.** Except for the reconstruction of the chapel portal, which still stands in the de Young's central court, and the unobtrusive incorporation of some of the ruins in retaining walls and rockeries around the park, the majority of the stones have never been reassembled, largely due to lack of funds. There is also a gift shop and a **Tea House,** serving tea, soft drinks, juices, and cookies. ♦ Admission; reduced admission for seniors and children (6-12); free for children 5 and under; free daily 9AM-9:30AM Mar-Oct; 8:30AM-9AM, 5PM-

6PM (or until sunset) Nov-Feb. Daily. Near the Asian Art Museum (between Martin Luther King Jr. and JFK Drs.). 752.4227, gift shop 752.1171

## 18 THE DE YOUNG MUSEUM

A modern sanctuary for the de Young's world-renowned art collection, the new $177 million museum, with its massive copper sheathing and ribbons of windows, opened in October 2005. Designed by German architects **Herzog and de Meuron,** the spacious interior boasts interconnected galleries and courtyards. Wilsey Court, the vaulted-ceiling central gathering place with an Italian stone floor and a massive painting by Gerhard Richter, is named for fund-raiser Dede Wilsey, who donated $10 million and raised most of the private funding.

The de Young's diverse collections—encompassing American painting and decorative arts—include works by John Singleton Copley, Thomas Hart Benton, Winslow Homer, Mary Cassatt, Edward Hopper, Georgia O'Keeffe, Diego Rivera, Willem de Kooning, and Mark Rothko. Also on view are the arts of the Americas, the Pacific Islands, and Africa. Emerge from the galleries to admire the new sculpture garden and terrace. The beloved original building closed in 2000 after suffering irreparable damage from the 1989 earthquake. The **Hamon Tower** on the observation floor (the copper-clad "thumb" rising above the trees) is free. ♦ 50 Hagiwara Tea Garden Dr. 863.3330, 866/912.6326. www.thinker.org

Within the de Young Museum:

### DE YOUNG CAFE

★★★$ At this special café you'll want to kick back and enjoy the view. The patio overlooks the **Barbro Osher Sculpture Garden,** so all senses are stimulated. The kitchen serves ingredients grown or produced within 150 miles of the de Young. Seasonal dishes brim with fresh, local produce straight from the farm. Try the Niman Ranch lamb with pomegranate sauce, the Dungeness crab cakes, or the salad with roasted winter root vegetables. Also recommended are the cheese platter and the Marin Sun Farms grass-fed beef. Art-glass light fixtures dangle from the ceiling like yo-yos. The black metal chairs look like polygons from outer space but are surprisingly comfortable. ♦ Californian ♦ Tu-Su, 9:30AM-4PM ⚫

## 19 CALIFORNIA ACADEMY OF SCIENCES

Closed until late 2008. When the $430 million project is completed, the Academy of Sciences will be a new 410,000-square-foot structure with a living roof planted with 1.7 million native plants. The public will be able to interact with scientists as they work in two large project labs. The new **Steinhart Aquarium** will have a two-story swamp and a 212,000-gallon tank with a living Philippine coral reef. The academy was founded in 1853 just following the Gold Rush, and is the West's oldest scientific institution. ♦ South side of the Music Concourse (between Middle Dr E and JFK Dr). 750.7145 Some museums have been temporarily relocated to 875 Howard St (between Fourth and Fifth Sts). www.calacademy.org

## 20 TENNIS COURTS

Some 21 courts, just north of the **Children's Playground,** draw players of all levels of expertise. ♦ Nominal fee. Reservations required. Off Bowling Green Dr (at Middle Dr E). Advance reservations 753.7101; same-day reservations 753.7001

## 21 STOW LAKE

🐧 This is the largest lake in the park and the only place to rent bicycles, rowboats, paddleboats, and motorboats. Bring your own food to picnic by the shore, or pick up something at the small concession stand. ♦ Boathouse and snack bar: Daily. Stow Lake Dr (between Martin Luther King Jr. and JFK Drs). 752.0347

Within Stow Lake:

### STRAWBERRY HILL

🐧 Located in the middle of Stow Lake is this artificial island, which once stored water for the park. The cascading **Huntington Falls** add to the picturesque setting. On its shores is the elaborate **Chinese Pavilion,** a gift from the government of Taiwan in 1984 and a popular spot for weddings, relaxation, and reflection. Footbridges connect from the shore, and a winding road leads to the island's 428-foot-high peak, from which there are good views of the city.

## 22 STRYBING ARBORETUM

🐧 This arboretum is a quiet sylvan retreat, with many paths among the 6,000 or so species of trees, plants, and shrubs, both native and exotic. Be sure to visit the **Garden of Fragrance** for visually impaired nature lovers, watched over by a statue of Saint Francis of Assisi. Labels are in braille and plants are selected especially for their taste, touch, and smell. Maps are available at the **Strybing Bookstore** at Ninth Avenue and Lincoln Way, and tours are given daily.

---

Restaurants/Clubs: Red | Hotels: Purple | Shops: Orange | Outdoors/Parks: Green | Sights/Culture: Blue

# SAN FRANCISCO IN FACT...

To learn more about the history, residents, architecture, and life in general in this popular West Coast city, here are a few pages worth flipping through before you tour the town.

### Fiction

**Dead Languages** by David Shields (Knopf, 1989). Growing up in the 1960s in San Francisco, a stutterer struggles in a family of articulates. Some of his cures are amusing, some sad. A latter-day *Catcher in the Rye*.

**Dead Man** (Warner Books, 1994) and **Menaced Assassin** (Warner Books, 1993) by Joe Gores. The author was actually a private detective in San Francisco before he became an award-winning screenwriter and author.

**Dreaming** by Herbert Gold (Donald I. Fine, 1988). Hutch Montberg loves the California lifestyle he has so carefully constructed for himself, but now he's in trouble with the mob. This is the life and death of a salesman, West Coast edition. Gold tunes into the customs, speech, and settings of the hip bourgeoisie of San Francisco.

**Face Value** by Lia Matera (Pocket Books, 1995). In this Laura DiPalma mystery, multiple murders and delightfully complex characters help carry a plot that moves from a striptease bar in the city to a guru's mysterious island retreat.

**The Maltese Falcon** by Dashiell Hammett (Knopf, 1930). In this famous detective story, private eye Sam Spade roams the city looking for a bird statue said to be worth a fortune.

**The Mistress and Other Stories** by Gina Berriault (Dutton, 1965). In each of these 15 short stories, an intellectual San Francisco man or woman experiences a moment of truth during the course of mundane home or social activity.

**The San Francisco Comic Strip Book of Big-Ass Mocha** by Don Asmussen (Russian Hill Press, 1997). In this first compilation of *San Francisco Comic Strip* by this leading cartoonist, Asmussen shares the zany side of city life. To prepare for your visit, read "A Reader's Guide to Muni," "San Francisco's Coffee Houses," and "Don Johnson & Other Myths."

**2nd Chance** by James Patterson (Little, Brown, 2002). International best-selling author James Patterson sets this novel in San Francisco, where detective Lindsay Boxer joins with the Women's Murder Club to trap a serial killer. She enters San Francisco's underworld, where Patterson's shocking twists and customary suspense confront her at every turn. *1st to Die* is the author's first title in the Women's Murder Club series.

**Strangers at the Gate** by Leonard Gross (Random House, 1995). The sights and sounds of San Fran-

♦ Free. Daily. Ninth Ave (off Lincoln Way). 661.1316

## 23 SHAKESPEARE GARDEN

Flowers and plants mentioned in Shakespeare's sonnets and plays are featured in this garden. ♦ Martin Luther King Jr. Dr (at Middle Dr E)

## 24 BASEBALL DIAMONDS

You may play on the two baseball diamonds in the **Big Rec Ball Field** with advance reservations, or, if you prefer softball, there's a first-come, first-served softball diamond near the **Children's Playground.** ♦ Off Martin Luther King Jr. Dr (at Seventh Ave). 831.2700

## 25 SAN FRANCISCO COUNTY FAIR BUILDING

Known as the **Hall of Flowers** to locals, this building is used for special events ranging

from cat shows to floral exhibitions. ♦ Ninth Ave (off Lincoln Way)

## 26 CHILDREN'S PLAYGROUND

One of the first public playgrounds to be built in an American park, this includes a gloriously restored carousel housed in a turn-of-the-twentieth-century Greek temple. The animals and turning platform were made in New York by the Herschell-Spillman Company around 1912, and came to San Francisco sometime after the 1939 World's Fair on Treasure Island. The brilliantly colored menagerie consists of 62 animals, 2 chariots, 1 turning tub, and 1 rocker, all revolving to various show tunes, polkas, and mazurkas coming from the 55-year-old organ. Children under 39 inches ride free if accompanied by a paying adult. ♦ Carousel: nominal fee. Daily, June-Sept; Th-Su, Oct-May. Off Martin Luther King Jr. Dr (near Kezar Dr)

cisco pervade this tale of a murder investigation involving tens of thousands of illegal immigrants fleeing Hong Kong in anticipation of Communist China's takeover in 1997.

**Tales of the City/More Tales of the City/Further Tales of the City** by Armisted Maupin (HarperCollins, 1987/1989/1994). The Oscar Wilde inscription in *Tales of the City* says it all: "It's an odd thing, but anyone who disappears is said to be seen in San Francisco."

### Nonfiction

**The Best of Herb Caen: 1960-1975** (Chronicle Books, 1991) and **Herb Caen's San Francisco: 1976-1991** (Chronicle Books, 1992) by Herb Caen. From the time he began writing for the *San Francisco Chronicle* more than 50 years ago, Caen has been the undisputed voice of the city and one of the country's best-known columnists. His best and most enduring columns are collected in those books.

**Captain Richardson** by Robert Ryal Miller (LaLoma Press, 1995). This biography of William A. Richardson, an English maritime officer who "jumped ship" in San Francisco Bay in 1822 to begin a new life in California, illuminates much of the history of California during the Mexican and Gold Rush eras.

**Hometown San Francisco** by Jerry Flamm (Scottwell Associates, 1994). History, biography reminiscence, and anecdote are woven together to form a tapestry of San Francisco from 1906 to the midcentury, when it was a wide-open town.

**San Francisco Almanac** by Gladys Hansen (Chronicle Books, 1995). Name your subject—movies, sports, maritime history, Victorian houses—and you're sure to find it in this gold mine of information.

**San Francisco, the City's Sights and Secrets** by Leah Garchik (Chronicle Books, 1995). Garchik provides a philosophic tour of both the well-known and little-known delights of "everybody's favorite city." More than 150 glorious photographs of the city as it is today are included, as well as historical black-and-white photos and lively text.

**San Francisco, the Painted City** by Harry L. Jones (Gibbs-Smith, 1992). This book contains a collection of unique views of such famous sites as **Coit Tower** and **Telegraph Hill,** the **Golden Gate Bridge, Chinatown, Fisherman's Wharf, Golden Gate Park,** the **Financial District,** and the **Transamerica Pyramid.** One hundred and fifty years of history are seen through artists' eyes.

**This Is San Francisco** by Robert O'Brien (Chronicle Books, 1994). Here is an affectionate, lively, carefully researched chronicle of the city from its inception to the end of World War II; an unabashedly romantic portrait of San Francisco's streets, neighborhoods, and people in the "present day" 1940s.

## 27 KEZAR STADIUM

This 10,000-seat facility is used for community activities, high school sports, soccer, and track. ♦ Kezar Dr (at Martin Luther King Jr. Dr)

---

Restaurants/Clubs: Red | Hotels: Purple | Shops: Orange | Outdoors/Parks: Green | Sights/Culture: Blue

# THE RICHMOND/ THE PRESIDIO

**E**ndless rows of stucco dwellings line the avenues of the staunchly middle-class and family-oriented Richmond District. The area contains more residential land than any other in San Francisco, and that's how the residents want it to stay. In fact, political donnybrooks have been aimed at developers who wanted to knock down single-family homes and replace them with multiple units.

In another era The Richmond was known as the dunes, and it took all day to reach **Seal Rocks** by railroad and horse-drawn carriage from downtown. Before 1900 most of the San Franciscans in the windy, foggy Richmond were the deceased inhabitants of the **Municipal Cemetery** or the **Chinese Cemetery**. After a street was cut through the area in 1863, however, a few roadhouses opened, and the first of what would turn into a series of **Cliff Houses** was built by Sam Brannan, though it soon burned to the ground.

Then along came Adolph Sutro, an engineer who made his fortune in the Comstock Lode. As mayor of the city, he set about to open The Richmond for development and created a Victorian fantasy castle on the bluff to replace the Cliff House that had been destroyed. Then he erected a fabulous group of glass-enclosed, oceanside swimming pools called the **Sutro Baths;** planted **Sutro Forest;** and built his own house and elaborate gardens, which he opened to the public. After providing such incentives for people to visit the area, the "Father of The Richmond" built a steam railroad on **California Street** to ease their way. Now only ruins mark the place where the once spectacular baths were situated, and a gazebo, a stone parapet, and a few marble statues are all that remain of the Sutro Estate. But Sutro's project served its purpose—to attract potential residents to the district. Thousands of houses were built here between 1910 and 1930. While many are bland stucco homes of no distinction, one neighborhood stands out: **Sea Cliff.** This long-established enclave of the well-to-do, tucked between **Lincoln Park** and **The Presidio**, contains many grand mansions, a number of them built on sheer rock cliffs overlooking the **Pacific Ocean.**

After World War I, hundreds of Russians and East European Jews moved into The Richmond District. Their religious centers still form the major landmarks: **Temple Emanu-El,** on **Arguello Boulevard** at **Lake**

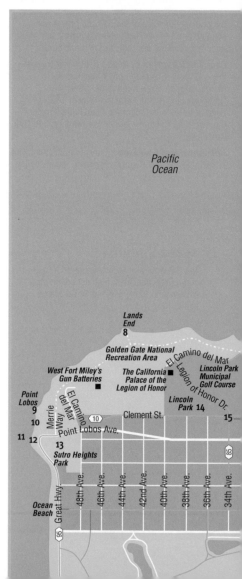

**Street,** and the gold-domed **Cathedral of the Holy Virgin,** on **Geary Boulevard** at **26th Avenue.** Russian restaurants and Jewish businesses continue to thrive alongside the enterprises of the Japanese, who moved in after World War II. More Japanese live here than in any other neighborhood. And so many Chinese have bought houses along **Clement Street** that the stretch between **First** and **11th Avenues** is called New Chinatown.

Clement Street mingles the traditions of Asia and Europe in a profusion of Chinese restaurants, Italian pizzerias, Irish bars and bookstores, Russian bakeries, Asian markets, and Middle Eastern and German delis. Austrians, Armenians, Hungarians, Ukrainians, Czechs, and Caucasian refugees from Shanghai and Singapore are all united into Clement's warmhearted community. The concentration of inexpensive restaurants is staggering, and given the keen competition, there's a lot of turnover.

**The Presidio,** on the other hand, is a district apart. This former military outpost is more than 200 years old and encompasses 1,480 acres of prime recreational land. A large portion of the area became part of the **Golden Gate National Recreation Area (GGNRA).** In addition to verdant scenery and a variety of views, it has two great beaches **(Ocean**

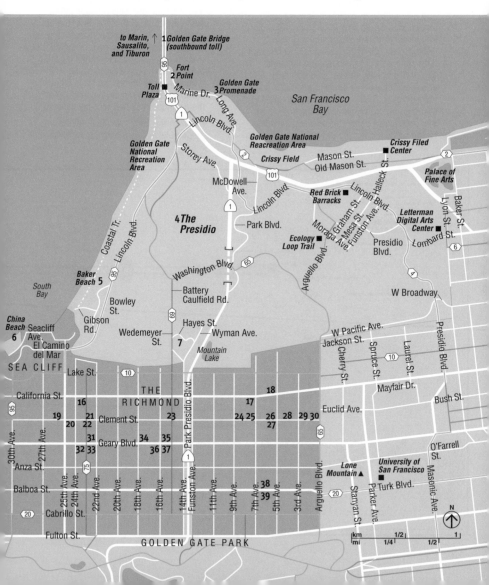

Beach and **Baker Beach)**, old-time fortifications, a golf course, a lake, and picnic sites everywhere. The shoreline promenade at **Crissy Field** passes the restored tidal marsh, recently reclaimed from an asphalt-covered industrial area.

## 1 GOLDEN GATE BRIDGE

San Francisco's pride and joy (see plan below) is undoubtedly one of the most beautiful bridges in the world, on account of its spectacular location, graceful lines, Moderne detailing, and emblematic color. The clear span of more than 4,200 feet was the longest in the world until 1959, when New York City's Verrazano Narrows Bridge was built. Although there is some controversy about who actually designed the bridge—some scholars say an engineer named Charles Ellis should get the credit—Joseph Strauss was chief engineer of the project, which took four and a half years and $35 million to complete. It was finally inaugurated on 28 May 1937, when President Roosevelt punched a telegraph key in the White House, giving the cue 3,000 miles away for a clamor of bells, sirens, and foghorns, squadrons of navy planes, and the most enormous peacetime concentration of naval strength ever. Over 200,000 pedestrians had swarmed across the structure the day before, and an endless parade of politicos' vehicles traversed the bridge the day after its opening.

At midspan, the roadway is 260 feet above the water, a height requested by the navy to allow its battleships to pass beneath. One of the piers is located in the water and the other is on the Marin shore. The main cables are 36.5 inches in diameter. The bridge was designed to withstand winds of more than 100 miles per hour and to be able to swing at midspan as much as 27 feet. The best views are from Vista Point on the Marin side and from **Fort Point** below on the San Francisco side.

On 24 May 1987, more than 200,000 pedestrians took over again to celebrate the bridge's 50th anniversary. Winners in a hard-fought battle with local bureaucracies, they took advantage of the closure of the bridge for a few hours and walked across, their weight flattening the center span, causing the bridge to drop 10 feet. The celebration included marching bands, poster contests, steelworkers from where the bridge steel was made, fireworks displays, more politicos, and the lighting of the 746-foot-tall towers.

Although the bridge was built for the automobile age, its designers wisely included

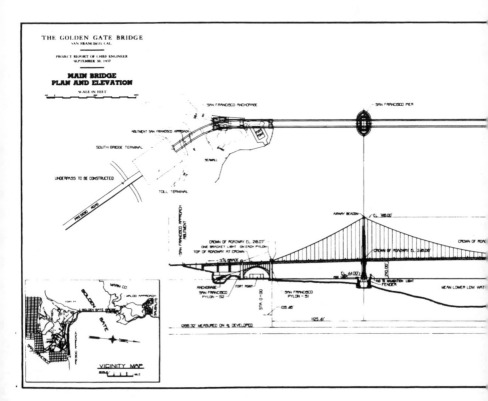

sidewalks, recognizing that it must be crossed on foot to be properly appreciated. The bridge is 1.2 miles across, and the walk, round-trip, takes about an hour. Pedestrians use the walk on the east side daily from 5AM to 9PM. Bicyclists share the path Monday through Friday, but must use the west side on the weekend. Don't forget to take a sweater—it's awfully windy up there. There's a convenient parking area east of the **Toll Plaza,** and nearby, a glass roundhouse containing a **Visitors' Center.** One of the two surrounding gardens is a memorial to the bridge workers; the other is a friendship garden that pays tribute to Pacific Rim nations.

Since its opening, the bridge has become as symbolic of San Francisco as the Eiffel Tower is of Paris. On the darker side, both structures have an unenviable record for suicides.

But the bridge itself is in good health and has aged well. With the additional girders installed in 1987 and new suspender ropes, it is stronger than ever and just as beautiful—the most photographed man-made structure built in the world. ♦ Hwy 101

## 2 FORT POINT

The fort lies under the southern end of the Golden Gate Bridge and was built between 1853 and 1861 to guard San Francisco from sea attack. It houses a museum filled with old swords, guns, cannons, uniforms, and historic photographs of earlier days. There are guided tours (advance reservations required); Civil War cannon-loading and firing demonstrations are held at noon when the museum is open. ♦ Free. F-Su. Off Lincoln Blvd (at Long Ave; take Long Ave to Marine Dr). 556.0505 ♿

At Fort Point:

## COASTAL TRAIL

On a sunny day, this trail, stretching from the Golden Gate Bridge to the **Cliff House,** is a must for bikers, joggers, and heavy-duty walkers. It's not the easiest trail to follow, with several splits, dead ends, and a detour through actor/comedian Robin Williams's neighborhood of Sea Cliff, but the tranquillity and the spectacular scenery make it another of the many reasons for San Franciscans' ongoing love affair with their city. ♦ Starts at Fort Point and ends at Point Lobos

## 3 GOLDEN GATE PROMENADE

The promenade extends from **Fort Point** underneath the Golden Gate Bridge past **Crissy Field** tidal marsh, along the **Marina Green** to **Aquatic Park,** and provides three and a half miles of spectacular bay views. It's also popular for biking, fishing, sailboarding, and sunbathing. ♦ Between Fort Point and Aquatic Park

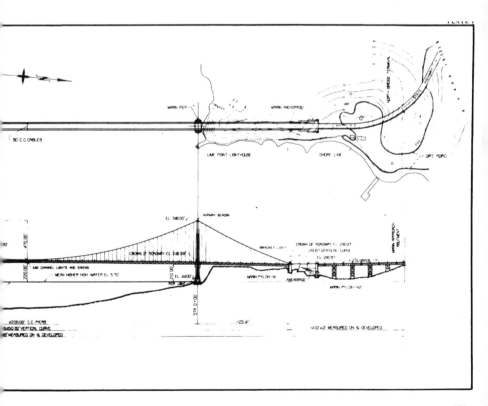

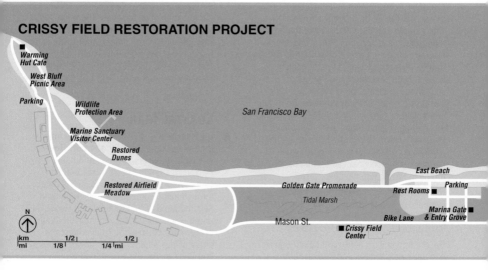

CRISSY FIELD RESTORATION PROJECT

Warming Hut Cafe

West Bluff Picnic Area

Parking

Wildlife Protection Area

San Francisco Bay

Marine Sanctuary Visitor Center

Restored Dunes

Restored Airfield Meadow

East Beach

Golden Gate Promenade

Rest Rooms

Parking

Tidal Marsh

N

Marina Gate & Entry Grove

Bike Lane

Mason St.

Crissy Field Center

km / mi    1/2    1/8    1/4    1/2    mi

## 4 THE PRESIDIO

Located at the entrance to the Golden Gate on the northernmost point of the San Francisco peninsula, **The Presidio** was a military outpost for more than 200 years. In the 1770s, while American colonists were writing the Declaration of Independence, the Spanish rulers of Mexico established a series of missions and military posts on the West Coast. The farthest north of these posts was this spot. The original installation was a walled camp 100 yards square surrounded by a palisade-type wall.

When the Mexicans gained their independence in 1822, they took over the site until it was forcibly possessed in 1846 by the United States. Originally, the 1,400-acre area consisted of bare hills and rocks. In the 1880s it was planted with pine and eucalyptus trees that today form one of the most beautiful wooded areas in the city. Union regiments trained here during the Civil War. After the 1906 earthquake and fire, it became a refugee camp for the homeless and injured. During World War II it was the headquarters of the Fourth Army and Western Defense Command.

After serving for more than 200 years as a military outpost under three flags, San Francisco's Presidio today is a national park, its 1,491 acres of brick buildings and forest combining the urban and the rural. The **Golden Gate National Recreation Area (GGNRA)** oversees the city's northern waterfront.

Established in 1972, the GGNRA encompasses 34,000 acres and is one and a half times larger in area than San Francisco. The park covers more than 68 square miles of land and water, including 28 miles of the Pacific Ocean, Tomales Bay in Marin, and the San Francisco coastline. Its diverse natural environment offers

sandy beaches, rugged headlands, grasslands, forests, lakes, marshes, and streams. While the area around **Fort Mason** in San Francisco has been developed, the rest of the expansive preserve is maintained as closely as possible in its natural state by the National Park Service. Places to visit include Baker Beach off Lincoln Boulevard and the gun emplacements **Battery Chamberlain, Battery Crosby,** and **Batteries Cranston, Marcus Miller,** and **Boutelle** near the Golden Gate Bridge. A Historical Trail Guide produced by the National Park Service features the many historic and scenic points; additional information is available at The Presidio Visitor Center, Building 50, on Moraga St at Arguello St (Officers' Club on the Main Post), 561.4323, or online: www.nps.gov/prsf. ◆ Main entrances: Lombard St (at Lyon St), Presidio Blvd (at Broadway), Arguello Blvd (at Jackson St), Lincoln Blvd (at 25th Ave), and Golden Gate Bridge Toll Plaza

Within The Presidio:

## PRESIDIO ARMY MUSEUM

Formerly the **Old Station Hospital** and built in 1857, this is the oldest surviving building in The Presidio. On view are numerous uniforms, weapons, photographs, and other memorabilia pertaining to the army's history in San Francisco. The museum was closed indefinitely at press time due to funding issues. ◆ Free. W-Su. Lincoln Blvd (at Funston Ave). 561.4323 ♿

## FUNSTON AVENUE OFFICERS' HOUSING

This group of houses along Funston Avenue constitutes some of the oldest and—depending on whom you ask—finest Victorian structures in San Francisco. Built in 1862, these elegant wood-frame structures housed army officers for over a century. ♦ Off Lincoln Blvd

## RED BRICK BARRACKS

Built in the Georgian style between 1895 and 1897, the stately brick barracks flanking the **Parade Ground** off Montgomery Avenue served as the enlisted men's first permanent barracks at The Presidio. ♦ Off Funston Ave (at Lincoln Blvd)

## THE ECOLOGY LOOP TRAIL

This sheltered pathway winds through groves of cypress, redwood, and eucalyptus. Follow it south from the old Officers Club and Visitors' Center. After half a mile, take the spur trail to **Inspiration Point,** where in clear weather you can see all the way to Mount Tamalpais.

## LETTERMAN DIGITAL ARTS CENTER

George Lucas is The Presidio's most illustrious tenant. He moved his special-effects group, Lucasfilm, to these new headquarters in 2005. The building contains multi-million-dollar digital-effects computers and a large private-screening theater. Lucas devoted as much expense to the beautiful native-grass meadow and meandering paths for visitors to enjoy. Visitors can stop at the café but cannot tour the building. Lombard St (near the Lyon St gate). www.lucasfilm.com

## 4 CRISSY FIELD

What was once a strip of cracked asphalt is now a 100-acre shoreline park perfect for walking, sailboarding, jogging, in-line skating, biking, and swimming. Follow the footbridge across the 20-acre tidal marsh and admire the groves of native cypress trees among the dunes. ♦ Marine Drive. 561.4730. www.crissyfield.org

Within Crissy Field:

## CRISSY FIELD CENTER

Learn about the **Crissy Field** transformation from military airstrip to tidal lagoon. The story of how Ohlone Indians used plants in the sand dunes is also preserved. Ohlone Indian descendants who are docents at the center give lectures and workshops on traditional tribal life. Highly recommended are the workshops that show how Indians made kayaks from tule reeds and rope from natural fibers. ♦ Daily ♦ 603 Mason St (at Halleck St) from the west end of Marina Blvd. 561.7690. www.crissyfield.org

## DISH

★★★$ Stop at this cozy café for gourmet sandwiches, market-fresh salads, and homemade muffins. ♦ American ♦ M-F, breakfast and lunch. No credit cards accepted. Inside the San Francisco Film Centre in Suite 108. 39 Mesa St (at Lincoln Blvd). 561.2336 (At press time, a new restaurant, **The Presidio Social Club,** is opening for dinner.)

## SENSPA

This spa has an Eastern theme and personalized treatments. Rare for a spa is its 13,000 square feet of tranquility. The first session of wellness coaching is free. ♦ 1161 Gorgas at O'Reilly Ave. 441.1777. www.senspa.com

## WARMING HUT CAFE

★★$ Pastries, soups, and sandwiches made using organic greens and homemade bread, not to mention the views of Golden Gate Bridge, make this a hopping lunch spot. ♦ American ♦ Daily, breakfast and lunch. On Torpedo Wharf, only steps from the parking lot at the west end of Mason St. 561.3042

## 5 BAKER BEACH

Although swimming is dangerous at this mile-long stretch of sandy shore, the fishing is fine, especially for striped bass. There are picnic and barbecue facilities, as well as drinking water and rest rooms, but no camping. Dogs on leashes are allowed. ♦ Daily, sunrise to 7PM. Main entrance at SW corner of Gibson Rd (off Lincoln Blvd)

At Baker Beach:

## BAKER BEACH BUNKERS

These concrete bunkers were built to defend the Golden Gate Bridge from aerial attack during World War II. ♦ Battery Chamberlain (next to Baker Beach)

## 6 CHINA BEACH

Nuzzled into a cove is one of the few San Francisco beaches where swimming is permitted. Popular with locals, this small stretch of sand was named after the Chinese fishers who used to camp here. No dogs are allowed. There are public rest rooms and limited parking. ♦ Daily, sunrise to 7PM. At the end of Seacliff Ave (off El Camino del Mar)

## 7 ARION PRESS LIVING MUSEUM OF PRINTING

Arion Press, the nation's largest fine printing press, publishes deluxe, limited-edition books featuring the work of prominent illustrators. A gallery displays artist books and prints. Tour the historic production facilities, the type foundry, pressroom, and bookbindery. Reservations required. Fee. ♦ Th, 3PM. 1802 Hayes

---

Restaurants/Clubs: Red | Hotels: Purple | Shops: Orange | Outdoors/Parks: Green | Sights/Culture: Blue

St (near 15th Ave). 668.2548. www.arionpress.com &

## 8 LAND'S END

The wonderful views from this promontory should be appreciated by the skilled hiker only. ♦ Park at Point Lobos Ave and Merrie Way and follow the marked trails, or go to the lot at El Camino del Mar and Point Lobos Ave adjacent to the *USS San Francisco Memorial* and follow the trail to Land's End

## 9 POINT LOBOS

The beautiful westernmost tip of San Francisco was named by the Spanish after the sea lions, whom they called *lobos marinos* (sea wolves). ♦ Follow the trails from the parking lot at El Camino del Mar and Point Lobos Ave

## 10 SUTRO BATHS

Opened in 1896 by Adolph Sutro, this three-acre spa resembled the baths of imperial Rome in scale and splendor. Six saltwater swimming pools heated to different temperatures sparkled beneath a colored-glass roof. The building was destroyed in a spectacular fire in 1966. Today the remains look like classical ruins. An algae-covered puddle is all that is left of the baths, but the National Park Service is considering a laser-image reconstruction of the once majestic structure. ♦ Follow the trails from the parking lot at El Camino del Mar and Point Lobos Ave

## 11 SEAL ROCKS

Four hundred feet offshore and below the **Cliff House,** the rocks swarm with sea lions and various seabirds. Watching them loll about is a favorite Sunday pastime for San Franciscans. ♦ Offshore from the Cliff House (off the Great Hwy)

## 12 CLIFF HOUSE

San Francisco families used to make day trips from the big city to sun at this resort spot, originally built in 1863. Later the house became associated with local powerbrokers, crime bosses, and their molls. When the schooner *Parallel,* loaded with dynamite, crashed on the rocks below, one whole wing of the building was lost in the explosion. Seven years later, on Christmas Day, the original building burned to the ground.

Adolph Sutro rebuilt it in 1895, and this one also burned within the year. Little remains of the fifth and last building on the site, which opened in 1909. Architecturally insensitive remodeling and repair work have obliterated the building's original character. It now houses the **Cliff House Restaurant,** and a small National Park Service visitors' center (556.8371). A few years ago, architects restored the 1909 structure and added a new light-filled, modernist building with two-story glass walls. The blend of vintage and modern has brought fresh energy and new generations to the old gathering place. ♦ 1090 Point Lobos Ave (at the Great Hwy). 386.3330. www.cliffhouse.com

Within the Cliff House:

## CAMERA OBSCURA

Children love this replica of Leonardo da Vinci's invention. The camera is trained on **Seal Rocks** and Ocean Beach and the image magnified on a giant parabolic screen. ♦ Nominal charge. Daily, weather permitting. 750.0415 &

## 13 SUTRO HEIGHTS PARK

Its bluff-top site overlooking the **Cliff House** and ocean beyond makes this park an ideal spot for sunsets and beach views. This was formerly the home and grounds of Adolph Sutro, a mining engineer, mayor, and one of the city's great benefactors. He bought much of the seafront property in the city and planted a forest of eucalyptus on Mount Sutro. The park has a haunting charm, with fragments of statuary lying half-hidden among the groves of fir, Monterey cypress, and Norfolk Island pine. Take a close look at the rock cliffs. Because of slides, the slope has been reinforced with concrete and finished to look just like the real rock. ♦ Point Lobos Ave (at 48th Ave)

## 14 LINCOLN PARK

Some 270 verdant acres on the Point Lobos Headlands provide striking views of the bay and Golden Gate Bridge. ♦ Main entrance: Clement St (at 34th Ave)

Within Lincoln Park:

## LINCOLN PARK MUNICIPAL GOLF COURSE

Tee off at this 18-hole public course that offers sweeping views of the Golden Gate Bridge. ♦ Daily, sunrise to sundown. 34th Ave (at Clement St). 221.9911

## WEST FORT MILEY'S GUN BATTERIES

This former military site is fun to explore. Picnic and barbecue facilities, drinking water, and rest rooms are available. ♦ Lincoln Park (next to the VA Hospital). Ranger station 556.8371

## THE CALIFORNIA PALACE OF THE LEGION OF HONOR

Having undergone a $36 million seismic retrofitting and modernization in 1995, this museum commands a broad view of the city and the bay from its hilltop site in the park. Originally built in 1916 by **George Applegarth,** the building's design is based on the Palais de la Légion d'Honneur in Paris, and was given to the city in 1924 by Mr. and Mrs. Adolph Spreckels in memory of California's dead in World War I. The museum features paintings, sculpture, and decorative arts presented in a chronological sequence, illustrating the development of European art from the medieval period through the beginning of the 20th century. In addition, there are six subterranean galleries as well as a garden café. ♦ Lincoln Park (enter on Clement St and 34th Ave). 750.3600 &

### 15 TSING TAO

★★$ This plain Chinese restaurant is distinguished by good food at remarkably low prices. The chili-pepper prawns are a favorite. Consider also the braised chicken legs, the hot-and-sour soup, and the shredded pork with garlic and eggplant in Szechuan sauce. The waiters are as helpful as can be, so don't hesitate to question them about dishes that sound good. ♦ Mandarin/ Szechuan ♦ Daily, lunch and dinner. 3107 Clement St (at 32nd Ave). 387.2344 &

### 16 PIZZETTA 211

★★★$ People line up for thin-crust Neapolitan pizza with savory toppings such as fresh mozzarella with pine nuts and rosemary. The menu changes weekly, as do seasonal offerings from local sources. Be prepared for the four-table dining room and small counter, but it's second home for the city's pizza addicts. Cash only. ♦ Pizza ♦ W-M, dinner. 211 23rd Ave (at California St). 379.9880. www.pizzetta211.com &

### 17 THE VILLAGE MARKET

A popular destination for the Pacific Heights–Presidio folks, this chic natural-foods market boasts a giant fountain at the entrance. It offers organic fresh and frozen fruits and vegetables, coffees, specialty mustards, canned truffles, and some organic wines. ♦ Daily. 4555 California St (at Eighth Ave). 221.0445 &

### 18 MANDALAY

★$$ The city's first Burmese restaurant is best suited to the gastronomically curious. Green-tea salad and satay dishes are among the interesting menu choices. ♦ Burmese ♦ Daily, lunch and dinner. 4348 California St (at Sixth Ave). 386.3895. www.mandalaysf.com &

### 19 INDIA CLAY OVEN

★★$$ The miraculous clay oven, fired up to 1,000 degrees, turns out tandoori chicken, tasting charred, moist, and smoky. It's served with raita and *naan* or paper-thin lentil *papadum*. The vegetable korma is filled with

nuts and farmer's cheese, and the lamb curry is also good. Order from the lunch menu rather than the all-you-can-eat lunch buffet. ♦ Indian/Pakistani ♦ Daily, lunch and dinner. 2436 Clement St (at 25th Ave). 751.0505. www.indiaclayoven.com &

### 20 SHIMO

★★$$ Chef Shimo-san expertly carves fish and seafood that is so fresh, it nearly jumps off your plate. Start lunch or dinner off with the *ama ebi* (raw prawns), *saba* (mackerel), or *mirugai* (briny clams). The tempura treats have the lightest touch of sesame oil. ♦ Japanese ♦ Daily, dinner. 2339 Clement St (at 25th Ave). 752.4422

### 20 BILL'S PLACE

★$ One of the most popular hamburger joints in the neighborhood also makes old-fashioned milk shakes—a far cry from what's offered by fast-food chains. Eat on the back patio in good weather. ♦ American ♦ Daily, lunch and dinner. 2315 Clement St (between 24th and 25th Aves). 221.5262 &

### 21 YET WAH

★$$ Several branches of this restaurant chain are scattered around the Bay Area, but they are all under different ownership and offer very different dining experiences. This outpost has larger quarters and a more civilized ambience than the popular Chinatown branch. Specialties include glazed walnut prawns, scallops with ginger and garlic, chicken chow mein, and lemon chicken. ♦ Mandarin ♦ Daily, lunch and dinner. 2140 Clement St (at 23rd Ave). 387.8040. Also at 5238 Diamond Heights Blvd (at Gold Mine Dr). 282.0788 &

### 22 NARAI

★★$$ This is one of the few places in San Francisco to offer Chou Chow cooking, a Cantonese offshoot that makes use of chili peppers, duck, goose, and citrus fruit. As the owners are Thai (but of Chou Chow extraction), the menu also includes Thai food. Among the offerings are chicken and coconut-milk soup and *larb ped,* chicken infused with lime and chilies. One of the Chinese delights is pompano, lightly breaded with rice flour, deep-fried, and sprinkled with garlic. ♦ Chinese/Thai ♦ Tu-Su, lunch and dinner. 2229 Clement St (between 23rd and 24th Aves). 751.6363 &

### 22 MESCOLANZA

★★$$ Decorated with painted columns and arches and white tablecloths, this always-packed place attracts a loyal and enthusiastic clientele who come for the first-rate fare. The pizza's cracker-crisp crust doesn't need fancy toppings, and the gnocchi rival any Italian grandmother's. ♦ Italian ♦ Daily, dinner. Reservations recommended. 2221 Clement St (between 23rd and 24th Aves). 668.2221 &

### 23 CHAPEAU!

★★$$ The bon vivant of Clement Street, Philippe Gardelle loves his work, greeting customers with Gallic charm to his jewel-box dining room. The magic that begins at the door carries over to the kitchen's efforts in steaming bowls of cassoulet (with lamb, duck, and garlic sausage) and platters of roasted pork loin (with French green lentils) and duck à l'orange. Linger over the warm chocolate cake with crème anglaise or rhubarb and Grand Marnier tart. One letdown: California wines dominate the wine list. ♦ French ♦ Tu-Su, dinner. Reservations recommended. 1408 Clement St (at 15th St). 750.9787 &

### 24 CLEMENT STREET BAR AND GRILL

★★$$ The kitchen specializes in creative pastas, grilled meats, and fowl, all at reasonable prices. The dark wood paneling, plants, and linen tablecloths contribute to the pleasant, relaxed ambience. ♦ American ♦ Tu-F, lunch and dinner; Sa, Su, brunch and dinner. Reservations recommended. 708 Clement St (at Eighth Ave). 386.2200 &

### 25 HAIG'S DELICACIES

In addition to coffees and teas, this long-established specialty shop carries a marvelous collection of olives, Middle Eastern baked goods, and other pantry foods from India, Europe, and the Middle East. ♦ M-Sa. 642 Clement St (between Seventh and Eighth Aves). 752.6283 &

### 26 ROCKET ROOM

Extremely popular with the postcollege crowd, this bawdy but friendly bar books a variety of dance bands—from reggae to indie rock—Wednesday through Sunday. The bottom floor has pool tables and dartboards, while the top floor is for dancing. ♦ Cover. Daily until 2AM. 406 Clement St (at Fifth Ave). 387.6343 &

### 27 TAIWAN RESTAURANT

★★$ This airy, contemporary Deco restaurant serves Taiwanese food, not often seen in San Francisco. Taiwanese cuisine rejects the fire of Hunan and Szechuan in favor of subtle sweet/salty and garlicky flavors. Not to be missed are the pork-filled boiled dumplings or roasted chicken. ♦ Taiwanese ♦ Daily, lunch and dinner; F, Sa, until midnight. Reservations recommended. 445 Clement St (at Sixth Ave). 387.1789 &

### 27 TOY BOAT DESSERT CAFÉ

★$ In addition to selling windup toys, this delightful little ice-cream parlor makes delicious coffees, Italian sodas, and desserts. Especially good are the peanut-butter-and-chocolate-cookie sandwich and the mildly tart Key lime pie. ♦ Coffeehouse/ice-cream parlor ♦ Daily. 401 Clement St (at Fifth Ave). 751.7505 &

### 28 MAI'S

★★$$ There are things on the menu here not to be missed by any Asian-food gourmet. The *la lot* beef (exotically seasoned charcoal-grilled ground beef wrapped in a leaf resembling that of a grape) is spectacular. Also try the imperial rolls and the chicken salad. ♦ Vietnamese ♦ Daily, lunch and dinner. 316 Clement St (between Fourth and Fifth Aves). 221.3046 &

### 28 BLUE DANUBE

This popular 1960s-style coffeehouse usually plays classical music. When the weather is sunny, a wall of glass doors overlooking Clement Street is opened wide. ♦ Coffeehouse ♦ Daily. 306 Clement St (at Fourth Ave). 221.9041 &

### 29 PLOUGH & STARS

A real Irish bar with live Irish music every night, it's at its wildest, of course, on St. Patrick's Day. ♦ Daily until 2AM. 116 Clement St (at Third Ave). 751.1122. www.theploughandstars.com &

### 30 SATIN MOON FABRICS

This shop provides a wide selection of designer fabrics for those who know how to sew a fine seam. ♦ Tu-Sa. 32 Clement St (near Arguello Blvd). 668.1623 &

### 31 AZIZA

★★★$$$ One of San Francisco's hot spots, Aziza is Moroccan heaven with blue and white arches, Italian fabrics, and exotic furnishings. The hand-carved tables come from the Moroccan town of Essouira and date back to the 1930s and 1940s. Chef Mourad Lahlou's Moroccan menu plays up the Bay Area's organic produce and free-range meats. Menu highlights include saffron Cornish hen with Moroccan pink olives, braised lamb shank with honey and kumquat sauce, and baked goat cheese. ♦ M-W, dinner. Moroccan ♦ 5800 Geary Blvd (at 22nd Ave). 752.2222. www.aziza-sf.com

### 32 KHAN TOKE THAI HOUSE

★★★$$ Diners leave their shoes at the entrance and are seated at low, intricately carved tables positioned over pits that accommodate their legs. Among the specialties are coconut-chicken soup with succulent pieces of chicken and mushrooms; prawn salad with touches of lime and lemongrass; and duck salad with its earthy flavor and texture, thanks to the powdered rice sprinkled on top. With a good wine list and food prices only slightly higher than at more modest Thai places, this makes a fine setting for special occasions. ◆ Thai ◆ Daily, dinner. 5937 Geary Blvd (at 24th Ave). 668.6654

### 33 TON KIANG

★★$$ The long menu specializes in the food of China's Hakka region, but is rounded out with Cantonese and northern Chinese selections; helpful servers will guide you through it all. Best bets are the clay-pot dishes: braised pork in a rich sauce lightened with tofu and vegetables, or delicious squares of pork-stuffed tofu stewed with carrots, celery, and pieces of pork. ◆ Hakka/Cantonese ◆ Daily, lunch and dinner. 5821 Geary Blvd (at 22nd Ave). 387.8273. Also at 3148 Geary Blvd (at Spruce St). 752.4440 ♿

### 34 PARC HONG KONG

★★★$$ Fish tanks in back display the daily seafood selection, but don't expect much help from the harried staff. Top menu choices are Peking duck; crab bathed in wine sauce; minced squab in lettuce cups; wok-charred calamari topped with fried peppers; roast chicken; dry-braised green beans; and roast baby pig with pickled vegetables (a frequent special). ◆ Cantonese ◆ Daily, lunch and dinner. Reservations recommended. 5322 Geary Blvd (between 17th and 18th Aves). 668.8998 ♿

### 35 KABUTO SUSHI

★★★$$ Don't be put off by the spare look of this Richmond District restaurant. Chef-owner Sachio Kojima presides like a samurai at his sushi bar, slicing myriad strips of raw fish to the delight of the sushi aficionados who nightly line his bar. He serves both traditional and creative versions of sushi, which is always the freshest available. Aside from sushi and sashimi, you can order barbecued eel, conch cooked in sake broth, and *yosenabe:* seafood cooked in vegetable broth. ◆ Japanese ◆ Tu-Sa, dinner. 5116 Geary Blvd (between 15th and 16th Aves). 752.5652

### 36 RUSSIAN RENAISSANCE RESTAURANT

★$$$ The walls and ceiling here are something of a landmark—and even worth a visit in themselves. They're covered with murals depicting scenes from Russian folklore and history, a 14-year labor of love by artist Serge Smernoff. Among the specialties are chicken Kiev and veal scallopine with eggplant and mushrooms. All entrées include soup, salad, dessert, and coffee. ◆ Russian ◆ W-Su, dinner. 5241 Geary Blvd (at 17th Ave). 752.8558

### 37 OLD SHANGHAI RESTAURANT

★★$$ A favorite Chinese restaurant, this place is known for its steamed fish and excellent egg rolls. It also crosses into a few other provinces and does a commendable Peking duck and Mongolian beef. ◆ Chinese ◆ M, W-Su, dinner. 5145 Geary Blvd (between 15th and 16th Aves). 752.0120 ♿

### 38 CINDERELLA BAKERY, DELI AND RESTAURANT

★$ Despite the name, this is not a romantic restaurant. But if you are looking for mushroom pie, pierogi, and the best borscht in the city, this is the place to come. Service can be slow and waiters aloof, however. On a sunny day you may want to take a loaf of Russian black bread and containers of Russian appetizers to Golden Gate Park for a picnic. ◆ Russian ◆ Tu-Sa, lunch and dinner. 436 Balboa St (between Fifth and Sixth Aves). 751.9690 ♿

### 39 CHIU'S CAFE

★★$$ Classic fare with some subtle twists is the hallmark of the China House menu. For vegetarian pot stickers, delicate wrappers enclose a crunchy mix of greens and herbs; for Snow Mountain chicken soup, a mound of egg whites floats on the rich, vegetable-laden broth—a sensory delight. Lion's head consists of two huge, delicately textured pork balls resting on a mound of creamy cabbage cooked in an intense broth. ◆ Chinese ◆ Daily, dinner. Reservations recommended. 501 Balboa St (at Sixth Ave). 387.6038 ♿

---

**Restaurants/Clubs: Red | Hotels: Purple | Shops: Orange | Outdoors/Parks: Green | Sights/Culture: Blue**

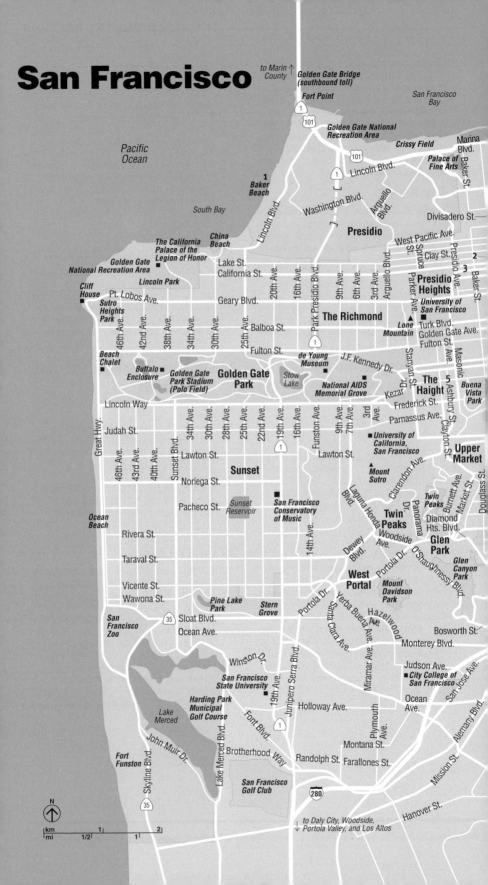

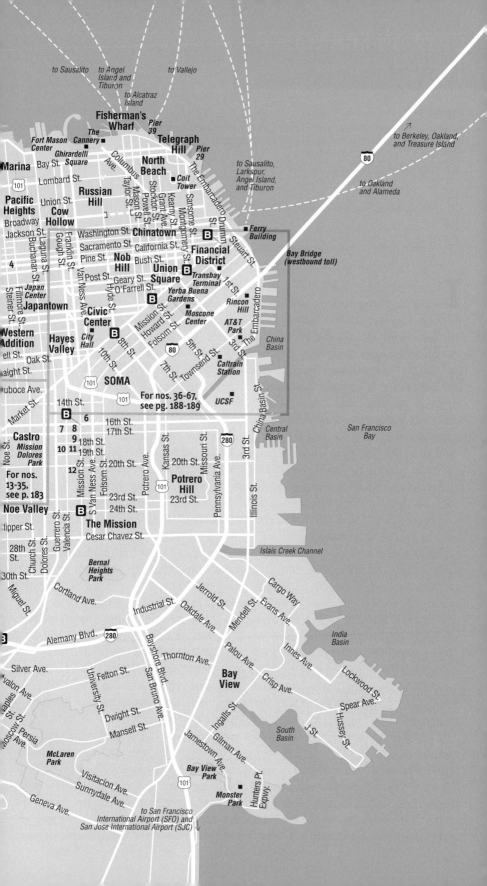

# GAY SAN FRANCISCO

## Symbols

While all of the establishments in this section are gay-friendly and popular with gay visitors and locals, those that are specifically gay-oriented are identified with the following symbols:

♂  predominantly/exclusively gay-male–oriented

♀  predominantly/exclusively lesbian-oriented

♂
♀  predominantly/exclusively gay-oriented with a male and female clientele

The "world's gay and lesbian capital" in the minds of many, San Francisco is also one of the US's most striking and beautiful cities. The setting is dramatic enough, with the hills, the bay, and the famous fog. Throw in the uniquely charming architecture, world-class restaurants and cultural institutions (including one of the best Asian art museums in the country), and a vibrant multicultural mix, and it's clear why this city of just 780,000 has become a favorite destination for all manner of travelers, both novice and seasoned—but perhaps none more than gays and lesbians.

When the famous gold rush began at Sutter's Mill in 1848, San Francisco became known as a place to get rich quick—and to spend it all, as the miners and other high rollers flooded to the pleasure palaces of the Barbary Coast. Such was its reputation as "Sodom by the Sea" that, when the famous 1906 earthquake leveled the city, the moral guardians of the time saw the righteous hand of God at work.

But the city rebuilt and continued to cultivate a freewheeling reputation through the years, becoming a magnet for the counterculture, including the flower children and their "Summer of Love" in the late 1960s, and the thousands of gays and lesbians who flocked here to escape intolerance and find a vibrant subculture that promised freedom, acceptance, and belonging. Queer San Francisco grew from a half-hidden demimonde to a militant community demanding its rights to something approaching a pillar of the establishment today. With homosexuals estimated at some 27% of the city's population, current mayor Gavin Newsom is just the latest in a long line of progressive local officials who embrace gay and lesbian San Franciscans as a powerful and positive force in the city's political, cultural, and economic life. There are two openly gay and lesbian members of the powerful Board of Supervisors (Bevan Duffy and Tom Ammiano) and many more throughout the municipal government. San Francisco has long been at the forefront of instituting antidiscrimination legislation for homosexuals and transgendered people. In 1997, the city even took on such powerful entities as **United Airlines** and the Catholic Church over equal treatment of their employees.

The gay community of San Francisco is predominantly young (the average age is 31), and pervasive. Unlike other cities, which have only one or two gay-popular neighborhoods, gays and lesbians live in every part of this metropolis. There are, however, a few hot spots, like lesbian-popular **Noe Valley** and the **Mission;** guppie-laden **Pacific Heights;** the anything-goes **SoMa (South of Market);** and such areas outside the city proper as **Berkeley.** But homo central is definitely the **Castro.** First settled by gay men in the early 1970s, along with New York City's Christopher Street, this roughly 14-square-block area became a defining symbol of gay America. Today the Castro is less male and more diverse, but still a lively center of the city's gay culture.

Visitors to the Bay Area will find that in many parts of the city's gay and lesbian community a small-town intimacy reigns, with people placing more value on personal growth, spiritual exploration, and human rights than in most other urban areas. But like New Englanders, the locals can have a certain surface reserve that is easily cracked if you make the first move. Many folks still tend to be politicized but are less "in your face" about it these days. Lesbians play a larger and more visible role here than ever, and there are plenty of suitable venues for visiting lesbians to enjoy.

Through all its travails—earthquakes and epidemics, gold rushes and market crashes, strikes and sit-ins—San Francisco has preserved a sense that it is in America's progressive cultural and social vanguard. It's easy for visitors to get swept up in that feeling too, as they explore the ins and outs of the gayest city in the US.

## 1 NORTH BAKER BEACH

The easiest to find of San Francisco's gay/lesbian nude beaches, this bit of sandy shore is located between **The Presidio** and **Lincoln Park.** Walk north along the ridge toward the Golden Gate Bridge (the trail can be tricky, so watch your step); you'll see the beach below. The sand is especially fine and the water is great for in-the-buff bodysurfing, but the surf can be dangerous at times.
♦ Daily, sunrise to 7PM. Main entrance at end of Gibson Rd (off Bowley St)

## 2 THE LION PUB

Dark wood, lots of plants, and a roaring fire (not to mention great martinis) make this friendly, low-key Pacific Heights bar and lounge a favorite with the 20 to 50 crowd. Wednesday's "Macho Night" is quite popular, and on weekends the crowd is almost all male.
♦ Daily, 4PM–2AM. 2062 Divisadero St (at Sacramento St). 567.6565

## 3 ELLA'S

★★★ $ The exceptional fare and reasonable prices have folks lining up just about every day for just about every meal at this comfy, gay-owned neighborhood eatery with simple tables, an open kitchen, and a counter bedecked with flowers. The menu offers a fresh take on old faves—an open-faced turkey sandwich livened with sage dressing, or chicken salad with carrots, cucumbers, and curry vinaigrette. The very popular brunch features spiced oatmeal-apple pancakes, fried cheese grits with eggs and toast, and a ham and mushroom omelette with cider-roasted onions and Swiss cheese.
♦ American ♦ M-F, breakfast, lunch, and dinner; Sa, Su, brunch and dinner. 500 Presidio Ave (at California St). 441.5669 &

## 4 PACIFIC HEIGHTS HEALTH CLUB

With separate-but-equal facilities for men and women (both gay/lesbian and straight), this first-rate gym is more for a serious workout than for cruising—not that it doesn't happen. The free weights, machines, and personal trainers are just about all you could ask for in a health club. Besides sauna, steam room, Jacuzzi, and tanning beds, there's also a retractable roof to let the sunshine in. ♦ M-Sa, 6AM–10PM; Su, 7AM–10PM. 2356 Pine St (between Fillmore and Steiner Sts). 563.6694

## 5 HAIGHT-ASHBURY

Haight-Ashbury is actually an intersection but it's also the general name for the Upper Haight, or Haight Street west of Divisadero. This strip of Haight Street, between beautiful **Buena Vista Park** and **Golden Gate Park,** is where the hippie movement was born in the late 1960s and still keeps its counterculture feel. It's a great place to shop for cutting-edge street fashion, grab a bite to eat, or just stroll and see the sights. Buy crystals and tie-dye clothes from the boutiques but be careful of what you buy off the street kids; for fifty bucks you'll probably get a bag of oregano.

## 6 THEATER RHINOCEROS

The oldest gay and lesbian theater company in America (founded by Alan Estes in 1977) is known for its innovative stagings of performance art, comedy, musicals, and drama. The main theater, which has premiered works by Charles Ludlum, Jane Chambers, and the Five Lesbian Brothers, seats about 150 people and puts on a five-work season September through June; there's a smaller studio theater in the basement. The name comes from the "lavender rhino" (gentle and peaceful until

---

Restaurants/Clubs: Red | Hotels: Purple | Shops: Orange | Outdoors/Parks: Green | Sights/Culture: Blue

provoked), a symbol of the early gay rights movement in Boston. ◆ Box office: Tu-Su. 2926 16th St (between S Van Ness Ave and Mission St). 861.5079

## 7 BLONDIE'S BAR AND NO GRILL

♀ Specializing in jazz, swing, and martinis, most days the dim, purple-neon-lit club attracts a cosmopolitan mix of genders and orientations (though some nights up to half the crowd might be lesbians). ◆ Daily, 2PM–2AM. 540 Valencia St (between 17th and 16th Sts). 864.2419

## 8 ESTA NOCHE

♂ Young Hispanic guys and those in search of *amor latino* dance to a salsa beat in this Mission District spot, mixing with the transvestites who put on awesome Wednesday-night drag shows that define camp. Weekend nights are also popular here. ◆ Cover F-Su, 9PM–3AM. M-Th, 1PM–2AM; F-Su, 1PM–3AM. 3079 16th St (between Mission and Valencia Sts). 861.5757 &

## 9 GOOD VIBRATIONS

You can probably find out everything you've always wanted to know about sex—and then some—at this women-owned and -operated co-op, which they describe as a "clean, well-lighted place" for sex books, toys, and videos. The emphasis here is on health, education, quality, and hot sex; the staff is helpful and informative and the selection is huge. ◆ Daily. 603 Valencia St (between 18th and 17th Sts). 522.5460

## 10 SAN FRANCISCO WOMEN'S CENTER—WOMEN'S BUILDING

The strength and history of women united is depicted in a beautiful mural covering part of the building. The center is a particularly important resource for women of color and lesbians, with regular meetings, readings, workshops, and events. ◆ M-F. 3543 18th St (between Valencia and Guerrero Sts). 431.1180

## 11 CLUB LEXINGTON

♀ One of San Francisco dykedom's more recent additions—and its only seven-day-a-week nightspot—is a cozy space with a few artsy touches (wriggly bars on the windows,

In March 1996, Mayor Willie Brown presided over the first mass gay and lesbian wedding—some 200 couples—ever sponsored by a US city.

The city's official song, "I Left My Heart in San Francisco," was penned by a homesick gay couple, Douglass Cross and George Cory, in 1954.

light fixtures suggestive of mammaries, and wavy toilet paper dispensers in the rest room) tarting up the green-and-red-painted premises of what's essentially a neighborhood barroom. The lively mix of girls, ranging in age from 21 to 61, tend to be a bit of an artsy bunch—the neighborhood being what it is—and the jukebox is eclectic, throwing out tunes from 1960s Motown to the Butthole Surfers. ◆ Daily, 3PM–2AM. 3464 19th St (between Mission and Valencia Sts). 863.2052

## 12 OSENTO

A sanctuary for unwinding and/or socializing, all to a sound track of soft, relaxing music, this women's day spa offers patrons a large Japanese-style hot tub, a sauna, a steam hut, massage service, and a meditation room; there's a bracing outdoor cold-plunge, and a deck for nude sunbathing. ◆ Admission. Daily, 1PM–1AM. 955 Valencia St (between 21st and 20th Sts). 282.6333

## 13 EROS

♂ A goodly range of guys between 20 and 50 prowl around this two-story safe-sex club, a sort of bathhouse without the private rooms. Downstairs is a lounge with skin flicks, sauna, steam room, and showers, while the upstairs offers various cushioned alcoves—albeit little real privacy—for doing what comes naturally. Don't forget to bring an ID. ◆ Admission. M-Th, Su, 4PM–midnight; F, Sa, 4PM–4AM. 2051 Market St (between Dolores and 14th Sts). 864.3767

## 14 SPARKY'S

★$ One of the few in the city to remain open around the clock, this friendly neighborhood diner is a great place for late-night munchies or an afternoon burger. There's usually a line after the bars close, when the food and the crowd look their best. It's conveniently located across the street from **The Pilsner,** so that if you don't find beefcake you can always get a pancake. ◆ Diner ◆ Daily, 24 hours. 242 Church Street (between 15th and Market Sts). 626.8666

## 15 THE PILSNER

♂ Since the ban on smoking in bars took effect, this neighborhood hangout has become very popular. The large backyard patio is great on a sunny day and ideal to grab a cigarette. The pool table, jukebox, and friendly local crowd keep this bar busy every night; and the variety of draft beers keep the crowd happy. Very busy on weekends, the Pilsner offers both cruising and conversation. Daily, 9AM–2AM. ◆ 225 Church St (between 15th and Market Sts). 621.7058

## 15 CHOW

★★$ The prices in this comfortable yet trendy diner-style room are so reasonable that you can almost afford to buy the local art right off the walls, but the food, mostly Italian but ranging all over the map, can be excellent, from standard quick pastas and wood-fired pizzas and daily sandwich and vegetarian specials to Asian-inspired starters like a Thai-style noodle salad or wontons. Or go all out beginning with rock-salt–roasted mussels and ending with Rose's warm ginger cake with pumpkin ice cream and caramel sauce. A wide range of microbrews and wines by the glass help wash it down. No reservations are taken, but call ahead to put your name on the wait list. ◆ Italian ◆ Daily, lunch and dinner. 215 Church St (between 15th and Market Sts). 552.2469

## 16 2223 Market

★★★$$ One of the few upscale restaurants in the Castro, this place draws a friendly, eclectic, and heavily gay clientele. Dinner crowds line up for chef Melinda Randolph's culinary delights on the order of wild-mushroom fettuccine and roasted chicken with garlic mashed potatoes, or a sophisticated grilled salmon with mustard-braised lentils and broccoli rabe with roasted-red-pepper *rouille*. The ever-changing pizza menu is a winner too, as are the huge colorful murals that bring a Mardi Gras atmosphere to mind. ◆ Californian/continental ◆ M-F, dinner; Sa, Su, brunch and dinner. Reservations recommended on weekends. 2223 Market St (between Sanchez and 16th Sts). 431.0692 &

## 17 Café Flore

★★$ Possibly the closest thing to a sidewalk café this side of Paris, this highly popular hangout (sometimes dubbed Café Hairdo) is a great place to meet people or just sit over a coffee, beer, or white wine with a bored existential look on your face. Writers, artists, and other creative types abound here. Tasty, inexpensive salads, burgers, and daily specials are served, and the only thing missing is a good gas heater on the outside patio for cold days. ◆ Café ◆ Daily. 2298 Market St (at Noe St). 621.8579 &

## 18 The Gym SF

♂ Cruisy, high energy, and boys-only, both branches of this gym offer a good selection of free weights, Universal equipment, and personal training, as well as a sauna and cardio machines. The clientele at the Hayes Street location (which has a Jacuzzi) is a bit older. ◆ M-F, 6AM–10PM; Sa, Su, 8AM–6PM. 2275 Market St (between Sanchez and 16th Sts). 863.4700. Also at 364 Hayes St (between Franklin and Gough Sts). 863.4701

## 19 Bagdad Café

★$ One of the few in the city to remain open around-the-clock, this friendly neighborhood diner is a great place to grab a quick bite anytime. There are lots of streetside windows for people watching, and art and photography exhibits from local talent on the walls. On the downside, the food (on the order of salads, burgers, and a breakfast menu served all day) can be hit or miss. ◆ Diner ◆ Daily, 24 hours. 2295 Market St (at Noe St). 621.4434 &

## 20 Inn On Castro

♂ $$ With just five rooms (each with private bath), this is one of the smaller guest houses in the city (and almost exclusively gay male); its intimacy, though, is a big part of its charm. The Edwardian exterior contrasts with the contemporary look inside, featuring classic modern furniture, track lighting, and the original art of one of the owners. Upstairs, breakfast is served on an extensive and ever-changing collection of imported china and stoneware. ◆ 321 Castro St (between Market and 16th Sts). 861.0321 &

## 21 Under One Roof

♂
♀ Staffed entirely by volunteers, this gift shop donates 100% of its proceeds to AIDS charities. It offers a lovely array of clothes, greeting cards, candleholders, hand-crafted

collectibles, and one-of-a-kind items. During the Christmas season it becomes a winter wonderland, featuring some of the most unusual and festive decorations in the city. ◆ Daily. 549 Castro St (between 17th and 16th Sts). 252.9430

## 21 DETOUR JET

♂ Locals either love or hate this lounge and upscale dance bar. Sunday nights are especially hot, and the tunes are always on the cutting edge. ◆ Daily, 4PM–2AM. 2348 Market St (between Noe and Castro Sts). 861.6053 &

## 22 GOLD'S GYM

♂ This popular co-ed facility not only has the usual panoply of weights, machines, aerobics, and personal training, but is also one of the gayest and cruisiest gyms for men in the city. The guys are buff, friendly, and frisky; check out the Jacuzzi. ◆ M-F, 6AM–10PM; Sa, Su, 8AM–8PM. 2301 Market St (at Noe St). 626.4488

## 23 THE CAFÉ

♂ Excellent is the music and hot are the friendly
♀ young guys and gals in attendance at this fun dance bar up a flight of stairs. When not cruising, shooting pool, or writhing on the small dance floor, the patrons cheer and whistle from the balcony overlooking the intersection of Market and Castro at every muscle, drag, or leather queen that walks by. Lines can be a block long on Friday and Saturday night, so come early; the 4PM Sunday tea dance is also copacetic. ◆ Daily, 12:30PM–2AM. 2367 Market St (between Noe and Castro Sts). 861.3846

## 24 MARCELLO'S PIZZA

★★$ Practically an institution, this small but very popular joint makes some of the tastiest pizza around. Choose from such innovative toppings as clams, pesto chicken, pineapple and ham, roasted rosemary potato and onion, or more traditional variations. Calzones, hot grilled subs, and salads are also on the menu. ◆ Pizza/takeout ◆ Daily, until 1AM. 420 Castro St (between 18th and Market Sts). 863.3900 &

## 25 CASTRO THEATER

The city declared this remarkable Spanish Colonial structure a landmark in 1977, calling it San Francisco's finest example of a 1920s movie palace. Inside, the 1,600-seat theater sports an awesome plaster ceiling resembling a giant cloth canopy. The loyal, enthusiastic audience revels in the theater's opulence and the thrill of seeing favorite classics as they were originally presented. If you're lucky, you'll be at a performance where the theater's multipipe organ rises from the orchestra pit and the organist regales moviegoers before the show. Special events are also staged here, such as concerts of the **Gay Men's Chorus,** and numerous film festivals, including the International Gay and Lesbian Film Festival. ◆ 429 Castro St (between 18th and 17th Sts). 621.6120 &

## 25 TWIN PEAKS

♂ Also known as the Glass Coffin, this landmark
♀ gay bar founded in 1972 is one of the oldest in the Castro, and the first to put in huge picture windows so folks could see and be seen. These days, the crowd around the beautiful antique wooden bar is a friendly, relaxed mix of guys and gals mostly in the age 40–60 range. ◆ Daily, noon–2AM. 401 Castro St (at 17th St). 864.9470 &

## 25 ORPHAN ANDY'S

★$ Filling breakfast fare, sandwiches, and burgers rule at this around-the-clock coffee shop where Day-Glo hair, piercings, and tattoos are de rigueur. It's a lifesaver during or after a night of partying, though at 4AM the staff and patrons can get a bit edgy. Check out the jukebox with its one-of-a-kind recordings scattered within a diverse selection of pop and rock. ◆ Diner ◆ Daily, 24 hours. 3991 17th St (between Hartford and Castro Sts). 864.9795

## 25 HARVEY MILK PLAZA

A small brick plaza in front of the **Castro and Market Muni** station was dedicated in 1985 to the slain civil rights leader and former member of the San Francisco Board of Supervisors. At the railway's entrance is a plaque giving a thumbnail history of Milk's career in the city—from 1973 when he opened a camera store at 575 Castro (now occupied by a shop called **Skin Zone**) up to his assassination at **City Hall** in November 1978. The memorial concludes movingly with a quote from Milk: "I am all of us." ◆ Market and Castro Sts

## 26 THE PARKER GUEST HOUSE

♂ $$ One of the Castro's newer all-homo prop-
♀ erties is run by Bob O'Halloran, an alumnus of the local Joie de Vivre hotel chain, and his lover Bill Boeddiker, in a three-story, yellow manse of brick, stone, and wood dating from 1909. The combination of a loving renovation and can-do hospitality makes for a winning stay with guests (an even mix of men and women), who are free to relax in the library—complete with fireplace and piano—or outside on the large sundeck, the landscaped lawn, gardens, or brick patio. The five rooms are a mix of contemporary and antiques—depending on the floor—but all share floral themes, earth tones, and pinewood. Four of the guest rooms have private baths and all offer voice mail and modem ports. Breakfast is included. ◆ 520 Church St (between 18th and 17th Sts). 621.3222, 888/520.7275

# A RIVER RUNS THROUGH GUERNEVILLE

Near **Sonoma** wine country about 1.5 hours north of San Francisco is the town of **Guerneville** (pop. 3,500) and the resort area of **Russian River,** which takes its name from the river running through it. With its shops, restaurants, bars, and inns, Guerneville has been the area's main gay and lesbian gathering place since the 1970s, and its attractions—redwood forests, wineries, and coastal beaches—keep San Franciscans coming back, especially in summer. The most popular "resorts" are basic, but socially oriented. Small cabins, campsites, and motel rooms are the most common lodging.

Premier among the local homo resorts is the casual and cruisy **Dawn Ranch Lodge** ($$; 16467 River Rd, 707/869.0656, www.dawnranch.com) in Guerneville. At the edge of the river, this rustic 15-acre compound for men and women offers simple accommodations in 50 cabins and cottages, as well as 100 campsites. On-site facilities include a pool, sundeck, private beach, small gym, a restaurant, the **Bunkhouse** country-western bar, and the **Signs** disco. Day-trippers are also welcome.

Also on **River Road,** though less elaborate, the friendly, mixed male and female, and laid-back **Willows** ($$; 5905 River Rd, 707/869.2824, 800/953.2828) sits at the river's edge, and offers 60 tent sites, 13 bedrooms with television and VCRs, a living room with fireplace, and a library with a grand piano. Breakfast is provided, and guests enjoy a private beach, sundeck, hot tub, sauna, nude sunbathing, and canoes.

Slightly smaller, and nestled on three lush wooded acres within walking distance of town, **Highlands** ($$; 14000 Woodland Dr, between Morningside Dr and Woodland Rd, 707/869.0333) is a popular spot for men and women, offering privacy and a swimsuit-optional pool and hot tub. There are 16 cabins and rooms (some with kitchens and fireplaces), as well as tent sites.

For a friskier, party atmosphere, try the mostly male **Russian River Resort** ($$; Fourth and Mill Sts, 707/869.0691, 800/417.3736). The 24 rooms

here are small and plain, but the guys come to party and play to a loud dance beat by the pool, in the hot tub, at the poolside bar, or in the indoor video bar. There's also a great restaurant that serves lunch and dinner daily, and has nightly piano music. The premises are open to nonguests as well. The "Triple R" is also the proud sponsor of Leather Weekend each August.

If luxury and gourmet food are more appealing, then the mixed gay/lesbian/straight **Applewood Inn & Restaurant** ($$$$; 13555 Hwy 116, 707/869.9093) may be just the place. A two-minute drive from downtown Guerneville, this beautiful inn offers 17 nonsmoking rooms and suites equipped with fireplaces and either a Jacuzzi or two-person shower. The pool's open in season, and the hot tub year-round. The restaurant ($$$) is one of the best in **Sonoma County.**

Apart from the nightlife at the resorts, there are a handful of eating, drinking, and dancing spots, such as the gay-lesbian **Molly's Country Club** (14120 Old Cazadero Rd, off Rte 116, west of town, 707/869.0511), with a restaurant, bar, country-western dancing, and house music on weekends. A fun place, it sponsors Western Weekend in October. Another option, in Guerneville, is the **Rainbow Cattle Company** (16220 Main St, 707/869.0206), a men's bar that opens at dawn. The gay- and lesbian-friendly **Sweet's Café** ($$; 16251 Main St, 707/869.3383), open daily in downtown Guerneville, serves light fare and offers fabulous people watching.

To get to the Russian River area by car, take **Highway 101** over the **Golden Gate Bridge** past **Santa Rosa,** then take the exit marked River Rd and go west for 20 minutes until you reach Guerneville. For more information, contact the **Russian River Chamber of Commerce** (707/869.9000), the **Gay and Lesbian Business Association** (707/869.4522), or the **Sonoma County Visitors' Information Services** (707/523.8075); and allow us to modestly recommend **ACCESS™ California Wine Country.**

## 27 BAR ON CASTRO

♂ Redecorated with plenty of space to lounge, this is a friendly bar for cruising or conversation. Pull up an ottoman and watch the DJ spin, or shoot some pool with friends. Tables in the front and a smoking patio in the back (closed at 11PM) help keep the boy traffic circulating.♦ M-F, 3PM–2AM; Sa, Su, noon–2AM. 456B Castro St (between 18th and Market Sts). 626.7220

## 27 440 CASTRO

♂ The smell of leather can be as intoxicating as the drinks in this friendly neighborhood

---

Restaurants/Clubs: Red | Hotels: Purple | Shops: Orange | Outdoors/Parks: Green | Sights/Culture: Blue

joint where basic black doubles as décor and dress code. Porn films grace the video screens while a chronologically diverse mix of guys cruise, chat, or work the pool tables or pinball machines. Hang out with the less hard-core boys up front or join the serious leathermen in the back bar. ♦ M-F, 9AM–2AM; Sa, Su, 6AM–2AM. 440 Castro St (between 18th and Market Sts). 621.8732

## 27 ALL AMERICAN BOY

♂ The local outpost of this gay-oriented men's clothing shop specializes in fun, California-casual clothes and accessories for men. For that supermacho look, try on the butchy-kitschy line of going-out gear inspired by Tom of Finland. ♦ M-Sa, 10AM–9PM; Su, 11AM–7PM. 436 Castro St (between 18th and Market Sts). 861.0444

## 27 IN-JEAN-IOUS

♂
♀ It's not just jeans at this friendly gay-owned shop, but all manner of activewear, club wear, shoes, hats, and accessories. The T-shirt collection is funnier than most, and a major best-seller is a local artist's campy takes on the popular Barbie doll: Imagine Big Dyke Barbie, Drag Queen Barbie, and Trailer Trash Barbie. ♦ M-Sa, 10AM–9PM; Su, 11AM–7PM. 432 Castro St (between 18th and Market Sts). 864.1863

## 28 18TH STREET BAR

♂ This longstanding Castro watering hole caters mostly, but not exclusively, to an African-American clientele. There's a friendly and very cruisy mix of chaps of all ages milling about the big horseshoe-shaped bar or the busy pool table. It's no wonder people keep coming back, as the bartenders and staff here truly make everyone feel at home. ♦ Daily, 7AM–2AM. 4146 18th St (between Castro and Collingwood Sts). (At press time the new number was unavailable) &

## 29 FUZIO

★★$$ The first of a new chain to take pastas from around the globe and puts them in one yummy restaurant. Casual and friendly, the crowd is as cute as the food is good. The firecracker pork fusilli is spicy hot and the Chinese chicken salad is cool and fresh. The full bar and very affordable prices keep the boys and girls waiting in line, so have a drink and enjoy the sights. ♦ M-Th, Su, 11AM–10PM; F, Sa, 11AM–11PM. 469 Castro St (at 18th St). 863.1400 &

## 29 A DIFFERENT LIGHT

♂
♀ The warm and welcoming local branch of America's largest gay and lesbian bookseller is a must-visit. The latest in fiction, nonfiction, poetry, self-help, magazines, cards, videos, music, and (of course) erotica are stocked here. Gay, lesbian, and transgender authors

give regular readings as well. Karen Bornstein, Quentin Crisp, Eileen Myles, and Robert Tiard are just a few such scribblers. ♦ Daily, 10AM–11PM. 489 Castro St (at 18th St). 431.0891, 800/343.4002 &

## 30 CASTRO COUNTRY CLUB

♂ A popular alternative to the bar scene (especially for nondrinkers), this mostly male place charges a nominal cover for a whole day's access to a friendly, relaxed space reminiscent of a family room. You'll find screened movies, comfy lounging areas, occasional art openings, and even a sundeck. The crowd on the front steps on weekends is deliciously cruisy. ♦ Cover. M-Th, Su, 11AM–11PM; F, Sa, 11AM–11PM. 4058 18th St (between Hartford and Castro Sts). 552.6102

## 31 THE EDGE

♂ A kind of disco lounge in the Twilight Zone, this dance palace seems stuck in the 1970s with its black walls, chrome, and mustachioed clones heavy on denim and leather. Mostly the guys boogie and cruise (each other, or the passing flesh on 18th Street through the window). ♦ Daily, noon–2AM. 4149 18th St (between Castro and Collingwood Sts). 863.4027 &

## 32 HARVEY'S

♂
♀ ★$ Local cops trashed this longtime gay gathering spot, known back in 1979 as the **Elephant Walk,** in response to the "White Nights" riots at **City Hall** (provoked by the light sentence meted out to Harvey Milk's assassin). Today the place has turned into a sort of homo Hard Rock Café, what with an eclectic and growing collection of homosexual memorabilia that includes items having to do with Liberace, Sylvester, Greg Louganis, the Lady Bunny, José Sarria, Agnes Moorehead, Barbara Stanwyck, Harvey Milk, and many, many others. The fare is simple, running toward burgers, pasta, and salads, but the real star at brunch is Eggs Harvey, poached and served with spinach and herb gravy on a sun-dried–tomato focaccia. The bar attracts a nice mix of locals and tourists, and the martinis are some of the best (and biggest) in town. ♦ American ♦ Restaurant: daily, brunch and dinner. Bar: daily, 11AM–2AM. 500 Castro St (at 18th St). 431.4278 &

## 32 BADLANDS

♂ One of the most popular bars in the Castro attracts a motley bunch of twenty- to forty-something guys, most of whom just stand around and stare. It sports a new upscale dance floor. The hi-energy tunes (spun periodically by live DJs) are some of the best around, though oldies (and rock-bottom beer specials) on Sunday draw a major crowd. ♦ M-F, 2PM–2AM. 4121 18th St (between Castro and Collingwood Sts). 626.9320

## 33 JAGUAR

♂
♀
The staff at this erotic emporium is so eager to please that they've been known to demonstrate the use of cockrings and nipple clamps. Whether or not you opt for such personal attention, it's fun (and sometimes educational) to browse for sex supplies, gift items, cards, magazines, and novelties. ♦ M-Th; F, Sa, 10AM-midnight; Su, 10AM-11PM. 4057 18th St (between Hartford and Castro Sts). 863.4777

## 33 THE MIDNIGHT SUN

♂ What's billed as the oldest gay video bar in the country (it was started in 1969) still packs in upwardly mobile queers in their twenties and thirties. With a galvanized metal exterior, high ceilings, huge projection screens, and a L-O-U-D sound system, the place can be cruisy enough; sometimes, though, the *Absolutely Fabulous, Barbarella,* and *Sound of Music* clips prove too distracting. Saturday comedy night is the most popular, and movie musical Tuesday doesn't do too badly, either. ♦ Daily, noon-2AM. 4067 18th St (between Hartford and Castro Sts). 861.4186 ♿

## 34 LUNA RESTAURANT

★★★$$ The garden at the casual, romantic "Full Moon Café" is a lovely place to dine alfresco, and is especially popular with brunchers. Apart from such morning favorites as the delicious oatmeal-almond French toast, there's a great selection of salads, sandwiches, and pastas, as well as imaginative entrées like sesame-encrusted catfish with lentil bean cake in a tomato coulis. The beer and wine list is superb. ♦ New American ♦ M, brunch; Tu-Su, brunch and dinner. Reservations recommended on weekends. 558 Castro St (between 19th and 18th Sts). 621.2566

## 35 MISSION DOLORES PARK

🅟 Just a short stroll from the Castro, this patch of green is the perfect place to sunbathe with the boys on a warm day while taking in a stunning view of the city skyline. Just watch out for the dope-pushing kids at the park entrance, and don't linger after dark. ♦ Bounded by Dolores and Church Sts, and 20th and 18th Sts

## 36 CLUB FUGAZI

OK, so it's touristy and lowbrow, but Steve Silver's *Beach Blanket Babylon* is still lots o' campy fun and one production every visitor (especially every queer visitor) should see. Featuring the biggest hats, biggest hair, and most outlandish costumes you're likely to ever see onstage, this show has been wowing

audiences for more than two decades and is still going strong. No one under 21 is admitted except for the Sunday matinee. ♦ Admission. Daily. Reservations required three to four weeks in advance. 678 Green St (between Stockton and Powell Sts). 421.4222 ♿

## 37 THE CINCH SALOON

♂
♀
A kitschy, pseudo-Southwestern décor combines with pool tables, computer games, a jukebox, and a large-screen TV to make this a comfortable neighborhood hangout. The staff and patrons (mostly in their thirties and forties) are very friendly, and the owners sponsor numerous benefits throughout the year in addition to the regular roster of events—beer busts, buffet nights, 49ers Sundays, pool tournaments, and holiday drag shows. ♦ Daily, 6AM-2AM. 1723 Polk St (between Clay and Washington Sts). 776.4162 ♿

## 38 THE SWALLOW

♂ One of San Francisco's few remaining piano bars is still a classy, popular pick for a friendly cast ranging from Gen-X to late Baby Boomer guys (and a few gals), who love to sit around the piano and along the long bar belting out Broadway and pop classics. They're accompanied by ivory tinklers who seem to know just about every song ever written. ♦ Daily, 9PM-1AM. 1750 Polk St (between Clay and Washington Sts). 775.4152

## 39 N' TOUCH

♂ Disco-era mirrors and flashing lights are big at this long, narrow dance bar popular with San Francisco's many young gay Asians and their admirers. Strippers are on hand several nights a week, and Tuesday's karaoke night is quite the thing. ♦ Daily, 3PM-2AM. 1548 Polk St (between California and Sacramento Sts). 441.8413

## 40 LE MERIDIEN HOTEL

$$$$ This 360-room hotel in the downtown financial district is way up on the list of best (and gay-friendliest) places to stay in the city, especially if you're in town on business and need such standard extras as two phones and 24-hour room service. Two Mercedes are also available to shuttle you through the downtown area, and the hotel offers a full business center and 14 meeting rooms. Afternoon tea and caviar are served in the lobby lounge; the lobby bar features a pianist nightly from 6:30PM-10PM, and the elegant, woody **Park Grill** restaurant is open for breakfast, lunch, and dinner. ♦ 333 Battery St (between Sacramento and Commercial Sts). 392.1234, 800/233.1234 ♿

---

Restaurants/Clubs: Red | Hotels: Purple | Shops: Orange | Outdoors/Parks: Green | Sights/Culture: Blue

## 41 101 CALIFORNIA STREET

With the **Bank of America** building and the **Transamerica Pyramid,** this cylindrical structure codesigned by gay architect **Philip Johnson** is the third major landmark in the Financial District. Completed in 1983, its silvery reflective glass looks especially beautiful when seen from the bay at dusk. Although the lobby is rather ungainly, a sloping glass wall slicing across the 90-foot-tall columns makes a dramatic sight. The north-facing plaza on California Street is flanked by two mid-rise blocks cut on the diagonal. Inside, the sleek **Atrium** restaurant makes a sophisticated dining experience for lunch or dinner. ♦ At Davis St

## 42 KIMO'S

♂ The perfect place to people-watch on Polk (thanks to lots of windows), this place serves cocktails priced to sell—for breakfast, even. The upstairs bar is complemented by a dance floor and stage where strippers and dragsters do their thing. ♦ Daily, 8AM–2AM. 1351 Polk St (at Pine St). 885.4535

## 43 HOTEL TRITON

$$$ Within striking distance of Union Square and Chinatown, the 140 smallish rooms here are stocked with playful and sophisticated modern furniture decorated in a pink-and-gold color scheme. This wacky hotel has a gay-friendly staff and hosts numerous gay and lesbian events throughout the year, including Wigstock West. It also works hard to make nice with the fashion and entertainment industry, so expect to see some glitzoids loitering about. There's no restaurant. ♦ 342 Grant Ave (between Sutter and Bush Sts). 394.0500, 800/433.6611 ♿

## 44 QUEEN ANNE HOTEL

$$ One of the city's most comfortable and unique hostelries had already had numerous lives when it was converted to a hotel in 1981—first as **Miss Mary Lake's School for Girls** in 1890, then as the **Cosmos** men's club, and finally as the Episcopal **Girls Friendly Society Lodge.** Today, each of the 49 rooms and suites is individually designed and furnished with antiques; eight have wood-burning fireplaces, and one has two. Complimentary continental breakfast is included, as are afternoon tea, sherry, and cookies. ♦ 1590 Sutter St (at Octavia St). 441.2828, 800/227.3970

## 45 POLK STREET

The stretch between Geary and California Streets known as Polk Gulch was the focus of the city's gay population until most of the

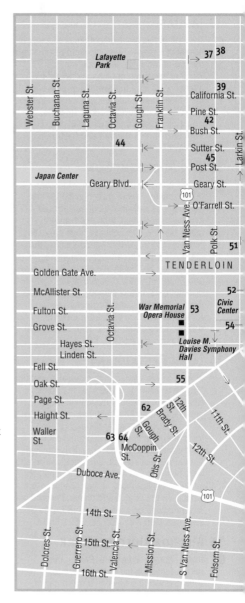

action moved to the Castro district. Currently, that portion of Polk is in transition, populated by drifters and young male hustlers, and much of the glitz of the 1970s has been lost to shops whose wares are in questionable taste. North of California Street it gets better, with a mix of old neighborhood food stores, antiques shops, bookstores, restaurants, and charming specialty shops. ♦ Between Geary and Lombard Sts

## 46 THE PRESCOTT HOTEL

♂ $$$ Close to Union Square, this 166-room hotel boasts an Edwardian décor in deep

♀ jewel tones and a first-rate, friendly staff. The guest rooms, however, are smallish, but offer such amenities as minibars, hair dryers, and terry-cloth robes, and complimentary wine, hors d'oeuvres, coffee, and tea are served. Best of all, guests will have better luck than ordinary mortals getting a table at **Postrio,** Wolfgang Puck's exciting on-premises restaurant (which also does room service). ♦ 545 Post St (between Mason and Taylor Sts). 563.0303, 800/283.7322 ♿

## 47 DOTTIE'S TRUE BLUE CAFÉ

★★★$ Breakfast just doesn't get much better than the freshly baked breads, scones, and muffins at this beloved spot—and the fresh poached eggs with corned beef is the best in town at this place that looks like a 1940s diner. The gay owners who recently took it over have increased the vegetarian offerings, especially at lunch; try the black-bean chili, the vegetable tarts, or the scrumptious roasted eggplant sandwich with goat cheese and tomatoes. ♦ American ♦

---

Restaurants/Clubs: Red | Hotels: Purple | Shops: Orange | Outdoors/Parks: Green | Sights/Culture: Blue

M, W-F, breakfast and lunch; Sa, Su, brunch. 522 Jones St (between O'Farrell and Geary Sts). 885.2767 &

### 48 NEIMAN MARCUS

Give in to those base shopping urges while taking in the work of gay architect **Philip Johnson,** who designed this controversial structure built on the corner of Union Square in 1982. The only remnant of the turn-of-the-century **City of Paris** store that occupied the site is an enormous glass dome, incorporated as part of the **Rotunda** restaurant. At Yuletide, the store erects the most dramatic Christmas tree in the city. ♦ M-Sa; Su, noon–6PM. 150 Stockton St (at Geary St). 362.3900 &

### 49 CENTER FOR THE ARTS

The gay and lesbian communities are well represented at this 55,000-square-foot contemporary arts center, part of the beautiful **Yerba Buena Gardens** complex. To date, the exciting array of exhibitions, screenings, and performances has featured a variety of artists, from **Pomo Afro Homos** to the **Stephen Petronio** dance company and the **San Francisco Gay Men's Chorus.** ♦ 701 Mission St (at Third St). Program information 978.2787

### 50 SAN FRANCISCO MUSEUM OF MODERN ART (SFMMA)

In January 1995, in celebration of its 60th year, the museum relocated its collection from the **Veteran's Building** in the **Civic Center** to new, larger quarters across from **Yerba Buena Gardens.** Its handsome brick box home was designed by the internationally acclaimed Swiss architect **Mario Botta** and features a 125-foot cylindrical skylight that channels light down to the first-floor atrium court. More than 17,000 works are housed on the museum's four floors; such queer and bisexual artists as Georgia O'Keeffe, Larry Rivers, Frida Kahlo, Jasper Johns, Robert Mapplethorpe, Andy Warhol, and Duane Michaels are represented in the permanent collection, along with the likes of Picasso, Matisse, Kandinsky, Calder, and Noguchi. And don't miss Jeff Koons's exquisitely campy statue *Michael Jackson and Bubbles.* ♦ Admission; free first Tuesday of the month; half-price Thursday evening. M, Tu, F-Su, 11AM–6PM; Th, 11AM–9PM. Tours daily. 151 Third St (at Minna St). 357.4000

### 51 THE PHOENIX HOTEL

$$ A one-acre oasis of respectability in a downscale neighborhood, this gay-owned 44-room inn feels much like a resort. It has a pool, garden, and outdoor café; massage and other spa services are also available on-site.

Popular with artsy and celebrity types, the rooms feature the works of Bay Area artists, and there's a hot new **Bambuddha** lounge for afternoon and evening cocktails. On-site parking and continental breakfast are included. ♦ 601 Eddy St (at Larkin St). 776.1380, 800/248.9466 &

### 52 ABIGAIL HOTEL

$$ Built in 1926 to house members of visiting theater groups, this Howard Johnson's hotel was remodeled in 1990 in an arty European style. There's a cozy, British feeling, complete with antiques, down comforters, and turn-of-the-century English art. While still not quite luxurious, the 61-room hotel is a good value and conveniently located to many cultural attractions and performance venues, including **Louise M. Davies Symphony Hall** and the **War Memorial Opera House.** ♦ 246 McAllister St (between Hyde and Larkin Sts). 861.9728, 800/243.6510

### 53 SAN FRANCISCO PERFORMING ARTS LIBRARY & MUSEUM (PALM)

With a gallery and collection focusing on the Bay Area, this nonprofit institution naturally has works by a bushel of theater queens, including Leonard Bernstein, Jerry Herman, Cole Porter, and Lorenz Hart. Make an appointment to view videos or listen to recordings. ♦ Free. W, 1–7PM; Th, F, 11AM–5PM; Sa, noon–5PM. 401 Van Ness Ave (between Grove and McAllister Sts). 255.4800 &

### 54 JAMES C. HORMEL GAY AND LESBIAN CENTER

♂ Located in a wood-paneled circular room in
♀ the seven-story **San Francisco Public Library** (known to locals as New Main), this center is a landmark in homosexual history: It is the first facility of its kind in the world to be housed in a public institution. Named for its single largest benefactor, a member of the Hormel meatpacking dynasty (and controversial ambassadorial nominee), the center is dedicated to research on gay and lesbian culture. Highlights of the collection include material from filmmakers Rob Epstein and Peter Adair, journalist Randy Shilts, and pioneering lesbian publishers Barbara Grier and Donna McBride of Naiad Press, and of course the personal papers and memorabilia of martyred San Francisco supervisor Harvey Milk. A dramatic 22-foot trompe-l'oeil ceiling mural by Charley Brown and Mark Evans, *Into the Light,* depicts gays and lesbians and the names of famous homos throughout history. ♦ M, F, Sa; Tu-Th, 9AM–8PM; Su, noon–5PM. 100 Larkin St (at Grove St), third floor. 557.4400

# SAN FRANCISCO SUN 'N' SURF

Expect anything! San Francisco's beaches can be sun drenched one day and enshrouded in fog the next. Always scenic and beautiful, some of the city's beaches are ideal for swimming, while others are limited to sunbathing and picnicking due to treacherous conditions along the rocky coastline. A chancy proposition on those beaches with treacherous conditions, yes, but you can always count on some warm and sunny days when the surf is calm. Here are some of San Francisco's favorites:

**Baker Beach** This mile-long beach, off 25th Avenue, is part of the Golden Gate National Recreation Area. Although it is a good-weather sandy beach, dangerous waves make swimming off-limits. Its views of the Bay Area entice hikers, fisherfolk, and picnickers.

**China Beach** Located at 29th Avenue between **Lincoln Park** and **The Presidio,** this 600-foot sandy beach cove was once a campsite for Chinese fishermen. Part of the **Golden Gate National Recreation Area,** the beach is popular for sunbathing and picnicking, and is one of the few swimming beaches in the city. Lifeguards are on duty during the summer.

**Land's End Beach** You'll find this secluded spot at **End Trail** off **Merrie Way** in the **Richmond District.** The no-swimming beach is difficult to reach, but the views are rewarding. Clothing is considered optional by the beach's mainly gay sunbathers.

**Ocean Beach** Located between **Lincoln Way** and **Fulton Street** on the westernmost edge of Golden Gate Park, this is the prime destination for locals and visitors alike. **Cliff House** provides a popular vantage point; just offshore is the outline of **Seal Rocks,** those stony offshore islands that are usually inhabited by shorebirds and a colony of sea lions. Bring binoculars for a closer look. On a clear day the **Farallon Islands,** some 30 miles distant, are also visible. Swimming is not allowed here because of dangerous tides and the undertow, but the wide sandy beach is fine for walking, jogging, and sunbathing.

**Phelan Beach** This cove-tucked small beach is used primarily for swimming and sunning and sports, with a lifeguard on duty April through October. You'll find it at **El Camino del Mar** in the **Richmond District.**

## 55 THE NEW CONSERVATORY THEATRE CENTER

This theater school and performing arts complex offers professional classes and productions. In addition to classrooms and rehearsal spaces, the center has three theaters and an art gallery featuring paintings, sculptures, and photographs in exhibitions that change quarterly. It's also home to the "Pride Season," a subscriber-based gay and lesbian performance program that has included the world premiere of the all-gay version of Jack Heifner's *Vanities,* a revival of John Herbert's 1967 classic *Fortune and Men's Eyes,* and Helen Eisenbach's *Lesbianism Made Easy.* ◆ Exhibits: Tu-Sa, noon–7PM. 25 Van Ness Ave (between Oak and Fell Sts). 861.8972

## 56 STORMY LEATHER

♀ Women into the bondage or the fetish look will groove on the well-made and elegant leather, rubber, and plastic goodies at this woman-owned boutique. Other accessories include handcuffs, whips, and such items from the toy chest, and there's a good selection of books, magazines, and greeting cards as well. ◆ M-Sa, noon–7PM; Su, 2–6PM.

1158 Howard St (between Seventh and Eighth Sts). 626.1672

## 57 RAWHIDE II

♂ The huge dance floor at this popular country
♀ and western spot is usually packed with two-steppers and a fiercely loyal following of dudes mostly in their thirties and forties. The animal heads staring out from the walls are supposed to create a "down-home" kind of feel, but they're actually rather creepy. Two-stepping and line dance lessons are offered Tuesday through Friday. ◆ Cover F-Su. M-Th, 4PM–2AM; F, Sa, noon–2AM; Su, 1PM–2AM. 280 Seventh St (at Folsom St). 621.1197

## 58 HOLE IN THE WALL

♂ Billing itself as a "nasty little biker bar," this place certainly acts the part, with chains and barbed-wire sculptures hanging from the ceiling, and spontaneous sexual combustion in dark corners. Hippies, bikers, drag queens, and leathermen meet here to play pool or pinball, or talk to their demons in private. The music ranges from industrial trance to punk to acid rock. Avoid the weekend lines; you can get just as good a taste of the place during the week. ◆ M, F-Su, 6AM–2AM; Tu-Th,

---

Restaurants/Clubs: Red | Hotels: Purple | Shops: Orange | Outdoors/Parks: Green | Sights/Culture: Blue

# SAN FRANCISCO GAY HISTORY 101

More than any other city, the history of the City by the Bay is the chronicle of gay America. Homosexuality in this part of northern California predates the European invasion, when Native American "two-spirit" people (also known as berdaches) were integral parts of local culture. Many years later, during the rough-and-tumble "Barbary Coast" era unleashed by the 1849 gold rush, the saloons, brothels, and vaudeville halls of a generally fluid society awash with single men gave rise to what was widely termed Sodom by the Sea (including a discreet homo demimonde).

Over the years, this world grew and flourished. While the **Dash**—San Francisco's first documented gay bar—was put out of business by the city in 1908, by the 1930s such gay watering holes as **Finocchio's** (established in 1929) and the **Black Cat Café** were a regular part of the city's social scene; some progressive newspapers even spoke out, condemning prejudice against homosexuals. Oppression and clandestinity continued, though, radicalizing homosexuals like Harry Hay, whose experiences during the San Francisco General Strike of 1933 sowed the seeds for his founding of the Mattachine Society, America's first effective gay-rights organization. World War II brought a huge surge in the Bay Area homo population, and in establishments (mostly along **Polk Street**) catering to them. In the late 1940s and 1950s, an official backlash against "perversion" led to police harassment of gay gathering places and even bookstores that sold gay-themed material like Allen Ginsberg's *Howl* (1955).

At the same time, the McCarthyite 1950s and the early 1960s saw the rise of several "homophile" organizations. In addition to the Mattachine Society, originally established in Los Angeles, and moved to San Francisco in 1957, there was the Daughters of Bilitis, founded here in 1955 by Phyllis Lyon and Del Martin, and the Society for Individual Rights, established in 1964. The Tavern Guild, the first gay and lesbian business group in the United States, was formed in 1962 to protect the interests of gay bar

owners and patrons. These early attempts at activism were further galvanized on New Year's Day in 1965 by "San Francisco's Stonewall," when police harassed and interfered with a legally sanctioned drag ball (even arresting some people—one of whom became California's first openly gay judge in 1983). Politicians, the media, and even some clergy criticized the cops, and as of that point bar raids largely ceased, politicos started courting the gay and lesbian vote, and homosexuals began to use "the system" to gain equal rights, even as more radical "gay liberation" groups began making their presence felt with pickets and protests.

In the early 1970s, gays and lesbians began to flock to a neighborhood known as **Eureka Valley** or the **Most Holy Redeemer Parish.** Rents were cheap, and as more homos moved in, more straights moved out. Soon this district was being called the Castro (after the old theater that dominated the street of the same name), and for many gays and lesbians this became the epicenter of their world.

Harvey Milk, the first openly gay official in San Francisco (elected to the Board of Supervisors in 1977), was often referred to as the Mayor of Castro Street. His own dreams of equal rights for gays and lesbians came to a brutal end when he and Mayor George Moscone were assassinated in 1978. But this tragedy brought the gay and lesbian communities together and helped forge an alliance that would mobilize again and again during the 1980s and 1990s in the fight against AIDS, breast cancer, and homophobic conservatives.

Today the Castro still attracts thousands of people, and some activists are trying to have it designated a national historic site. Others want to establish a Gay Walk of Fame, with pink triangles in the sidewalk inscribed with the names of well-known gays and lesbians. Such civic-mindedness is an important part of the fabric of gay life in San Francisco, and no doubt will help to ensure its survival as a vibrant community for generations to come.

---

noon–2AM. 289 Eighth St (between Folsom St and Clementina Alley). 431.4695

## 59 BLOW BUDDIES

♂ Until San Francisco rescinds its ban on bathhouses, this safe-sex club for the orally fixated is one of the few such venues in town. To the beat of trancelike music, the premises offer plenty of dark corners, a lounge, open-air backyard, and a range of men in all ages, shapes, and sizes. The best turnout is on Friday, Saturday, and Sunday. Bring an ID for admission. ♦ Cover. Th, 8PM–4AM; F, Sa, 9PM–6AM;

Su, 6PM–2:30AM. 933 Harrison St (between Fifth and Sixth Sts). 777.4323

## 60 ENDUP

♂ Make your disco nap a good one, because
♀ weekends are wild at this club, what with the great music and high energy. The all-day Sunday tea dance really packs them in both indoors and out on the relaxing patio. In between, Saturday's "Girl Spot" is the dyke dance event of the week. ♦ Cover. F, 10:30PM–5:30AM; Sa, 8PM–2AM; Su, 6AM–9PM. 401 Sixth St (at Harrison St). 487.6277, 263.4850; Girl Spot 337.4962

## 61 Coco 500

★★★$$ In a gay-popular SOMA bistro with glazed walls, Loretta Keller prepares such favorites as tempura-fried green beans, Catalan shrimp, and fresh grilled sardines. The slow-simmered and gently baked dishes are just the thing on a foggy day. Desserts are memorable, especially the summer berry pudding, with its dense, moist cakey texture and plenty of fruit. ♦ French/Californian ♦ M-F, lunch and dinner; Sa, dinner. Reservations recommended. 500 Brannan St (at Fourth St). 543.2222. www.coco500.com

## 62 Zuni Restaurant & Bar

★★$$$ Although the original menu of this dining spot featured Southwestern fare (hence the name), this multilevel contemporary restaurant with floor-to-ceiling windows now offers a Mediterranean style of cooking. Chef and co-owner Judy Rogers offers Malaspina oysters from British Columbia that can be washed down with a frosty espresso granita, followed by roast chicken with bread salad (bread and greens in a champagne vinaigrette). Or try one of the pizzas baked in the brick oven. The place usually attracts hordes of great-looking men and women of every sexual orientation. ♦ Californian/Mediterranean ♦ Tu-Su, lunch and dinner. Reservations recommended. 1658 Market St (between Franklin and Haight Sts). 552.2522 ♿

## 63 SF LGBT Community Center

Home to a staggering array of organizations that support the lesbian, gay, bisexual, and transgender community, this center holds exhibits, along with literary and other public events. It's also home to the city's only all-dance nonprofit, the Ballroom Party, where you can drop in for weekly dance lessons and attend swing, Latin, country, and ballroom dances. Another gathering place is **Three Dollar Bill Café**, 503.1532, providing sandwiches, snacks, and coffee. ♦ 1800 Market St (at Octavia St) 865.5555. www.sfgaycenter.org

Within the LGBT Community Center:

### Harvey Milk Institute

This continuing-ed program for the gay and lesbian community offers dozens of one- and two-day workshops focusing on a variety of relevant subjects. Fees vary, but most are within the $45-$95 range. Check online for dance parties with live music including Bottoms Up! Burlesque. 865.5664

## 64 Martuni's

Show-tune maniacs will get a kick out of this friendly, charming spot that draws a cast of characters who make the rounds of piano bars, getting progressively drunk and braying along to their pop Broadway favorites. The lighting's soft, the staff friendly, and the crowd in the front bar a nice mix of pretty guppies, lipstick lezzes, and older gents. At times, though, the music from the cabaret room in back can be just a tad intrusive. ♦ Daily, 2PM-2AM. 4 Valencia St (at Market St). 241.0205 ♿

## 65 The Stud

♂ Rock, funk, oldies, new wave, and world-beat music draw a big crowd to this funky
♀ hangout. The owner and sexy bartender Michael has turned the space into a fun party place for the cute, mixed clientele of men and women. Tuesday night's "Tranny Shack." "Stud" is an over-the-top drag show hosted by the hilarious Heklina. Many consider it the "trashiest" club night in town, with a mix of disco, drag, and dance tunes. Saturday night's "Sugar" Stud turns the small space into a hot, positive-energy dance club that stays pounding until four in the morning. The 20- to 30ish hip crowd is a great mix of gays and lesbians, and the music is cutting-edge fun. Life is sweet. ♦ Cover some nights. M-F, Su, 5PM-2AM; Sa, 5PM-4AM. 399 Ninth St (at Harrison St). 252.7833

## 66 San Francisco Eagle

♂ One of the best, and best-known, leather bars in the country, this grizzled old bird's been roping in a butch but friendly herd since 1972. The thirty- and forty-somethings can get frisky in this large, comfortable space complemented by a huge covered patio and a leather shop, but they generally do their acting out elsewhere. The Sunday afternoon beer bust is a major crowd-pleaser. ♦ M-F, 4PM-2AM; Sa, Su, noon-2AM. 398 12th St (at Harrison St). 626.0880 ♿

## 67 Gold's Gym

♂ This is the largest and most popular gym in San Francisco for gays and lesbians, and
♀ their straight friends. The huge space has any equipment you could possibly hope for and classes throughout the day. It's cruisy all the time, but the large facility allows you to escape predators easily if you're looking for a serious workout. Changing rooms are complete with showers, steam rooms, and dry saunas, but lockers fill up fast after work hours, when it gets very crowded. A small café in the front has light, healthy meals and power drinks for gym boys on the run. ♦ Admission. M-Th, 5AM-midnight; F, 5AM-11PM; Sa, 7AM-9PM; Su, 8AM-8PM. 1001 Brannan (at Ninth St). 552.4653

Restaurants/Clubs: Red | Hotels: Purple | Shops: Orange | Outdoors/Parks: Green | Sights/Culture: Blue

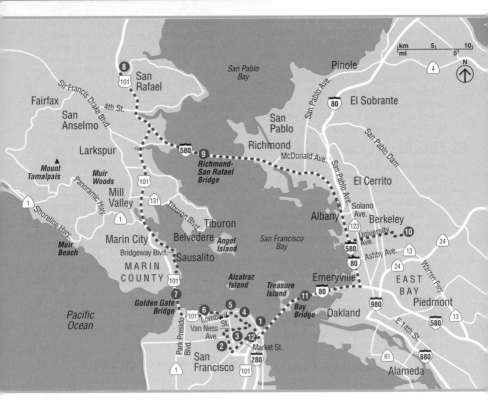

San Francisco is a haven for both Victorian architecture (including the "Painted Ladies"—Queen Anne houses with elaborate ornament highlighted in bright colors) and pioneering Modern and Postmodern structures, built after the 1906 earthquake and fire devastated the city.

## BAY AREA ARCHITECTURAL BLITZ

Before embarking on this driving tour of the Bay Area's architectural highlights, review a commercial road map of the area and familiarize yourself with the following directions. Plan on parking the car at some points so you can really admire the buildings.

This tour begins at the **(1) Ferry Building,** at the foot of **Market Street,** designed by architect **Arthur Page Brown** in 1894. Modeled after the Cathedral Tower in Seville, Spain, this building was for many years the tallest in San Francisco. Drive down Market past the **(1) Hyatt Regency Hotel,** a distinct component of the San Francisco skyline designed by **John Portman and Associates** in 1973, and the **(1) Crown Zellerbach Building,** a 1959 design by **Hertzka and Knowles** and **Skidmore, Owings & Merrill** set back from the street at

**Battery.** Make a "soft" right onto **Sutter Street** to see the **Citicorp Building,** a 1984 **William Pereira and Associates** design, with its lovely atrium. At **1 Sutter** (on your left) is the **Crocker Galleria,** a three-level, glass-barrel-vaulted shopping arcade modeled after Milan's vast Galleria Vittorio Emanuele, and on your right is the **Hallidie Building,** designed by **Willis Polk and Company** in 1917, which purports to have the world's first curtain-wall glass façade. Take a left at **Stockton Street,** and turn right on Market. Continue to **McAllister Street** and bear right to the **(2) Civic Center,** acclaimed as the most magnificent assortment of Beaux Arts buildings in the US. There you will see **City Hall,** the main part of the complex, designed in 1915 by **Bakewell and Brown; Louise M. Davies Symphony Hall,** designed by **Skidmore, Owings & Merrill,** which first opened in September 1980 and was remodeled in 1992; the glorious and opulent **Opera House,** which opened on 15 October 1932; and the **Veterans' Building,** former home of the **San Francisco Museum of Modern Art,** also by **Bakewell and Brown.** Turn right on **Franklin**

Street and left on **Geary** until you reach **(2) St. Mary's Cathedral** at Gough Street. Continue to **Laguna Street,** make a right, then right again on **California Street.** Continue across **Van Ness** and up **Nob Hill** to **Jones Street,** where Lewis P. Hobart's **(3) Grace Cathedral** is located. This lovely neo-Gothic church was modeled after Notre Dame in Paris. Head on to **Mason Street** to see the city's most illustrious hotels: the **(3) Mark Hopkins Inter-Continental** (familiarly known as The Mark), best known for **Timothy Pflueger's Top of the Mark** cocktail lounge with its panoramic vista of the bay and the city's hills, and the **Fairmont,** which opened in 1907 in celebration of the city's renaissance one year after the earthquake. Continue downhill on California to the **Financial District.** At Kearny Street view the **(3)** former **Bank of America World Headquarters,** a 1969 structure by **Wurster, Bernardi & Emmons Inc.** and **Skidmore, Owings & Merrill,** with **Pietro Belluschi** as design consultant, with its dark-red marble façade that changes colors with the time of day. Turn left on **Sansome Street** and left on **Washington** past the **(3) Transamerica Pyramid,** designed in 1972 by **William Pereira and Associates,** which has become a landmark because of its singular form and position at the end of **Columbus Avenue.** Take Columbus Avenue toward **North Beach**—en route notice the Art Deco-ish **(4) Coit Tower** on top of **Telegraph Hill,** and turn left on **North Point Street** until you reach **(5) Ghirardelli Square,** the converted chocolate factory that is now a shopping complex. The transformation was done by **Wurster, Bernardi & Emmons Inc.** and **Lawrence Halprin & Associates** from 1962 to 1967. Turn left on Van Ness, right on Bay, and head westward through the **Marina District** to **Marina Boulevard.** At **Lyon** and **Baker Streets** is Bernard Maybeck's **(6) Palace of Fine Arts,** with its characteristic Roman rotunda with two curvilinear columns. Next, head north on **Highway 101,** across the **(7) Golden Gate Bridge** into Marin County. Take the **Alexander Avenue** exit, veer right, and drive through downtown **Sausalito** (note the private homes clinging to the steep hillside). At the end of town, get back on Highway 101 north. You may want to make a side trip to **Tiburon** and **Belvedere,** where you'll see some of the most expensive housing in the country. Continue north on Highway 101 for 15 miles, past **San Rafael,** to the **North San Pedro Road** exit, to take a look at the **(8) Marin County Civic Center** by **Frank Lloyd Wright,** begun in 1957 (Wright died in 1959). Built atop the crests of three low hills, this was one of the American master's last efforts. Note the prevalence of the circle motif in the building's design, including the decorative grilles, pavements, and custom-designed furniture; be sure to walk up to the viewing deck next to the library. Then return south on Highway 101 through San Rafael and take the **I-580** exit. Drive across the **(9) Richmond–San Rafael Bridge;** look to the right and see **San Quentin** prison. Follow signs for **Oakland** through the industrial area along **Cutting** and **Hoffman Boulevards,** and join **I-80** at **Albany.** Exit at **University Avenue** and travel 11.5 miles east until you reach the **(10) University of California, Berkeley,** at **Oxford Street.** Turn right on Oxford and left on **Durant.** Park at the garage on Durant and **Telegraph Avenue** or on the street. On campus see the **(10) Campanile** (there's a great view of the Bay Area from the top) and the handsome granite-clad **(10) Mining and Metallurgy**

**Building** of 1907 by **John G. Howard,** who designed many buildings and other structures on campus. Afterward, drive up Durant to **Piedmont** and take a look at the **(10) Sigma Phi** frat house, designed by famed Arts and Crafts architects, the brothers **Greene & Greene.** Most of the old mansions on this strip are fraternity or sorority houses. Turn left on Piedmont, left on Bancroft Way, and continue down University Avenue. Follow University to I-80/I-580 southbound for San Francisco. Return to the city via I-80 across the **(11) Bay Bridge** (toll). Then exit on **Fremont Street,** take a left onto **Howard Street,** and go past **(12) Yerba Buena Gardens,** which include the mostly underground **Moscone Convention Center** by **Hellmuth, Obata & Kassabaum,** and the **Center for the Arts Galleries and Forum** by **Fumihiko Maki** and **Center for the Arts Theater** by **James Stewart Polshek,** which opened in 1993.

# HOUSE CALLS: SAN FRANCISCO'S PREMIER ESTATES

For a tour of some of the city's most notable residences (see map next page), start at the top of **(1) Telegraph Hill,** and walk down the **Filbert Steps** on the east side. Some of the oldest houses in San Francisco are perched precariously on these steep slopes—notice the Carpenter Gothic style of many. Access to these homes is only by footpath and steps. Turn right on **(2) Powell Street,** where you will see a particularly fine row of Postmodern houses on the west side of **(3) Vandewater Street,** a short alley between Powell and **Mason Streets,** half a block south of **Bay Street.** Note the condominiums by **Esherick, Homsey, Dodge & Davis,** at **No. 22; Donald MacDonald, No. 33;** and **Daniel Solomon, No. 55.** All three structures were built in 1981. Turn left onto Mason Street, right onto **Francisco Street,** and continue across **Columbus Avenue** up **Russian Hill** to **Leavenworth Street.** Turn left here and cross **Union Street** to the corner of **(4) Green Street,** where you can see one of the best examples of 1930s-style apartment towers.

Continue on Leavenworth Street until **California Street,** turn right, and follow the cable-car tracks to **Van Ness Avenue;** cross Van Ness and continue to **Franklin Street.** Turn right and look for the superb Queen Anne-style **(5) Haas-Lilienthal House** at **2007** Franklin Street (tours are available) in affluent Pacific Heights, with many substantial dwellings on its slopes. From Franklin Street, turn left on **Broadway.** You will pass a series of apartment towers and mansions as you approach **The Presidio,** and many fine Victorian houses on the surrounding streets. Take a left on **Fillmore Street,** then a right on **(6) Clay Street** to see the row of false-fronted Italianate houses between **Fillmore** and **Divisadero Streets** opposite **Alta Plaza Park.**

Now turn right on Divisadero Street, continue to the summit of the hill, and take a left at **Pacific Avenue.** The famous **(7) 3200 Pacific** block between **Presidio Avenue** and **Walnut Street** boasts houses by **Bernard**

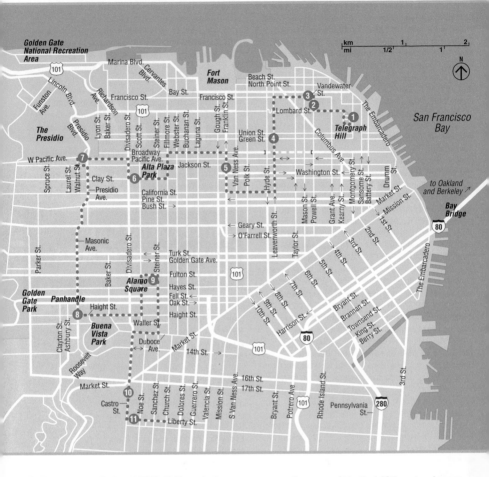

Maybeck, Ernest Coxhead, Willis Polk, and others. Turn left on Walnut Street, left on **Jackson Street,** and right on Presidio Avenue, which zigzags and becomes **Masonic Avenue** (veer right when the road divides, or, if you miss the split, turn right onto **Geary Boulevard** and left onto Masonic Avenue). Cross the **Panhandle of Golden Gate Park** to **Haight Street,** which runs through the **(8) Haight-Ashbury District,** with its many ornate late-Victorian houses, some painted in bright colors that emphasize their elaborate façades. Turn left onto **Haight Street** to **Scott Street,** turn left, and then right onto **Fulton Street** six blocks away, where you can see the group of identical 19th-century houses on the east side of **(9) Alamo Square.** Turn right onto **Steiner Street.** Head south to **Duboce Avenue** and take a right. Proceed to **Castro Street,** turn left, and then continue to **Market Street.** At Market and Castro is **(10) Castro Commons,** a condominium complex completed in 1982, designed by **Daniel Solomon & Associates.** A gridded wall separates the triangular courtyard from busy Market Street. Four blocks farther south along Castro Street at **(11) Liberty Street** is a good cross section of older San Francisco dwellings of various styles.

# DAY TRIPS

**B**eyond San Francisco's immediate boundaries are the thriving, vital cities of the **East Bay,** where the weather in summer is often warmer and sunnier than in fog-covered San Francisco. **Berkeley,** across the **Bay Bridge,** is home to the state's prestigious branch of the **University of California.** Oftentimes derisively called Berserkley by nonresidents and residents alike, it is a city with a political matrix that's frequently radical and either totally out of sync with the rest of the nation or on the cutting edge of political change.

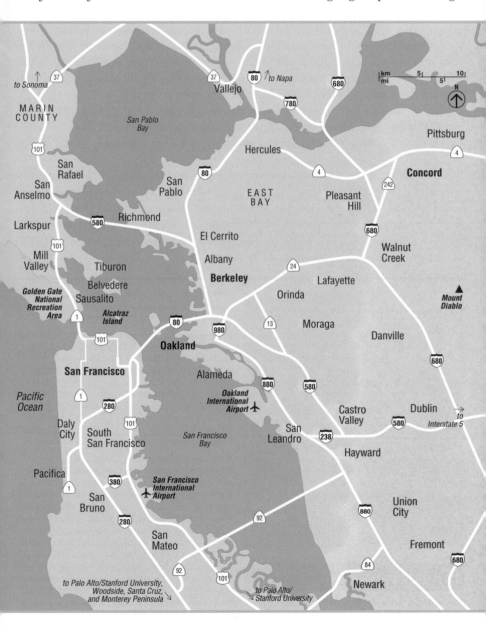

Also across the Bay Bridge is **Oakland,** a metropolis locked in a struggle to combat drugs and poverty—not to mention overcoming the ravages of 1991's devastating fire in the hills—and working hard to enlarge its position as a strong shipping, commercial, and convention center.

In contrast, on the northern side of the **Golden Gate Bridge** are the softly undulating hills of mellow **Marin County.** Cross the bridge, and the first town you'll reach is **Sausalito,** a little gem of a place frequently compared to the hill towns on the Riviera. Once a fishing village, Sausalito is now an upscale community of suburbanites who enjoy their pretty hillside homes, abundant greenery, and quaint village atmosphere.

The prosperous **Peninsula** area to the south of San Francisco is home to **Stanford University,** one of California's finest private institutions of learning, and **Silicon Valley,** the center of the worldwide Internet and computer industry. It is also home to many Bay Area millionaires, who have settled in such posh communities as **Hillsborough, Los Altos, Woodside,** and **Portola Valley.** One of the most magnificent mansions in the area, **Filoli,** with its superb gardens, is now a landmark open to the public.

About two and a half hours south of the city lies the magnificent **Monterey Peninsula,** home of the popular **Monterey Bay Aquarium,** the charming seaside village of **Carmel** (where Clint Eastwood was once mayor), and some of the most stunning coastal scenery in the world.

Finally, if you're a wine connoisseur, no trip to the Bay Area would be complete without a visit to **Napa, Sonoma,** and **Mendocino** wine country. In addition to possessing some of the world's finest vineyards, the Napa and Sonoma areas are home to lovely inns, marvelous massage centers, idyllic scenery, and enough good restaurants to warrant a special trip. For a complete guide to this beautiful region, consult *ACCESS Wine Country California,* also from ACCESS Press.

## MARIN COUNTY

Blessed with a sense of whimsy and an affluent, educated, and creative populace, Sausalito doesn't march lockstep with most suburban communities. In the 1970s the town's mayor was Sally Stanford, who had retired to the bayside community after years of running San Francisco's premier bordellos, lending new meaning to the term *Madam Mayor.* Stanford died in 1982.

To really savor the day, take a ferry ride to Sausalito, starting at San Francisco's **Ferry Building** (located at the foot of Market Street and The Embarcadero; call 923.2000) or at **Fisherman's Wharf** (for scheduling information, call 705.5555). You can also get there in a half hour via **Golden Gate Transit** buses (923.2000) or by automobile across the Golden Gate Bridge. If you decide to drive, be aware that parking in Sausalito is difficult and the city's traffic cops are uncannily vigilant. Parking is likely to be easiest on the hilly streets.

When you've debarked from the ferry in Sausalito, walk left along the shoreline (called **Bridgeway Boulevard**), and drink in the bay views and glorious vistas of San Francisco. Right by the ferry pier, which is in the heart of downtown Sausalito, you'll see the small **Viña del Mar Park,** named for Sausalito's sister city in Chile. The park delights the eye with statues of elephants and a fountain that came from the Panama-Pacific Exposition of 1915. You may take a photo in front of the park, but you may not walk in. (It's been closed to the public for many years because it drew drug addicts and other unsavory characters.) For visitors with an extended agenda, stay at the **Hotel Sausalito** (16 El Portal at Bridgeway, 332.0700, 888/442.0700, www.hotelsausalito.com), a romantic French Riviera-style inn with 16 rooms and suites overlooking Viña del Mar Park. Or try the nearby **Inn Above**

**Tide** (30 El Portal, 332.9535), which features sweeping views of the bay. Bridgeway Boulevard is still called **Old Town,** reflecting its status as a historic district where the first Portuguese fishers settled in the late 18th and early 19th centuries. Walk past **Scoma's** (588 Bridgeway Blvd, 332.9551), a popular seafood restaurant with a branch in San Francisco, and **Horizons,** nearby (558 Bridgeway, 331.3232), one of the best places in town to enjoy a drink on the deck. Stop if you're ravenous, but be forewarned that the view is often more satisfying than the meal. Just beyond the waterside restaurants, look out onto the bay and see if the seal sculpture by Bay Area artist Benny Bufano is visible (it pops out at low tide). Walk back along the side of the street with all the shops, some of them charming, some just selling touristy whatnots and junk. Take a short detour to explore the shops along **Princess Street.** If you feel energetic, keep on walking—Princess leads to the back streets, which are lined with galleries and lovely homes. If you get lost, just keep walking downhill and you'll eventually be back on Bridgeway.

Nearby is the convivial **Bar with No Name,** more popularly known as the **No-Name,** for the obvious reason; no sign identifies the place (757 Bridgeway Blvd, 332.1392). Sometimes there's live jazz, and invariably there's a local clientele swapping conversation around communal tables.

If you're feeling flush, have breakfast or dinner at the **Casa Madrona** (801 Bridgeway Blvd, 331.5888, www.casamadrona.com), a delightful little hotel that meanders up the hillside where **Poggio** offers a terrace for alfresco dining. The food is Italian/Mediterranean.

Continue walking along Bridgeway Boulevard or hop aboard one of the buses that frequently makes its way along the street, checking first to see if it stops at the **Bay Model** (Marinship Way, off the east side of Bridgeway Blvd, 332.3871). Be sure to have plenty of change in your pocket—the buses require exact fare.

The Bay Model is a working model of the whole San Francisco Bay and the Delta region. It features interactive exhibits, self-guided tours, and a permanent exhibit of the World War II shipyard "Marinship." It is open Tuesday through Sunday from Memorial Day to Labor Day; the rest of the year it's open Tuesday through Saturday. Arrangements for tours may be made for groups of 10 or more by calling in advance. Admission is free.

Docked near the Bay Model is the *Wapama* (pictured below), a steam-powered 1915 schooner that once hauled lumber and passengers. *Wapama* tours take place Saturday at 11AM; on Saturday at 12:30PM there's also a tour of the *Hercules,* a venerable old steam

tub (free admission; children under 12 years of age are not permitted on the vessel tours).

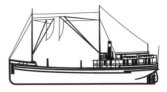

Farther north along Bridgeway Boulevard is a community of floating homes (Sausalito doesn't like to call them houseboats). Turn onto **Gate 6 Road.** (If you end up on the freeway, you've gone too far.) The greatest concentration of homes can be seen at **Gates 5, 6,** and **6½.** Some are spacious, some are funky, some are exquisite little waterborne jewels. One even has a helipad (you'll find it on **Issaquah Dock,** at the very end). Issaquah Dock, at Gate 6, also has more serious gardeners than any of the other piers. Arguments continue to rage between those charged with protecting the bay and the "anchor-outs," those who live freely anchored out in the water on what in some cases appear to be floating junkyards. (Anchor-outs prefer to drop anchor in the bay rather than tie their boats to the docks.)

Tiburon, shortened from the Spanish Punta de Tiburon (Shark Point), has a quaint **Main Street.** It appears much like a New England fishing village, especially if you arrive on the late-morning ferry from Fisherman Wharf's Pier 43½. **Ark Row** has a collection of Victorian-era houseboats.

# MUIR WOODS, MOUNT TAMALPAIS, AND POINT REYES

Muir Woods, on Shoreline Highway in **Mill Valley,** is a national monument located in the middle of **Mount Tamalpais State Park.** Both are open daily until sunset (Park Ranger Station, Pan-Toll, is at 801 Panoramic Hwy, Mill Valley, 388.2070; Muir Woods information 388.2596; recorded information 388.2595). Within the approximately 559 acres of redwoods are many trails, some paved and wheelchair-accessible.

Those who can stay for only a short time can see many of the highlights in one to two hours. Within Muir Woods are some of the tallest and oldest coast redwood trees in the state, and a stand of virgin redwoods. The oldest tree has been around for 1,100 years; the tallest is 257 feet high. This tranquil wonderland of proud, giant trees also includes **Redwood Creek,** where steelhead and salmon come to spawn and then die (there's no fishing). A **Visitors' Center,** built in the rustic 1930s style of cedar and stone, was deliberately designed to look inconspicuous. It's located at the park's main entrance, and includes a snack bar and gift shop.

Hardy types can hike from Muir Woods to the surrounding **Mount Tamalpais State Park.** Mount Tam, as it's popularly known, rises majestically 2,221 feet above sea level. The park includes a variety of terrain, and is renowned for its sensational panoramic views on clear days and its abundance of colorful wildflowers during the springtime. There are many trails, suitable for hikers of all levels. The park is home to a variety of wildlife: herds of deer, many types of birds, some snakes (including the seldom-encountered rattlers), and the rarely seen bobcats and mountain lions.

There is no public transportation going into the woods or park, but among the companies that offer private tours to the redwoods are **A Day in Nature** (673.0548), **Great Pacific** (626.4499), and **Ocean View Hiking Tours** (383.4252). If you are driving from San Francisco, take **Highway 101** north across the Golden Gate Bridge and turn off at the **Stinson Beach–Highway 1** exit. Follow the signs to the area's parking lots.

If hiking Mount Tam doesn't do you in, you might want to tackle some of the scenic trails a little farther north at the **Point Reyes National Seashore.**

There's backcountry camping, stables, a lighthouse on a spit of land that affords great whale watching in season (approximately January through April), and miles and miles of stunning unspoiled seashore.

If all this touring has given you an appetite, Marin boasts at least two outstanding restaurants: **The Lark Creek Inn** (234 Magnolia Ave, Larkspur, 924.7766), where owner/chef Bradley Ogden turns out magnificent American regional cuisine in a sublime country setting; and the informal, exuberant **Buckeye Roadhouse** (15 Shoreline Hwy, near Hwys 101 and 1, Mill Valley, 331.2600), run by the same team that owns the very popular **Fog City Diner** in San Francisco and **Mustards Grill** in Yountville.

# University of California, Berkeley

Across the Bay Bridge in the bustling East Bay lies Berkeley, which manages to combine an East Coast intellectual energy with a Californian New Age consciousness.

A city of ideas, both worthy and wacky, Berkeley rates a visit because of its outstanding university, restaurants, and cultural programs, as well as its quirky lifestyle. This is also the site of some of the Bay Area's best bookstores, including **Cody's** (2454 Telegraph Ave, at Haste St, 510/845.7852) and **Black Oak Books** (1491 Shattuck Ave, at Vine St, 510/486.0698).

The easiest way to reach Berkeley from San Francisco is by **BART** (www.bart.gov), a half-hour ride from downtown. Get off at the Berkeley station and walk east for three blocks on Bancroft Way to reach the southern end of the campus. The **Visitor Information Center** is located in **University Hall, Room 101,** at University Avenue and Oxford Street. Free student-led campus tours, lasting approximately one and three-quarters hours, include the interior of the main library, a typical classroom, the interiors of most of the sports facilities, the exterior of the **University Art Museum,** and a typical 500-seat lecture hall. The tours are on Monday, Wednesday, and Friday at 10AM and 1PM, and occasionally on Saturdays (510/642.5215). Reservations are not necessary, but it's a good idea to confirm scheduled tours, as the campus closes between semesters and on holidays. There is a modest charge for the ride to the top of the Campanile (pictured), the campus tower that provides an aerial view of the Bay Area. To fully appreciate the intellectual energy that swirls around this campus, visit when classes are in session.

After the tour, go on to explore some of the campus offerings in greater depth. **The University Art Museum,** just off campus in a 1970 building designed by **Mario Ciampi,** has a good collection emphasizing 20th-century painting and sculpture. The museum is open Wednesday through Sunday; admission, free on Thursday 11AM to noon and 5PM to 9PM (2626 Bancroft Way, 510/642.0808). Within the museum you'll find the **Pacific Film Archive,** a large movie library, and the **George Gund Theater,** which schedules a wide range of international films during the week (www.bampfa.berkeley.edu).

The university's **Phoebe Hearst Museum of Anthropology** is in **Kroeber Hall** (Bancroft Way and College Ave, 510/642.3682; www.hearstmuseum.berkeley.edu). Named after its principal benefactor, the museum focuses on cultural anthropology. A gift store sells ornaments, books, and ethnic arts and crafts. It is open daily; nominal admission; free Thursday.

The **Lawrence Hall of Science** (Centennial Dr, near Grizzly Peak Blvd, www.lawrencehallofscience.org) is a memorial to Ernest O. Lawrence, the first **University of California** professor to win a Nobel Prize (he won for physics in 1939). A favorite destination for visitors, the hall contains an interactive science museum, traveling science exhibitions, and a planetarium. Opened in 1968, it was designed by the San Francisco firm **Anshen and Allen** in an octagonal shape to represent the eight branches of physical science. Two levels of the building offer splendid views. If you have time, there's a 50-minute show in the planetarium. (Children under six are not admitted.) The hall is open daily; nominal admission. The planetarium's shows are on Saturday and Sunday at 1PM, 2:15PM, and 3:30PM; additional nominal admission.

The **University of California's Botanical Garden** is located in **Strawberry Canyon,** just above the stadium (510/643.2755, www.botanicalgarden.berkeley.edu). There are wonderful views of the bay from this site. Free tours take place Saturday and Sunday at 1:30PM and last about an hour. The garden is arranged according to the plants' geographical origins, and includes a redwood grove, a large native-plants section, South African plants, Asian plants, and economic plants (those used for food, fiber, and medicine). Another area is dedicated to plants that eat insects, a desert and rain-forest house filled with orchids, cacti, and succulents, and a garden of rosebushes. There's a nice lawn for sun worshiping and tables for picnicking.

Just outside the university campus, on ever-popular **Telegraph Avenue,** the street scene is alive with street musicians, small shops, and food, jewelry, and clothing vendors (you can still buy top-quality tie-dyed T-shirts, pants, and undergarments here).

Seven blocks north of the campus is **Chez Panisse** (1517 Shattuck Ave, 510/548.5525), generally regarded as the birthplace of Californian cuisine and the training ground for many famous Bay Area chefs. Although some critics sniff that her place isn't what it used to be, celebrity owner/chef Alice Waters is determined to maintain her high standards and keep her menus fresh and original. Even if you don't care to splurge for the expensive prix-fixe meals downstairs, be sure to try the lighter meals—which include inventive pizzas and calzones—upstairs at the **Chez Panisse Café**, and across the street at the Cheeseboard (510/549.3055), which offers breakfast at a stand-up counter or at benches outside.

# OAKLAND

Even though Gertrude Stein scathingly said of her hometown that "there is no there there," in fact, there is quite a bit here to see and enjoy. Oakland has a thriving port (it has taken substantial business away from the port of San Francisco), wonderful historic buildings, a restored **Old Town,** and charming hillside neighborhoods.

The easiest way to get to Oakland is by **BART.** The ride is a mere 12 minutes from San Francisco's **Powell Street** station to the city center, where you'll get off at **12th Street and Broadway.** The restored **Old Oakland** area is on the right of Broadway, and Oakland's **Chinatown** (still unspoiled by tourism) sits on the left. Chinatown is dotted with restaurants, herbalists, and shops catering to the needs of daily life. In addition to the Chinese, the neighborhood is home to many other Asian immigrants. Old Oakland, bounded by **8th** and **10th Streets,** and **Broadway** and **Washington Streets,** is a historic Victorian neighborhood of structures dating from 1868 to 1881. The buildings have been restored and developed by architects **Storek & Storek** as a retail and office complex. The **Pro Arts Gallery** (550 Second St,

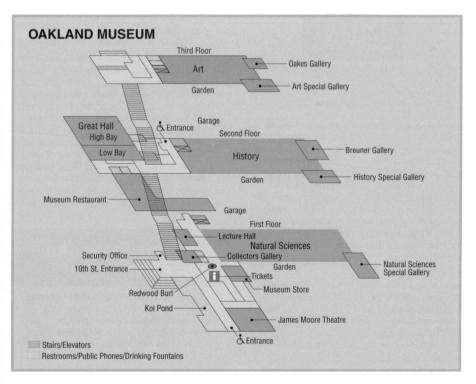

OAKLAND MUSEUM

510/763.4361) features the work of Bay Area artists, and mounts exhibitions and major art events, including the famous Open Studios in June.

If you're thirsty, head for the **Pacific Coast Brewing Co.** (906 Washington St, between 9th and 10th Sts, 510/836.2739). The brewmasters will draw one of the specialty brews or any of the 19 other beers in stock while you relax, possibly over some pub grub or a game of darts.

On Oakland's waterfront is **Jack London Square,** a rather contrived but pleasant waterfront development, and, nearby, the **Jack London Village,** another touristy oasis, featuring several shops and a museum. Between the village and the square is Jack London's transplanted sod-roofed log cabin, where he once passed a Yukon winter, another attraction open to the public. One of the most authentic watering holes in the area is **Heinold's First and Last Chance Saloon** (56 Jack London Sq, 510/839.6761), a favorite hangout of the celebrated writer. At the dock is **Scott's Seafood Grill & Bar** (2 Broadway, 510/444.3456), one of the outstanding seafood restaurants in the area. For earthier waterfront ambience, try the produce warehouse district, covering about 24 blocks east of the square and south of Broadway. The **FDR Pier** (Clay St and The Embarcadero) gives good views of working port operations, as do **Port View Park,** next to the **Seventh Street Terminal,** and **Middle Harbor Park** (at Middle Harbor Rd).

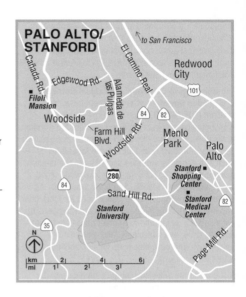

**HEINOLD'S**
FIRST & LAST CHANCE SALOON
*Since 1883*

Also worth a visit is the historic **Paramount Theater** (21st St and Broadway), a spectacular example of Art Deco architecture by **Timothy Pflueger.** Inside the movie palace, which has been converted to general entertainment use (conventions, symphonies, theater, ballet, classic movies, and such), there's a mind-blowing assemblage of gilt, silver railings, columns, and marble. Two-hour tours are offered the first and third Saturday of each month at 10AM, but not on holidays or when an activity is planned within the theater. No reservations are required. There is a small charge, and no children under age 10 are allowed. For more information, call 510/465.6400.

Definitely try to make room for a trip to **The Oakland Museum** (10th and Oak Sts, 510/238.2200, www.museumca.org), about a 15-minute walk from the **Paramount Theater.** Covering a four-block site, the multilevel building (see the plan, previous page) with terraced gardens was designed by **Kevin Roche.** The structure incorporates galleries of ecology, history, and art, all of which emphasize California's diversity. The

museum is open Wednesday through Sunday; donation.

Science buffs and stargazers are flocking to the new **Chabot Space & Science Center** (10000 Skyline Blvd, 510/530.3480, www.chabotspace.org) in the Oakland Hills near Joaquin Miller Park. You can explore the center, experience the Tien MegaDome Theater, and watch the night sky in the Ask Jeeves Planetarium.

Another point of interest is **Lake Merritt** (bordered by Lakeside Dr, Lakeshore Ave, and Grand Ave; information www.oaklandcitycenter.com; Boating Center 510/238.2196), offers boat rentals, sailing lessons, a strolling/jogging path, a garden center, and a bird sanctuary. If you're ready to sit back and relax for a while, catch a movie at the grandiose **Grand Lake Theatre** (Grand Ave and Lake Park, 510/452.3556)—they don't make 'em like this anymore. And, finally, top off your day with a meal at the **Bay Wolf Café** (3853 Piedmont Ave, 510/655.6004, www.baywolf.com), a lively, upscale restaurant serving Californian cuisine with French and Italian influences.

# PALO ALTO/STANFORD UNIVERSITY

Fueled by the intellectual fires at **Stanford University,** Palo Alto is an oasis of energy and culture in the suburban desert. (Okay, it's a mixed metaphor and a trifle hyperbolic, but you get the idea.) Movie houses play foreign and art films, restaurants serve a variety of international cuisines to a casual-chic crowd, a bookstore and a cappuccino place mark every corner, and everything from child-care centers to exercise facilities reflects cutting-edge thinking. Furthermore, there's excellent shopping, from a lively downtown with trendy boutiques to the **Stanford Shopping Center,** a mall so magnificent that more than one local has asked that her ashes be scattered here.

Rail service on **Caltrain** will get you to the peninsula. (Get off at **Palo Alto** and then walk downtown through the pocket park to the shopping center.) For rail schedule information, check www.caltrain.com, or call 800/660.4287 (in the Bay Area). If you plan on doing a lot of local exploration, the best way to approach this area is by automobile. Take **Highway 280,** heading south, exiting at **Sand Hill Road.** It's the turnoff right after **Woodside Road.** Take Sand Hill Road east for 10 traffic lights, and you'll find yourself at the **Stanford Shopping Center** (between Sand Hill and Quarry Rds, west of El Camino Real). The shopping center is also served by **SamTrans** bus 7F. The ride takes about an hour from San Francisco. For scheduling information, call 800/660.4287 (in the Bay Area).

The **Stanford Shopping Center** (www.stanfordshop.com) is a retailing paradise and one of the most attractive mercantile complexes to be found, incorporating 150 stores in an open mall. It is anchored by several of the leading department and specialty stores in the Bay Area, including **Bloomingdale's** (650/463.2000), **Macy's** (650/326.3333), **Nordstrom** (650/323.5111), and **Neiman Marcus** (650/329.3300). After you've shopped yourself into a state of hunger, there's **Bravo Fono** (650/322.4664), a lovely spot for lunch and memorable homemade ice cream. **Max's Opera Café** (650/323.6297) serves overstuffed deli sandwiches, and **Long Life Noodle** (650/324.1110) offers Asian fare.

Although dedicated shoppers can easily spend the entire day at this mall-to-end-all-malls, Palo Alto's thriving downtown shouldn't be neglected. In addition to a host of interesting boutiques (mostly along **University Avenue** and its cross streets), Palo Alto is home to a number of fine restaurants, including the ever-popular **Il Fornaio** (Italian; 520 Cowper St, 650/853.3888),

_Maddalena's_

**Maddalena's** (French; 544 Emerson St, 650/326.6082), **MacArthur Park** (American; 27 University Ave, 650/321.9990), and **Café Pro Bono** (Italian; 2437 Birch St, 650/326.1626). And if you're an old-movie buff, be sure to take in a classic flick at the wonderfully restored **Stanford Theater** (221 University Ave, 650/324.3700; www.stanfordtheater.org), which warms up audiences with lively organ music on weekend nights.

One-hour tours of Stanford University, one of California's most prestigious private educational institutions, are given free of charge daily, at 11AM and 3:15PM. It's best to call ahead (650/723.2560) to be sure that tours are being offered, as the university closes to the public

for holidays, semester breaks, and final exams. The tour begins at the information booth in front of the **Main Quad** (at the end of **Palm Dr**). Tours cover the central campus area, including administration buildings, classrooms, student union, bookstore, art gallery, chapel, **Hoover Tower,** and the main quadrangle area. The tower's observation platform (open daily from 10AM to 11AM and from 1PM to 4:30PM; nominal admission) offers panoramic views of the area. The **Stanford Memorial Chapel** and the **Leland Stanford Jr. Museum** both suffered structural damage during the 1989 earthquake. The museum is still closed, but the church reopened in 1992. Tasty, inexpensive food is offered at the **Tresidder Student Union** on campus, which includes a coffeehouse, cafeteria, and bakery counter.

Visitors can also tour the **Stanford Linear Accelerator Center (SLAC),** a world-class physics laboratory with a mind-blowing two-mile-long linear electron accelerator. Tours are available by appointment only (www.slac.stanford.edu; sign up online); not recommended for children under 11.

# WOODSIDE

Located in the exclusive community of **Woodside,** this mansion was built between 1916 and 1919 by architect **Willis Polk** for prominent San Franciscans Mr. and Mrs. William B. Bourn II. The 16 acres of gardens were laid out by Bruce Porter, with the subsequent help of Isabella Worn. The homesite was chosen partly because it was near the Spring Valley Water Company, headed by Bourn, and partly because it reminded him of Ireland's Lakes of Killarney. The Bourns lived at the mansion until their deaths in 1936, whereupon the estate was acquired by Mr. and Mrs. William P. Roth, who kept it until 1975. Mrs. Roth then deeded it to the National Trust for Historic Preservation. The mansion is an important example of American country-house architecture, and is one of the few in the state intact in its original setting. The house and gardens are within the **Crystal Springs Watershed,** south of San Francisco. The now-mature gardens reflect the meticulous care during the nearly 40 years the Roths occupied the estate. The garden is a successful blend of the formal and the natural. A focal point is the Italian Renaissance **Tea House,** designed by **Arthur Brown Jr.,** who also designed the nearby Carriage House, dominated by a bell tower. The structure houses a collection of antique carriages.

**Filoli** is best reached by taking Highway 280 to the **Edgewood Road** exit, then turning right on Cañada Road. Follow Cañada Road and keep an eye peeled for the small, unobtrusive sign on the right side of the road. The gate on the left side is where you enter. The house and gardens are open for guided tours Tuesday through Saturday from mid-February to mid-November; advance reservations are required, and there is an admission charge. You may also take the self-guided tours every Friday and the first Saturday and second Sunday of every month from March through November; reservations are not required and there is no admission fee. Limited wheelchair access is available, but prior notification is requested to ensure that special entrance arrangements can be made. Guided hikes through the property are available by reservation from September through June. Children accompanied by an adult are welcome.

One hour south of San Francisco on scenic Highway 1 is **Costanoa Coastal Lodge and Camp,** an upscale camp connected to four state parks, 30,000 acres of foot trails, and a spectacular wildlife preserve. Includes spa facilities. 2001 Rossi Rd at Hwy 1, Pescadero, 650/879.1100, 877/262.7848, 800/738.7477, www.costanoa.com.

# SANTA CRUZ

Ninety minutes south of San Francisco on the coast, the laid-back, college-town feel of Santa Cruz has a lot to do with the University of California, Santa Cruz (www.ucsc.edu). Its eight colleges form an impressive campus nestled among the redwoods. For more Californiana, check out the history of one of the area's central attractions at the **Surfing Museum** (Lighthouse Pt, off Westcliff Dr, 831/420.6289; www.santacruzsurfingmuseum.org). But the real reason you should stop here is to ride on the Giant Dipper at the **Santa Cruz Beach Boardwalk** (www.beachboardwalk.com), considered by most wooden-roller-coaster aficionados to be the best in the world.

The best food in this town is not found at fancy French restaurants. For a casual meal on a rose-garden patio, stop in at **The Crêpe Place** (1134 Soquel Dr, at Seabright Dr, 831/429.6994; www.thecrepeplace.com), where you can choose from a variety of crepes or create your own combination. The ultimate in Santa Cruz hippie-vegetarian fast food can be found at **Dharma's** (4250 Capitola Rd, between 42nd and 43rd Aves, 831/462.1717; www.dharmaland.com)—known as McDharma's until the litigious burger company sued over the *Mc.*

# MONTEREY PENINSULA

The peninsula is two and a half to three hours from San Francisco, but the scenic drive makes getting there half the fun. **Interstate 280** is rightfully known as America's most beautiful interstate, and it provides the quicker route south. Exit Interstate 280 at **Highway 17** to **Santa Cruz,** then pick up **Highway 1** south to **Monterey** and **Carmel.** It takes longer to follow Highway 1 all the way down the coast, but the quaint towns make the drive worthwhile.

The capital of Hispanic California, Monterey has preserved its heritage. Discover downtown's Spanish architecture on the **Path of History,** a three-mile walking tour. Maps are available from the **Visitors' Information Center** (401 Camino el Estero, at Del Monte Ave). Monterey's sardine canneries inspired John Steinbeck's description "a poem, a stink, a grating noise, a quality of light, a tone, a habit, a nostalgia, a dream." His **Cannery Row** (on the bay between David Ave and the Coastguard Pier, south to Lighthouse Ave),

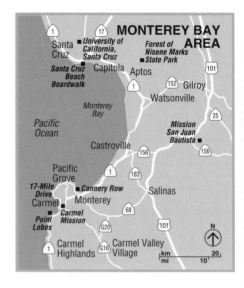

shut down by the depletion of the local sardine schools, has been renovated into a collection of shops, galleries, and restaurants, with much of the area's old character (but not the stench) preserved. A modern but must-see attraction is the **Monterey Bay Aquarium** (886 Cannery Row on the bay, 831/648.4888, www.mbayaq.org), a renowned collection highlighting the local underwater ecology, including Monterey's giant kelp forests (see the floor plan page 205).

Carmel, just south of Monterey, is the home of the **Carmel Mission** (3080 Río Rd, 831/624.1271, www.carmelmission.org), one of the most beautiful and well preserved of the California missions. It was founded in 1770 by Friar Junípero Serra and is his final resting place. Poets and painters later discovered the spectacular coast around Carmel that had attracted the Spanish settlers, and formed an artists' community that thrives to this day. Although undeniably touristy, Carmel has been preserved as a small Mediterranean-type village, with no street addresses on downtown buildings and no traffic signals (but *lots* of traffic, especially on weekends). Former mayor Clint Eastwood was an integral part of the fight to prevent development. Stop in at Clint's **Hog's Breath Inn** restaurant (San Carlos St between Fifth and Sixth Aves, 831/625.1044, www.hogsbreathinn.net), though he probably won't be around. For a romantic and scenic stay-over, try the **Highlands Inn** (Highland Dr, off Hwy 101, 408/624.3801), where Sean Penn and Madonna honeymooned. The lounge at the stately old hotel is a wonderful place to enjoy a cocktail as the sun sets.

The Monterey Peninsula you've seen on TV, and really shouldn't miss in person, can be found on the **17-Mile Drive.** The circular tour takes you past grand and pricey homes, past some of the world's

## MONTEREY BAY AQUARIUM

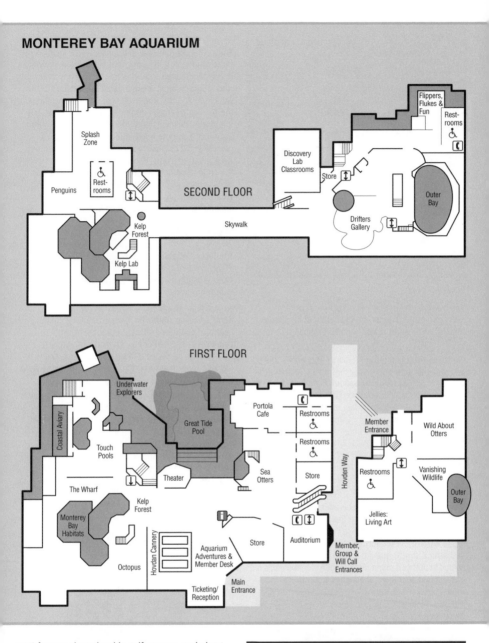

**SECOND FLOOR**

Splash Zone · Penguins · Restrooms · Kelp Forest · Kelp Lab · Skywalk · Discovery Lab Classrooms · Store · Flippers, Flukes & Fun · Restrooms · Outer Bay · Drifters Gallery

**FIRST FLOOR**

Coastal Aviary · Touch Pools · The Wharf · Monterey Bay Habitats · Octopus · Kelp Forest · Hovdan Cannery · Underwater Explorers · Great Tide Pool · Theater · Aquarium Adventures & Member Desk · Ticketing/Reception · Main Entrance · Store · Sea Otters · Store · Auditorium · Portola Cafe · Restrooms · Restrooms · Hovden Way · Member, Group & Will Call Entrances · Member Entrance · Restrooms · Jellies: Living Art · Wild About Otters · Vanishing Wildlife · Outer Bay

---

most famous championship golf courses, and along California's stunning central coastline. If you can't bear to leave this area or pass up the great golfing, check in at the expensive **Lodge at Pebble Beach** along the 17-Mile Drive (800/654.9300, www.pebblebeach.com).

If you're feeling a mite peckish, try one of the following stellar peninsula restaurants: **Fresh Cream** (Heritage Harbor complex at Pacific and Scott Sts, Monterey, 831/375.9798, www.freshcream.com), or **Casanova** (Fifth St between Mission and San Carlos Sts, Carmel, 831/625.0501, www.casanovarestaurant.com).

# WINE COUNTRY

Any visit to the Bay Area should include a few relaxing days of wine tasting, bike riding, and even hot-air ballooning in the wine country. The valleys of this primarily northern California region stretch from the Pacific coast to the Sierra Nevada, carpeting the area with more than 400,000 acres of vineyards. Fabled **Napa** and **Sonoma Counties**, just one and a half to two hours north of San Francisco, are dotted with nearly 300 wineries producing such premium wines as Chardonnay, Cabernet Sauvignon, Zinfandel, Syrah, and Pinot Noir, as well as charming bed-and-breakfast inns

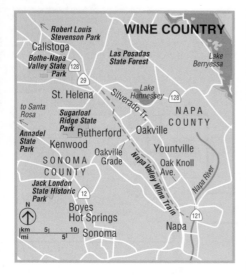

If you don't mind rousing the ire of the locals, you might want to go for a ride on the **Napa Valley Wine Train.** This controversial enterprise, which involves three-hour dining, drinking, and sightseeing excursions in Pullman lounge cars, was fought by many valley folk who feared it might change the serious nature of the wine industry. You won't see much of Napa while on the train—passengers don't disembark en route—but the food is delicious and the surroundings are quite luxurious. For more information, contact the train company (1275 McKinstry St, 707/253.2111, www.winetrain.com). If you opt for a great meal without the choo-choo ride, **Bistro Don Giovanni** (4110 St. Helena Hwy, 707/224.3300) is a popular spot for gourmet dining in the city of Napa. Napa wineries include the family-run **Trefethen Vineyards** (1160 Oak Knoll Ave, 707/255.7700, www.trefethen.com), **Stag's Leap Wine Cellars** (5766 Silverado Trail, 707/944.2020, www.stagsleapwinery.com), and **The Hess Collection Winery** (4411 Redwood Rd, 707/255.1144, www.hesscollection.com), which offers a high-powered art collection as well as a number of popular wines.

Almost halfway into the valley as you drive from San Francisco, **Yountville** is where the wine country begins to stir the emotions. George Yount, who came here in search of new frontiers, was the first US citizen to be ceded a Mexican land grant—the 12,000 acres making up the heart of Napa Valley called **Rancho Caymus.**

While in Yountville, try wine-country cuisine at **Hurley**'s (6518 Washington St, 707/944.2345), French fare at **Bouchon** (6534 Washington St, 707/944.8037), or exuberant Californian cuisine at **Mustards Grill** (7399 St. Helena Hwy, 707/944.2424). The **Vintage Inn** (6541 Washington St, 707/944.1112, 800/351.1122) and the bed-and-breakfast-style **Maison Fleurie** (6529 Yount St, 707/944.2056) are two good bets for lodging. Nearby wineries include **Domaine Chandon** (1 California Dr, 707/944.2280), which produces sparkling wine by the traditional *méthode champenoise* and also has a very highly regarded (and expensive) restaurant; the venerable **Robert Mondavi Winery** (7801 St. Helena Hwy, Oakville, 707/963.9611); and the **Beaulieu**

Vineyard (1960 St. Helena Hwy, Rutherford, 707/963.2411).

**Saint Helena,** a friendly town in the heart of the vineyards, has come alive in the past few years with some exceptional restaurants and inns. Walking down Main Street is like taking a step back in time—it's easy to imagine long white dresses and parasols emerging from the arched doorways of the stone buildings. Main Street is a portion of the valley's main highway, and has been a significant thoroughfare all the way back to the days of the horse and buggy. The stone bridges and buildings in

and some of the best restaurants in the country. September and October are the height of the grape harvest, and the aroma of fermenting wine is everywhere.

Another option is a hot-air balloon. This art of riding above the ground was discovered by the French aristocracy in 1783. (The first balloon flight was made by a sheep, a duck, and a rooster!) Today, the wine country's stunning scenery has turned ballooning in northern California into big business. It's a costly experience, but one you won't soon forget. **The Balloon Tours** (707/538.7359, 888/238.6359) can provide this bird's-eye view of the vineyards. In Vallejo, at **Six Flags Marine World** (2001 Marine World Pkwy, 707/644.4000), you can ride the vertical velocity, a spiraling, suspended impulse coaster.

Most wineries offer tastings and tours around the storage casks. Some take you through limestone caves carved out long ago by Chinese laborers. Though some of the wines can probably be purchased more cheaply at discount shops, one advantage to buying at the source is that you might discover one you like that's not easily found elsewhere. Production of these special wines, often called reserves, is usually limited by the wineries. Most now charge a small fee for tastings, but tours are usually free.

The town of Napa, the largest in the wine country, was laid out in 1848 by Nathan Coombs, who got the property from Nicholas Higuerra, holder of the original Spanish land grant. It was the activity surrounding the Gold Rush that spurred the city's growth. After the first harsh winter in the gold fields, miners sought refuge in town and found work in the cattle and lumber industries. The first settlers planted vineyards from cuttings given to them by padres of the Sonoma and San Rafael Missions, and from those modest beginnings, the surrounding valley's reputation as the center of the American wine industry evolved. For free maps and brochures on valley attractions, contact the **Napa Valley Conference & Visitors' Bureau** (707/226.7459, www.napavalley.org).

the area were constructed by European stonemasons and Chinese laborers in the late 19th century. Outlaw Black Bart, who led a dual life as a schoolteacher and a poet when he wasn't robbing stagecoaches, was the most notorious character to parade through Main Street before his capture in 1883. Author Robert Louis Stevenson and his new bride also passed through the town. The newlyweds spent most of the summer of 1880 in nearby **Calistoga.**

St. Helena is heaven on earth for serious foodies. Some good—no, make that great—dining choices: **Terra** (1345 Railroad Ave, 707/963.8931), **Ristorante Tra Vigne** (1050 Charter Oak Ave, 707/963.4444), and **Trilogy** (1234 Main St, 707/963.5507). The Rhineland-inspired **Beringer Vineyards** (2000 Main St, 707/963.7115) and, by appointment only, **Frog's Leap**

(3358 St. Helena Hwy, 707/963.4704) are among the wineries worth a visit.

With its geysers, hot springs, and lava deposits, Calistoga is a clear-cut reminder of the valley's tempestuous geological beginnings. Some of the eruptions formed the gray stone with which the Italian and Chinese workers built bridges and wineries. The first spa at Calistoga was built by Sam Brannan, California's first millionaire. He designed a spectacular hotel, now known as **Indian Springs,** to attract wealthy San Franciscans. Brannan also brought the first railroad to the valley and donated a costly engine to the first fire department. He coined the name Calistoga by combining the names California and Saratoga (the famous New York resort). Set in the middle of the wine country, this small town, with its Western-style main street still intact, is known for its mineral water and mud baths. Almost every motel or inn is equipped with at least a Jacuzzi. Contact the **Calistoga Chamber of Commerce** (1458 Lincoln Ave, 707/942.6333, www.calistogafun.com) for a list of spas.

Quaint Calistoga hotels include the **Larkmead Country Inn** (1103 Larkmead La, 707/942.5360) and the **Mount View Hotel** (1457 Lincoln Ave, 707/942.6877). There are also some very good restaurants here, including **All Seasons Café** (1400 Lincoln Ave, 707/942.9111) and the **Brannan's Grill** (1374 Lincoln Ave, 707/942.2233). Be sure to tour **Sterling Vineyards,** which is entered via a scenic tramway (1111 Dunaweal La, 707/942.3300); the **Clos Pegase** winery (1060 Dunaweal La, 707/942.4981) and its art gallery,

designed by **Michael Graves;** and the gracious **Château Montelena** (1429 Tubbs La, 707/942.5105).

In nearby **Sonoma Valley** lies the historic town of **Sonoma** with its eight-acre plaza, the largest in California. The plaza, laid out by General Mariano Vallejo in 1835, is ringed by boutiques, restaurants, and galleries. The stone structure dominating the area is **City Hall,** built to look the same on all sides. Wonderful adobe structures from the Mexican era, Western-type edifices, and stone buildings surround the plaza. Vallejo's soldiers trained here, and this was the site of the 25-day Bear Flag Party revolution in 1846 (still celebrated each 14 June). Contact the **Sonoma Valley Visitors' Bureau** (453 First St E, 707/996.1090, 866/996.1090, www.sonomavalley.com) for maps and information about the valley.

When you get hungry from all this touring, try **The General's Daughter** (400 West Spain St, between Fourth St W and Fifth St W, 707/938.4004), housed in a Victorian built in 1864 for General Vallejo's daughter; and the **Red Grape** (529 First St W, 707/996.4103), serving thin-crust pizza in an outdoor patio. **MacArthur Place Inn & Spa** is a renovated estate offering 33 guest rooms (29 E MacArthur St, 707/938.2929, 800/722.1866, www.macarthurplace.com). A little farther afield in Sonoma County is **John Ash & Co.** (4330 Barnes Rd, Santa Rosa, 707/527.7687), where both the food and the prices are breathtaking. This area is also rich in pleasant accommodations, including the **Thistle Dew Inn** (171 W Spain St on the Plaza, 707/938.2909), the **Victorian Garden Inn** (316 E Napa St, Sonoma, 707/996.5339, 800/543.5339), and the luxurious **Sonoma Mission Inn & Spa** (18140 Sonoma Hwy, Boyes Hot Springs, 707/938.9000, 800/862.4945). This is a true spa, available for day use, created in the European tradition and based on the benefits of the property's thermal mineral springs. The inn's historic golf course provides the most beautiful golf experience in the wine country.

The town of **Healdsburg** (north of the town of Sonoma off Hwy 101) sustains the charm of small-town life. **Honor Mansion** (14891 Grove St, Healdsburg, 707/433.4277, 800/554.4667) offers Victorian splendor and a gourmet breakfast in the mansion's formal dining room. While in Healdsburg, visit the villa and gardens of **Ferrari-Carrano Vineyard & Winery** (8761 Dry Creek Rd, Healdsburg, 707/433.7266).

Among the valley's noteworthy vintners are **Benziger Family Winery** (1883 London Ranch Rd, Glen Ellen, 707/935.4046), which offers a free vineyard tram tour; **Gundlach-Bundschau** (2000 Denmark St, Sonoma, 707/938.5277), a historic and lovely winery; the **Buena Vista Winery** (1800 Old Winery Rd, Sonoma, 707/938.1266); the **Matanzas Creek Winery** (6097 Bennett Valley Rd, Santa Rosa, 707/528.6464); and **Kenwood Vineyards** (9592 Sonoma Hwy, Kenwood, 707/833.5891).

# HISTORY

**1579**   Sir Francis Drake anchors on the northern California coast.

**1595**   Captain Sebastian Cermeno claims the land for Spain and names it Puerto de San Francisco.

**1769**   Spanish explorers, led by Don Gaspar de Portola, discover **San Francisco Bay.**

**1775**   Explorers Ayala and Canizares enter **San Francisco Bay.**

**1776**   Padre Junípero Serra founds the **Mission of St. Francis** on the shore of **Lake Dolores**, already home to the Costanoan Indians. Captain Juan Bautista begins building **The Presidio.**

**1792**   George Vancouver anchors off **Yerba Buena Cove**, the spot from which San Francisco grew.

**1794**   The protective **Castillo de San Joaquin** is established on the site of **Fort Point**, now overshadowed by the approach to the **Golden Gate Bridge**.

**1806**   California is declared a province of the Republic of Mexico.

**1835**   Homes are built at Yerba Buena Cove on the site of the present downtown **Financial District**. The rest of the city, with its 43 hills, is occupied largely by *ranchos*.

**1846**   The American flag is raised in **Portsmouth Square**, and **Yerba Buena** becomes San Francisco. Captain John C. Fremont coins the term *Golden Gate*.

**1848**   The Gold Rush begins. The first commercial bank is established in San Francisco, and the first American public school opens in the city.

**1850**   Legislature creates Bay region counties: San Francisco, **Contra Costa**, **Marin**, **Santa Clara**, **Sonoma**, **Solano**, and **Napa**. The city of San Francisco is incorporated. California is admitted to the Union.

**1854**   The first lighthouse is built on **Alcatraz Island**. Principal streets in San Francisco are lighted with coal gas for the first time.

**1855**   **St. Ignatius College** (later the **University of San Francisco**) is founded.

**1860**   The first Pony Express rider arrives in San Francisco from Saint Joseph, Missouri. A telegraph line opens between San Francisco and Los Angeles.

**1862**   Direct telegraph between San Francisco and New York is established. San Francisco supports the Union Army; a company of cavalry, known as the California Hundred, sails east. The San Francisco and San Jose Railroad formally opens.

**1864**   Young reporter Mark Twain begins writing about life in San Francisco for *Morning Call.*

**1867**   The first steamer sails from San Francisco to Alaska.

**1869**   The transcontinental railroad is completed, providing new trade and travel routes to the West.

**1870**   **Golden Gate Park** is established by Order 800, an act to provide for the improvement of public parks in the City of San Francisco.

**1872**   The first Japanese ship arrives in San Francisco loaded with tea.

**1873**   Ground is broken for the world's first cable street railroad on **Clay Street**.

**1875**   The Northern Pacific Coast Railroad is inaugurated, running from San Francisco to Tomales, via **Sausalito**.

**1876**   Electricity lights up San Francisco just in time for author Jack London's birth.

**1898**   The **Ferry Building** opens.

**1904**   The Bank of Italy, later to become Bank of America, is created by Italian merchant A.P. Giannini.

**1906**   Earthquake and fire destroy much of the city.

**1915**   The Panama-Pacific International Exhibition, commemorating the opening of the Panama Canal, opens in San Francisco. More than 18 million people attend.

**1927**   **San Francisco International Airport** opens.

**1933**   **Coit Tower** is erected.

**1934**   5 July is "Bloody Thursday," when a head-on confrontation between the Industrial Association scabs, the International Longshoremen's Union, and the police takes place.

**1936**   The **San Francisco–Oakland Bay Bridge** opens.

**1937**   The **Golden Gate Bridge** opens.

**1939**   **Treasure Island** is created for the Golden Gate International Exposition; the **Maritime Museum** opens.

**1945**   The United Nations Charter is founded in San Francisco.

**1960**   **Candlestick Park** opens.

**1963**   After nearly one hundred years, **Alcatraz** is closed because of old age.

**1967**   The "Summer of Love" comes to San Francisco: hippies, the Free Speech Movement, drugs, and the sexual revolution.

**1972**   The **Golden Gate National Recreation Area** is established; the **Bay Area Rapid Transit (BART)** System opens.

**1974**   **BART** makes its first run through the Transbay tube.

**1978**   Mayor George Moscone and Supervisor Harvey Milk are shot to death in their offices.

**1982**   The **San Francisco 49ers** win **Superbowl XVI** against Cincinnati. They repeat their victory 2, 7, 8, and 13 years later.

**1986**   The Downtown Plan limits building in San Francisco.

**1989**   A 7.1 earthquake at Loma Prieta, east of **Santa Cruz**, rocks San Francisco and Oakland.

**1993**   **Yerba Buena Gardens,** the multimillion-dollar arts and cultural center, officially opens.

**1994**   Most of the 200-year-old **Presidio**, the nation's oldest continuously used military post, is transferred from the army's jurisdiction to become part of the **Golden Gate National Recreation Area**.

**1998**   E-line, a Muni light-rail system, opens along The Embarcadero.

**2000**   The city's new baseball stadium, opens. The International Terminal opens at San Francisco Airport.

The Internet explosion reaches its height. Between 1999 and 2000 venture capital firms invested $50.1 billion in Bay Area start-ups. In 2000, 158 Harvard Business School graduates took jobs here. Craig's List posted 542 Internet jobs. But by January 2001, most companies folded.

**2003**   **The Asian Art Museum** opens at the Civic Center. BART to San Francisco International Airport opens.

**2004**   San Francisco becomes the first US city to issue marriage licenses to same-sex couples. Thousands of gay couples say "I do." Barry Bonds hits his 700th home run at AT&T Park.

**2006**   Total visitor and convention spending reaches $7.37 billion.

# INDEX

## A

A.A. Cantin Architects, 30
Abigail Hotel $$, 19, 190
Absinthe Brasserie and Bar **$$, 22
Academy of Art University Galleries, 40
Accessibility for the disabled, 5
Accommodations, 10
Acme Chophouse ***$$$, 36
Acorn Books, 84
Acquerello ****$$$, 83
African American Art and Cultural Center, 132
Airlines, Oakland International Airport, 7
Airlines, San Francisco International Airport, 6
Airlines, San Jose International Airport, 8
Airports, 5
Airport services, Oakland International Airport, 7
Airport services, San Francisco International Airport, 5
Airport services, San Jose International Airport, 8
Alabaster, 23
Albona **$$, 97
Alcatraz Island, 107
Alemany Farmers' Market, 143
Alioto's **$$$, 92
All American Boy, 186
Allegro Ristorante Italiano **$$$, 81
Alliance Française, 86
Alta Plaza Park, 120, 195
Ambiance, 151
Amoeba Music, 134
Amphora Wine Merchant, 22
Anchorage, 94
Anchor Brewing Co., 140
Anchor Oyster Bar & Seafood Market **$$, 149
Andalé Taqueria **$, 112
Andalu ***$$, 138
Anderson, John, 150
Andrew Rothstein Fine Foods **$$, 81
Andrews Hotel $$, 44
Angel Island, 106
Anjou **$$$, 44
Anshen and Allen, 200
Antonio's Antiques, 36
Apartment Towers, 116

Applegarth, George, 68, 121, 174
Apple Store, 57
Aqua ***$$$, 66
Aquarium of the Bay, 93
Aquatic Park, 93
Archbishop's Mansion Inn $$$, 131
Architecture Tours, 194 (chapter and map), 196 (map)
Argonaut Hotel $$, 93
Arion Press Living Museum of Printing, 173
Arthur Beren, 50
Arts Commission Gallery, 25
Asakichi, 130
Asian Art Museum, 20
A16 ***$$, 111
AT&T Park, 27, 36
Atrium **$$$, 66
Audiffred Building, 28
Aulenti, Gae, 20
Australian Fair, 40
Axum Cafe *$, 133
Aziza ***$$$, 176

## B

Bacar ***$$$, 36
Bacco Ristorante Italiano **$$, 150
Backen, Arrigoni & Ross, 97, 116
Badlands, 186
Bagdad Café *$, 183
Baker Beach, 173
Baker Beach Bunkers, 173
Bakewell and Brown, 17, 20, 194
Bakewell, John, Jr., 17
Balboa Café *$$, 114
Balclutha, 90
Banana Republic, 42
Bank of American World Headquarters, 195
Bank of America World Headquarters, 64
Bank of California, 65
Bank of Canton of California, 60
Barney's Gourmet Hamburgers *$, 112
Barney's New York, 55
Bar on Castro, 185
BART (Bay Area Rapid Transit), 6, 7, 8
Baseball Diamonds, 166
Basic Brown Bears, 94
Bath Sense, 121

Bay Area. See inside front cover (map)
Bay Area Architectural Blitz, 194 (map)
Bay Area Rapid Transit (BART), 6, 7, 8
Bay Bridge, 29, 195
Bayfront Theater, 111
Bay Model, 199
635 Bay Street, 96
Bayview Opera House, 143
Beach Chalet, 162
Bead Store, 147
Beaulieu Vineyard, 206
Bechelli's Coffee Shop **$, 112
Belden Place, 67
Bell'occhio, 37
Bell Tower **$, 82
Belluschi, Pietro, 64, 195
Belvedere, 195
Benkyodo Confectioners *$, 128
Benziger Family Winery, 207
Beringer Vineyards, 207
Berkeley, 200
Bernal Heights, 136 (chapter and map)
Best Western Miyako Inn $$, 128
Best Western Tuscan Inn $$$, 96
Betelnut ***$$, 114
Betsey Johnson, 53
Beyond Expectations ***$, 121
B44 **$$, 67
Bicycles, 9
Big 4 Restaurant *$$$, 85
Bill Graham Civic Auditorium, 22
Bill's Place *$, 175
Bistro 69 *$$, 51
Bistro Aix **$$, 113
Bistro Clovis **$, 25
Bix ***$$$, 108
Black Oak Bookstore, 103
Blazing Saddles, 91
Bliss & Faville, 37, 55, 65, 116
3200 Block of Pacific Avenue, 195
Blondie's Bar and No Grill, 182
Blow Buddies, 192
Blue & Gold Fleet, 93
Blue Bottle Coffee Co., 24
Blue Danube, 176
Blue Light Café **$$, 114
Bocce Café *$$, 101
Bodega Bistro, 18
Body, 149
Body Manipulations, 138
Body Shop, 112

Bong Su Restaurant and Lounge **$$, 34
Books Inc., 19
Borders Books and Music, 46
Botanical Garden, University of California (Berkeley), 201
Botta, Mario, 27, 31, 33, 190
Bottega Veneta, 53
Bottom of the Hill *$, 140
Boudin at the Wharf, 92
Bound Together, 135
Brain Wash *$, 36
Brand X Antiques, 149
Brandy Ho's **$, 104
Britex Fabrics, 53
Broadway, 102
2000 Broadway, 116
Brooks Brothers, 47
Brown, Arthur, Jr., 17, 29, 97, 203
Brown, Arthur Page, 61, 120, 124, 194
Buca Giovanni *$$$, 80
Buddha's Universal Church, 73
Buena Vista $$, 95
Buena Vista Park, 135
Buena Vista Winery, 207
Buffalo Exchange, 142
Buffalo Paddock, 162
Buffalo Whole Foods & Grain Company, 149
Burgee, John, 52, 63, 66
Burnham and Root, 68
Burnham, Daniel, 16, 157
Buses, 6, 7, 8, 9
130 Bush Street, 68
Bus Stop, 115

## C

Cable Car Museum, 82
cable cars, 9
Café, 184
Café Andrée **$$, 41
Café Bastille *$, 67
Café Claude **$, 42
Cafe de Stijl **$, 99
Café Du Nord **$$, 146
Café Flore **$, 183
Café for All Seasons **$$, 157
Café Gratitude **$, 141
Café Jacqueline **$$, 100
Café Kati ***$$$, 128
Café Mozart ****$$$$, 87
Café Pescatore **$$, 96
Café Tiramisù **$$, 67
Caffè Greco *$, 102
Caffè Macaroni **$$, 105
Caffè Museo *$, 32
Caffè Puccini *$, 102

Caffè Sport $$, 101
Caffè Trieste *$, 102
Cahill, B.J., 131
California Academy of Sciences, 165
California Culinary Academy *$$, 18
California Federal Bank (88 Kearny Street), 69
California Historical Society, 30
California Palace of the Legion of Honor, 174
580 California Street, 64
345 California Street, 65
101 California Street, 66, 188
California Welcome Center, 93
Calistoga, 207
Calistoga Chamber of Commerce, 207
Calzone's *$$, 102
Camera Obscura, 174
Cameron House, 75
Campanile, 195
Campton Place $$$$, 44
Campton Place Restaurant ***$$$$, 44
Cannery, 94
Cannery Row, 204
Canteen **$$, 87
Capp's Corner *$$, 101
Carl-Warnecke and Associates, 57
Carmel Mission, 204
Carnelian Room *$$$$, 64
Car rentals, 7, 8
Cartier, 46
Cartoon Art Museum, 30
Cartwright Hotel $$, 41
Casebolt House, 115
Castro, 144 (chapter and map)
440 Castro, 185
Castro Country Club, 186
Castro Street shopping, 148 (map)
Castro Theatre, 147, 184
Castro Village Wine Company, 150
C.A. Thayer, 90
Cauchot, Maurice, 37
CAV Wine Bar & Kitchen *$$, 25
Center for the Arts, 190
Center for the Arts Galleries and Forum, 195
Center for the Arts Theater, 195
Cha Cha Cha ***$$, 134
Chancellor Hotel $$$, 42
Chanel, 50
Chapeau! **$$, 176
Charles Campbell Gallery, 97
Château Montelena, 207
Cheesecake Factory **$$, 55
Chestnut Street, 113
Chevys Fresh Mex *$$, 61

Chevys (South of Market) **$$, 33
Chez Nous ***$, 125
Children's Playground (Golden Gate Park), 166
Child's Play, 163
China Basin Building, 37
China Beach, 173
Chinatown, 70 (chapter and map)
Chinatown Kite Shop, 75
China Trade Center Art Gallery, 74
Chinese Historical Society of America, 74
Chiu's Cafe **$$, 177
Chow **$, 182
Christofle, 51
Ciampi, Mario, 57, 200
Cinch Saloon, 187
Cinderella Bakery, Deli and Restaurant, 177
Citicorp Building, 194
Citicorp Center, 69
Citizen Cake ***$$, 21
Citrus Club ***$, 134
City Hall, 20, 194
City Lights Booksellers & Publishers, 103
Civic Center, 16 (chapter and map), 194
Clement Street Bar and Grill **$$, 176
Cliff House, 174
Cliff's Variety, 149
Clift Hotel $$$$, 51
Climate, 10
Clos Pegase, 207
Club 1015, 35
Club Fugazi, 100, 187
Club Lexington, 182
Coach Leather, 47
Coastal Trail, 171
Coco500 ***$$, 35, 193
Coit Memorial Tower, 97, 195
Comix Experience, 133
Commodore Sloat School, 159
Condor Lounge $$, 102
Conservatory of Flowers, 164
Contemporary Jewish Museum, 29
Convent of the Sacred Heart, 116
Cookin,', 133
Cordon Bleu Vietnamese Restaurant **$, 83
Cortez Restaurant and Bar ***$$, 51
Cosmopolitan Cafe *$$, 28
Cost Plus World Market, 96
Country Cheese, 133
Cover to Cover Booksellers, 150
Cowell Theater, 111
Cow Palace, 143
Coxhead, Ernest, 108, 117, 196

Crab House *$$, 93
Crissy Field, 173
Crissy Field Center, 173
Crissy Field Restoration Project, 172 (map)
Crocker Galleria, 69
Crown Plaza Hotel $$$, 41
Crown Zellerbach Building, 69, 194
Crustacean **$$, 83
Crystal Springs Watershed, 203
Curlett, William, 55
Curran Theatre, 52

**D**

D&M Liquors, 124
DAAN Chinese Herbs and Acupuncture, 73
Daniels, Mark, 157
Daniel Solomon & Associates, 96, 121, 196
Danilo Italian Bakery, 101
David Stephen, 50
Day, Clinton, 55
Day Trips, 197 (chapter and map)
Delancey Street Restaurant **$$, 35
Delfina ****$$$, 139
de Matran, Nilus, 99
Designer Consigner, 121
Detour Jet, 184
de Young Cafe ***$, 165
de Young Museum, 165
Different Light, 149, 186
Dim Sum and Then Some, 76
Dining Room ***$$$$, 86
Diptyque, 50
Disabled travelers, accessibility, 5
Discount Cameras, 53
Dish ***$, 173
329 Divisadero Street, 133
DMJM, 34
DNA Lounge, 37
Does Your Mother Know?, 149
Donald MacDonald & Associates, 96
Donatello Hotel $$$, 45
Donovan, John L., 29
Dosa Restaurant **$$, 141
Dottie Doolittle, 121
Dottie's True Blue Café ***$, 54, 189
DPD Restaurant **$$, 72
Drewes Meats, 153
Drinking, 10
Driving, 7, 8, 9
Duxiana, 128

**E**

Eames & Young, 106
E'Angelo **$$, 112
Eastern Bakery, 75
Ebisu **$$, 156
Ecology Loop Trail, 173
Edge, 186
Edmund G. Brown State Office Building, 19
Edwardian San Francisco Hotel $, 25
871 Fine Arts Gallery and Bookstore, 53
t18th Street Bar, 186
Eileen Fisher, 123
Elaine Magnin Needlepoint, 121
Elbo Room, 139
electric car, 9
Electric Tour Company, 95
electric trolley buses, 9
Elisa's Beauty & Health Spa, 151
Elite Café **$$, 124
Ella's ***$, 124, 181
El Río, 142
Embarcadero Center, 60
Emergencies, 14
Empire Plush Room, 87
Emporio Armani Boutique, 55
Empress of China **$$$, 74
Endup, 193
Eric's **$, 153
Erika Meyerovich Gallery, 46
Eros, 182
Esherick Homsey, Dodge & Davis, 97, 195
Esta Noche, 139, 182
Eureka, 90
Eureka Restaurant and Lounge *$$, 149
Evelyn's Antique Chinese Furniture, 24
Executive Hotel Mark Twain $$$, 55
Exploratorium, 110

**F**

Fairmont $$$$, 84, 195
Farallon ****$$$$, 45
Farallon Islands, 106
Far-Out Fabrics/Mendel's Art Supplies and Stationery, 134
Faz Restaurant **$$, 28
F. Dorian, Inc., 22
FDR Pier, 202
Federal Office Building, 19
Federal Reserve Bank of San Francisco, 61

Fee and Munson, 59
Feinstein, Dianne, 23 (bests)
Ferrari-Carrano Vineyard & Winery, 207
Ferries, 9
Ferry Building, 61, 194
Ferry Building Line, 67
Ferry Plaza Farmers' Market, 62
Fields Book Store, 84
Filbert Steps, 98
Fillmore Street, 120
Fillmore Street Shopping, 122 (map)
Filoli Mansion, 203
Financial District, 58 (chapter and map), 195
Fino Bar and Ristorante **$$, 44
Fior d'Italia *$$$, 97
Fioridella, 82
Firefly ***$$, 150
Firewood Café **$, 149
Fisherman's and Seamen's Memorial Chapel, 90
Fisherman's Wharf, 92
Fisherman's Wharf/Telegraph Hill/North Beach, 88 (chapter and map)
Fishman, Kimberly (bests), 135
Fleur de Lys ****$$$$, 40
Flicka, 125
Flight 001, 23
Florio **$$, 125
Fly Trap ***$$, 32
Fog City Diner **$$, 98
Folk Art International, Xanadu Gallery and Boretti Amber & Design, 50
Foreign Cinema ***$$, 142
Forest Hill, 157
Forest Hill Association Clubhouse, 157
Forrest Jones, 123
Fort Mason Center, 110
Fort Point, 171
440 Castro, 185
Fournou's Ovens ***$$$$, 86
Four Seasons Hotel San Francisco $$$$, 30
Fraenkel Gallery, 53
210 Francisco Street, 97
Frank Lloyd Wright Building, 50
Freed, James Ingo, 17
Fringale Restaurant **$$$, 35
Frjtz Fries and DJ Art Teahouse **$, 23
1198 Fulton Street, 131
Funston Avenue Officers' Housing, 172
Fuzio **$$, 186

# G

Galeria de la Raza/Studio, 142
Galleria Park Hotel $$$, 68
Gallery Paule Anglim, 53
Gamescape, 133
Gaylord India Restaurant **$$$, 94
Gay San Francisco, 183 (map), 188 (map), 189 (map)
Geary Theater, 52
Geilfuss, Henry, 133
Gensler & Associates, 34, 98
Germania Street Houses, 133
Getting Around San Francisco, 8
Getting to and from Oakland International Airport (OAK), 7
Getting to and from San Francisco Airport (SFO), 6
Getting to and from San Jose International Airport (SJC), 8
Getting to San Francisco, 5
Ghirardelli Chocolate Manufactory and Soda Fountain, 95
Ghirardelli Square, 94, 195
Gift Center, 37
Gira Polli **$, 99
Gleneagles Golf Course, 143
Glover Street Duplex, 81
Goat Hill Pizza **$, 140
Golden Gate Bridge, 170, 195
Golden Gate Fortune Cookies, 72
Golden Gate Golf Course, 162
Golden Gate Park, 160 (chapter and map)
Golden Gate Park Riding Academy, 162
Golden Gate Park Shuttle, 164
Golden Gate Promenade, 171
Golden Gate Theatre, 57
Gold's Gym, 184, 193
Good Vibrations, 182
Gordon Biersch **$$, 29
Grace Cathedral, 84, 195
Graffeo Coffee Roasting Co., 98
Grand Central Station Antiques, 37
Grand Hyatt Hotel $$$$, 42
Grandview ***$$$, 42
Grant Avenue, 75
Grant Plaza Hotel $, 75
Graves, Michael, 207
Great American Music Hall, 18
Great Eastern Restaurant *$, 72
Greene & Greene, 195
Green Room, 94
Greens ***$$$, 111
Green's Sports Bar, 81
Grove-Fillmore *$, 124
Gucci, 52
Gump's, 47

Gundlach-Bundschau, 207
The Gym SF, 183

# H

H&M, 55
Haas-Lilienthal House, 121, 195
Hackett Freedman Gallery, 42
Hahn's Hibachi *$, 113
Haight-Ashbury District, 181
Haight/Japantown, 126 (chapter and map)
Haig's Delicacies, 176
Hallidie Building, 69, 194
Hallidie Plaza, 57
Handlery Union Square $$$, 52
Harbor Court Hotel $$, 29
Hard Rock Café *$$, 93
Harris' Restaurant **$$$, 82
Harry and David, 47
Harry's Bar **$, 124
Harvey Milk Institute, 193
Harvey Milk Plaza, 184
Harvey's *$, 186
Hawthorne Lane ***$$$, 32
Hayes Street Grill **$$$, 22
Hayes Valley, 16 (chapter and map)
Heart of the City Farmers' Market, 21
Hellmuth, Obata & Kassabaum, 34, 46, 98, 195
Helmand Restaurant ***$$, 103
Herb Caen Way..., 92
Herbst Theater, 19
Hercules, 90
Hermès of Paris, 50
Hertzka and Knowles, 69, 195
Hess Collection Winery, 206
Hibernia Bank, 19
Hidden Cottage $$, 152
Hilton San Francisco Financial District $$$, 73
Hing Lung Chinese Cuisine **$, 72
Historic streetcars, 9
History, 208
Hobart Building, 69
Hobart, Lewis P., 32, 84, 195
Hole in the Wall, 191
Holey Bagel, 152
Holiday Inn Express and Suites $$, 96
Hon's Wun Tun House *$, 75
Hood, Bobbie Sue, 80
Hoover Tower, 203
Hortica, 149
Hotaling Place, 105
Hotel Adagio $$, 51
Hotel Beresford $, 40

Hotel Beresford Arms $, 87
Hotel Bijou $, 57
Hotel Bohème $$, 101
Hotel Carlton $, 87
Hotel Del Sol $$, 113
Hotel des Arts $, 40
Hotel Diva $$, 52
Hotel Drisco $$, 119
Hotel Griffon $$$, 28
Hotel Majestic $$$, 129
Hotel Milano $$$, 33
Hotel Nikko San Francisco $$$$, 55
Hotel Palomar $$$$, 31
Hotels, rating, 5
Hotel Triton $$$, 39, 188
Hotel Union Square $$, 56
Hotel Vitale $$$, 28
Hours, 10
House Calls: San Francisco's Premier Estates, 194 (map)
House **$$, 102
House of Nanking ***$$, 72
House of Prime Rib ***$$, 82
Howard, John Galen, 22, 155, 159, 195
Howells and Stokes, 67
Hunan *$$, 103
Hunter-Dulin Building, 69
Huntington Hotel $$$, 84
Huntington Park, 84
Hyatt Regency Hotel $$$$, 61, 194
Hyde Street Bistro ***$$, 82
Hyde Street Pier, 90

# I

Ikenobo Ikebana Society, 131
Il Fornaio **$$, 98
Il Pollaio $, 100
Imperial Fashion, 75
Imperial Tea Court, 71
India Clay Oven **$$, 175
Industrial Indemnity Building, 66
Information, essential, 10
Ingleside, 159
In-Jean-Ious, 186
Inn at the Opera $$$, 20
Inn at Union Square $$$, 46
Inn on Castro $$, 147, 183
InterContinental Hotel $$$, 34
Irish Bank Bar & Restaurant **$$, 40
Irving Street, 156
Isobune Sushi **$$, 130
Italian French Bakery, 100
Ixia, 147
Izzy's Steaks & Chops **$$$, 112

## J

Jack London's Birthplace, 36
Jack London Square, 202
Jack London Village, 202
Jackson Court $$, 119
Jackson Fillmore Trattoria ***$$, 120
Jackson Square Historic District, 105
Jade Galore, 73
Jaguar, 187
James C. Hormal Gay and Lesbian Center, 190
James Stewart Polshek and Partners, 33, 61
Japan Center, 129
Japanese Tea Garden, 164
Japantown, 126 (chapter and map)
Jardinière ***$$$, 20
Jasmine Tea House **$, 143
Jeanty at Jack's ***$$$, 63
Jeremys, 35
Jewish Museum of San Francisco, 31
JFK Drive, 164
John Berggruen Gallery, 44
John McLaren Park, 143
Johnny Rockets *$, 112
John Portman and Associates, 60, 61, 194
John S. Bolles and Associates, 143
John's Grill **$$, 56
Johnson, Fain, and Pereira Associates, 28
Johnson, Philip, 52, 63, 66, 188, 190
John Walker & Co. Liquors, 69
Joji's House of Teriyaki *$, 115
Jonathan-Kaye by Country Living, 121
Jones, Inigo, 94
Joseph Esherick & Associates, 94
Joseph Schmidt Confections, 147
Judy's Cafe **$, 112
Juicy News, 120
Julie's Supper Club *$$, 36
Julius' Castle *$$$$, 97
JW Marriott Hotel San Francisco $$$, 45

## K

Kabuki Springs & Spa, 129
Kabuto Sushi ***$$, 177
Kahn House, 99
Kaplan/McLaughlin/Diaz, 37, 61, 98, 106, 135

Katzman, Robert and Marilyn, 56 (bests)
Kavanaugh, Matthew, 132
Kay Cheung Restaurant **$, 73
88 Kearny Street (California Federal Bank), 69
Kelham, George, 61, 65, 68
Kensington Park Hotel $$, 45
Kenwood Vineyards, 207
Kezar Stadium, 167
Khan Toke Thai House ***$$, 176
Kimo's, 188
King George Hotel $$$, 54
Kinokuniya Book Store, 130
Kinokuniya Stationery & Gifts, 130
Knowles, William, 108
Koji Osakaya **$$, 130
Kokkari **$$$, 106
Kouchak's Rugs of Yesterday, 123
Kuleto's Italian Restaurant **$$, 54

## L

La Bodega *$, 102
La Boulange de Polk *$, 80
La Canasta ***$, 114
Lacoste Boutique, 53
La Folie ****$$$$, 80
Lake Merced, 159
Lake Merritt, 202
La Luna Inn $, 113
La Méditerranée ***$, 147
L'Amour dans le four **$$, 113
Lands End, 174
Lansburgh, G. Albert, 57
La Raccolta, 101
Lark in the Morning, 94
La Rondalla **$$, 141
La Rosa, 134
La Scene Café and Bar **$$$, 52
La Traviata ***$$, 142
Laurel Village Café *$, 124
La Victoria Mexican Bakery and Grocery, 142
Lawrence Hall of Science, 200
Lawrence Halprin & Associates, 57, 94, 195
Le Central **$$$, 40
Leland Stanford Jr. Museum, 203
Le Meridien Hotel $$$$, 61, 187
Lem House, 121
Le Petit Robert *$$, 80
Letterman Digital Arts Center, 173
Levi's Plaza, 98
Liberty Café and Bakery **$$, 143
Liberty Hill Historic District, 141
Lights, Camera, Action: SF On-Screen, 116

Likewise Cafe **$, 149
Limelight, 37
Limòn **$$, 139
Limousines, 7, 8
Lincoln Park, 174
Lincoln Park Municipal Golf Course, 174
Li Po, 73
Little Thai Restaurant *$, 80
Liverpool Lil's *$, 113
Lombard Street, 79
London Wine Bar $$, 63
Long and Winding Roads, 131
Lord and Burnham, 164
L'Osteria del Forno ***$, 101
Louise M. Davies Symphony Hall, 21, 194
Lovejoy's Tea Room **$$, 152
Lower Polk Street, 83
Lucca Delicatessen, 112
LuLu ***$$, 34
Lumsden, Anthony J., 31
Luna Restaurant ***$$, 187

## M

MacDonald, Donald, 133, 195
Macondray Lane, 80
Macy's, 55
Mad Dog in the Fog *$, 133
Magic Theatre, 111
Magnolia Pub & Brewery **$$, 134
Maharishi Ayurveda Health Spa, 96
Maiden Lane, 50
Main Events, 12
Mai's **$$, 176
Maki, Fumihiko, 27, 33, 195
Maki ***$$, 131
170-80 Manchester Street, 142
Mandalay *$$, 175
Mandarin ***$$$, 95
Mandarin Oriental San Francisco $$$$, 65
Manora's Thai Cuisine ***$$, 37
Map key, 5
Marc by Marc Jacob's, 124
Marcello's Pizza **$, 147, 184
Margaret O'Leary, 42
Marina, 108 (chapter and map)
Marina District, 195
Marina Green, 110
Marina Inn $$, 113
Marin County, 198 (map)
Marin County Civic Center, 195
Mario's Bohemian Cigar Store *$, 100
Market Bar **$$, 62
388 Market Street, 67

444 Market Street, 68
Mark Hopkins InterContinental San Francisco $$$$, 85
Mark Hopkins Inter-Continental San Francisco $$$$, 195
Marnee Thai **$, 156
Marquis Associates, 99, 110, 159
Martuni's, 193
Masa's ****$$$$, 39
Matanzas Creek Winery, 207
MatrixFillmore, 114
Matsu Temple, 72
MaxMara, 47
Max's Diner and Bakery *$, 34
Max's Opera Café *$$, 19
Maxwell $$, 52
Maybeck, Bernard, 108, 110, 117, 157, 159, 195
Maybeck Building, 98
Maykadeh **$$, 101
McCormick & Kuleto's **$$$, 95
McDonald's Bookstore, 57
McLaren Lodge, 164
Mecca ***$$$, 146
Mendel's Art Supplies and Stationery/Far-Out Fabrics, 134
Mendelsohn, Eric, 120
Merchant, William S., 32
Mescolanza **$$, 175
Metier, 42
Metreon, 33
Metro Hotel $, 133
Metro light-rail vehicles, 9
Metro streetcars, 9
Meyer, Frederick, 36
Michael Mina ***$$$$, 47
Middle Harbor Park, 202
Midnight Sun, 149, 187
Mifune **$, 130
Mikado, 130
Miki Boutique, 131
Milk Bar, 134
Millennium ***$$, 51
Miller & Pflueger, 30, 67
Mills Building and Mills Tower, 68
Mining and Metallurgy Building, 195
Miseki Jewelry, 130
Mission District Murals, 142
Mission Dolores, 139
Mission Dolores Park, 141, 187
Mission/Potrero Hill/Bernal Heights, 136 (chapter and map)
Mission Street, 138
Mitchell Brothers O'Farrell Theatre, 18
Miyako Hotel $$$, 129
Molinari's, 102

Monarch Hotel $$, 18
Money, 10
Monster Park, 143
Monte Cristo Bed and Breakfast $, 128
Monterey Bay Aquarium, 204, 205 (map)
Monterey Bay Area, 204 (map)
Monterey Peninsula, 204
505 Montgomery Street, 63
655 Montgomery Street, 59
722 Montgomery Street, 106
1360 Montgomery Street, 98
Monticello Inn $$, 56
Moose's ***$$$, 99
Morgan, Julia, 48
Morton's ***$$$, 46
Moscone Convention Center, 34, 195
Moshi Moshi **$, 140
Mosser Victorian Hotel of Arts and Music $$, 31
Mount Davidson, 158
Mount Tamalpais, 199
Mount Tamalpais State Park, 199
Mudpie, 115
Muir Woods, Mount Tamalpais, and Point Reyes, 199
Municipal Railway (MUNI), 9
Museo Italo-Americano, 111
Museum of Craft and Folk Art, 31
Museum of the African Diaspora, 30
My Boudoir, 124
Myth ***$$$, 104

N

Naan 'n' Curry **$, 156
Naomi's Antiques to Go, 82
Napa Valley Conference & Visitors Bureau, 206
Napa Valley Winery Exchange, 54
Napa Valley Wine Train, 206
Narai **$$, 175
Narumi Japanese Antiques, 125
National Maritime Museum, 93
Neiman Marcus, 52, 190
Neptune Society Columbarium, 131
Neutra, Richard, 99
New Asia *$, 72
New Conservatory Theatre Center, 191
New Langton Arts, 37
New Sang Sang Market, 72
Next-to-New Shop, 123
Niebaum-Coppola Café **$$, 104
Niketown, 46
Nobby Clarke's Folly, 149

Nob Hill Café **$, 83
Nob Hill Masonic Center, 84
Nob Hill Restaurant **$$$$, 85
Nob Hill/Russian Hill, 78 (chapter and map)
Noe's Sports Bar & Grill, 152
1051 Noe Street, 151
Noe Valley, 150
Noe Valley/Castro/Upper Market, 144 (chapter and map)
Noe's Nest, 152
North Beach, 88 (chapter and map)
North Beach Museum, 102
North Beach Pizza **$, 100
North Dutch Windmill, 162
N' Touch, 187

O

Oakland, 195, 201
Oakland International Airport (OAK), 7
Oakland Museum, 201 (map), 202
1111 Oak Street, 133
Oakville Grocery, 94
Obiko, 40
Ocean Beach, 162
Ocean Front Walker, 150
Octagon House, 115
Octavia Boulevard, 22
Octavia's Haze Gallery, 22
ODT Theatre, 140
Old Chinatown Lane, 73
Old Chinese Telephone Exchange Building, 73
Old Navy, 31
Old Shanghai Restaurant *$$$, 177
Old St. Mary's Cathedral, 75
Omni San Francisco Hotel $$$, 65
O'Neill's Irish Pub, 36
One Maritime Plaza, 60
One Market Restaurant ***$$$, 28
One Stop Party Shop, 153
1000 Block of Vallejo Street, 81
The Opal San Francisco $$, 18
Opera House, 194
Orchard Garden Hotel $$, 39
O'Reilly's Holy Grail Bar and Restaurant *$$, 86
Oriental Pearl Restaurant **$, 74
Orientation, 4
Original Cow Hollow Farmhouse, 114
Orphan Andy's *$, 184
Orpheum Theater, 21

Osaka Japanese Restaurant ***$$, 125
Osento, 182
Osteria ***$$, 123
Ovation at the Opera **$$$$, 20

## P

Pacific Avenue, 104
Pacific Bay Inn $, 54
Pacific Coast Stock Exchange, 67
Pacific Heights, 108 (chapter and map)
Pacific Heights Conference Center & Culinary Arts Institute, 124
Pacific Heights Health Club, 181
Pacific Heights Mansions, 115
Pacific Heritage Museum, 60
Pacific Telephone Building, 30
Pacific Telesis Center, 69
Pacific-Union Club, 84
Paffard, Keatings, Clay, 79
294 Page Street, 133
Palace of Fine Arts, 110, 195
Palio d'Asti **$$, 63
Palio Paninoteca **$, 63
PALM (San Francisco Performing Arts Library and Museum), 190
Palo Alto, 202 (map)
Pampanito Submarine, 92
Pane e Vino ***$$, 115
Panhandle, 164
Pao Café **$$, 141
Parc Hong Kong ***$$, 177
Parker Guest House $$, 184
Park Grill **$$$, 61
Park Hill Condominiums, 135
Parking, 11
Pasha *$$$, 81
Pasquale Iannetti Gallery, 41
Pasta Pomodoro **$, 100
Path of History, 204
Patisserie Delange, 128
Pauline's Pizza **$$, 138
Paul Thiebaud Gallery, 98
Pazzia **$$, 34
Peace Pagoda, 130
Pearl City Seafood **$$, 72
Peek-a-bootique, 150
Peet's Coffee & Tea, 124
Pei Cobb Freed and Partners, 17, 21
300 Pennsylvania Street, 141
Perbacco Ristorante and Bar **$$, 66
Perry's Downtown **$$, 68

Perry's *$$, 115
Personal safety, 11
Pescheria **$$, 153
Petite Auberge $$, 39
Pflueger, Timothy, 29, 41, 147, 195, 202
Phelan Building, 55
Phoebe Hearst Museum of Anthropology, 200
Phoenix Hotel $$, 18, 190
Pickwick Hotel $$, 33
Pier 23 Café **$$, 98
Pier 39, 91 (map), 92
Pilsner, 182
235 Pine Street, 67
Pipe Dreams, 134
Piperade ***$$, 99
Pissis, Albert, 19
Pizzeria Delfina **$$, 140
Pizzetta 211 ***$, 175
Place Pigalle *$, 22
Plough & Stars, 176
Plum Paths for Pedal Pushers in the City by the Bay, 146
PlumpJack Café **$$$, 114
PlumpJack Wines, 113
Point Lobos, 174
Point Reyes, 199
Point Reyes National Seashore, 200
Polk Street, 188
Polk, Willis, 16, 19, 31, 68, 81, 84, 108, 117, 196, 203
Polly Ann Ice Cream, 157
Polshek, James Stewart, 27, 195
Ponzu ***$$, 54
Pork Store Café *$, 134
Portals of the Past, 162
Portman, John C., Jr., 45
Portsmouth Square, 74
Postrio ****$$$, 44
Post Street Theater, 45
Potrero Hill, 136 (chapter and map)
Pot Sticker *$$, 74
Prada, 53
Prescott Hotel $$$, 44, 188
Presidio, 168 (chapter and map), 172, 195
Presidio Army Museum, 172
Priteca, B. Marcus, 21
Pro Arts Gallery, 201
Publications, 11
Puccini and Pinetti **$$, 56
Punch Line, 59

## Q

Queen Anne Hotel $$, 129, 188

## R

Radisson Hotel Fisherman's Wharf $$, 94
Rainbow Grocery and General Store, 36
Rainforest Café **$, 94
Ramp **$$, 140
Randall Museum, 146
Range ***, 141
Rawhide II, 191
Real Food Company (Russian Hill), 81
Recycled Records, 135
Red & White Fleet, 92
Red Blossom Tea Company, 74
Red Brick Barracks, 173
Red Vic Movie House, 134
Red Victorian Bed & Breakfast Inn $$, 134
Redwood Room *$$, 51
Remodeled Warehouses, 99
Renaissance Parc Fifty Five $$$$, 55
Rental cars, 7, 8
Repeat Performance Resale Shop, 120
Restaurant Gary Danko ****$$$$, 95
Restaurants, 11
Restaurants, rating, 5
Restored Victorian Row Houses, 128
Return to Tradition, 123
Rex $$, 41
610 Rhode Island Street, 140
Rhododendron Dell, 163
Richart, 41
Richmond-San Rafael Bridge, 195
Richmond/The Presidio, 168 (chapter and map)
Rincon Center, 28
Ripley's Believe It or Not! Museum, 92
Ristorante Ideale ***$$, 102
Ristorante Milano ***$$, 82
Ritz-Carlton Residences and Club, 53
Ritz-Carlton San Francisco $$$$, 86
River Runs Through Guerneville, 185
Robert Mondavi Winery, 206
Roche, Kevin, 202
Rocket Room, 176
Roller, Albert F., 19
Rolo, 36
Rooftop Pleasures, 48
Roosevelt Tamale Parlor **$, 142
Roos House, 117

Rose Garden, 163
Rose's Cafe ***$, 114
Rotunda *$$, 53
Roxie, 139
Royal Globe Insurance Building, 67
Rubicon ***$$$, 63
Ruby Skye, 52
Russ Building, 68
Russian Hill, 78 (chapter and map)
Russian Hill Antiques, 81
Russian Renaissance Restaurant
     *$$$, 177
Ruth Asawa Fountain, 42

S

Saarinen, Eliel, 30
Sacramento Street, 121
353 Sacramento Street, 63
Safety, personal, 11
Sailors' Union of the Pacific
     Building, 32
Saks Fifth Avenue, 46
Sam's Grill **$$, 68
San Francisco, 2 (map), 178
     (map). See also inside front
     cover (map)
San Francisco Ballet Association
     Building, 20
San Francisco Bar-B-Que **$, 140
San Francisco Brewing Company $,
     104
San Francisco Conservatory of
     Music, 24
San Francisco County Fair Building,
     166
San Francisco Craft & Folk Art
     Museum, 111
San Francisco Eagle, 193
San Francisco Fire Department
     Pumping Station, 36
San Francisco Flower Mart, 37
San Francisco Gas Light Company
     Building, 111
San Francisco Gay History, 192
San Francisco Herb Company,
     138
San Francisco Hilton and Towers
     $$$$, 54
San Francisco History Room and
     Special Collections
     Department, 21
San Francisco in Fact..., 166
San Francisco International Airport
     (SFO), 5
San Francisco Marriott Fisherman's
     Wharf $$$$, 96
San Francisco Marriott Hotel $$$$,
     31

San Francisco Museum of Modern
     Art Rental Gallery, 111
San Francisco Museum of Modern
     Art (SFMMA), 31, 190
San Francisco on Tap, 64
San Francisco Performing Arts
     Library and Museum (PALM),
     21, 190
San Francisco Public Library, 21
San Francisco Public
     Transportation. See inside
     back cover (map)
San Francisco Railway Museum, 28
San Francisco's Islands, 106 (map)
San Francisco's Premier Estates,
     194 (map)
San Francisco State University,
     159
San Francisco Sun 'n' Surf, 191
San Francisco Ticket Box Office
     Service, 47
San Francisco Women's Center-
     Women's Building, 182
San Francisco Zoo, 158 (map)
San Jose International Airport
     (SJC), 8
Sanppo **$$, 129
San Quentin, 195
San Rafael, 195
San Remo Hotel $, 97
Santa Cruz, 204
Santa Cruz Beach Boardwalk,
     204
Satin Moon Fabrics, 176
Sausalito, 195
Savoy Hotel $$, 51
Savoy Tivoli $, 100
Schultze and Weaver, 69
Scoma's **$$, 91
Scooter, 9
Sea Change, 36
Seal Rocks, 174
Sears Fine Food **$$, 42
Security Pacific Bank Hall, 65
SenSpa, 173
Seven Hills of San Francisco,
     132
700 Block of Steiner Street, 132
76 Tower Union Oil Company
     Building, 32
SF LGBT Community Center, 193
SFMMA (San Francisco Museum of
     Modern Art), 190
SFMoMA (San Francisco Museum
     of Modern Art), 31
SFO (San Francisco International
     Airport), 5
Shakespeare Garden, 166
Shakespeare in the Park, 163
Shalimar **$, 83

Shell Building, 68
Sheraton at Fisherman's Wharf
     $$$, 96
Shige Kimono, 130
Shimo **$$, 175
Shopping, 11
Showplace Square, 138
Shreve & Co., 46
Shuttles, 6, 7, 8
Sigma Phi frat house, 195
Sigmund Stern Memorial Grove,
     159
Silks ****$$$, 65
Simon Martin-Vegue Winkelstein
     Morris Associated Architects,
     21
Sir Francis Drake Hotel $$$, 41
Six Flags Marine World, 206
SJC (San Jose International
     Airport), 8
Skates on Haight, 133
Skidmore, Owings & Merrill, 19
Sky's the Limit, 104
SLAC (Stanford Linear Accelerator
     Center), 203
Slanted Door ***$$$, 62
Slim's, 37
Smoking, 11
Soko Hardware, 129
Solomon, Barbara Stauffacher, 103
     (bests)
Solomon, Daniel, 81, 140, 195
SOMA (South of Market), 26
     (chapter and map)
Sonoma Valley Visitors' Bureau,
     207
South of Market (SOMA), 26
     (chapter and map)
South Park Café **$$, 35
Spa Bar, 32
Sparky's *$, 182
Specialty's Café and Bakery, 68
Spike's Coffees and Teas, 150
Spreckels Lake, 162
Spreckels Mansion (Pacific
     Heights), 121
Spreckels Mansion (The Haight),
     135
Stag's Leap Wine Cellars, 206
Stanford Court, a Renaissance
     Hotel $$$$, 85
Stanford Linear Accelerator Center
     (SLAC), 203
Stanford Medical Center, 203
Stanford Memorial Chapel, 203
Stanford Shopping Center, 203
Stanford University, 202 (map)
Stanyan Park Hotel $$, 135
Starlet, 125
Star Lunch *$, 73

601 Steiner Street, 132
Stella Pastry & Caffè, 101
Sterling Vineyards, 207
St. Francis Fountain **$, 142
St. Francis Wood, 159
St. Francis Yacht Club, 110
St. Helena, 206
Stinking Rose *$$, 102
St. Mary's Cathedral, 18, 195
Stockton Street, 74
Stone/Marraccini/Patters, 19
Stonestown Galleria, 159
Storek & Storek, 201
Stormy Leather, 191
Stout, William, 142
Stow Lake, 165
Straits Restaurant **$$, 33
Strawberry Hill, 165
Streetcars, 9
Streetcars of Desire, 43
Streetlight, 152
Street plan, 11
St. Regis Hotel San Francisco
    $$$$, 30
Strybing Arboretum, 165
Stud, 37, 193
Studio 24, 142
Sue Fisher King, 123
Sunset/Twin Peaks, 154 (chapter
    and map)
Suppenküche **$$, 23
Supperclub San Francisco, 34
Surfing Museum, 204
Sutro Baths, 174
Sutro Heights Park, 174
Sutro TV Tower, 157
450 Sutter Street Office Building,
    41
Swallow, 187
Swan Oyster Depot ***$$, 83
Swedenborgian Church, 120
Sweinfurth, A.C., 120
SW Hotel $, 72

T

Tablespoon **$$, 81
Tadich Grill ***$$, 66
Taggert, Paulette, 81
Taiwan Restaurant **$, 176
Taniguchi, Yoshiro, 130
Taquería La Cumbre *$, 138
Taraval Street, 157
Tartine Bakery, 139
Taxes, 11
Taxis, 7, 10
Taylor, James Knox, 35
Taylor's Refresher ***$, 62
Tea Time, 151

Teatro ZinZanni ****$$, 97
Ted Baker, 53
Telegraph Hill, 88 (chapter and
    map)
Telegraph Terrace, 97
Telephone numbers, essential,
    14
Temple, 30
Tennis Courts (Golden Gate Park),
    165
Ten Ren Tea Co., Ltd., 73
Terrace **$$$, 86
Teuscher Chocolates of Switzerland,
    42
Thai House **$, 150
Theatre Rhinoceros, 139, 181
Thep-Phanom **$, 133
3200 Block of Pacific Avenue,
    117
Thomas Brothers Maps, 105
Thomas Reynolds Gallery, 125
Tiburon, 195
Tickets, 11
Ti Couz **$, 139
Tien Hou Temple, 74
Tiffany & Co., 46
Time zone, 14
Tipping, 14
Tommaso's Ristorante Italiano
    **$$, 104
Tommy Toy's ***$$$, 59
Tonga Restaurant and Hurricane
    Bar $$, 84
Ton Kiang **$$, 177
Top of the Mark, 85, 195
Toronado, 133
Tosca Café *$, 103
Tours, 14
Toy Boat Dessert Café *$, 176
Train Depot, 37
Transamerica Pyramid, 60, 195
Transbay Terminal, 29
Transportation, 5
Transportation, public, unlimited
    access options, 10
Treasure Island, 107
Trefethen Vineyards, 206
Trolleys to Yesteryear, 24
Tsing Tao **$, 175
Tuggey's, 152
Tully's Coffee Co., 151
21st Amendment Brewery, 35
24th St. Cheese Co., 152
3733-3777 and 3817-3871 22nd
    Street, 150
3780 23rd Street, 150
2223 Market ***$$, 183
Twin Peaks, 154 (chapter and
    map), 157
Twin Peaks (Castro), 147, 184

U

Under One Roof, 183
Underwood, Gilbert Stanley, 28,
    106
Union Square, 38 (chapter and
    map), 47
Union Street, 115
Union Street Inn $$$, 114
Union Street Shopping, 118
    (map)
United Nations Plaza, 21
Universal Café ***$$, 140
University Art Museum, 200
University of California, Berkeley,
    195, 200 (map)
University of California, San
    Francisco, 27, 157
Upper Fillmore/Pacific
    Heights/Marina, 108 (chapter
    and map)
Upper Market, 144 (chapter and
    map)
Urban Pet, 121
US Appraiser's Building, 106
US Court of Appeals Building, 35
US Custom House, 106

V

Valencia Street, 139
Vallejo Street, 81
Valley Tavern, 150
Vandewater Street, 96
Velvet Da Vinci Gallery, 82
Venticello Ristorante ***$$$, 82
Veranda *$$, 56
Vermont Street, 140
Vesuvio, 103
Veteran's Building, 194
Victorian House, 124
Victoria Pastry Co., 102
Vietnam II **$, 18
Views, 48
Villa Florence $$, 54
Village Market, 175
Viña de Mar Park, 198
Virgin Megastore, 57
Visitors' Information, 14
Visitors' Information Center, 15
VIVANDE Porta Via ***$$, 124
Volare Trattoria **$$, 100

W

Walking, 10
Warfield Theater, 57
War Memorial Opera House, 20

War Memorial Veteran's Building, 19
Warming Hut Cafe **$, 173
Warnecke, John Carl, 19
Warwick Regis Hotel $$$, 51
Washington/Battery Street Building, 59
Washington Square, 99
Washington Square Inn $$, 99
3778 Washington Street, 120
Wattle Creek Winery, 95
Wave Organ, 110
Wax Museum, 94
Wells Fargo Bank Building, 55
Wells Fargo History Museum, 65
Westfield San Francisco Centre, 32
West Fort Miley's Gun Batteries, 174
Westin San Francisco Market Street $$$$, 30
Westin St. Francis Hotel $$$$, 47
West Portal Avenue, 157
W. Graham Arader III Gallery, 105
Wharf Inn $, 94
Wheelchair accessibility, 5
White Horse Tavern and Restaurant **$$, 40
White Swan Inn $$$, 39
Whittier Mansion, 120
Whittlesey, Charles F., 81
W Hotel San Francisco $$$$, 32
Wilkes Bashford, 41
William Cross Wine Merchants and Wine Bar, 81
William Pereira and Associates, 60, 69, 194, 195
Williams-Sonoma, 46
William Stout Architectural Books, 105
Willis, Beverly, 20
Willis Polk and Company, 48, 68, 69, 194
Willows Inn $, 146
Wine Country, 206 (map)
Wok Shop, 75
Woodside, 203
World Ginseng Center, 73
Wright, Frank Lloyd, 50, 195
Wurster, Bernardi & Emmons Inc., 64, 94, 195

Y

Yabbies Coastal Kitchen ***$$$, 80
Yank Sing ***$$, 29
Yeast Also Rises, 156
Yerba Buena Gardens, 27, 33, 195
Yerba Buena Island, 107
Yerba Buena Square, 34

Yet Wah *$$, 175
Yoné, 100
York Hotel $$, 87
Young Performers Theatre, 111
Yountville, 206
Yountville-Clothes for Children, 121
Yuet Lee Seafood Restaurant **$, 71
Yves Saint Laurent, 50

Z

Zara, 46
Zarzuela **$$, 80
Zazie **$$, 135
Zeitgeist, 138
Zinc Details, 125
Zingari **$$$, 45
Zuni Restaurant & Bar ***$$$, 25, 193

## RESTAURANTS

Only restaurants with star ratings are listed below. All restaurants are listed alphabetically in the main (preceding) index. Always call in advance to ensure a restaurant has not closed, changed its hours, or booked its tables for a private party. The restaurant price ratings are based on the average cost of an entrée for one person, excluding tax and tip.

**** An Extraordinary Experience
*** Excellent
** Very Good
* Good

$$$$ Big Bucks ($28 and up)
$$$ Expensive ($18-$28)
$$ Reasonable ($10-$18)
$ The Price Is Right (less that $10)

****

Acquerello $$$, 83
Café Mozart $$$$, 87
Delfina $$$, 139
Farallon $$$$, 45
Fleur de Lys $$$$, 40
La Folie $$$$, 80
Masa's $$$$, 39
Postrio $$$, 44
Restaurant Gary Danko $$$$, 95
Silks $$$, 65
Teatro ZinZanni $$, 97

***

Acme Chophouse $$$, 36
Andalu $$, 138
Aqua $$$, 66
A16 $$, 111
Aziza $$$, 176
Bacar $$$, 36
Betelnut $$, 114
Beyond Expectations $, 121
Bix $$$, 105
Café Kati $$$, 128
Campton Place Restaurant $$$$, 44
Cha Cha Cha $$, 134
Chez Nous $, 125
Citizen Cake $$, 21
Citrus Club $, 134
Coco500 $$, 35, 193
Cortez Restaurant and Bar $$, 51
de Young Cafe $, 165
Dining Room $$$$, 86
Dish $, 173
Dottie's True Blue Café $, 54, 189
Ella's $, 124, 181
Firefly $$, 150
Fly Trap $$, 32
Foreign Cinema $$, 142
Fournou's Ovens $$$$, 86
Grandview $$$, 42
Greens $$$, 111
Hawthorne Lane $$$, 32
Helmand Restaurant $$, 103
House of Nanking $$, 72
House of Prime Rib $$, 82
Hyde Street Bistro $$, 82
Jackson Fillmore Trattoria $$, 120
Jardinière $$$, 20
Jeanty at Jack's $$$, 63
Kabuto Sushi $$, 177
Khan Toke Thai House $$, 176
La Canasta $, 114
La Méditerranée $, 147
La Traviata $$, 142
L'Osteria del Forno $, 101
LuLu $$, 34
Luna Restaurant $$, 187
Maki $$, 131
Mandarin $$$, 95
Manora's Thai Cuisine $$, 37
Mecca $$$, 146
Michael Mina $$$$, 47
Millennium $$, 51
Moose's $$$, 99
Morton's $$$, 46
Myth $$$, 104
One Market Restaurant $$$, 28
Osaka Japanese Restaurant $$, 125
Osteria $$, 123

Pane e Vino $$, 115
Parc Hong Kong $$, 177
Piperade $$, 99
Pizzetta 211 $, 175
Ponzu $$, 54
Ristorante Ideale $$, 102
Ristorante Milano $$, 82
Rose's Cafe $, 114
Rubicon $$$, 63
Slanted Door $$$, 62
Swan Oyster Depot $$, 83
Tadich Grill $$, 66
Taylor's Refresher $, 62
Tommy Toy's $$$, 59
2223 Market $$, 183
Universal Café $$, 140
Venticello Ristorante $$$, 82
VIVANDE Porta Via $$, 124
Yabbies Coastal Kitchen $$$, 80
Yank Sing $$, 29
Zuni Restaurant & Bar $$$, 25, 193

**

Absinthe Brasserie and Bar $$, 22
Albona $$, 97
Alioto's $$$, 92
Allegro Ristorante Italiano $$$, 81
Anchor Oyster Bar & Seafood Market $$, 149
Andalé Taqueria $, 112
Andrew Rothstein Fine Foods $$, 81
Anjou $$$, 44
Atrium $$$, 66
Bacco Ristorante Italiano $$, 150
Bechelli's Coffee Shop $, 112
Bell Tower $, 82
B44 $$, 67
Bistro Aix $$, 113
Bistro Clovis $, 25
Blue Light Café $$, 114
Bong Su Restaurant and Lounge $$, 34
Brandy Ho's $, 104
Café Andrée $$, 41
Café Claude $, 42
Cafe de Stijl $, 99
Café Du Nord $$, 146
Café Flore $, 183
Café for All Seasons $$, 157
Café Gratitude $, 141
Café Jacqueline $$, 100
Café Pescatore $$, 96
Café Tiramisù $$, 67
Caffè Macaroni $$, 105
Canteen $$, 87
Chapeau! $$, 176
Cheesecake Factory $$, 55

Chevys (South of Market) $$, 33
Chiu's Cafe $$, 177
Chow $, 182
Clement Street Bar and Grill $$, 176
Cordon Bleu Vietnamese Restaurant $, 83
Crustacean $$, 83
Delancey Street Restaurant $$, 35
Dosa Restaurant $$, 141
DPD Restaurant $$, 72
E'Angelo $$, 112
Ebisu $$, 156
Elite Café $$, 124
Empress of China $$$, 74
Eric's $, 153
Faz Restaurant $$, 28
Fino Bar and Ristorante $$, 44
Firewood Café $, 149
Florio $$, 125
Fog City Diner $$, 98
Fringale Restaurant $$$, 35
Frjtz Fries and DJ Art Teahouse $, 23
Fuzio $$, 186
Gaylord India Restaurant $$$, 94
Gira Polli $, 99
Goat Hill Pizza $, 140
Gordon Biersch $$, 29
Harris' Restaurant $$$, 82
Harry's Bar $, 124
Hayes Street Grill $$$, 22
Hing Lung Chinese Cuisine $, 72
House $$, 102
Il Fornaio $$, 98
India Clay Oven $$, 175
Irish Bank Bar & Restaurant $$, 40
Isobune Sushi $$, 130
Izzy's Steaks & Chops $$$, 112
Jasmine Tea House $, 143
John's Grill $$, 56
Judy's Cafe $, 112
Kay Cheung Restaurant $, 73
Koji Osakaya $$, 130
Kokkari $$$, 106
Kuleto's Italian Restaurant $$, 54
La Rondalla $$, 141
La Scene Café and Bar $$$, 52
L'Amour dans le four $$, 113
Le Central $$$, 40
Liberty Café and Bakery $$, 143
Likewise Cafe $, 149
Limòn $$, 139
Lovejoy's Tea Room $$, 152
Magnolia Pub & Brewery $$, 134
Mai's $$, 176
Marcello's Pizza $, 147, 184
Market Bar $$, 62
Marnee Thai $, 156
Maykadeh $$, 101

McCormick & Kuleto's $$$, 95
Mescolanza $$, 175
Mifune $, 130
Moshi Moshi $, 140
Naan 'n' Curry $, 156
Narai $$, 175
Niebaum-Coppola Café $$, 104
Nob Hill Café $, 83
Nob Hill Restaurant $$$$, 85
North Beach Pizza $, 100
Oriental Pearl Restaurant $, 74
Ovation at the Opera $$$$, 20
Palio d'Asti $$, 63
Palio Paninoteca $, 63
Pao Café $$, 141
Park Grill $$$, 61
Pasta Pomodoro $, 100
Pauline's Pizza $$, 138
Pazzia $$, 34
Pearl City Seafood $$, 72
Perbacco Ristorante and Bar $$, 66
Perry's Downtown $$, 68
Pescheria $$, 153
Pier 23 Café $$, 98
Pizzeria Delfina $$, 140
PlumpJack Café $$$, 114
Puccini and Pinetti $$, 56
Rainforest Café $, 94
Ramp $$, 140
Roosevelt Tamale Parlor $, 142
Sam's Grill $$, 68
San Francisco Bar-B-Que $, 140
Sanppo $$, 129
Scoma's $$, 91
Sears Fine Food $$, 42
Shalimar $, 83
Shimo $$, 175
South Park Café $$, 35
St. Francis Fountain $, 142
Straits Restaurant $$, 33
Suppenküche $$, 23
Tablespoon $$, 81
Taiwan Restaurant $, 176
Terrace $$$, 86
Thai House $, 150
Thep-Phanom $, 133
Ti Couz $, 139
Tommaso's Ristorante Italiano $$, 104
Ton Kiang $$, 177
Tsing Tao $, 175
Vietnam II $, 18
Volare Trattoria $$, 100
Warming Hut Cafe $, 173
White Horse Tavern and Restaurant $$, 40
Yuet Lee Seafood Restaurant $, 71
Zarzuela $$, 80

Zazie $$, 135
Zingari $$$, 45

## $

Axum Cafe $, 133
Bagdad Café $, 183
Balboa Café $$, 114
Barney's Gourmet Hamburgers $, 112
Benkyodo Confectioners $, 128
Big 4 Restaurant $$$, 85
Bill's Place $, 175
Bistro 69 $$, 51
Bocce Café $$, 101
Bottom of the Hill $, 140
Brain Wash $, 36
Buca Giovanni $$$, 80
Café Bastille $, 67
Caffè Greco $, 102
Caffè Museo $, 32
Caffè Puccini $, 102
Caffè Trieste $, 102
California Culinary Academy $$, 18
Calzone's $$, 102
Capp's Corner $$, 101
Carnelian Room $$$$, 64
CAV Wine Bar & Kitchen $$, 25
Chevys Fresh Mex $$, 61
Cosmopolitan Cafe $$, 28
Crab House $$, 93
Eureka Restaurant and Lounge $$, 149
Fior d'Italia $$$, 97
Great Eastern Restaurant $, 72
Grove-Fillmore $, 124
Hahn's Hibachi $, 113
Hard Rock Café $$, 93
Harvey's $, 186
Hon's Wun Tun House $, 75
Hunan $$, 103
Johnny Rockets $, 112
Joji's House of Teriyaki $, 115
Julie's Supper Club $$, 36
Julius' Castle $$$$, 97
La Bodega $, 102
La Boulange de Polk $, 80
Laurel Village Café $, 124
Le Petit Robert $$, 80
Little Thai Restaurant $, 80
Liverpool Lil's $, 113
Mad Dog in the Fog $, 133
Mandalay $$, 175
Mario's Bohemian Cigar Store $, 100
Max's Diner and Bakery $, 34
Max's Opera Café $$, 19
New Asia $, 72
Old Shanghai Restaurant $$$, 177

O'Reilly's Holy Grail Bar and Restaurant $$, 86
Orphan Andy's $, 184
Pasha $$$, 81
Perry's $$, 115
Place Pigalle $, 22
Pork Store Café $, 134
Pot Sticker $$, 74
Redwood Room $$, 51
Rotunda $$, 53
Russian Renaissance Restaurant $$$, 177
Sparky's $, 182
Star Lunch $, 73
Stinking Rose $$, 102
Taquería La Cumbre $, 138
Tosca Café $, 103
Toy Boat Dessert Café $, 176
Veranda $$, 56
Yet Wah $$, 175

## HOTELS

The hotels listed below are grouped according to their price ratings; they are also listed in the main index. The hotel price ratings reflect the base price of a standard room for two people for one night during the peak season.

$$$$ Big Bucks ($250 and up)
$$$ Expensive ($200-$250)
$$ Reasonable ($150-$200)
$ The Price Is Right ($100-$150)

## $$$$

Campton Place, 44
Clift Hotel, 51
Fairmont, 84, 195
Four Seasons Hotel San Francisco, 30
Grand Hyatt Hotel, 42
Hotel Nikko San Francisco, 55
Hotel Palomar, 31
Hyatt Regency Hotel, 61, 194
Le Meridien Hotel, 61, 187
Mandarin Oriental San Francisco, 65
Mark Hopkins InterContinental San Francisco, 85
Mark Hopkins Inter-Continental San Francisco, 195
Renaissance Parc Fifty Five, 55
Ritz-Carlton San Francisco, 86
San Francisco Hilton and Towers, 54
San Francisco Marriott Fisherman's Wharf, 96

San Francisco Marriott Hotel, 31
St. Regis Hotel San Francisco, 30
Stanford Court, a Renaissance Hotel, 85
W Hotel San Francisco, 32
Westin San Francisco Market Street, 30
Westin St. Francis Hotel, 47

## $$$

Archbishop's Mansion Inn, 131
Best Western Tuscan Inn, 96
Chancellor Hotel, 42
Crown Plaza Hotel, 41
Donatello Hotel, 45
Executive Hotel Mark Twain, 55
Galleria Park Hotel, 68
Handlery Union Square, 52
Hilton San Francisco Financial District, 73
Hotel Griffon, 28
Hotel Majestic, 129
Hotel Milano, 33
Hotel Triton, 39, 188
Hotel Vitale, 28
Huntington Hotel, 84
Inn at the Opera, 20
Inn at Union Square, 46
InterContinental Hotel, 34
JW Marriott Hotel San Francisco, 45
King George Hotel, 54
Miyako Hotel, 129
Omni San Francisco Hotel, 65
Prescott Hotel, 44, 188
Sheraton at Fisherman's Wharf, 96
Sir Francis Drake Hotel, 41
Union Street Inn, 114
Warwick Regis Hotel, 51
White Swan Inn, 39

## $$

Abigail Hotel, 19, 190
Andrews Hotel, 44
Argonaut Hotel, 93
Best Western Miyako Inn, 128
Buena Vista, 95
Caffè Sport, 101
Cartwright Hotel, 41
Condor Lounge, 102
Harbor Court Hotel, 29
Hidden Cottage, 152
Holiday Inn Express and Suites, 96
Hotel Adagio, 51
Hotel Bohème, 101
Hotel Del Sol, 113
Hotel Diva, 52
Hotel Drisco, 119

Hotel Union Square, **56**
Inn on Castro, **147, 183**
Jackson Court, **119**
Kensington Park Hotel, **45**
London Wine Bar, **63**
Marina Inn, **113**
Maxwell, **52**
Monarch Hotel, **18**
Monticello Inn, **56**
Mosser Victorian Hotel of Arts and Music, **31**
The Opal San Francisco, **18**
Orchard Garden Hotel, **39**
Parker Guest House, **184**
Petite Auberge, **39**
Phoenix Hotel, **18, 190**
Pickwick Hotel, **33**
Queen Anne Hotel, **129, 188**
Radisson Hotel Fisherman's Wharf, **94**
Red Victorian Bed & Breakfast Inn, **134**
Rex, **41**
Savoy Hotel, **51**
Stanyan Park Hotel, **135**
Tonga Restaurant and Hurricane Bar, **84**
Villa Florence, **54**
Washington Square Inn, **99**
York Hotel, **87**

**$**

Edwardian San Francisco Hotel, **25**
Grant Plaza Hotel, **75**
Hotel Beresford, **40**
Hotel Beresford Arms, **87**
Hotel Bijou, **57**
Hotel Carlton, **87**
Hotel des Arts, **40**
Il Pollaio, **100**
La Luna Inn, **113**
Metro Hotel, **133**
Monte Cristo Bed and Breakfast, **128**
Pacific Bay Inn, **54**
San Francisco Brewing Company, **104**
San Remo Hotel, **97**
Savoy Tivoli, **100**
SW Hotel, **72**

Wharf Inn, **94**
Willows Inn, **146**

## FEATURES

Child's Play, **163**
Dim Sum and Then Some, **76**
Lights, Camera, Action: SF On-Screen, **116**
Long and Winding Roads, **131**
Main Events, **12**
Plum Paths for Pedal Pushers in the City by the Bay, **146**
River Runs Through Guerneville, **185**
Rooftop Pleasures, **48**
San Francisco Gay History **101, 192**
San Francisco in Fact... ,**166**
San Francisco on Tap, **64**
San Francisco Sun 'n' Surf, **191**
Seven Hills of San Francisco, **132**
Sky's the Limit, **104**
Streetcars of Desire, **43**
Tea Time, **151**
Trolleys to Yesteryear, **24**
Yeast Also Rises, **156**

## BESTS

Feinstein, Dianne, **23**
Fishman, Kimberly, **135**
Katzman, Robert and Marilyn, **56**
Solomon, Barbara Stauffacher, **103**

## MAPS

Architecture Tours, **194, 196**
Bay Area. *See inside front cover*
Bay Area Architectural Blitz, **194**
Bernal Heights, **136**
Castro, **144**
Castro Street shopping, **148**
Chinatown, **70**
Civic Center, **16**
Crissy Field Restoration Project, **172**
Day Trips, **197**
Fillmore Street Shopping, **122**
Financial District, **58**

Fisherman's Wharf/Telegraph Hill/North Beach, **88**
Gay San Francisco, **183, 188, 189**
Golden Gate Park, **160**
Haight/Japantown, **126**
Hayes Valley, **16**
House Calls: San Francisco's Premier Estates, **194**
Japantown, **126**
Marina, **108**
Marin County, **198**
Mission/Potrero Hill/Bernal Heights, **136**
Monterey Bay Aquarium, **205**
Monterey Bay Area, **204**
Nob Hill/Russian Hill, **78**
Noe Valley/Castro/Upper Market, **144**
North Beach, **88**
Oakland Museum, **201**
Pacific Heights, **108**
Palo Alto, **202**
Pier 39, **91**
Potrero Hill, **136**
Presidio, **168**
Richmond/The Presidio, **168**
Russian Hill, **78**
San Francisco, **2, 178**. *See also inside front cover*
San Francisco Public Transportation. *See inside back cover*
San Francisco's Islands, **106**
San Francisco's Premier Estates, **194**
San Francisco Zoo, **158**
SOMA (South of Market), **26**
South of Market (SOMA), **26**
Stanford University, **202**
Sunset/Twin Peaks, **154**
Telegraph Hill, **88**
Twin Peaks, **154**
Union Square, **38**
Union Street Shopping, **118**
University of California, Berkeley, **200**
Upper Fillmore/Pacific Heights/Marina, **108**
Upper Market, **144**
Wine Country, **216**